MARK TWAIN AT HIS BEST

A Comprehensive Sampler

WITH FOUR ITEMS IN
BOOK FORM FOR THE FIRST TIME

——————————◦∻◦——————————

Selected and Edited
with an Introduction by

Charles Neider

DOUBLEDAY & COMPANY, INC.
GARDEN CITY, NEW YORK
1986

To Joseph H. Silverman

818.409
T969

Copyright © 1986 by Charles Neider.
Library of Congress Cataloging-in-Publication Data
Twain, Mark, 1835–1910.
    Mark Twain at his best.
    Includes index.
    I. Neider, Charles, 1915– .
PS1302.N43 1986   818'.409   85-29328
ISBN 0-385-19836-1

CONTENTS

NOVELS

ESSAYS

LETTERS

SPEECHES

AUTOBIOGRAPHY

INTRODUCTION
by Charles Neider

I'm writing this in 1985, the Mark Twain Year—the 150th anniversary
of his birth, the 75th of his death and the centenary of the American
edition of *Adventures of Huckleberry Finn*. The other day a friend of
mine in San Francisco who works in nuclear medicine and subscribes
to surprising publications—I offer the *Antarctican Society Newsletter*
and *Sky & Telescope* as examples—sent me a notice from the current
(August) issue of the latter magazine. The notice itself is not surprising, for it deals with the return of Halley's Comet this year to the
closest vicinity of our planet after a respectable absence of three quarters of a century. These close approaches are known in the trade as
"perihelion-passages," as I learned from the notice.

My friend sent me the notice not because she thinks I'm a perihe-
lion-passage freak but because of my interest in Mark Twain. The
chief message of the notice is that the Turks and Caicos Islands of the
British West Indies have issued a commemorative stamp honoring
1985 as the 150th anniversary of Mark Twain's birth. Judging by the
black-and-white photocopy she sent me, it seemed a very handsome
stamp.

Being in New York several days later, I bought a sheet of the stamps
and was pleased to discover it's even more handsome than I had
thought. I also learned the stamp was printed in Lichfield, England.
There's nothing unsophisticated about it, nothing to suggest it was
issued by tiny Caribbean islands. The comet's head is a large sphere of
bluish ice. The bluish tail whips around to the right in a massive,
muscular shape suggestive of a whale's. And there's Clemens astride
the sphere, riding the comet as if it were a bucking bronco and making
me think of the time (in *Roughing It*) when he bought an old Mexican

plug at auction and discovered, once he was on its back, that it was a notorious bucking bronc.

In the stamp he seems to hang onto something with his left hand. A closer look reveals it to be a glowing, smoking cigar held elegantly between two fingers. His right hand is raised high, as if in triumph. His right hand holds a quill pen. There's no doubt about who this is: flowing white hair, beetling white brows, white killer mustache, youthful figure. He's wearing a light-brown suit, a string tie, and a handkerchief in his lapel. Behind him is the black sky of outer space, with white and bluish stars here and there.

Until my friend's notice arrived I had never heard of the Turks and Caicos Islands (pronounced kaykos; population 8,000). I got out a map of the West Indies and after some searching with a magnifying glass located them. A little below the Tropic of Cancer, a little above the Dominican Republic is where they are. But wherever they are exactly, my heart now warms with their gesture regarding a man who many believe is America's greatest writer.

Do I think the stamp was issued for idealistic reasons? Ah, what do you take me for? Do I think it was issued for commercial ones? Certainly. Nevertheless it's a fine stamp, well and boldly conceived, and I take my hat off to you, Turks and Caicos, for knowing the greatness and cash value of the man who was once among us, among all of us and not just among his countrymen, and who figuratively had the guts to ride the great comet whose successive perihelion-passages coincided with his coming and going: 1835 and 1910.

I have been reading Clemens a long time, but there is so much of him that is absolutely first-rate on a wild and gut comic level, and first-rate also in the most serious ways, some of them tragic, ways that stand up decade after decade and generation after generation, that I still often react to him in a very fresh way, with surprise. In humor I don't believe anyone else in American literature, and possibly any other literature, can touch him. His friend William Dean Howells, in a moving small volume written soon after Clemens's death in the spring of 1910, called him "the Lincoln of our literature." I would add, "And the Shakespeare of our humor." He is a healing force, a literary medicine, an international health treasure of incalculable worth. Once again I bless his memory for the endless chuckles, belly laughs, emotions and thoughts he has given me—for more than half a century.

I feel privileged to offer this volume, this selection of very choice pieces, the choicest of the choice, in this period of greatly renewed interest in Mark Twain and his work. The book is designed not only for old and faithful readers of Mark Twain, the many who year after year and decade after decade find him irresistible, a truly American genius whose audience is worldwide, but also for the generations of readers who will want to explore and discover him on their own. A comprehensive sampler drawn from the body of his best work, it should serve as a guide to the massive structure of his work while at the same time entertaining (and often instructing) both sets of readers.

Whatever a short story may be, we can say with some assurance what it isn't. It isn't a fragment of autobiography or biography. It's not a report, unalloyed, of a historical event. It's not a joke or a hoax pure and simple. It's not a moral sermon, whether taken down from the pulpit or not. It's not, in short, any of the small bits of writing which used to be produced in the Old West for newspaper and magazine fillers and of which Clemens turned out a healthy share. A short story is something which, through the long process of literary evolution, has come to exist in and for itself. It has laws of its own; it is sovereign in its field. And it was already sovereign when Clemens began to write.

He had the artistic temperament without much of the artistic conscience. His genius was essentially Western, its strength the land, the people, their language and their humor. What he lacked was a studied Eastern conscience to refine the great ore he mined. Perhaps such a conscience would have inhibited and eventually ruined him. Probably he knew best what was necessary for him. What he had, he had in great measure: the naked power of the man with the gift of gab. He knew what a yarn was, and what it was for, and what to do with it. He didn't think that a good yarn needs prettifying, and he told it straight, without trimmings. His high jinks are remarkable—his love of mugging, monologue, dialect, caricature, irony, sometimes sarcasm. He's a great proponent of the tall story, piling details on until the story comes crashing down—or rather makes you *think* it's going to crash, but to your surprise, survives. At his best he's uproarious, and he's often at his best in his stories, as you'll see.

He's relaxed, and his mood is infectious. He rarely tries to overreach himself, to strain after an effect of greatness. This lesson of being relaxed while writing, although a dangerous one for young writers, is an invaluable one for the mature ones. The right balance of pressure when one is about to sit down to work—one's health, one's relation to the material, one's linguistic resilience, the play of one's mind—is really what's called inspiration. The balance is everything. The container, which is one's own complex state, must exactly suit the thing contained, which is the raw material about to be transfigured into art.

Clemens grew up a journalist, like Dickens, and was one of those hearty nineteenth-century scribblers who strayed into literature almost without realizing it. He had the journalist's instinct, in the way Defoe had and in the way Hawthorne and James didn't. This isn't necessarily a handicap in the creation of literature. Insofar as it stimulates a sense of audience, of common scene and the use of native speech and lore—insofar, that is, as it inspires one to attempt a colloquy in common terms but with uncommon genius, it's a definite and rare gift. Clemens's writing was almost always a means to an end. He had few impersonal objectives in mind in the way of form, experiment, texture, design. He had the common touch and knew it was a blessing. He was enriched by it and made world-famous.

It's a large part of his greatness that he heard so well. His dialogue and dialect are extraordinary. One sometimes wonders if he had a phonographic memory. His ability to imitate styles of speech, with a vast array of accurate detail, is remarkable. His official biographer, Albert Bigelow Paine, has written, "At dinner, too, it was his habit, between the courses, to rise from the table and walk up and down the room, waving his napkin and talking—talking in a strain and with a charm that he could never quite equal with his pen. It is the opinion of most people who knew Mark Twain personally that his impromptu utterances, delivered with that ineffable quality of speech, manifested the culmination of his genius."

Clemens and the oral tradition: both are related to the frontier. Yet some of his chief literary faults stem directly from this side of his genius—an occasional looseness of texture, a kind of stage or vaudeville timing for effect, an overindulgence in burlesque, a sense as if he were lecturing from a platform. Early in his public career he achieved success as a lecturer and as a maker of speeches, and no doubt this success, this practice, this buttressed confidence in a talent he long must have known he possessed, had a crucial influence on his work. There is a certain transparency in his work, like that found in fairy tales. You sense the machinery behind the silken screen. But in this very transparency there is a kind of potency also found in fairy tales, a foreknowledge of events, a delight in repetition, in the spelling out of the known, a sort of tribal incantation. When Clemens is at his best, with his drawl and idiom and dialect, he is unique, inspired, at times zany, and very often wonderful.

Clemens's best books are those with a Western scene. They owe their humor, their geniality and their wisdom to his Western orientation. The sentimentality of the frontier, which ranged all the way from an exaggerated regard for females to the most deadly sort of sadism; the lack of form in social behavior, together with certain codes of behavior which smack of juvenile delinquents; the relative contempt for the written as against the spoken word, the racy language; the attitudes toward dudes and the East, the two being almost synonymous; the impatience with the ways and principles of law—all these characteristics of the American frontier are to be found in Clemens's best work, and they are the motor of that work.

Clemens has a wonderful wisdom. He's so essentially sane that it's exhilarating to be in his company. By his way of life he seemed to say, "I'm of the tribe of writers but I'm saner than they. I know how to savor life." You expect a man like that to live a long life. He did, like Tolstoy, and like Tolstoy managed very often to write without contrived effects. His personal influence during his lifetime was great. His literary legacy has also been considerable, not only among humorists but also among American novelists. Hemingway's prose of action and language of speech owe much to Clemens. Hemingway said that American literature begins with one book, *Huckleberry Finn*—an obvious exaggeration in his fashion but indicative of his regard for Clemens. When he is at his best, Clemens is a muscular writer who calls a spade a spade, a writer intent on making an accurate correspondence between reality as he has experienced it and reality as it emerges in his books. Clemens often gives the impression of being only incidentally a great writer. The writing follows upon his life—when he is at his best. This is far from the example of Henry James and Gustave Flaubert, who seemed to live only for their work and whose passion, intelligence and religion were dissolved and sacrificed in their work: something which can be said of James Joyce, too, and to a large extent of Marcel Proust.

"The Notorious Jumping Frog" is the story which first brought Clemens to national attention. Although an early work, it's in his most finished manner, as if he had all his great talent at the very start: tall tale, suspense, rich vernacular vocabulary, an astonishing ear for dialect. In the third paragraph he describes how a frontier tale was told, and incidentally how he himself would later behave on the lecture platform. He's talking about Simon Wheeler.

"He never smiled, he never frowned, he never changed his voice from the gentle-flowing key to which he tuned his initial sentence, he never betrayed the slightest suspicion of enthusiasm; but all through the interminable narrative there ran a vein of impressive earnestness and sincerity, which showed me plainly that, so far from imagining that there was anything ridiculous or funny about his story, he regarded it as a really important matter, and admired its two heroes as men of transcendant genius in *finesse.*"

"A Day at Niagara" is wonderful satire, fresh, gutsy, zesty, and very funny. It has all the punch of the best parts of *The Innocents Abroad,* which isn't surprising, for it first appeared in 1869, the same year in which the travel book did. What a gift of gab, what marvelous rhetoric, what a genius in handling the English language, Clemens displays here.

"Any day, in the hands of these photographers, you may see stately pictures of papa and mamma, Johnny and Bub and Sis, or a couple of country cousins, all smiling vacantly, and all disposed in studied and uncomfortable attitudes in their carriage, and all looming up in their awe-inspiring imbecility before the snubbed and diminished presentment of that majestic presence whose ministering spirits are the rainbows, whose voice is the thunder, whose awful front is veiled in clouds, who was monarch here dead and forgotten ages before this hackful of small reptiles was deemed temporarily necessary to fill a crack in the world's unnoted myriads, and will still be monarch here ages and decades of ages after they shall have gathered themselves to their blood-relations, the other worms, and been mingled with the unremembering dust."

The keenness of his ear for American dialect and his remarkable ability to set such dialect down on paper are vividly evidenced in "A True Story," so authentic and moving a narrative that it highlights an important part of his genius.

Clemens published three "McWilliams" stories: "Experience of the McWilliamses with Membranous Croup," "Mrs. McWilliams and the Lightning" and the story in the present collection, "The McWilliamses and the Burglar Alarm," which is my favorite, and one of his very best stories—in humorous invention, flowery flights of inappropriate language (for example, the first burglar), and ability to make one chuckle aloud with surprising, punchy jokes. As for "The Stolen White Elephant," its superb invention and nutty satire are totally charming.

Clemens's sketches never won for themselves the illustrious reputation gained by his other kinds of writing, but no one interested in American humor can long remain indifferent to them. They constituted a substantial share of his literary apprenticeship and developed so thoroughly into a flair of genius that they made their way into his important books long after he had decided he had broken their spell. Some of his well-wishers were embarrassed by his sketches and were ready to consign them to oblivion. Paine, in discussing a collection of items titled *Sketches New and Old* (1875), said, "Many of them are amusing, some of them delightful, but most of them seem ephemeral. If we except 'The Jumping Frog,' and possibly 'A True Story' (and the latter was altogether out of place in the collection), there is no reason to suppose that any of its contents will escape oblivion." William Dean Howells praised the book in the *Atlantic* on its publication, however. Although the sketches are a minor side of Clemens's genius, they are a particularly brilliant and representative one.

He began writing them at an early age, before he left Hannibal, Missouri, and the newspapers of the day made their publication possible. The blights of bigness and sameness had not yet reached the papers. There were no press associations and no syndicates. Each paper had an intimate, personal, local tone rare today and reflected the personality of its editor, also of the town or area in which it was read. Today a reader's only, slim hope of a hearing is in the Letters to the Editor section of the editorial pages. In those earlier times the papers welcomed contributions from their readers, particularly pithy paragraphs from clever men. If you were bright enough you could work your way up to whole sketches. The reward was a haven from anonymity.

It wasn't only a question of appearing in your local paper. Because papers didn't jealously guard their copyright status, if you were good other papers would pick up your items and reprint them with your name, and your fame might spread across a whole region, as it did in the case of Mark Twain. Those paragraphs of comment, news, observation, hoax, skit and sketch were Clemens's apprenticeship on the American literary scene, although it's doubtful that he ever regarded them in so portentous a manner. He used what was available to him in outlet and matter, and the result is that his beginnings and career were so different from those of the masters of the predominant New England school and from those of the emerging Henry James. If anyone strayed into literature (the phrase is Thomas Mann's as applied to himself) it was Clemens.

But fame, however mild, was only the first part of the reward. Later there was payment in greenbacks and gold. Thus Clemens wrote sketches for the Hannibal *Journal,* the New Orleans *True Delta,* the *Territorial Enterprise* of Virginia City, Nevada, the San Francisco *Morning Call* and *Daily Alta California,* for the *Californian* and the *Golden Era* and the Buffalo *Express* and the *Galaxy.* Beginning in the fifties, he continued writing them into the seventies. He traveled a familiar road to fame, that of Artemus Ward, Josh Billings and Petroleum Vesuvius Nasby, all humorists, all commentators and all lecturers and showmen. Once one's fame was established in the paragraphic way, the lecture circuit beckoned with its gold as it competed with other forms of entertainment: the minstrel show, the music hall, the variety show, the circus. The humorous lecturer in those days was invariably a showman and invariably "quaint" in matter and style. He availed himself of the appurtenances of showmanship: pseudonyms, advance agents, puff advertisements, colored lithographs, droll posters.

Lectures had a wide audience, for they were written up in the newspapers and often quoted at length. Just as Clemens the lecturer was aggrandized by Clemens the writer of sketches, so the writer of sketches benefited from the lecturer, by the creation of a greater market for his wares. And just as the lectures were influenced by the competing forms of entertainment, so they in turn influenced them. The sketches in particular established Mark Twain's fame as "the wild humorist of the Pacific slope" and "the moralist of the Main." In them we find more than mere echoes of the variety shows he no doubt enjoyed during his years of piloting on the great river (he didn't pilot showboats, but they flourished on the river in his time) and of the Negro minstrel shows he so loved. The "nigger show," as it was known, with its formalized dialogue between the middle man (who was the straight man) and the end men Tambo (for tambourine) (also Banjo for banjo) and Bones (for castanets) made itself felt in Clemens's early writings, and even in his later ones.

According to Paine, Clemens gave up the writing of sketches in 1871, when he relinquished his humor column in the monthly *Galaxy.* Around this time he also sold his one-third interest in the Buffalo *Express.* He was pressed for time now and wanted to devote himself more thoroughly to the writing of books. His old sketches kept appearing in his books, however—in *Punch, Brothers, Punch!* (1878), *The Stolen White Elephant* (1882), *The £1,000,000 Bank-Note* (1893), and several others. At the same time, new sketches were written for the travel books—thirteen for *A Tramp Abroad* (1880), two for *Life on the Mississippi* (1883) (but one of these was lifted from a novel in progress, *Huckleberry Finn),* and two for *Following the Equator* (1897).

Clemens's sketches contain his brand of humor in what is perhaps its purest form. Here more than elsewhere he indulged in fun for its own sake. It's true that in his *Autobiography* he denied he had ever been a humorist of the "mere" sort, but his practice belied him. In a discussion of a pirated edition of *Mark Twain's Library of Humor* he said, "This book is a very interesting curiosity, in one way. It reveals the surprising fact that within the compass of these forty years wherein I have been playing professional humorist before the public, I have had for company seventy-eight other American humorists. Each and every one of the seventy-eight rose in my time, became conspicuous and popular, and by and by vanished. A number of these names were as familiar in their day as are the names of George Ade and Dooley today—yet they have all so completely passed from sight now that there is probably not a youth of fifteen years of age in the country whose eye would light up with recognition at the mention of any one of the seventy-eight names. . . . In this mortuary volume I find Nasby, Artemus Ward, Yawcob Strauss, Derby, Burdette, Eli Perkins, the 'Danbury News Man,' Orpheus C. Kerr, Smith O'Brien, Josh Billings and a score of others, maybe two score, whose writings and sayings were once in everybody's mouth but are now heard of no more and are no longer mentioned. . . . Why have they perished? Because they were merely humorists. Humorists of the 'mere' sort cannot survive. Humor is only a fragrance, a decoration. Often it is merely an odd trick of speech and of spelling, as in the case of Ward and Billings and Nasby and the 'Disbanded Volunteer,' and presently the fashion passes and the fame along with it. There are those who say a novel should be a work of art solely and you must not preach in it, you must not teach in it. That may be true as regards novels but it is not true as regards humor. Humor must not professedly teach and it must not professedly preach, but it must do both if it would live forever. By forever, I mean thirty years. . . . I have always preached. That is the reason that I have lasted thirty years. If the humor came of its own accord and uninvited I have allowed it a place in my sermon but I was not writing the sermon for the sake of the humor. I should have written the sermon just the same, whether any humor applied for admission or not."

The reader need only read the present sketches to see that Clemens fortunately didn't always consider it necessary to "preach." Nor did he always consider humor only a fragrance. Is laughter indeed only a fragrance? And is frowning the substance of life? Some of Clemens's "merely" humorous things have survived "forever"—because of their play of fancy, their wit, their fresh and idiomatic prose. The vogue of coy illiteracy practiced by Ward and Billings was bound to die, if only because it represented not a way of seeing life but of exploiting tricks of style and manner. Clemens saw life as a strange and comic affair, and that's why his humor needs no surface help. Also, his statement notwithstanding, he was graced by the power to enjoy the comic aspect of things for its own sake, and to enjoy laughter as few have enjoyed it, with invective when he was aroused, but for the most part with a kindliness which makes the use of his great gift seem little short of epic.

"Punch, Brothers, Punch!" is one of the funniest and most charming of his sketches. He catches the beguiling aspects of the rhymes brilliantly, hypnotically. His biting humor, sarcasm and invective are very evident in "Fenimore Cooper's Literary Offenses," which almost incidentally shows his ability at literary, even textual, criticism. Closely reasoned and highly sustained in its arguments, it's juicy with wit, sarcasm and truth. As for "Instructions in Art," with its lovely, inimitable drawings, this has always been an irresistibly funny and beguiling piece for me.

Clemens wrote five travel books, three of foreign travel—*The Innocents Abroad* (1869), *A Tramp Abroad* (1880) and *Following the*

Equator (1897)—and two of domestic travel—*Roughing It* (1872) and *Life on the Mississippi* (1883)—or not quite two, inasmuch as one fifth of *Roughing It* is concerned with his experiences in the Sandwich Islands. Three of his travel books are widely read and admired today: *The Innocents Abroad, Roughing It* and *Life on the Mississippi.* The other two are just as widely neglected.

Few great novelists have had so inauspicious a beginning as a novelist as he had. The same cannot be said of him as a writer of travel books—witness the great success, both financial and critical, of his first full-length book, which was also his first travel book, *The Innocents Abroad.* In a number of cases Clemens wrote a novel after a great expenditure of creative energy on a travel book, with the result that these novels suffered from the drop in temperature. In some respects Clemens was a novelist *manqué.* This cannot be said of him as a writer of travel books. In the latter respect we're dealing with what may be called the essential, rock-bottom Clemens, Clemens as humorist and creative journalist.

He was a fresh, youthful, excited traveler in *The Innocents Abroad,* which accounts in large measure for the book's bounce, humor, insight and verbal felicity. He was even more youthful and excited on his Western travels, described in *Roughing It,* although the latter was much more an exercise in recall than the former. He was more wideeyed, exuberant, open to experience in his Western years than he was subsequently, and he successfully projected his impressions and experiences when he wrote the Western books. In the first half (speaking approximately) of *Life on the Mississippi,* which he composed as a unit some years before he wrote the second one, he went back still farther in his life and again captured, with extreme vividness and authenticity, the excitement of his youth and of his early love of travel, this time as a pilot on the river. Perhaps the finest of his travel writings is to be found in this first half, in which he probed farthest back into his life.

After *Roughing It* and after the publication in the *Atlantic,* 1875, of "Old Times on the Mississippi," those first nostalgic chapters of what was to become *Life on the Mississippi,* he undertook to gather materials for and to write *A Tramp Abroad.* Now, as in *The Innocents Abroad,* he was writing about concurrent, not recalled, time. But by now he was tired of travel and he forced himself to do it as a professional duty in order to produce a book to increase or at least sustain the income which he found had become so necessary to offset his considerable and still burgeoning domestic expenses. When he revisited the Mississippi in order to gather materials with which to complete *Life on the Mississippi,* he again was to write about concurrent time and out of professional duty and again he was a tired traveler. It is therefore no surprise that the second half of the river book lags far behind the first in every respect: suspense, narrative power, poetry, importance of subject matter, perception, style. *Following the Equator* was the most dutiful of his travel books. More than any of the others it was written for professional, not inner, reasons. Also, by now the process of travel threatened to overwhelm him. And he was past sixty and burdened by debts. Once again, when he wrote *Following the Equator,* he was writing about concurrent time.

I'm suggesting that as he probed farther back in his life he wrote with greater harmony, illumination, power, style. And that as he grew more bored and tired as a traveler his travel writings showed the result, first in the lesser experiences which he derived from travel, second in a dulled critical sense with regard to what he was composing, and third in a kind of desperation to fill up space to meet the requirements of subscription publishing.

His travels began early in his eighteenth year, when, telling his mother he was going up to St. Louis to earn a little money, he went *through* St. Louis to New York, where the Crystal Palace Fair was in progress in the hot months of 1853. It must have been quite an experience for the Missouri boy, who had been working for his brother Orion on the Hannibal *Journal,* to make his way from his lodgings on Duane Street up to Sixth Avenue and 42nd Street, to where Bryant Park now stands, and to stare at the progress of nations as displayed there at an admission price of fifty cents. We can imagine young Clemens with his southwestern drawl and country manners, full-throated, strong-nosed, keen-eyed, with long, thick, carelessly barbered reddish hair and country clothes, making his way uptown in that mob of urbanites, going from the sticky heat, the smells and noise of downtown to the suburban flavors of 42nd Street and the site of the reservoir which drew its water from the Croton Aqueduct, where more than half a century later he was to observe the great building of the public library go up, he then white-haired, absorbed in dictating his autobiography, and tending to avoid the publicity which almost anywhere in the world surrounded the sobriquet of Mark Twain and the person to whom that name belonged.

He worked in New York at the printing trade (on Cliff Street), then in Philadelphia (where he was aware, certainly, of the giant footsteps of another printer who had been there before him), made a brief trip to Washington and returned to Missouri after an absence of almost fifteen months. He may have had his qualms about being out in the great world, but if he did he kept them out of his letters to his family. He was then, as he was later, a good traveler, a fellow who slept and ate well almost anywhere and who didn't easily succumb to depression. However, he liked his comforts, particularly in the years of his success, and among them he ranked companionship very high. He rarely traveled without a friend if he could help it, and he believed that a good guide was indispensable to his happiness.

But this was in his affluent years. As a young man of eighteen he took up his trade in St. Louis for a while, then joined Orion in Keokuk, Iowa, for a two-year printing stint on another of Orion's ill-fated ventures. When he tired of life in Keokuk under the melancholy and restrictive influence of Orion, ten years his senior, he was at no loss as to how to make his fortune. He would go to the headwaters of the Amazon, collect coca and return home rich. The inspiration had come from reading William Lewis Herndon's volume about his explorations of the valley of that mighty river.

It pained him to tell Orion of his plans, for he knew he would receive only arguments, sincerely offered (Orion wasn't easily capable of insincerity), yet difficult to deflect without hurting Orion's feelings. He was always an outspoken critic of Orion, at times to Orion himself. He had confided his Amazon plans to his mother, who advised him to handle the matter as he had handled an earlier one, the trip to New York. She reminded him of how diplomatic he had been with *her*. Why not tell Orion that he was going as far as New York—or whatever the port was going to be?

He went to Cincinnati and worked at his trade until April 1857 (he wasn't yet twenty-two), then took a boat down the Mississippi to New Orleans, ready to sail for the Amazon. The only trouble was, as he explained much later in his autobiography, "When I got to New Orleans I inquired about ships leaving for Pará and discovered that there weren't any and learned that there probably wouldn't be any during that century." There was only one thing to do: to make his fortune by piloting. And so he persuaded a reluctant Horace Bixby to take him on as a cub and to teach him the sinuous, treacherous, shifting day life and night life of that other great river, the Mississippi.

He was taught the river and in the process he learned a cross section of American life he could hardly have studied elsewhere. He got to know shoals, bars and towheads; towns and hamlets by the score; men by the hundred who would teem in his memory, types found on the river and in the river's basin; and he got to know the cosmopolis of New Orleans, with its foreign flavor. The river commingled American types as California does today. He learned the taste of independence and high pay, both of which were the rewards of Mississippi piloting. But the real fortune he made wasn't yet evident. It consisted of the optimism of his best years and of a keen sense of the American condition, qualities of mind and character which were to determine the output of his genius. Not to mention the vast volume of American talk which his extraordinarily acute ear was exposed to.

He would have continued on the river indefinitely, perhaps, for piloting and the river were the loves of his life, but the Civil War put an end to piloting on the river. Clemens, after a two-week stint in the Confederate Army in Missouri (during which he was exhausted by continual retreating, as he claimed later), decided to sit out the war. Orion, whose luck and destiny would be as bleak as Sam's would be bright, had recently been appointed Secretary of Nevada Territory, and so Clemens accompanied him on a stagecoach journey to Nevada. The brothers took the stage at St. Joseph on July 26, 1861, and it was only after five and a half years of roaming in Nevada, California and the Sandwich (Hawaiian) Islands, with a trip across the Isthmus of Panama to New York, before Clemens saw St. Louis and Hannibal again. When he began the trip he guessed that it would last about three months. He was an unknown former printer and former river pilot with an uncertain future. At the trip's conclusion his fame as an eccentric humorist, established to some degree in the West, was already beginning to spread eastward.

These were the years later to be recorded in *Roughing It,* the determining years of literary apprenticeship, of gathering materials, of learning the trades of newspaper correspondence and lecturing. No longer a printer and a pilot, Clemens became an amateur miner and scribbler, meanwhile observing and memorizing the life of the silver-mining frontier and that of the Sandwich Islands as he had observed and memorized the life of the river and its basin. Prospecting and mining became a passion which died, but the writing, beginning with letters to the Virginia City *Territorial Enterprise* signed "Josh," grew to the proportions of regular correspondence under the name of "Mark Twain." Clemens was a reporter in San Francisco, a correspondent in Hawaii for the Sacramento *Union,* a successful Pacific Coast lecturer and the author of the "Jumping Frog" story. By 1867 he had almost gained the fortune he had lost by not collecting coca along the Amazon. He had made it by giving up printing in favor of journalism, and dialect humor in favor of the plain, deeper humor which had already established his fame as "the wild humorist of the Pacific Slope." He was now ready to blow upon the embers of his destiny and to light a great conflagration in the literary skies of his native land.

Shortly before sailing from San Francisco for New York on December 15, 1866, the thirty-one-year-old Clemens had gotten the notion to go around the world and write a series of newspaper letters as he went, letters which would pay his way, serve as raw material for possible lectures and perhaps even as the basis of a book. By the time he sailed, his idea was more than a notion. A prominent San Francisco newspaper, the *Daily Alta California,* had agreed to print his letters at $20 each. It was no great risk for the paper to take, for he was by now known to be one of the best correspondents available, with a brilliant and idiomatic descriptive gift in addition to what was even rarer, an apparently inexhaustible store of humor, a usually benign humor which when the need was felt could transform itself into an awesome invective, all with a flavor uniquely American.

His letters began at once, at sea, and continued from New York. In New York, having learned of the *Quaker City* excursion to the Holy Land, he abruptly changed his plans and prepared to join it. The excursion was well suited to his genius and became the basis of his extraordinary first book of travel, *The Innocents Abroad.* The excursion lasted from June 8 to November 19, 1867, and the immediate result for Clemens was some fifty letters to the *Alta,* half a dozen to the *New York Tribune* and one to the *New York Herald.*

The Innocents Abroad was composed in the first half of 1868 and was issued by the American Publishing Company of Hartford in July 1869. Clemens was now in his thirty-fourth year. Between the completion of the manuscript and its publication he traveled extensively on a lecture tour and also courted his future wife, Olivia Langdon, becoming engaged to her on February 4, 1869. *The Innocents Abroad* was a great success. The United States had been on the receiving end of a procession of sour-eyed visitors from Europe and had gotten the wincing habit as a result. It was time to return the compliment with a flourish. Clemens had the apprenticeship and the background for the task. Above all, he had the appetite and the skill.

The prose of *The Innocents Abroad* sings. It's not Melville's supercharged, somewhat feverish, rhetorical kind of singing but, rather, the singing of overarching good health and spirits. Clemens was delighted to join the excursion, to write the travel letters, to write the book, and he evidenced his delight in his improvisations, his very funny inventions. Hadn't the *New York Herald* called him editorially "that most amusing American genius"?

We quickly sense the euphoria of this gifted writer whose mind has been stimulated by strange, colorful scenes and who is brimful of his awakened and still unfolding powers, powers which reveal themselves in the fresh, tireless language energy of the book, in the broad and sophisticated vocabulary and in the easy ability to achieve many kinds of effect. Much of the pleasure we derive from the book stems from his sheer gift of gab, the gift of itinerant preachers, healers, salvation-mongers, circus barkers, minstrel men. Nor can we overlook the book's technical skill, for example the subtle shifts of tense from past to present to give sudden vividness to scene and description, or the wise, sly avoidance of much use of the first-person pronoun, suggesting that the author's opinions and reactions are typical.

I still enjoy "An Ancient Playbill," which shows his gift for mimicking things linguistic, as in pretending to review the ancient show at the Coliseum. I love it when he lets out the stops in his uproarious imagination and riproaring rhetoric, as he does when he discusses Michael Angelo in "Guying the Guides." The humor throughout this piece is very broad and very engaging, as are his youthful energy, his linguistic self-confidence, and his ability to write with tongue in cheek while wearing a cocked hat. And I love "The Turkish Bath" precisely for its unsubtle humor based on his disenchantment with romantic notions of travel in far places. "The Benton House" is one of those interruptions in his travel books that stand out for their charm and their ability to catch us by surprise. He's in an Egyptian hotel—when suddenly he whisks us to a hotel in a small American town with an utterly beguiling sketch. "The Pyramid of Cheops" is deliciously wild. We're supposed to feel sorry for the Egyptian poor, but he turns every-

1

thing upside down when he expresses his harassment by all the requests for "bucksheesh," and in so doing deromanticizes the Old World he's visiting.

Roughing It, published in February 1872, is an invaluable social history of the silver-mining days, for even if its facts are sometimes open to question the essential truth of its portrait isn't. Its language is looser, thinner, freer and more idiomatic than that of *The Innocents Abroad.* If the greater variety of scenes of *The Innocents* is part of the latter's charm, the more poetic vein and the tone of a great fable are to the advantage of *Roughing It.* Clemens was able to regard certain of his experiences in such a way that they took on infinitely greater scope and resonance than the other actors in them would have dreamed they could possess. His special dimension was always his great, earthy humor, often cast in a vernacular style that doesn't easily date.

"When the Buffalo Climbed a Tree" is a fine example of the tall tale done with great gusto. "A Hundred and Ten Tin Whistles" is a riotous example of Clemens's invention, his ability to stretch outward to the far reaches of the absurd and do it with a straight face and with all the flying buttresses of realism. It's astonishing how carefully and minutely he'll work out all the details and create an airy structure that's deliciously absurd, yet which has definite remnants of truth. "The Alkali Desert" shows his brilliant descriptive ability. "Mr. Arkansas" is one of my favorite sketches—not because the landlord's wife so cowers the frontier bully (Arkansas) that she permanently removes him from his self-appointed, sadistic perch, but because of the broad, wild strokes with which Clemens portrays him. There's catharsis here. Clemens is venting something pent up inside him, and because of his great literary gifts, so are we.

A brilliant showpiece contrasting a formal language with an earthy one can be found in "Buck Fanshaw's Funeral," a wonderful dialogue between a frontier veteran and a young minister, in which there's a total breakdown in communication because the two are speaking in different tongues. Scotty Briggs, the frontiersman, says in one of his exchanges, "Well, you've ruther got the bulge on me. Or maybe we've both got the bulge, somehow. You don't smoke me and I don't smoke you. You see, one of the boys has passed in his checks and we want to give him a good send-off, and so the thing I'm on now is to roust out somebody to jerk a little chin-music for us and waltz him through handsome."

The minister replies, "My friend, I seem to grow more and more bewildered. Your observations are wholly incomprehensible to me. Cannot you simplify them in some way? At first I thought perhaps I understood you, but I grope now. Would it not expedite matters if you restricted yourself to categorical statements of fact unencumbered with obstructing accumulations of metaphor and allegory?"

After another pause and some reflection Scotty says, "I'll have to pass, I judge. . . . You've raised me out, pard. . . . Why, that last lead of yourn is too many for me—that's the idea. I can't neither trump nor follow suit."

"The Story of the Old Ram" is the kind of fiction that Clemens characteristically threw into a book of nonfiction as if it belonged exactly there. Later he made the old ram even more famous on the lecture platform under the title of "His Grandfather's Old Ram." Near the end of his life he discussed the story in his autobiography, retelling it precisely as he remembered it from the platform and pointing up the great and crucial differences between the printed version and the spoken one. That this particular yarn was very important to him is evidenced by the fact it occupies more than six pages of *The Autobiography of Mark Twain.*

Laughing with Clemens can sometimes be a strange and complex experience, as it is in reading this tale. I'm still embarrassed to find something funny in the image of Miss Wagner, an old spinster who had one eye, one leg and was "as bald as a jug," and in addition "was considerable on the borrow, she was," which is to say she was a seasoned borrower of glass eye, wooden leg and wig. Clemens understood profoundly the comedy inherent in other people's misfortunes, for example the laughter caused by seeing someone slip on a banana peel.

A glass eye and a wooden leg are hardly funny in themselves. It's the astonishing things that Clemens does with them that lifts the story above the level of stupid frontier cruelty. His comic invention is marvelous and unflagging. He piles up an incredible array and variety of details, to the extent that we realize he's exercising a remarkable gift and not simply being realistic and cruel. Furthermore, in the printed version of this story he hides behind the figure of Jim Blaine, the drunker miner, the narrator. In the platform story he discarded him, or rather acted him, using the Western dialect and mannerisms and his own inimitable deadpan and drawl and making important use of improvised timing and pauses, varying them subtly to suit each audience.

In *Roughing It* it was old Miss Jefferson who used to lend her glass eye to Miss Wagner, "that hadn't any, to receive company in; it warn't big enough, and when Miss Wagner warn't noticing, it would get twisted around in the socket, and look up, maybe, or out to one side, and every which way, while t'other one was looking as straight ahead as a spy-glass. Grown people didn't mind it, but it 'most always made the children cry, it was so sort of scary. She tried packing it in raw cotton, but it wouldn't work, somehow—the cotton would get loose and stick out and look so kind of awful that the children couldn't stand it no way. She was always dropping it out, and turning up her old deadlight on the company empty, and making them oncomfortable, becuz *she* could never tell when it hopped out, being blind on that side, you see. So somebody would have to hunch her and say, 'Your game eye has fetched loose, Miss Wagner, dear'—and then all of them would have to sit and wait till she jammed it in again—wrong side before, as a general thing, and green as a bird's egg, being a bashful cretur and easy sot back before company. But being wrong side before warn't much difference, anyway, becuz her own was sky-blue and the glass one was yaller on the front side, so whichever way she turned it didn't match nohow."

The reason Clemens gets away with all this is that his invention is so freewheeling, wild, that it distances him (and us) from the reality and therefore from simple bad taste. At the same time it releases something in us, perhaps some powerful repression, taboo. The glass eye is an instrument gone haywire, a machine with a life of its own. Designed to help Miss Wagner, it victimizes her, in this respect being a little like the society she lives in. Meanwhile Clemens's invention is so gifted we're lost in admiration, and our own good taste nods.

His audacity is an important aspect of his comic genius. Making jokes about a person with a glass eye is obviously not something one does in polite society. But of course the frontier society of *Roughing It* wasn't polite. Frontier humor could be rough, and often it was directed at minorities. In the present case the minority is woman, about whom the men could be endlessly sentimental as well as thickly insensitive. At his best Clemens is uproarious, a great comic virtuoso who delights in sharing the pyrotechnics of his genius.

A great deal of his humor, as well as his essential, larger genius (which includes that of the great novelist), depends on his alive language, strongly idiomatic and flavored with the vernacular. His language dates less than that of any other American writer I can think of. The simple, spoken English language holds up much better than the literary one. It's a hardier instrument, and actually more difficult to manage, for it quickly reveals false tones, unsteady ones, and the least touch of strutting, cake-walking, putting on the dog. Clemens understood instinctively, as did Charles Darwin, the virtues of sober English prose, unadorned with literary sequins, and why the four-letter words have lasted for centuries, only in our own most recent time being debased by overuse. In addition, his wild effects often stem from his extraordinarily rich and wide-ranging vocabulary and his vigorous and unexpected use of verbs, all usually proffered deadpan.

Clemens had a very proper side too, but even when he was being proper and even when he was largely divorcing himself from his Western roots, as he was when he wrote *A Tramp Abroad,* he could be irresistibly funny. There are few things in any literature, probably, as astonishingly comic and sustained as "The Awful German Language" in that book. To be a comic virtuoso in so sustained a way meant that he was also a comic architect of genius. *A Tramp Abroad* lacks the tension, the fire, the brilliant detail, the vocabulary, the energy and the invective of *The Innocents Abroad,* but in terms of stretches of sustained humor, of heights of humor, of sustained virtuoso performance, *The Innocents Abroad* doesn't come near it. In *A Tramp Abroad,* Clemens can make fun of Europe and its human types but he also has a devastating eye out for those of his compatriots who are exported embarrassments. In "American in Europe" he puts himself into the young man's head and invents all kinds of wild nonsense which he thrusts into the young man's mouth. The piece is perfectly done.

Life on the Mississippi was published in May 1883. "Upon the whole," wrote Howells after his friend's death in 1910, "I have the notion that Clemens thought this his greatest book." A long, sustained calm and a profound reservoir of power supplanted the ebullience of *The Innocents Abroad.* In the river book humor for the most part was subdued. Clemens was so absorbed in writing about the life of the river basin which he understood and loved that he dispensed with jokes, burlesques and gimmicks. The river book is a period piece of an aspect of the nation's youth which couldn't have been done better by another hand. Clemens owed the river years much. They had given him two great disciplines from which he had benefited as a writer: close observation and memory practice.

The book enlarged his reputation, especially in Europe, as an author who was a good deal more than just an inspired wit or buffoon. Thomas Hardy remarked to Howells at a dinner in England, "Why don't people understand that Mark Twain is not merely a great humorist? He's a very remarkable fellow in a very different way." And he went on to praise the Mississippi book.

There are so many fine things in *Life on the Mississippi* that it wasn't easy to make selections from it. I have included "The Boys' Ambition" because it's so nostalgically and wonderfully autobiographical. The details are enchanting, and very rich, and magical. The effect of reading the piece is like that of hearing special music. Clemens's language music, the golden tones of his reminiscences, resonate hauntingly in one's memory. "The House Beautiful" is priceless with its immense aggregate of period details, many of them presented satirically, all of them resoundingly hitting the mark to form an authentic portrait of a long-vanished river time. I've included "The Art of Inhumation" because it's so typical of a wildly audacious, almost coarse side of Clemens. Who else would be capable of carrying on so successfully (I'm tempted to add and so charmingly) about the joys of an undertaker in a bullish (in terms of business) time?

One of the first things we can say about Clemens as a novelist is that he didn't regard novel-writing as his essential calling—in the way that Flaubert, Mann, James, Dostoyevsky, Faulkner, Hemingway and other writers did. He came to novel-writing almost accidentally and didn't give it the major part of his literary energy. He didn't *begin* as a novelist. He wrote his first novel, *The Gilded Age,* only after he had poured out a great deal of literary energy on his first two books of nonfiction, and when he did begin, he began as only a half novelist, for he coauthored *The Gilded Age* with his Hartford friend and neighbor Charles Dudley Warner. *The Gilded Age* was conceived not only as a kind of accident but as a sort of joke as well.

Few great novelists have had such an inauspicious beginning, and the history of the novel doesn't reveal for us many prominent examples of coauthorship. If Clemens's beginnings as a novelist were weak, it shouldn't surprise us, for if he lacked any great instinct as a novelist it was that instinct which we call the artistic conscience. He didn't hesitate to take liberties in his novels and in his fiction in general which he would have hesitated to take in his nonfiction. He had a respect for nonfiction which he often seemed to lack for fiction. He told Rudyard Kipling in 1890, "I never read novels myself except when the popular persecution forces me to—when people plague me to know what I think of the last book that everyone is reading. . . . Personally I never care for fiction or story books. What I like to read about are facts and statistics of any kind. If they are only facts about the raising of radishes they interest me."

He regarded himself from first to last as a reporter who had clear and quite stern responsibilities to his public, whatever the jigs and high kicks he performed in an overflow of good spirits, health and a desire to amuse. He thought of himself as an entertainer but as a serious one. And, as he said in his last years in his autobiography, his humor was only incidental to his purpose: if it came, good, if not, it could be dispensed with, for he was concerned primarily with discussing a moral.

In general this purpose is true for his novels also. The difference is that his conception of the act of writing novels and of the act of reading them lacked that rigorous sense, that discipline, that artistic conscience, which one finds in his nonfiction books, loosely constructed though the latter may at times be. We note a significant pattern in the extraordinary years of his literary activity. Two books of nonfiction preceded *The Gilded Age*. Many of the nostalgic and by far the best chapters of *Life on the Mississippi* preceded *Tom Sawyer*. (By the way, I have not included *Tom Sawyer* in the present volume because, though I enjoy reading the book, it's so clearly inferior to its Mississippi River companion, *Huckleberry Finn*.) *A Tramp Abroad* preceded *The Prince and the Pauper*. And the composition of the major part and the publication of the whole of *Life on the Mississippi* preceded the publication of *Huckleberry Finn*. The sense we have that he poured out vast literary energy for his books of nonfiction and a lesser energy for his novels is supported not only by the matter of ebullience, scope and linguistic energy of the books of nonfiction but also by their greater length. But we mustn't push this comparison far, inasmuch as it's obvious that the fiction may be more compressed and more potent than the nonfiction.

The American yarn had important influences on Clemens. One of his triumphs in *Huckleberry Finn* was the introduction in breadth and depth of mock-oral language into the American novel and his mastering the American spoken idiom in print. In this accomplishment he was aided by an incomparable ear and a subtle memory. This particular triumph was dependent on his decision to tell the story from the point of view and in the language of its protagonist, a decision which had major consequences for the hairy-chest branch of the American novel. His singularity resided in the fact that he applied his training as a humorist to the medium of the novel. This seems now like an easy and fairly obvious transfer of energy. That it wasn't so even in the case of so gifted a writer may be judged by the fact that not many of his novels have the released, vernacular style of *Huckleberry Finn.* His taste was uncertain enough to allow him to declare late in his writing career that his favorite among his books was *Joan of Arc,* whose antique style is only one of its unattractive features.

One blatant proof of his uncertain artistic conscience is his tossing an important chapter, the raft episode, of *Huckleberry Finn* into *Life on the Mississippi* to fill out the latter, and his failure to rescue the chapter when he prepared *Huckleberry Finn* for publication. Inasmuch as I have recently published an edition of the novel which includes the raft chapter, I have in the present volume treated the chapter as part of the novel. "Keelboat Talk and Manners," the chapter's title, recalls and portrays the ring-tailed roarers of the old Southwest. This is Clemens at his very best, his most inspired. It may well be the novel's finest chapter.

It was George Washington Cable, fellow author and lecturer, who introduced Clemens to Malory's *Le Morte d'Arthur* and presented him with a copy of the book, a book which had a lasting effect on Clemens and which was the inspiration of *A Connecticut Yankee.* The choice of the Arthurian time (or what the author's imagination pretended was the Arthurian time, for there are many anachronisms in the novel) could hardly have been improved upon for the purposes of contrast and satire to be presented in Clemens's characteristic vein. Here was a European age of chivalry which he could deride as unchivalrous; of romance which he could portray as childish and silly; and of "justice" which he could denounce as inhuman. He could also indulge his talent for tall statement, his delight in roaming in time past, and his pleasure in handling a language so distant that it was humorously archaic.

His contrast of Europe and America recalls Henry James's contrast of the simplicity of contemporary American life with the graces of contemporary European society, often to the disadvantage of his home country. James's simplicity becomes in *A Connecticut Yankee* social decency and political equality, as well as unsentimental practicality; and the Jamesian view of European graces becomes something more oppressive than mere empty gestures whose chief basis is inherited title and wealth.

Many of the descriptions in *A Connecticut Yankee* are extraordinarily vivid and solid, yet their solidity doesn't spoil the illusion of a fairy tale being told or of a tour de force being performed. There are many virtues in the novel although they largely reside in the first half, after which the narrative becomes episodic and the style rather thin. There are chapters, such as Eleven, which display Clemens's special powers: speed of delivery, great invention, vast resources of humor, alertness to the idiomatic richness of his language.

A work of great humanitarianism and savage satire, the novel reveals as well as any of his works the quality and temper of his mind. It contains excellent and impassioned essays on the injustices inherent in certain social institutions; on man's willingness, perhaps desire, to be ruled or enslaved; and in general on man's inhumanity to man. It also contains his famous statement on the French Revolution, which he defended despite its horrors. In addition, there is much in the novel which has little if anything to do with the theme of social injustice; so much, as a matter of fact, that it requires a nice balance of judgment to decide which is the weightier, the social criticism or the play of fancy.

The novel was published toward the end of 1889, at a time when Clemens's own publishing company (Charles L. Webster & Co., New York) was in considerable need, for financial reasons, of a new book by him, and when he himself felt, for literary reasons, that it was high time he stepped on stage again. It was his first book to appear since *Huckleberry Finn.* It wasn't a book that came from his pen all in one rush, although there were times when it came quickly and well. Around its middle he grew tired and laid it aside for some two years before he worked up enthusiasm once more. Such behavior wasn't uncommon in his creative life. It even seemed to be the rule. As he himself wrote in 1906 in a note for his autobiography, "There has never been a time in the past thirty-five years when my literary shipyard hadn't two or more half-finished ships on the ways, neglected and baking in the sun; generally there have been three or four; at present there are five. This has an unbusiness-like look but it was not purposeless, it was intentional. As long as a book would write itself I was a faithful and interested amanuensis and my industry did not flag, but the minute that the book tried to shift to *my* head the labor of contriving its situations, inventing its adventures and conducting its conversations, I put it away and dropped it out of my mind."

His English publisher, Chatto & Windus, asked that the novel be edited for the English edition, having in mind no doubt that the English public wouldn't cotton to a burlesque of their Arthurian legends, much less to a severe criticism of their institution of the nobility. Clemens refused, and wrote in reply, ". . . the book was not written for America; it was written for England. So many Englishmen have done their sincerest best to teach us something for our betterment that it seems to me high time that some of us should substantially recognize the good intent by trying to pry up the English nation to a little higher level of manhood in turn." The volume was published according to his wishes and, not surprisingly, didn't find a hearty welcome in England.

A Connecticut Yankee is the first of Clemens's novels which doesn't follow an important work of nonfiction. It's chiefly for this reason that it possesses a great amount of energy: in invention, the speed of delivery of its humor, the multiplicity of themes, the venom and sweep of its social criticism, the acreage of corpses, the ebullience of language, the free and easy characterizations. It's one of the most successful of his creations, with fewer flaws than is usual in his books, and it's one of his most important works for several reasons: the success of its fancy, its coherence as a work of the imagination, the seriousness of its themes, and its purity and ease of language despite the fact the language isn't the wonderful vernacular of *Huckleberry Finn.*

It's a subversive book, for in it Clemens is saying that almost all laws and customs are relative, even our own, and that none are excusable if they are cruel. Nothing so enrages and finally disheartens him about "the damned human race" as its willingness to endure torment without resistance, and nothing so disgusts him as the priestly misuse of the conception of God, the use of God and religion to buttress a particular social structure based on subordination. Although on the surface Clemens was attacking the inhumanity of that more primitive time of the sixth century and of the lowly man's rotten condition in it, he was also making savage comments on the modern British system of nobility, preference, a powerful church, and oppression of the unwashed classes. In addition he was subtly alluding to the economic abuses of his own country—to the effects of capitalism, with its underpaid and overworked wage earners, its sweatshops—and to the social abuses of the South, both before and after the Civil War.

Clemens, like Cable, was a reconstructed Southerner. Howells characterized him after his death as "the most desouthernized Southerner" he ever knew, adding, "No man more perfectly sensed and more entirely abhorred slavery, and no one has ever poured such scorn upon the second-hand, Walter-Scotticized, pseudo-chivalry of the Southern ideal." Howells read galleys of the novel and gratified Clemens by praising the book handsomely, at first in private and then, shortly after its publication, in a review in *Harper's Magazine.* He wrote in the review, "Mr. Clemens, we call him, rather than Mark Twain, because we feel that in this book our arch-humorist imparts more of his personal quality than in anything else he has done. . . . The delicious satire, the marvelous wit, the wild, free, fantastic humor are the colors of the tapestry, while the texture is a humanity that lives in every fibre. . . . We can give no proper notion of the measureless play of an imagination which has a gigantic jollity in its feats, together with the tenderest sympathy."

Clemens's humor performs the subtlest of functions. It humanizes, leavens, anoints, lulls dissension. Through the sound of our common laughter it hints to us of our origin and destiny, our brotherhood, our vale of tears. Clemens as an essayist? A man of strong opinions. Self-educated and surprisingly well-read, especially in history. Bold, direct, impatient, restless. (We're describing him at his best.) A man who claims to loathe travel, yet who endures a great deal of it and gives the impression of liking it. An optimist by physiology and a pessimist through sustained observation of "the damned human race." Like Voltaire, a self-appointed correction officer for the species. (Some of Voltaire's *Philosophical Dictionary* sounds as if it had been written by Clemens, especially the section on "fatalism"—determinism or a variant of it.)

A haloed clown. A dogmatic, saddened, weary tragedian. A night watchman patrolling with his torch the dark streets of sham, cant and oppression. A bloodhound sniffing out injustice. A Bessemer oven blasting at it. A knight-errant cantering to the aid of unfranchised holocausting damsels in distress. A linx-eyed observer of his own foibles and the foibles of the race. A competent journalist who, like any professional, enjoys the exercise of his skill. An amateur literary man in every sense, including love of the vocation. A dogged researcher into the Case of Adam and Eve. A stout defender of Satan on the ground that Satan is the original underdog. "I have no special regard for Satan; but I can at least claim that I have no prejudice against him. It may even be that I lean a little his way, on account of his not having a fair show. All religions issue bibles against him, and say the most injurious things about him, but we never hear *his* side."

The man with the unruly mop and the assassin's drawl telling the nations how to behave. The printer's devil from Hannibal sounding off to the globe and, like Ambrose Bierce, finding it in the end mostly rotten, inherited as it is by man. No ivory tower man, occasionally no Humor for Humor's Sake man. At times a deliberate censor of his work, withholding it from public view through paying too much homage to the power of public opinion. Sometimes extending himself beyond the sphere of his competence, as in the Shakespeare essay, very human, which is to say quite foolish.

A man of moods and whims. He detests the French, derides the Italians, adores the English and covertly respects the Germans and the Austrians while overtly ridiculing their language and certain of their institutions, such as student dueling. He deplores dueling yet uses sarcasm on the French because they don't duel bloodily enough, not as bloodily as the Austrians. A republican, he waxes warm through contact with the English nobility and the Viennese court, enough to neutralize some of the acid of his thought and to cause him to set down statements which show his perspective to have blown away in the winds of monarchical excitement. In short he is masculine, personal, sarcastic, tender and nostalgic. He is also often funny.

"Aix, the Paradise of the Rheumatics," is extremely observant, informative, amusing, well written and charming. It offers a historical sense of the place as well as a contemporary one. Occasionally the humor is irrepressible, as when Clemens quotes someone on the progress of his diseases during the course of douche baths. "To the Person Sitting in Darkness" is a cutting, eloquent indictment of the behavior of great foreign powers in weak countries, and a virulent attack on the behavior of American missionaries in China after the Boxer Rebellion. This is Clemens the humanist, outspoken in his sympathy for the poor, downtrodden, afflicted, exploited, dispossessed, murdered. It's an important side of him.

The first collection of Clemens's letters appeared in 1917, seven years after his death. Since then there have been numerous other published collections: to his wife, to his friend William Dean Howells, to his publishers, to his friend Henry H. Rogers, and so on. He was a voluminous letter writer. His extant letters begin early. The 1917 edition has a letter from New York to his sister, Pamela Moffett, written when he was in his eighteenth year.

The letters in the present selection span the major portion of Clemens's professional life. The first is from his twenty-third year, the last from his seventieth. What a purview we get of his psyche and genius in reading them, and how suggestive some of the details are. Very early he had personal independence on his mind, which he achieved in unusual measure: as pilot, frontier silver-miner, newspaper correspondent, eminently successful lecturer and author. When he was fresh from the great river basin and the country's interior, he had a xenophobic view of foreigners. This jaundiced view, which perhaps had its genesis during his first visits to New York and Philadelphia when he was finishing his eighteenth year, would reward him handsomely through *The Innocents Abroad,* published sixteen years later, the remarkable travel book in which he repaid with interest but with the ameliorating power of humor the debt he felt America owed those visitors from overseas who had criticized his own country too archly, glibly. The Missouri upstart would someday become an Anglophile, a Germanophile, a Francophobe and, in terms of length of time spent abroad, one of the nation's early literary expatriates.

I have selected sixteen letters, the first an open letter, the others personal ones. The open one (October 11, 1869; he was almost thirty-four), to the New York Society of California Pioneers, is one of my favorites. In addition to striking aptly and strongly the note that would be orchestrated in *Roughing It,* it evidences his unsurpassed, instinctive timing and understatement. All the tones are right: irony, wryness, his style of poking fun at himself. Even though the text is relatively brief, we touch here the humorist as genius, who opens new psychological corridors for us, changing us permanently by an exposure to comic subtleties, the ballet of the humorous mind.

His is a fertile imagination. And what metaphors! "I ran tunnels till I tapped the Arctic Ocean and I sunk shafts till I broke through the roof of perdition." Where did he learn it all? But on the whole he didn't. We are privileged to observe the unexplainable, the possession of a wondrous gift. The letter is not without surprises, it keeps us off balance, begins soberly, quietly, humorlessly, then grows riotous with comedy, and ends with the pathos of aging and human change. No jokes at the end, only a marvelous humanity and a wisdom couched in haunting prose. ". . . and close this screed with the sincere hope that your visit here will be a happy one and not embittered by the sorrowful surprises that absence and lapse of years are wont to prepare for wanderers; surprises which come in the form of old friends missed from their places; silence where familiar voices should be; the young grown old; change and decay everywhere. . . ."

When he was in his twenty-third year he revealed an extraordinary ability to write with great accuracy and force about a devastating event extremely close to him, an ability suggesting a strange kind of psychic split. This was in his letter (June 18, 1858) about his younger brother Henry's death, written to Orion's wife, Mollie. Orion was Clemens's older brother, ten years his senior. What an overactive, Presbyterian conscience Mark Twain has, for he insists on blaming himself for Henry's terrible death in the explosion of the *Pennsylvania*'s boilers. (The *Pennsylvania* was a Mississippi River steamboat.) He himself, Sam Clemens, had been spared by a trifle. But part of his guilt is common to survivors of a calamity, the haunting question being, "Why was *I* spared, I who didn't deserve to be?"

Nine years later, also in June, in a letter to his mother and family written in New York on the eve of the *Quaker City* Holy Land excursion which was to make him famous and prosperous, he feels guilty toward Orion for not having "gouged an office" in the federal government for him, and his mind "is stored full of unworthy conduct toward Orion and towards you all." Still later (January 19, 1897) we see him writing with even greater power about the death of his daughter Susy (the letter is included here) than about Henry's death.

There isn't much humor in his early letters. But his writing flows, he's articulate, bursting with language and life. A large difference in content and style is noticeable when he begins writing from Nevada. His style now is freewheeling, his humor increasingly evident. It's as if his imagination exploded with the experience of plains, mountains, alkali desert and the get-rich-quick society of the silver-mining frontier. In his letter of August 15, 1862, written from Esmeralda, California, to his sister, Pamela Moffett, in St. Louis, we encounter a talent which is almost full-blown: the gift of gab, of phrase, the richness of material (really the richness of mind), the ageless gusto, the wild or understated Western humor. All is possible in the American West, for good or bad, he seems to be suggesting between the lines. He was in Esmeralda on a brief trip from Nevada, where he was spending most of his time.

These letters are like a second but even more intimate autobiography. Of course, not all his letters are equally good. I have selected those that are lively and interesting and which reveal various sides of him. It is doubtful that any were written with the thought of publication in mind. Reading the letters of his mature period, one understands that rarely if ever did he have to strain for humor. It seems to flow from his pores, and apparently he could afford to throw it away on even minor business mail, as in his letter to James Redpath, his lecture agent (August 8, 1871), written in Hartford: "I am different from other women. My mind changes oftener. People who have no mind can easily be steadfast and firm, but when a man is loaded down to the guards with it, as I am, every heavy sea of foreboding or inclination, maybe of indolence, shifts the cargo. . . . You must try to keep the run of my mind, Redpath, it is your business being the agent, and it always was too many for me. It appears to me to be one of the finest pieces of mechanism I have ever met with."

Other letters included here remind us, in case we had forgotten, that Clemens could use humor with deadly intent and effect, that his power of invective was awesome, perhaps especially in his unmailed replies to certain correspondence, as when (undated; addressee unknown) he wrote, "Dear Sir, What is the trouble with you? If it is your viscera, you cannot have them taken out and reorganized a moment too soon. I mean, if they are inside. But if you are composed of them, that is another matter. Is it your brain? But it could not be your brain. Possibly it is your skull: you want to look out for that. Some people, when they get an idea, it pries the structure apart."

Some of the letters which I have *not* included have parts that are particularly fine. I can't resist quoting from the one to Howells from Munich (November 17, 1878) in which he wrote, "She [Susy Clemens, his favorite daughter] is sorely badgered with dreams, and her stock dream is that she is being eaten up by bears. She is a grave and thoughtful child, as you will remember. Last night she had the usual dream. This morning she stood apart (after telling it) for some time, looking vacantly at the floor and absorbed in meditation. At last she looked up, and with the pathos of one who feels he has not been dealt by with even-handed fairness, said, 'But Mamma, the trouble is that I am never the *bear,* but always the *person.'* " And in his letter to Howells of November 28, 1879, he noted, ". . . reminds me of Susy's newest and very earnest longing—to have crooked teeth and glasses—'like Mamma.' I would like to look into a child's head once and see what its processes are."

I have selected six speeches. They reveal the breadth of Clemens's subject matter as a speaker, his inspired humor, his passionate humanity, and the loveliness, at times magnificence, of his style. After joking about the New England weather in the speech of that title, suddenly he writes incomparably, unforgettably. "If we hadn't our bewitching autumn foliage we should still have to credit the [New England] weather with one feature which compensates for all its bullying vagaries—the ice-storm: when a leafless tree is clothed with ice from the bottom to the top. Ice that is as bright and clear as crystal. When every bough and twig is strung with ice beads, frozen dew-drops, and the whole tree sparkles cold and white like the Shah of Persia's diamond plume.

"Then the wind waves the branches and the sun comes out and turns all those myriads of beads and drops to prisms that glow and burn and flash with all manner of colored fires, which change and change again with inconceivable rapidity from blue to red, from red to green, and green to gold. The tree becomes a spraying fountain, a very explosion of dazzling jewels, and it stands there the acme, the climax, the supremest possibility in art or nature of bewildering, intoxicating, intolerable magnificence. One cannot make the words too strong."

The first collection of Clemens's speeches, consisting of ninety-four items, was issued by Albert Bigelow Paine in 1910, the year of Clemens's death. The speeches were not in chronological order. As a matter of fact, they possess no order discernible to me. The volume contained a brief Preface by Howells but lacked an introduction by Paine, the friend of Clemens's last several years, his official biographer and literary executor. Most of the titles are by Paine or were accepted by him from sources at his disposal. Many give the impression of being more concerned with the occasion of a speech, rather than with its content. In Clemens's case, sometimes the guts of a speech had little relevance to the occasion, as when he was autobiographically

humorous at a benefit for victims of a social or natural disaster—
humorous but never insensitive, for he was profoundly imaginative
and compassionate.

The second collection of Clemens's speeches, brought out by Paine
in 1923, contained eighty-four items, most of which were drawn from
the earlier edition, while the rest made their first appearance in book
form. The speeches were now in chronological order. On the whole,
Paine retained the earlier titles. Occasionally he quietly retitled a
speech. He reprinted Howells's Preface and added an Introduction by
himself. The 1923 edition also appeared as Volume XXVIII of the
Definitive Edition of Clemens's works, published that same year.

Paine's editions were designed for the general reader. In 1976 the
University of Iowa Press brought out the third collection of Clemens's
speeches (the last one prior to my own, *Plymouth Rock and the Pilgrims),* this one intended primarily for scholars: *Mark Twain Speaking,* edited by Paul Fatout, a volume evidencing a full battery of schol-
arly apparatus and containing, in its 195 items and 688 pages
(excluding the Introduction), lectures and readings as well as
speeches. The text of the majority of the speeches is a "composite"
one, that is, the best that the editor, in his opinion, depending on
variant texts, could construct. The titles are often elusive regarding
both content and occasion. For example, I counted seven speeches
with the same title, "Curtain Speech."

A few words about the textual sources of Clemens's speeches: Some
of the speeches survive only in Paine's editions, and one is at a loss to
explain what happened to his sources. Others survive only in contemporary newspaper accounts and transcripts. Sometimes there is no
record of how a speech was originally written—or exactly delivered.
There is a distinction to be made here between prepared text and
actual delivery, for it was Clemens's practice to depart from his text
whenever he thought it advantageous to do so, to create an impromptu
effect or one of easy, graceful flexibility.

Which is to say that there is a paucity of, first, the perfect manuscript indications of what Clemens had in mind when he conceived a
speech, and, second, a paucity of clear indications as to the final,
spoken product. Sometimes there are variant texts of the same speech,
one text representing the prepared text which he may have handed in
advance to newspaper reporters, and another indicating what he actually said, or what some reporter believed he heard him say. And if

Clemens gave the same speech, or more or less the same, on more than one occasion, he was sure to invent variations of emphasis, phrasing and even, now and then, of anecdote.

Despite the foregoing, there is ample evidence that he rarely made speeches which were pure exercises in improvisation. He almost always wrote them out with as much care as he devoted to work meant for publication. In his time, key speeches and lectures were news. They were reported in the newspapers, and with a degree of stenographic accuracy. Because of his early fame as a speaker, not to mention his renown as an author, he soon realized that his lectures and speeches *were* news and often would be published whether he liked it or not (he liked it). To assure greater authenticity of text, he early formed the habit of making available to reporters in advance written or typed copies of his speeches. Later, on occasion he even made proof sheets available.

Having written the speeches, he memorized them with avid attention to detail concerning emphasis and delivery. In Howells's words, "He studied every word and syllable, and memorized them by a system of mnemonics peculiar to himself, consisting of an arbitrary arrangement of things on a table—knives, forks, salt-cellars; inkstands, pens, boxes, or whatever was at hand—which stood for points and clauses and climaxes, and were at once indelible diction and constant suggestion." When Clemens delivered his speeches and lectures, including the after-dinner ones, he suggested by his casual demeanor, and occasionally by stammers, pauses or slips of grammar, that they were impromptu, and he did so with great naturalness.

"He was a most consummate actor," Howells reported, "with this difference from other actors, that he was the first to know the thoughts and invent the fancies to which his voice and action gave the color of life." Howells went further. "He studied every tone and gesture, and he forecast the result with the real audience from its result with that imagined audience. Therefore, it was beautiful to see him and to hear him; he rejoiced in the pleasure he gave and the blows of surprise which he dealt; and because he had his end in mind, he knew when to stop."

So much for method and manner. As for matter, one cannot but agree with Howells that "it is good matter, glad, honest, kind, just." And so because the speeches were crafted carefully, because they were not mere momentary extemporized efforts, they rank in importance with his other short writings.

With so much distance between us and his time, it is fascinating to have a look at how he appeared to his contemporaries—appeared as a living presence—and also to catch glimpses of his effect on them. The *San Francisco Examiner* of October 3, 1866, under the headlines "Local Intelligence/Mark Twain's Lecture," had the following to say about his maiden platform appearance.

"Until last evening there were but few people in this city who knew what manner of man the correspondent of the Sacramento Union, whose letters, signed 'Mark Twain,' had so often amused them, might be. Nor had 'Mark' himself as yet drawn aside the curtain which concealed his individuality, or made his bow to the public that was so well acquainted with his mind, in *propria persona*. There was naturally a good deal of curiosity felt by all who knew his writings (and their name is legion) to ascertain if the man himself was like the ideal conjured up by his letters, if he spoke as he wrote, if he could enchain the interest of an audience by the utterances of his lips as he has so successfully done by the emanations of his pen. Many fears were expressed, to speak the truth, as to the issue of the experiment—for it *was* an experiment. He had never before, so far as we know, spoken in public, which was one disadvantage. And again it was not unnaturally feared that like many other clever humorists on paper, he would prove but a Dryas-dust in speech.

"Still his reputation was so great, and the desire to know how he would come out of the ordeal so strong and general, that the Academy of Music last night was crowded to its utmost capacity, with an audience who may be considered as having represented the most critical elements of a particularly fastidious community. Whatever that audience should endorse, would be a success. That appeared to us almost a certainty, as we looked around the house previous to the appearance of the lecturer. No doubt the audience was disposed to be good-humored; but also, no doubt, they were determined not to be bored with impunity, nor to endorse a humbugging lecturer because he was a good writer."

Clemens was almost thirty-one then, and stage-frightened, and he and his friends had taken the precaution to "paper" the house.

"He came before them; he began to speak, and, in five minutes, all doubt as to his ability as a lecturer was dispelled. The most delightful discovery made was, we think, this: that he spoke as he writes. The same unexpected jokes—the same inimitable drollery—the same strong sense embodied in quaint phraseology. He is sometimes a little too rough; of that there can be no doubt. He verges, indeed, occasionally upon coarseness; but his roughness is the roughness of the crude diamond through the opaque incrustation of which flashes ever and anew a ray of that fountain of light which is the essence of the gem.

"We have no intention of analyzing his lecture of last night. It is to be hoped that he will repeat it, and it is much better that people should judge by themselves as to the matter, than we should attempt to direct their tastes. With the style alone we are dealing now—and the style is excellent.

"We confess that we have always preferred Mark Twain to Artemus Ward, as a humorist. We do not much respect that species of wit which has sprung up into a school in the United States so recently, and the fun of which rests chiefly upon labored cacography. In nine cases out of ten, the jokes which have a show of humor when clothed in blundering orthography, would, divested of their ragged covering, and written in plain English, appear but dreary jests. But apart from writing, we like Mark Twain's style of delivery better than that of Artemus Ward. There is life, more quaintness and drollery in it; more evidence of a genius indeed, we think.

"And there is a power which Mark developed last night which adds very much to our estimate of his abilities. He can talk seriously as well as humorously, and his serious descriptions are, if possible, even better than his drolleries. His picture of the volcano of Kilauea was an admirable piece of word painting. It was eloquent, and it showed, at least for us, that Mark Twain is something more than a mere humorist; he is a poet. There is no true poet to whom humor is a stranger, and there can be no true humorist without something of the *divine afflatus* in his breast."

Curiously, aside from the mention of Kilauea, the *Examiner* writer has said nothing about the subject of Clemens's lecture: the Sandwich Islands, which Clemens had visited earlier that year for four months. (The Sandwich Islands was an earlier name for the Hawaiian Islands.) Nor does he mention that the islands were the subject of Clemens's letters to the *Sacramento Union*.

"Mark Twain has undergone the test," he concludes, "and has come out triumphant from the ordeal. He has received the hall mark of approbation from a public whose endorsement is not to be despised or lightly thought of, and he will hereafter be recognized as the greatest humorist, not only of the Pacific slope, but of the United States of America."

Reporting on the same lecture, the San Francisco *Daily Alta California* made many of the same points, and closed by saying, "Mark Twain has thoroughly established himself as the most piquant and humorous writer and lecturer on this coast, since the days of the lamented 'John Phoenix.' "

The East Coast was as charmed by the newly celebrated Clemens as the West Coast was. A little more than three years later he was still working the Sandwich Islands materials. The *Philadelphia Evening Bulletin* (December 8, 1869) regarded him as "the very best of the humorists of his class." It said he was more extravagant and preposterous than John Phoenix, and superior to Artemus Ward because he had a decent regard for the English language, and that Josh Billings was not to be compared with him.

"Mark Twain indulges in humor because it is his nature to do so," the *Evening Bulletin* said. "It is impossible to read his productions or to hear him speak without being impressed with the conviction that his cleverest utterances are spontaneous, natural, unpremeditated. Like all men of his temperament he has a hearty hatred of sham, hypocrisy and cant, whether in religion, social life or politics. Some of his sturdiest blows have been aimed at the follies of the times; and we believe that he may, if he chooses, exercise a very considerable influence as a reformer. Ridicule, cleverly used, is one of the most powerful weapons against pretension and humbug; for it not only robs them of their false dignity, but it appeals strongly to the popular reader, and finds ready acceptance where serious discussion would not be permitted. . . . There may be some who will regard his calling as of smaller dignity than that of other men. Perhaps this is the class with which he is at war. The mass of intelligent people will agree with us that genuine humor is as rare and excellent a quality as any other, and that it is as respectable to amuse mankind as to stupefy them."

A review in the Washington, D.C., *Daily Morning Chronicle* (December 9, 1869) is interesting because the writer was not entirely sold on Clemens. Again Clemens had delivered his Sandwich Islands lecture. The reviewer gave him high marks but ranked him below Artemus Ward.

Clemens worked his Sandwich Islands materials heavily but almost always with fresh turns, and with increasing fame. The newspapers seemed to be competing with each other to describe his manner as droll. An unidentified clipping of no date in the Mark Twain Papers at the University of California at Berkeley affords a particularly vivid picture of him on the lecture platform.

"The apparent unconscious drollery of the lecturer began almost with his opening sentences, in which he deprecated any criticisms upon his inability to explain, or even to understand, why the Sandwich Islanders were placed so far away from everywhere else. From that time forth he held the audience in his hand. His hearers never laugh in the wrong place. Perhaps this is because he never indicates either by voice or manner what he thinks the right place for a laugh; and hence his audience has to listen sharply. . . . After you have listened to his wild extravagances for an hour, you are astonished to perceive that he has given you new and valuable views of the subject discussed. Every sentence may be burlesque, but the result is fact. And what insures his success as a teacher is that his manner is so irresistibly droll that it conquers at the first moment the natural revolt of the human mind against instruction."

It is extremely interesting to glimpse Clemens not only as Americans saw him, but Europeans as well. The *Northern Whig* of Belfast, Ireland, in a clipping of no date (again in the Mark Twain Papers in Berkeley) provides a particularly detailed portrait. On the clipping Clemens wrote, "I can't get halls in Ireland on dates that are satisfactory—lose too much time—so I don't lecture in Ireland at all. —Mark." A probable date for the clipping is early January 1874.

"We regret to learn that in consequence of other engagements Mr. S. L. Clemens ('Mark Twain') has been compelled to relinquish the intention of giving his now celebrated 'lecture' in Belfast, prior to his return to America on the 13th inst. The people of Belfast have missed a great enjoyment, for Mr. Clemens's 'lecture' is perfectly unique, and is one of the most singular, most humorous, and most exhilarating discourses that can be imagined. It is, in point of fact, impossible to form, without having heard him, an adequate conception of the steady deliberate gravity with which Mark Twain for an hour and a half pours out an even stream of jokes, and stories, and ludicrous phrases, his countenance remaining stonily impassive, whilst his auditors are shaking and screaming with laughter. Hardly changing his position, never moving the muscles of his face, speaking in a tone which is almost melancholy, with what the French call 'tears in his voice,' when he is saying the funniest things, the lecturer is the only person in the room who preserves a semblance of gravity or maintains any personal dignity. The closest attention is demanded from the audience, for often the finest bits of humor and the best hits are quietly dropped out parenthetically, as if the speaker either wasn't aware there was any fun in them or didn't notice it himself. Hearing Mark Twain's lecture is a perfect cure for low spirits, and as a hearty laugh is a very good thing alike for body and mind, we are sorry that, for the present, at any rate, our readers are not to have a call from Mr. Clemens on his way home."

From the above quotations the reader may be led to think that Clemens was invariably successful with his platform lectures and after-dinner speeches. Such was not the case, however. His lecture tour of several months in the lyceum season of 1871–72 was on the whole disappointing until he switched from "Reminiscences of Some Uncommonplace Characters Whom I Have Chanced to Meet," and later a lecture on Artemus Ward, to Western materials garnered from his forthcoming *Roughing It.* And the after-dinner speech he gave in Boston in December 1877, titled "Whittier's Birthday," was by all odds his most painful experience in giving a speech, judging by his reaction to it. For a while he believed the reports that he had been "irreverent beyond belief, beyond imagination" (his own words) toward New England's literary idols, Emerson, Holmes, Longfellow and Whittier, all of whom had been present at that dinner. But the reader may judge for herself (or himself) the degree of his irreverence by examining both the speech and Clemens's emotional and copious comments on it which follow it.

The reader may wonder why, if this speech wasn't successful, I have included it here. The reason is that it's one of Clemens's best and most interesting speeches, as he himself later understood. Its "failure" was social only, and in a limited, parochial setting. He had the cards stacked against him. It was immaterial whether the butts of his jokes were tolerant. The social setting itself was unprepared to accept his performance in the genial, freewheeling spirit in which it was offered.

Once again it is fascinating to examine the contemporary records for the light they shed on Clemens and his time. For example, the *Boston Advertiser* of December 18, 1877, devoted much of its front together with Thomas Power O'Connor, known as Tay Pay. That evening the lord mayor tendered him a lavish banquet in the town hall. Clemens did not partake of the twelve-course dinner and assorted wines and brandies. Next day the *Liverpool Daily Post* explained why, but first it honored him with headlines: "Mark Twain in Liverpool/ Dines with the Lord Mayor/Distinguished Company at the Town Hall/Characteristic Speech by the Humorist."

After listing some of the prominent people who attended, the article noted, "When the guests reached the cloakroom they were informed by prominent printed notices that Dr. Clemens would arrive at the dinner between eight and half-past. It appears that Mark, having had a sleepless night, and feeling fatigued as the result of his journey down from London, had retired to bed for a brief rest at the London and North-Western Hotel before attending the dinner. At twenty-five minutes past eight o'clock, when the menu had been all but gone through, the Lord Mayor left the hall, and a few minutes later escorted Mark into the presence of the company, who received him very warmly. Mark was smoking the inevitable cigar."

About a fortnight later O'Connor, the Irish politician, journalist and founder of *T.P.'s Weekly*, described the effect of Clemens's speech on the large audience. "It may seem impossible to write anything new about Mark Twain; and yet I believe I have something to say about him that has never been said before. He is known as the great humorist; as the great master of tears as well as laughter; as the great reasoner—as shown in his dissection of the Christian Science myth; as a great controversialist—witness his scathing exposure of the atrocities of King Leopold in the Congo; but I have never yet seen any mention of the fact that he is one of the great orators of his time.

"This fact first dawned upon me when I heard him speak at the lunch over which Mr. Birrell presided. He had made a speech for half an hour or so which consisted entirely of rollicking jokes which sent the whole company into fits of laughter; and everybody might have expected that he was going to end on this note—that, in fact, he had no other note on which he could play but this. And then all of a sudden, with a transition so easy and so natural that you scarcely perceived it at first, he dropped the cap and bells, and one saw into the depths of the man.

"Like so many great humorists, Mark Twain is often sad; like all men of strong and deep emotion, he is incapable of recovering from

page to the celebrated dinner, with appropriate headlines. "Whittier's Birthday./Testimonial in Honor of the/Quaker Poet./Dinner at the Brunswick Hotel Last/Evening—Gathering of the Con-/tributors of the Atlantic Monthly." Poets were stars in Boston then, the equivalent (at least in terms of news) of our sports stars, film stars, or astronauts fresh from outer space.

Poor Clemens, with his Western jokes he set himself up to seem the upstart crow in such a company. And if New England's literary establishment felt threatened by him, it had good cause, for his was the rising literary power. A splendid dinner it certainly was, and the *Advertiser* writer made the most of it. At times his prose seems to drip with idolatry.

"The gathering of gentlemen at the Brunswick Hotel last evening was of a rare kind. December 17 was the twentieth anniversary of the founding of the Atlantic Monthly, and was also the day which rounded out the life of the poet Whittier to seventy full years. To celebrate these events the publishers of the Atlantic, Messrs. H. O. Houghton & Co., invited the contributors to the magazine, both the present and the past, to meet in a never before attempted gathering. No heartier response could have been wished. Contributors of 1877 and 1857 were present, and the company was without doubt the most notable that has ever been seen in this country within four walls. The oldest and best known poets of our country were there, and the absent Bryant sent a letter of regret.

"About six o'clock the contributors began to gather in one of the reception rooms of the Brunswick, and, after a social union and friendly acquaintance-making for an hour, the doors of the east dining hall were opened, and the real interest of the evening from then onward was in that room. It had been tastefully prepared for the testimonial. Most marked of its decorations was the new portrait of Whittier issued by the Atlantic proprietors, which, set in a luxurious gilt frame and wreathed with a wealth of ivy, hung from the wall over the centre of the table. At the left, and facing it upon the opposite wall, was a beautiful country scene, with an old-fashioned New England dwelling —Whittier's birthplace. At the head of the table was a rich vase of flowers, and the table ornaments down the whole length were fitting to this decoration.

"If a painter could have caught for his canvas the picture presented when the hosts and guests were all seated, the scene would, as reality, have rivalled the imaginary one of Shakespeare and his friends. At the head of the table sat the chief host, Mr. H. O. Houghton. At his right was the honored guest and centre of loyal, loving interest, Mr. Whittier. Next to him sat the Concord philosopher, and at Mr. Emerson's right was Mr. Longfellow. The trio—Whittier, Emerson, Longfellow—gave a reverend, almost holy air to the place, and their gray hairs and expressive, joyful faces formed a beautiful group. On Mr. Houghton's left was Dr. Oliver Wendell Holmes; next to him Mr. William D. Howells, the editor of the magazine, and at the extreme left Mr. Charles Dudley Warner."

The writer then gave the arrangement of the guests, adding, "How this list of guests compares with the invitations accepted and what persons were compelled to decline the invitation may be seen from the following." Then he presented a list of fifty-two acceptances and another list of forty-one regrets, after which he offered the menu.

"MENU. OYSTERS ON SHELL. *Sauterne*. SOUP. Purée of Tomatoes au Croutons. Consommé Printanier Royal. *Sherry*. FISH. Broiled Chicken Halibut à la Navarin. Potatoes à la Hollandaise. Smelts Panne, Sauce Tartare. *Chablis*. REMOVES. Capon à l'Anglaise. Rice. Cauliflower. *Champagne*. *Mumm's Dry Verzenay. Roederer Imperial*. Saddle of English Mutton à la Pontoise. String Beans. Turnips. ENTREES. Filet of Beef, larded, Sauce Financière. Epinards Veloutés. Vol au Vent of Oysters à l'Américaine. *Claret*. Squabs en compote à la Francaise, Tomatoes Sautées. Terrapin Stewed, Maryland Style. Sorbet au Kirsch. GAME. Broiled Partridges on Toast. Canvasback Ducks. Water Cresses. Sweet Potatoes. Dressed Lettuce. *Burgundy*. PASTRY. Charlotte Russe. Gelée au Champagne. Gâteaux Variés. Confectionery. FRUIT. DESSERT. COFFEE.

"Dinner was leisurely served, and the social part was by far the most prominent element. Each item on the bill of fare was served as a separate course, and the intervals between them were occupied by the guests in rising from their seats and circulating about, laughing and joking. Were there space and time for the detail it would be most interesting to sketch the noteworthy and constantly changing groups. Here was Mr. Longfellow talking with Mr. Emerson and Mr. Whittier; Colonel Higginson drawing his chair around for a tête-à-tête with Mr. Longfellow; Mr. E. P. Whipple and Mr. Whittier conversing earnestly; Mr. Houghton mingling with his guests; Dr. Holmes sparkling with vivacity for all who greeted him; and so on, down both sides of

the room; all through the evening the scenes were most rare, attractive and memorable.

"At quarter past ten Mr. Houghton called the tables to order for the after-dinner speaking to begin. By this time the company was enlarged by the presence of ladies, who had not before appeared upon the scene. The doors at the sides of the hall were opened, and the women who were staying in the hotel filled the entrances and were favored with seats even between the tables. In the rear was the cloud of black faces—for the waiters took a keen interest in all the proceedings."

The *Advertiser* then printed the speech by H. O. Houghton.

"Mr. Houghton's allusions to Mr. Whittier were applauded most rapturously. The tables rose to their feet and gave cheer upon cheer. Mr. Whittier bore his welcome with characteristic modesty and spoke a few words in reply. Mr. Whittier was received with prolonged applause, and the entire company rose to do him honor."

Then Longfellow read a note which Whittier had sent him when he did not expect to be present, and then "an exquisite little poem which Mr. Whittier had sent to be read." Next Houghton introduced Howells, who introduced Emerson. Emerson read Whittier's poem "Ichabod," and then Howells made a speech. Holmes read a poem, after which Howells introduced Charles Eliot Norton and then read extracts from a few letters of regret, among them one from John J. Piatt whose poem he carefully read aloud.

"The humorist of the evening was next introduced and the amusement was intense, while the subjects of the wit, Longfellow, Emerson and Holmes, enjoyed it as much as any."

The paper now printed Clemens's speech, and then there were poem by R. H. Stoddard, remarks by Charles Dudley Warner, and summary of other addresses as well as a presentation in print of so of the letters of regret. Clearly the *Advertiser* writer was having no of the implied scandal of irreverence. Perhaps he was whitewash Clemens's gaffe by treating him as a sort of court jester or fool, because of his special condition and role was allowed to say th forbidden to saner mortals.

The final speech in the present collection, "The *Begum of Ben* was one of the most felicitous and moving that Clemens ever n After declining a dinner offered by the lord mayor of Liverpool gland, because he was being so heavily feted in London, Clemen persuaded to change his mind. He went to Liverpool on July 10,

some of fortune's wounds. And there are two wounds from which he has not recovered—from which he will never recover—the death of his wife and the death of his daughter, Susan. It was to these great sorrows that suddenly he referred, and at once there came over the gathering, which had been shouting its tumultuous laughter a moment before, that great, deadly stillness which is always the truest sign of an audience being stirred to its uttermost depths. And it was not merely the beautiful language in which this reference to his great trouble was clothed that thrilled the audience, it was the perfect delivery and management of his voice which had a great gamut of melodies—a voice the most perfect singer or actor might envy. And then it was that I realised how tremendous was Mark Twain's power over an audience; and how richly he was endowed with that divine afflatus which makes one man able to play on every chord of the hearts of hundreds or thousands of other men who listen to him. It was to me almost a revelation.

"But it was at the banquet given by Lord Mayor Japp in Liverpool last week that I saw the final proof that Mark Twain ought to have been an orator by occupation as well as a writer."

O'Connor then quoted from his introduction of Mark Twain, in which he stressed Clemens's determined and successful efforts to pay all his debts to the penny. (Clemens's publishing firm, Charles L. Webster & Co., mentioned previously, had become bankrupt in the spring of 1894, and Clemens, accompanied by his wife, Livy, and his daughter Clara, had gone on a round-the-world lecture tour to pay off his debts.)

"I omit the brilliant witticisms with which the greater part of Mark Twain's reply was occupied; everybody is now accustomed to the fact that there is no living man can approach him in a humorous after-dinner speech; what I want to insist on is the other side—the purely oratorical side of the man.

"Therefore do I come at once to the serious passages in which the great speech finally ended. I had—as has been seen—alluded to the historic lecturing tour he had taken to pay his debt which another man had accumulated for him in the business of publisher, and this is how he alluded to the fact; it will be seen how recurrent is the memory of that beautiful character who was the lodestar of his life."

Here O'Connor quoted that part of Clemens's speech in which the latter credited his wife for insisting that he pay one hundred cents on the dollar.

"You can realise how suddenly all the temper of that audience was transformed, and how this beautiful and touching allusion to that wondrous type of all the stern sense of right, combined with all a woman's tenderness and devotion, moved the great audience which Mark Twain was addressing.

"From that moment forward, the speech was not mere speech; it was a rich symphony. He approached at last a peroration, the like of which I have rarely heard. Here it is."

And then O'Connor gave the last part of the speech, beginning with "Home is dear to us all."

"A wonderful bit of literature, you will see at once; but that is not the reason I transfer it to these columns; it is because of the extraordinary way in which it was delivered, and its marvelous effect.

"The audience sat suddenly in spellbound and almost painful silence, and the voice rang out on the stillness—very quiet, very self-controlled, but clear as the bells whose chimes reach you on a far-off hill from the belfry in the chapel of your native town. And at last the audience could restrain itself no longer; and when in rich, resonant, uplifted voice Mark Twain sang out the words: 'I am the Begum of Bengal a hundred and twenty-three days out from Canton,' there burst forth a great cheer from one end of the room to the other. It seemed an inopportune cheer, and for a moment it upset Mark Twain, and yet it was felicitous in opportuneness. Slowly, after a long pause, came the last two words—like that curious, detached and high note in which a great piece of music sometimes suddenly and abruptly ends— 'Homeward Bound.' Again there was a cheer; but this time it was lower; it was subdued; it was the fitting echo to the beautiful words— with its double significance—the parting from a hospitable land, the return to the native land—wail and paean, paean and wail. It is only a great littérateur that could conceive such a passage; it is only a great orator that could so deliver it."

To the best of my knowledge, four items, all from Clemens's autobiographical writings, appear in book form for the first time: "Duelling," "Of Cats and Billiards," "Captain Osborn's Odd Adventure," and "Oxford." These appeared in the *North American Review* in April, September and October 1907. I came upon them while studying the files of the magazine for 1906–7 in connection with the publication of the biography his daughter Susy wrote of him when she was thirteen and fourteen.

When Clemens died, in April 1910, he was widely regarded as the most prominent and characteristic American writer of his generation. He had a large and devoted public, a public which had some reason to expect from him, as a posthumous publication, an autobiography which was the equal if not the superior of any yet written in the United States. It had been known for some time that he was writing such a book, and a number of chapters had appeared in twenty-five installments of the *North American Review* of 1906 and 1907. But his public was disappointed, for he had some curious notions about writing an autobiography, notions which kept changing over the years except in one respect: they became ever more curious.

He began with composing sections by hand and ended with a series of autobiographical dictations. As early as the '70s he was writing fragments. Around 1873 he wrote a brief autobiographical sketch for Charles Dudley Warner. In 1877 he recalled the early days in Florida, Missouri. In 1885, on the death of General Ulysses S. Grant, he dictated a series of recollections of his meetings with the General. In 1890 he set down the Paige typesetting machine episode, that fiasco of his middle years, and his memories of his mother. In 1897–98, while in Vienna, he wrote the brilliant chapters on the early days spent on his uncle's farm. In 1899 he composed an autobiographical sketch for his nephew, Samuel Moffett, on the basis of which Moffett wrote a biographical essay for the Uniform Edition of Mark Twain's works, issued in the same year. In 1904 he wrote the notes on the Villa Quarto and the memory of John Hay while living on the outskirts of Florence, Italy. And in 1906 he undertook the sustained series of dictations which added so greatly to the autobiography's bulk.

The task alternately irked and pleased him. In 1877, at the age of forty-two, he resolved to begin his autobiography at once, in a formal way.

"I did begin it," he wrote in 1904, "but the resolve melted away and disappeared in a week and I threw my beginning away. Since then, about every three or four years I have made other beginnings and thrown them away. Once I tried the experiment of a diary, intending to inflate that into an autobiography when its accumulation should furnish enough material, but that experiment lasted only a week; it took me half of every night to set down the history of the day, and at the week's end I did not like the result.

"Within the last eight or ten years I have made several attempts to do the autobiography in one way or another with a pen, but the result was not satisfactory; it was too literary. . . .

"With a pen in the hand the narrative stream is a canal; it moves slowly, smoothly, decorously, sleepily, it has no blemish except that it is all blemish. It is too literary, too prim, too nice; the gait and style and movement are not suited to narrative. That canal stream is always reflecting; it is its nature, it can't help it. Its slick shiny surface is interested in everything it passes along the banks—cows, foliage, flowers, everything. And so it wastes a lot of time in reflection."

Later he experimented with newspaper clippings. "I shall scatter through this Autobiography newspaper clippings without end. When I do not copy them into the text it means that I do not make them a part of the Autobiography—at least not of the earlier editions. I put them in on the theory that if they are not interesting in the earlier editions, a time will come when it may be well enough to insert them for the reason that age is quite likely to make them interesting although in their youth they may lack that quality."

He was not afraid to wander. "In this autobiography it is my purpose to wander whenever I please and come back when I get ready." Once, he thought he had found the "right" way. "Finally in Florence, in 1904, I hit upon the right way to do an Autobiography: Start it at no particular time of your life; wander at your free will all over your life; talk only about the thing which interests you for the moment; drop it the moment its interest threatens to pale, and turn your talk upon the new and more interesting thing that has intruded itself into your mind meantime. . . .

"And so, I have found the right plan. It makes my labor amusement —mere amusement, play, pastime, and wholly effortless."

But early in 1906 he was having difficulties. "The difficulties of it grow upon me all the time. For instance, the idea of blocking out a consecutive series of events which have happened to me, or which I imagine have happened to me—I can see that that is impossible for me. The only thing possible for me is to talk about the thing that something suggests at the moment—something in the middle of my life, perhaps, or something that happened only a few months ago. It is my purpose to extend these notes to 600,000 words, and possibly more. But that is going to take a long time—a long time."

At other times he was proud of what he was composing.

"I intend that this autobiography should become a model for all future autobiographies when it is published, after my death, and I also intend that it shall be read and admired a good many centuries because of its form and method—a form and method whereby the past and the present are constantly brought face to face, resulting in contrasts which newly fire up the interest all along like contact of flint with steel. Moreover, this autobiography of mine does not select from my life its showy episodes, but deals merely in the common experiences which go to make up the life of the average human being, and the narrative must interest the average human being because these episodes are of a sort which he is familiar with in his own life and in which he sees his own life reflected and set down in print. The usual, conventional autobiographer seems to particularly hunt out those occasions in his career when he came into contact with celebrated persons, whereas his contacts with the uncelebrated were just as interesting to him and would be to his reader, and were vastly more numerous than his collisions with the famous.

"Howells was here yesterday afternoon and I told him the whole scheme of this autobiography and its apparently systemless system— only apparently systemless, for it is not that. It is a deliberate system and the law of the system is that I shall talk about the matter which for the moment interests me, and cast it aside and talk about something else the moment its interest for me is exhausted. It is a system which follows no charted course and is not going to follow any such course. It is a system which is a complete and purposed jumble—a course which begins nowhere, follows no specified route, and can never reach an end while I am alive, for the reason that if I should talk to the stenographer two hours a day for a hundred years I should still never be able to set down a tenth part of the things which have interested me in my lifetime. I told Howells that this autobiography of mine would live a couple of thousand years without any effort and would then take a fresh start and live the rest of the time.

"He said he believed it would and asked me if I meant to make a library of it.

"I said that that was my design but that if I should live long enough the set of volumes could not be contained merely in a city, it would require a state, and that there would not be any multibillionaire alive, perhaps, at any time during its existence who would be able to buy a full set, except on the installment plan.

"Howells applauded, and was full of praises and indorsement, which was wise in him and judicious. If he had manifested a different spirit I would have thrown him out of the window. I like criticism, but it must be my way."

And in a similar vein:

"This Autobiography of mine differs from other autobiographies— differs from *all* other autobiographies, except Benvenuto's, perhaps. The conventional autobiography of all the ages is an open window. The autobiographer sits there and examines and discusses the people that go by—not all of them, but the notorious ones, the famous ones; those that wear fine uniforms, and crowns when it is not raining; and very great poets and great statesmen—illustrious people with whom he has had the high privilege of coming in contact. He likes to toss a wave of recognition to these with his hand as they go by and he likes to notice that the others are seeing him do this, and admiring. He likes to let on that in discussing these occasional people that wear the good clothes he is only interested in interesting his reader and is in a measure unconscious of himself.

"But this Autobiography of mine is not that kind of autobiography. This Autobiography of mine is a mirror and I am looking at myself in it all the time. Incidentally I notice the people that pass along at my back—I get glimpses of them in the mirror—and whenever they say or do anything that can help advertise me and flatter me and raise me in my own estimation I set these things down in my Autobiography. I rejoice when a king or a duke comes my way and makes himself useful to this Autobiography, but they are rare customers, with wide intervals between. I can use them with good effect as lighthouses and monuments along my way, but for real business I depend upon the common herd."

And in March of 1907, while on vacation in Bermuda, he recorded still another objective of the autobiography. "I do not need to stay here any longer, for I have completed the only work that was remaining for me to do in this life and that I could not possibly afford to leave uncompleted—my Autobiography. Although that is not finished, and will not be finished until I die, the object which I had in view in compiling it is accomplished: that object was to distribute it through my existing books and give each of them a new copyright of twenty-eight years, and thus defeat the copyright statute's cold intention to rob them and starve my daughters. I have dictated four or five hundred thousand words of autobiography already and if I should die tomorrow this mass of literature would be quite sufficient for the object which I had in view in manufacturing it."

In his autobiography Clemens let out most of the stops in whatever disciplines he had managed to maintain during his writing career. Bernard DeVoto, at one time the editor of the Mark Twain Papers, believed that Clemens's failure to write a coherent autobiography was due to a certain dread. "When he invoked Hannibal [that is, his early years] he found there not only the idyll of boyhood but anxiety, violence, supernatural horror, and an uncrystallized but enveloping dread. Much of his fiction, most of his masterpiece *[Huckleberry Finn]*, flows from that phantasy-bound anxiety.

"I think that the impulse to write his autobiography was in part an impulse to examine and understand that dread. And I think that the impulse was arrested short of genuine self-revelation because the dread was so central in him that he could approach it only symbolically, by way of fiction."

But one doesn't need to rely on such a theory to account for Clemens's difficulties with his autobiography. His mind, rich in memory and nostalgia, kept seeking anecdotal forms of recollection, which did not easily suit the chronological organization of the classic autobiography. And it was a case of the storyteller irked by "facts," the dross which inhibited fancy. If the facts were at times the losers, that worried Clemens not at all. "I don't believe these details are right but I don't care a rap. They will do just as well as the facts," he once wrote in his autobiography. In this respect he had good company, even the meticulous Henry Adams. Speaking of a journey to Washington with his father as a twelve-year-old in 1850, Adams wrote in his own autobiography, "The journey was meant as education, and as education it served the purpose of fixing in memory the stage of a boy's thought in 1850. . . . This was the journey he remembered. The actual journey may have been quite different, but the actual journey has no interest for education. The memory was all that mattered. . . ."

Clemens's life was a long and rich one. It must have seemed to him an inexhaustible mine of recollection. The associations streamed from it in a million directions, and it was his quixotic hope to capture most of them with the irony, humor and storytelling gift which were his own way of regarding the human drama. He was justly staggered by the size of the task. But did he actually fail? True, he didn't use a comprehensive, strategic approach, kept winning battles at the cost of losing a war. But many works of art are approached in this way, yet reach a great culmination. If he had lived a few years longer he might have found a sufficient perspective to organize the autobiography and edit out all the irrelevant materials which his odd methods of composition had allowed to sneak in. The fact is that the greatness is *there* in the raw materials. You can edit the trivia out but you can't edit the greatness in. One of the ironies of art is that it's possible to win a war and lose the battles, and that it's more tragic to lose the battles than the war. Formal neatness and comprehensive sweep: and dead or dying details. The details in Clemens's autobiography are intensely alive.

He was trying to amuse himself: that was his chief aim during the dictations. (It was during the dictations, near the end of his life, that he let most of the trivia in. And the trivia is always set apart. There is no case of a brilliant section which contains it. Everything is distinctly of a piece: the good is good, the bad is clearly bad.) He had produced his share of work in the world. He had outlived most of the people he cared for. The world was in a bad way and he wasn't averse to leaving it. And so he reminisced—on his own terms, not according to some theory of autobiographical composition.

It was in 1906 that Albert Bigelow Paine began to have an influence on the autobiography. Meeting Clemens at a dinner in New York, he asked if he might visit him soon. At their next meeting he proposed to write the official biography of him, and Clemens agreed. As a result, Clemens undertook a series of autobiographical dictations, to be used partly by Paine as the basis of the biography and to be published in and for themselves at an appropriate time. The word "appropriate" in this connection turned out to have a surprisingly flexible meaning. At first it was Clemens's intention to publish no part of his autobiography until a century after his death. But in some parts of the typescript he indicated marginally that they were to wait for fifty years after his death; in others seventy-five; and in several places five hundred years after the year of composition. As if to prove his inconsistency, he soon set about publishing the chapters in the *North American Review* which I have already mentioned.

As editor of the Mark Twain Papers after Clemens's death, Paine had the unhappy choice of publishing the autobiography as he found it or of regarding it as raw material and bringing it to a more or less finished state. I say unhappy because he faced a special dilemma. What he found was a manuscript of unwieldy size, consisting of a series of extended notes—a bundle of things relevant and inspired mixed with things irrelevant and dull, all in so disorganized a condition as to be bewildering, although the sections and fragments in themselves were thematically, stylistically and factually complete. If Paine had published the manuscript as he found it he would have been charged with lack of understanding of his whole responsibility. If he had edited the manuscript he would probably have been criticized even more strongly. He decided to leave the responsibility with Clemens: except for the omissions he made whenever the spirit moved him, usually in the interest of propriety as he understood it, often failing to warn the reader that something had been left out.

He had another choice to make. Clemens had requested him to publish the autobiography not in chronological order but in the sequence in which it was written and dictated. What an extraordinary idea! As if the stream of composition time were in some mysterious way more revealing than that of autobiographical time! To gauge Paine's problem adequately we must keep in mind that Clemens had approached his autobiography from all directions simultaneously. Paine offered no details of the wording or manner of Clemens's request, nor did he suggest whether it was written or given orally, or whether made at the beginning of their relationship or near the end. And so we're unable to judge how much earnestness there was behind it. He merely noted, "The various divisions and chapters of this work, in accordance with the author's wish, are arranged in the order in which they were written, regardless of the chronology of events." As a result of this system, it's impossible to call to memory another autobiography by a major writer which made its debut so inauspiciously and in so confusing a manner.

The shortcomings of the two-volume edition, issued in 1924, were plain. The autobiography was incomplete, raw, badly arranged. It was a grab bag, a repository for anything and everything. Its chief flaw was that it correctly reflected Clemens's notions and methods. Beginning with fragments composed by hand as early as 1870, it ranged over sublime and ridiculous chapters down to dictations of April 1906.

Much of it was embarrassing: fragmentary notations on news stories of the day, exchanges of letters, opinions of the moment. Parts, such as the reminiscences of the uncle's farm, were among the best things Clemens had ever written, and cried out to be saved. But it was difficult to save such an inauspicious edition, and the good things in it began to be forgotten with the bad. In time there were literate readers, and admirers of Mark Twain, who barely realized he had tried his hand at an autobiography. Paine's hope of issuing more volumes in the autobiographical series was doomed.

Sixteen years after the appearance of Paine's edition, Bernard DeVoto issued *Mark Twain in Eruption,* which offered the public a large new portion of the autobiographical typescript. DeVoto didn't like Paine's edition, which he called shapeless and annoying. He didn't emulate Paine's technique of "sampling" the contents of the autobiography but instead depended on "omitting trivialities and joining together things that belonged together." He didn't hesitate to select, rearrange and edit. The organization of his volume was thematic. But the book he issued was supplementary to and conditioned by the edition of his predecessor, consequently it was as incomplete as Paine's two volumes.

Speaking of the order which he gave his volume, DeVoto said, "It is a loose order but it is the tightest one that can be given the Autobiography; and occasionally I have chosen to let the original order stand, at some cost in coherence." But he was in error. His thematic order was an imposed one and could not accurately be called the tightest which could be given the autobiography, the essence of whose internal order is time. The tightest order of any work is the order functional to it, inherent in it, which is in harmony with its subject.

DeVoto worked only with the unpublished parts of the typescript and as he did so he had occasion to make omissions. "I have left out what seems to me irrelevant or uninteresting," he wrote. Yet later in his Introduction he admitted that he left out certain passages because they contained matter which was "fantastic and injurious." He added that he had omitted other passages "because the exaggeration gets so far into phantasy that it becomes a trivial rage." I have been able to examine the passages in question and have reached the conclusion (not an unexpected one) that the wise course is to let Clemens have his say in these matters of high emotion.

In 1959 I brought out my own edition, *The Autobiography of Mark*

Twain. Working with the autobiographical manuscript as a whole, both unpublished and published parts, I weeded out a variety of material. I did this for several reasons: in order to make a wieldy volume which would meet certain requirements of the general reader, for whom the book was designed; to unburden the excellent parts of the dated, dull, trivial and journalese sections of the work; and to concentrate less on opinion and second-hand recollection and more on the more truly autobiographical, the more purely literary and the more characteristically humorous material. My volume is to a high degree anecdotal, but I believe this to be a virtue, rather than a defect, in that it correctly represents the creative slant of Clemens's mind. Also, the materials of my volume are arranged in chronological sequence.

"A Heavenly Place" is as wonderful for me now as when I first encountered it. What an immense array of details this portrait is, the kind that recall vividly the very texture of the life of that time and place, his uncle's farm, a Missouri farm around 1845. What a power of recollection Clemens has. And a great humanity pervading his recall, and the gentle, teasing irony, the irony always at his command. And the pathos—for example his mother on the subject of Sandy's (the slave boy's) singing, forgetting he was sold away from his family as a child. Clemens is very great in nostalgia. He recalls the poetically important things, the psychologically important ones, those that are still alive in him and which strike sparks in us. It's priceless stuff. The range and extent of his memory are impressive. And always, and with seeming ease, he finds the right language for his recollections. He's a master at remembering the physicality of life. And the details are tightly packed together. No padding. Exquisite economy. We have the sense of a mind pressured by richnesses crowding it, eager to unburden itself, and loving the language as the medium for doing this.

"Beginnings as an Author" is full of withering irony regarding his publishers (Webb and Bliss), written in his high style. It's fascinating to hear him speak about his literary/publishing beginnings, those of one of the great careers in American literature. But one must remember that he had a way of being suspicious and hard with respect to his publishers, and that his memory might not always be accurate regarding his dealings with them.

And now to return to where I began: the chapters from the *North American Review* which make their first book appearance. It's a pleasure at this late date, in this time of renewed celebration of Mark

Twain's greatness as a man and an author, to be able to offer the book reader not merely writings by him for the first time, but such charming ones.

Princeton, New Jersey
December 24, 1985

STORIES

THE NOTORIOUS JUMPING FROG
OF CALAVERAS COUNTY

In compliance with the request of a friend of mine, who wrote me from the East, I called on good-natured, garrulous old Simon Wheeler, and inquired after my friend's friend, Leonidas W. Smiley, as requested to do, and I hereunto append the result. I have a lurking suspicion that *Leonidas W.* Smiley is a myth; that my friend never knew such a personage; and that he only conjectured that if I asked old Wheeler about him, it would remind him of his infamous *Jim* Smiley, and he would go to work and bore me to death with some exasperating reminiscence of him as long and as tedious as it should be useless to me. If that was the design, it succeeded.

I found Simon Wheeler dozing comfortably by the bar-room stove of the dilapidated tavern in the decayed mining camp of Angel's, and I noticed that he was fat and bald-headed, and had an expression of winning gentleness and simplicity upon his tranquil countenance. He roused up, and gave me good day. I told him that a friend of mine had commissioned me to make some inquiries about a cherished companion of his boyhood named *Leonidas W.* Smiley—*Rev. Leonidas W.* Smiley, a young minister of the Gospel, who he had heard was at one time a resident of Angel's Camp. I added that if Mr. Wheeler could tell me anything about this Rev. Leonidas W. Smiley, I would feel under many obligations to him.

Simon Wheeler backed me into a corner and blockaded me there with his chair, and then sat down and reeled off the monotonous narrative which follows this paragraph. He never smiled, he never frowned, he never changed his voice from the gentle-flowing key to which he tuned his initial sentence, he never betrayed the slightest suspicion of enthusiasm; but all through the interminable narrative there ran a vein of impressive earnestness and sincerity, which showed me plainly that, so far from his imagining that there was anything ridiculous or funny about his story, he regarded it as a really important matter, and admired its two heros as men of transcendent genius in *finesse*. I let him go on in his own way, and never interrupted him once.

"Rev. Leonidas W. H'm, Reverend Le—well, there was a feller here once by the name of *Jim* Smiley, in the winter of '49—or maybe it was the spring of '50—I don't recollect exactly, somehow, though what makes me think it was one or the other is because I remember the big flume warn't finished when he first come to the camp; but anyway, he was the curiousest man about always betting on anything that turned up you ever see, if he could get anybody to bet on the other side; and if he couldn't he'd change sides. Any way that suited the other man would suit *him*—any way just so's he got a bet, *he* was satisfied. But still he was lucky, uncommon lucky; he most always come out winner. He was always ready and laying for a chance; there couldn't be no solit'ry thing mentioned but that feller'd offer to bet on it, and take ary side you please, as I was just telling you. If there was a horse-race, you'd find him flush or you'd find him busted at the end of it; if there was a dog-fight, he'd bet on it; if there was a cat-fight, he'd bet on it; if there was a chicken-fight, he'd bet on it; why, if there was two birds setting on a fence, he would bet you which one would fly first; or if there was a camp-meeting, he would be there reg'lar to bet on Parson Walker, which he judged to be the best exhorter about here, and so he was too, and a good man. If he even see a straddle-bug start to go anywheres, he would bet you how long it would take him to get to—to wherever he was going to, and if you took him up, he would foller that straddle-bug to Mexico but what he would find out where he was bound for and how long he was on the road. Lots of the boys here has seen that Smiley, and can tell you about him. Why, it never made no difference to *him*—he'd bet on *any* thing—the dangdest feller. Parson Walker's wife laid very sick once, for a good while, and it seemed as if they warn't going to save her; but one morning he come in, and Smiley up and asked him how she was, and he said she was considerable better—thank the Lord for his inf'nite mercy—and coming on so smart that with the blessing of Prov'dence she'd get well yet; and

Smiley, before he thought, says, 'Well, I'll resk two-and-a-half she don't anyway.'

"Thish-yer Smiley had a mare—the boys called her the fifteen-minute nag, but that was only in fun, you know, because of course she was faster than that—and he used to win money on that horse, for all she was so slow and always had the asthma, or the distemper, or the consumption, or something of that kind. They used to give her two or three hundred yards' start, and then pass her under way; but always at the fag end of the race she'd get excited and desperate like, and come cavorting and straddling up, and scattering her legs around limber, sometimes in the air, and sometimes out to one side among the fences, and kicking up m-o-r-e dust and raising m-o-r-e racket with her coughing and sneezing and blowing her nose—and *always* fetch up at the stand just about a neck ahead, as near as you could cipher it down.

"And he had a little small bull-pup, that to look at him you'd think he warn't worth a cent but to set around and look ornery and lay for a chance to steal something. But as soon as money was up on him he was a different dog; his under-jaw'd begin to stick out like the fo'castle of a steamboat, and his teeth would uncover and shine like the furnaces. And a dog might tackle him and bully-rag him, and bite him, and throw him over his shoulder two or three times, and Andrew Jackson—which was the name of the pup—Andrew Jackson would never let on but what *he* was satisfied, and hadn't expected nothing else—and the bets being doubled and doubled on the other side all the time, till the money was all up; and then all of a sudden he would grab that other dog jest by the j'int of his hind leg and freeze to it—not chaw, you understand, but only just grip and hang on till they throwed up the sponge, if it was a year. Smiley always come out winner on that pup, till he harnessed a dog once that didn't have no hind legs, because they'd been sawed off in a circular saw, and when the thing had gone along far enough, and the money was all up, and he come to make a snatch for his pet holt, he see in a minute how he'd been imposed on, and how the other dog had him in the door, so to speak, and he 'peared surprised, and then he looked sorter discouraged-like, and didn't try no more to win the fight, and so he got shucked out bad. He give Smiley a look, as much as to say his heart was broke, and it was *his* fault, for putting up a dog that hadn't no hind legs for him to take holt of, which was his main dependence in a fight, and then he limped off a piece and laid down and died. It was a good pup, was that Andrew Jackson, and would have made a name for hisself if he'd lived, for the stuff was in him and he had genius—I know it, because he hadn't no opportunities to speak of, and it don't stand to reason that a dog could make such a fight as he could under them circumstances if he hadn't no talent. It always makes me feel sorry when I think of that last fight of his'n, and the way it turned out.

"Well, thish-yer Smiley had rat-tarriers, and chicken cocks, and tomcats and all them kind of things, till you couldn't rest, and you couldn't fetch nothing for him to bet on but he'd match you. He ketched a frog one day, and took him home, and said he cal'lated to educate him; and so he never done nothing for three months but set in his back yard and learn that frog to jump. And you bet you he *did* learn him, too. He'd give him a little punch behind, and the next minute you'd see that frog whirling in the air like a doughnut—see him turn one summerset, or maybe a couple, if he got a good start, and come down flat-footed and all right, like a cat. He got him up so in the matter of ketching flies, and kep' him in practice so constant, that he'd nail a fly every time as fur as he could see him. Smiley said all a frog wanted was education, and he could do 'most anything—and I believe him. Why, I've seen him set Dan'l Webster down here on this floor—Dan'l Webster was the name of the frog—and sing out, 'Flies, Dan'l, flies!' and quicker'n you could wink he'd spring straight up and snake a fly off'n the counter there, and flop down on the floor ag'in as solid as a gob of mud, and fall to scratching the side of his head with his hind foot as indifferent as if he hadn't no idea he'd been doin' any more'n any frog might do. You never see a frog so modest and straightfor'ard as he was, for all he was so gifted. And when it come to fair and square jumping on a dead level, he could get over more ground at one straddle than any animal of his breed you ever see. Jumping on a dead level was his strong suit, you understand; and when it come to that, Smiley would ante up money on him as long as he had a red. Smiley was monstrous proud of his frog, and well he might be, for fellers that had traveled and been everywheres all said he laid over any frog that ever *they* see.

"Well, Smiley kep' the beast in a little lattice box, and he used to fetch him down-town sometimes and lay for a bet. One day a feller—a stranger in the camp, he was—come across him with his box, and says:

" 'What might it be that you've got in the box?'

"And Smiley says, sorter indifferent-like, 'It might be a parrot, or it might be a canary, maybe, but it ain't—it's only just a frog.'

"And the feller took it, and looked at it careful, and turned it round this way and that, and says, 'H'm—so 'tis. Well, what's *he* good for?'

" 'Well,' Smiley says, easy and careless, 'he's good enough for *one* thing, I should judge—he can outjump any frog in Calaveras County.'

"The feller took the box again, and took another long, particular look, and give it back to Smiley, and says, very deliberate, 'Well,' he says, 'I don't see no p'ints about that frog that's any better'n any other frog.'

" 'Maybe you don't,' Smiley says. 'Maybe you understand frogs and maybe you don't understand 'em; maybe you've had experience, and maybe you ain't only a amature, as it were. Anyways, I've got *my* opinion, and I'll resk forty dollars that he can outjump any frog in Calaveras County.'

"And the feller studied a minute, and then says, kinder sad-like, 'Well, I'm only a stranger here, and I ain't got no frog; but if I had a frog, I'd bet you.'

"And then Smiley says, 'That's all right—that's all right—if you'll hold my box a minute, I'll go and get you a frog.' And so the feller took the box, and put up his forty dollars along with Smiley's, and set down to wait.

"So he set there a good while thinking and thinking to himself, and then he got the frog out and prized his mouth open and took a tea-spoon and filled him full of quail-shot—filled him pretty near up to his chin—and set him on the floor. Smiley he went to the swamp and slopped around in the mud for a long time, and finally he ketched a frog, and fetched him in, and give him to this feller, and says:

" 'Now, if you're ready, set him alongside of Dan'l, with his fore paws just even with Dan'l's, and I'll give the word.' Then he says, 'One—two—three—*git!*' and him and the feller touched up the frogs from behind, and the new frog hopped off lively, but Dan'l give a heave, and hysted up his shoulders—so—like a Frenchman, but it warn't no use—he couldn't budge; he was planted as solid as a church, and he couldn't no more stir than if he was anchored out. Smiley was a good deal surprised, and he was disgusted too, but he didn't have no idea what the matter was, of course.

"The feller took the money and started away; and when he was going out at the door, he sorter jerked his thumb over his shoulder—

so—at Dan'l, and says again, very deliberate, 'Well,' he says, '*I* don't see no p'ints about that frog that's any better'n any other frog.'

"Smiley he stood scratching his head and looking down at Dan'l a long time, and at last he says, 'I do wonder what in the nation that frog throw'd off for—I wonder if there ain't something the matter with him—he 'pears to look mighty baggy, somehow.' And he ketched Dan'l by the nap of the neck, and hefted him, and says, 'Why blame my cats if he don't weigh five pound!' and turned him upside down and he belched out a double handful of shot. And then he see how it was, and he was the maddest man—he set the frog down and took out after that feller, but he never ketched him. And—"

[Here Simon Wheeler heard his name called from the front yard, and got up to see what was wanted.] And turning to me as he moved away, he said: "Just set where you are, stranger, and rest easy—I ain't going to be gone a second."

But, by your leave, I did not think that a continuation of the history of the enterprising vagabond *Jim* Smiley would be likely to afford me much information concerning the Rev. *Leonidas W.* Smiley, and so I started away.

At the door I met the sociable Wheeler returning, and he button-holed me and recommenced:

"Well, thish-yer Smiley had a yaller one-eyed cow that didn't have no tail, only just a short stump like a bannanner, and—"

However, lacking both time and inclination, I did not wait to hear about the afflicted cow, but took my leave.

1865

A DAY AT NIAGARA

Niagara Falls is a most enjoyable place of resort. The hotels are excellent, and the prices not at all exorbitant. The opportunities for fishing are not surpassed in the country; in fact, they are not even equaled elsewhere. Because, in other localities, certain places in the streams are much better than others; but at Niagara one place is just as good as another, for the reason that the fish do not bite anywhere, and so there is no use in your walking five miles to fish, when you can depend on being just as unsuccessful nearer home. The advantages of this state of things have never heretofore been properly placed before the public.

The weather is cool in summer, and the walks and drives are all pleasant and none of them fatiguing. When you start out to "do" the Falls you first drive down about a mile, and pay a small sum for the privilege of looking down from a precipice into the narrowest part of the Niagara River. A railway "cut" through a hill would be as comely if it had the angry river tumbling and foaming through its bottom. You can descend a staircase here a hundred and fifty feet down, and stand at the edge of the water. After you have done it, you will wonder why you did it; but you will then be too late.

The guide will explain to you, in his blood-curdling way, how he saw the little steamer, *Maid of the Mist,* descend the fearful rapids— how first one paddle-box was out of sight behind the raging billows and then the other, and at what point it was that her smokestack toppled overboard, and where her planking began to break and part asunder—and how she did finally live through the trip, after accomplishing the incredible feat of traveling seventeen miles in six minutes, or six miles in seventeen minutes, I have really forgotten which. But it was very extraordinary, anyhow. It is worth the price of admission to hear the guide tell the story nine times in succession to different parties, and never miss a word or alter a sentence or a gesture.

Then you drive over to Suspension Bridge, and divide your misery between the chances of smashing down two hundred feet into the river below, and the chances of having the railway-train overhead smashing down onto you. Either possibility is discomforting taken by itself, but, mixed together, they amount in the aggregate to positive unhappiness.

On the Canada side you drive along the chasm between long ranks of photographers standing guard behind their cameras, ready to make an ostentatious frontispiece of you and your decaying ambulance, and your solemn crate with a hide on it, which you are expected to regard in the light of a horse, and a diminished and unimportant background of sublime Niagara; and a great many people *have* the incredible effrontery or the native depravity to aid and abet this sort of crime.

Any day, in the hands of these photographers, you may see stately pictures of papa and mamma, Johnny and Bub and Sis, or a couple of country cousins, all smiling vacantly, and all disposed in studied and uncomfortable attitudes in their carriage, and all looming up in their awe-inspiring imbecility before the snubbed and diminished present-ment of that majestic presence whose ministering spirits are the rain-bows, whose voice is the thunder, whose awful front is veiled in clouds, who was monarch here dead and forgotten ages before this hackful of small reptiles was deemed temporarily necessary to fill a crack in the world's unnoted myriads, and will still be monarch here ages and decades of ages after they shall have gathered themselves to their blood-relations, the other worms, and been mingled with the unremembering dust.

There is no actual harm in making Niagara a background whereon to display one's marvelous insignificance in a good strong light, but it requires a sort of superhuman self-complacency to enable one to do it.

When you have examined the stupendous Horseshoe Fall till you are satisfied you cannot improve on it, you return to America by the new Suspension Bridge, and follow up the bank to where they exhibit the Cave of the Winds.

Here I followed instructions, and divested myself of all my clothing, and put on a waterproof jacket and overalls. This costume is pictur-esque, but not beautiful. A guide, similarly dressed, led the way down a flight of winding stairs, which wound and wound, and still kept on winding long after the thing ceased to be a novelty, and then termi-nated long before it had begun to be a pleasure. We were then well down under the precipice, but still considerably above the level of the river.

We now began to creep along flimsy bridges of a single plank, our persons shielded from destruction by a crazy wooden railing, to which I clung with both hands—not because I was afraid, but because I wanted to. Presently the descent became steeper, and the bridge flim-sier, and sprays from the American Fall began to rain down on us in fast increasing sheets that soon became blinding, and after that our progress was mostly in the nature of groping. Now a furious wind began to rush out from behind the waterfall, which seemed deter-mined to sweep us from the bridge, and scatter us on the rocks and among the torrents below. I remarked that I wanted to go home; but it was too late. We were almost under the monstrous wall of water thun-dering down from above, and speech was in vain in the midst of such a pitiless crash of sound.

In another moment the guide disappeared behind the deluge, and, bewildered by the thunder, driven helplessly by the wind, and smitten by the arrowy tempest of rain, I followed. All was darkness. Such a mad storming, roaring, and bellowing of warring wind and water never crazed my ears before. I bent my head, and seemed to receive the Atlantic on my back. The world seemed going to destruction. I could not see anything, the flood poured down so savagely. I raised my head, with open mouth, and the most of the American cataract went down my throat. If I had sprung a leak now I had been lost. And at this moment I discovered that the bridge had ceased, and we must trust for a foothold to the slippery and precipitous rocks. I never was so scared before and survived it. But we got through at last, and emerged into the open day, where we could stand in front of the laced and frothy and seething world of descending water, and look at it. When I saw how much of it there was, and how fearfully in earnest it was, I was sorry I had gone behind it.

The noble Red Man has always been a friend and darling of mine. I love to read about him in tales and legends and romances. I love to read of his inspired sagacity, and his love of the wild free life of mountain and forest, and his general nobility of character, and his stately metaphorical manner of speech, and his chivalrous love for the dusky maiden, and the picturesque pomp of his dress and accoutrements. Especially the picturesque pomp of his dress and accoutrements. When I found the shops at Niagara Falls full of dainty Indian beadwork, and stunning moccasins, and equally stunning toy figures representing human beings who carried their weapons in holes bored through their arms and bodies, and had feet shaped like a pie, I was filled with emotion. I knew that now, at last, I was going to come face to face with the noble Red Man.

A lady clerk in a shop told me, indeed, that all her grand array of curiosities were made by the Indians, and that they were plenty about the Falls, and that they were friendly, and it would not be dangerous to speak to them. And sure enough, as I approached the bridge leading over to Luna Island, I came upon a noble Son of the Forest sitting under a tree, diligently at work on a bead reticule. He wore a slouch hat and brogans, and had a short black pipe in his mouth. Thus does the baneful contact with our effeminate civilization dilute the picturesque pomp which is so natural to the Indian when far removed from us in his native haunts. I addressed the relic as follows:

"Is the Wawhoo-Wang-Wang of the Whack-a-Whack happy? Does

the great Speckled Thunder sigh for the war-path, or is his heart contented with dreaming of the dusky maiden, the Pride of the Forest? Does the mighty Sachem yearn to drink the blood of his enemies, or is he satisfied to make bead reticules for the pappooses of the paleface? Speak, sublime relic of bygone grandeur—venerable ruin, speak!"

The relic said:

"An' is it mesilf, Dennis Hooligan, that ye'd be takin' for a dirty Injin, ye drawlin', lantern-jawed, spider-legged divil! By the piper that played before Moses, I'll ate ye!"

I went away from there.

By and by, in the neighborhood of the Terrapin Tower, I came upon a gentle daughter of the aborigines in fringed and beaded buckskin moccasins and leggins, seated on a bench with her pretty wares about her. She had just carved out a wooden chief that had a strong family resemblance to a clothespin, and was now boring a hole through his abdomen to put his bow through. I hesitated a moment, and then addressed her:

"Is the heart of the forest maiden heavy? Is the Laughing Tadpole lonely? Does she mourn over the extinguished council-fires of her race, and the vanished glory of her ancestors? Or does her sad spirit wander afar toward the hunting-grounds whither her brave Gobbler-of-the-Lightnings is gone? Why is my daughter silent? Has she aught against the paleface stranger?"

The maiden said:

"Faix, an' is it Biddy Malone ye dare to be callin' names? Lave this, or I'll shy your lean carcass over the cataract, ye sniveling blaggard!"

I adjourned from there also.

"Confound these Indians!" I said. "They told me they were tame; but, if appearances go for anything, I should say they were all on the warpath."

I made one more attempt to fraternize with them, and only one. I came upon a camp of them gathered in the shade of a great tree, making wampum and moccasins, and addressed them in the language of friendship:

"Noble Red Men, Braves, Grand Sachems, War Chiefs, Squaws, and High Muck-a-Mucks, the paleface from the land of the setting sun greets you! You, Beneficent Polecat—you, Devourer of Mountains—you, Roaring Thundergust—you, Bully Boy with a Glass Eye—the paleface from beyond the great waters greets you all! War and pestilence have thinned your ranks and destroyed your once proud nation. Poker and seven-up, and a vain modern expense for soap, unknown to your glorious ancestors, have depleted your purses. Appropriating, in your simplicity, the property of others has gotten you into trouble. Misrepresenting facts, in your simple innocence, has damaged your reputation with the soulless usurper. Trading for forty-rod whisky, to enable you to get drunk and happy and tomahawk your families, has played the everlasting mischief with the picturesque pomp of your dress, and here you are, in the broad light of the nineteenth century, gotten up like the ragtag and bobtail of the purlieus of New York. For shame! Remember your ancestors! Recall their mighty deeds! Remember Uncas!—and Red Jacket!—and Hole in the Day!—and Whoopdedoodledo! Emulate their achievements! Unfurl yourselves under my banner, noble savages, illustrious guttersnipes—"

"Down wid him!" "Scoop the blaggard!" "Burn him!" "Hang him!" "Dhround him!"

It was the quickest operation that ever was. I simply saw a sudden flash in the air of clubs, brick-bats, fists, bead-baskets, and moccasins —a single flash, and they all appeared to hit me at once, and no two of them in the same place. In the next instant the entire tribe was upon me. They tore half the clothes off me; they broke my arms and legs; they gave me a thump that dented the top of my head till it would hold coffee like a saucer; and, to crown their disgraceful proceedings and add insult to injury, they threw me over the Niagara Falls, and I got wet.

About ninety or a hundred feet from the top, the remains of my vest caught on a projecting rock, and I was almost drowned before I could get loose. I finally fell, and brought up in a world of white foam at the foot of the Fall, whose celled and bubbly masses towered up several inches above my head. Of course I got into the eddy. I sailed round and round in it forty-four times—chasing a chip and gaining on it— each round trip a half-mile—reaching for the same bush on the bank forty-four times, and just exactly missing it by a hair's-breadth every time.

At last a man walked down and sat down close to that bush, and put a pipe in his mouth, and lit a match, and followed me with one eye and kept the other on the match, while he sheltered it in his hands from the wind. Presently a puff of wind blew it out. The next time I swept around he said:

"Got a match?"

"Yes; in my other vest. Help me out, please."

"Not for Joe."

When I came round again, I said:

"Excuse the seemingly impertinent curiosity of a drowning man, but will you explain this singular conduct of yours?"

"With pleasure. I am the coroner. Don't hurry on my account. I can wait for you. But I wish I had a match."

I said: "Take my place, and I'll go and get you one."

He declined. This lack of confidence on his part created a coldness between us, and from that time forward I avoided him. It was my idea, in case anything happened to me, to so time the occurrence as to throw my custom into the hands of the opposition coroner on the American side.

At last a policeman came along, and arrested me for disturbing the peace by yelling at people on shore for help. The judge fined me, but I had the advantage of him. My money was with my pantaloons, and my pantaloons were with the Indians.

Thus I escaped. I am now lying in a very critical condition. At least I am lying anyway—critical or not critical. I am hurt all over, but I cannot tell the full extent yet, because the doctor is not done taking inventory. He will make out my manifest this evening. However, thus far he thinks only sixteen of my wounds are fatal. I don't mind the others.

Upon regaining my right mind, I said:

"It is an awful savage tribe of Indians that do the beadwork and moccasins for Niagara Falls, doctor. Where are they from?"

"Limerick, my son."

1869

A TRUE STORY

Repeated word for word as I heard it

It was summer-time, and twilight. We were sitting on the porch of the farmhouse, on the summit of the hill, and "Aunt Rachel" was sitting respectfully below our level, on the steps—for she was our servant, and colored. She was of mighty frame and stature; she was sixty years old, but her eye was undimmed and her strength unabated. She was a cheerful, hearty soul, and it was no more trouble for her to laugh than it is for a bird to sing. She was under fire now, as usual when the day was done. That is to say, she was being chaffed without mercy, and was enjoying it. She would let off peal after peal of laughter, and then sit with her face in her hands and shake with throes of enjoyment which she could no longer get breath enough to express. At such a moment as this a thought occurred to me, and I said:

"Aunt Rachel, how is it that you've lived sixty years and never had any trouble?"

She stopped quaking. She paused, and there was a moment of silence. She turned her face over her shoulder toward me, and said, without even a smile in her voice:

"Misto C——, is you in 'arnest?"

It surprised me a good deal; and it sobered my manner and my speech, too. I said:

"Why, I thought—that is, I meant—why, you *can't* have had any trouble. I've never heard you sigh, and never seen your eye when there wasn't a laugh in it."

She faced fairly around now, and was full of earnestness.

"Has I had any trouble? Misto C——, I's gwyne to tell you, den I leave it to you. I was bawn down 'mongst de slaves; I knows all 'bout slavery, 'case I ben one of 'em my own se'f. Well, sah, my ole man—dat's my husban'—he was lovin' an' kind to me, jist as kind as you is to yo' own wife. An' we had chil'en—seven chil'en—an' we loved dem chil'en jist de same as you loves yo' chil'en. Dey was black, but de Lord can't make no chil'en so black but what dey mother loves 'em an' wouldn't give 'em up, no, not for anything dat's in dis whole world.

"Well, sah, I was raised in ole Fo'ginny, but my mother she was raised in Maryland; an' my *souls!* she was turrible when she'd git started! My *lan'!* but she'd make de fur fly! When she'd git into dem tantrums, she always had one word dat she said. She'd straighten herse'f up an' put her fists in her hips an' say, 'I want you to under-stan' dat I wa'n't bawn in de mash to be fool' by trash! I's one o' de ole Blue Hen's Chickens, *I* is!' 'Ca'se, you see, dat's what folks dat's bawn in Maryland calls deyselves, an' dey's proud of it. Well, dat was her word. I don't ever forgit it, beca'se she said it so much, an' beca'se she said it one day when my little Henry tore his wris' awful, and most busted his head, right up at de top of his forehead, an' de niggers didn't fly aroun' fas' enough to 'tend to him. An' when dey talk' back at her, she up an' she says, 'Look-a-heah!' she says, 'I want you niggers to understan' dat I wa'n't bawn in de mash to be fool' by trash! I's one o' de ole Blue Hen's Chickens, *I* is!' an' den she clar' dat kitchen an' bandage' up de chile herse'f. So I says dat word, too, when I's riled.

"Well, bymeby my ole mistis say she's broke, an' she got to sell all de niggers on de place. An' when I heah dat dey gwyne to sell us all off at oction in Richmon', oh, de good gracious! I know what dat mean!"

Aunt Rachel had gradually risen, while she warmed to her subject, and now she towered above us, black against the stars.

"Dey put chains on us an' put us on a stan' as high as dis po'ch—twenty foot high—an' all de people stood aroun', crowds an' crowds. An' dey'd come up dah an' look at us all roun', an' squeeze our arm, an' make us git up an' walk, an' den say, 'Dis one too ole,' or 'Dis one lame,' or 'Dis one don't 'mount to much.' An' dey sole my ole man, an' took him away, an' dey begin to sell my chil'en an' take *dem* away, an' I begin to cry; an' de man say, 'Shet up yo' damn blubberin',' an' hit me on de mouf wid his han'. An' when de las' one was gone but my little Henry, I grab' *him* clost up to my breas' so, an' I ris up an' says, 'You sha'n't take him away,' I says; 'I'll kill de man dat tetches him!' I says. But my little Henry whisper an' say, 'I gwyne to run away, an' den I work an' buy yo' freedom.' Oh, bless de chile, he always so good! But dey got him—dey got him, de men did; but I took and tear de clo'es mos' off of 'em an' beat 'em over de head wid my chain; an' *dey* give it to *me,* too, but I didn't mine dat.

"Well, dah was my ole man gone, an' all my chil'en, all my seven chil'en—an' six of 'em I hain't set eyes on ag'in to dis day, an' dat's twenty-two year ago las' Easter. De man dat bought me b'long' in Newbern, an' he took me dah. Well, bymeby de years roll on an' de waw come. My marster he was a Confedrit colonel, an' I was his family's cook. So when de Unions took dat town, dey all run away an' lef' me all by myse'f wid de other niggers in dat mons'us big house. So de big Union officers move in dah, an' dey ask me would I cook for *dem.* 'Lord bless you,' says I, 'dat's what I's *for.*'

"Dey wa'n't no small-fry officers, mine you, dey was de biggest dey *is;* an' de way dey made dem sojers mosey roun'! De Gen'l he tole me to boss dat kitchen; an' he say, 'If anybody come meddlin' wid you, you jist make 'em walk chalk; don't you be afeared,' he say; 'you's 'mong frens now.'

"Well, I thinks to myse'f, if my little Henry ever got a chance to run away, he'd make to de Norf, o' course. So one day I comes in dah whar de big officers was, in de parlor, an' I drops a kurtchy, so, an' I up an' tole 'em 'bout my Henry, dey a-listenin' to my troubles jist de same as if I was white folks; an' I says, 'What I come for is beca'se if he got away and got up Norf whar you gemmen comes from, you might 'a' seen him, maybe, an' could tell me so as I could fine him ag'in; he was very little an' he had a sk-yar on his lef' wris' an' at de top of his forehead.' Den dey look mournful, an' de Gen'l says, 'How long sence you los' him?' an' I say, 'Thirteen year.' Den de Gen'l say, 'He wouldn't be little no mo' now—he's a man!'

"I never thought o' dat befo'! He was only dat little feller to *me* yit. I never thought 'bout him growin' up an' bein' big. But I see it den. None o' de gemmen had run acrost him, so dey couldn't do nothin' for me. But all dat time, do' *I* didn't know it, my Henry *was* run off to de Norf, years an' years, an' he was a barber, too, an' worked for hisse'f. An' bymeby, when de waw come he ups an' he says: 'I's done barberin',' he says, 'I's gwyne to fine my ole mammy, less'n she's dead.' So he sole out an' went to whar dey was recruitin', an' hired hisse'f out to de colonel for his servant; an' den he went all froo de battles everywhah, huntin' for his ole mammy; yes, indeedy, he'd hire to fust one officer an' den another, tell he'd ransacked de whole Souf; but you see *I* didn't know nuffin 'bout *dis.* How was *I* gwyne to know it?

"Well, one night we had a big sojer ball; de sojers dah at Newbern was always havin' balls an' carryin' on. Dey had 'em in my kitchen, heaps o' times, 'ca'se it was so big. Mine you, I was *down* on sich doin's; beca'se my place was wid de officers, an' it rasp me to have dem common sojers cavortin' roun' my kitchen like dat. But I alway' stood aroun' an' kep' things straight, I did; an' sometimes dey'd git my dander up, an' den I'd make 'em clar dat kitchen, mine I *tell* you!

"Well, one night—it was a Friday night—dey comes a whole platoon f'm a *nigger* ridgment dat was on guard at de house—de house was headquarters, you know—an' den I was jist a-*bilin'!* Mad? I was jist a-*boomin'!* I swelled aroun', an' swelled aroun'; I jist was a-itchin' for 'em to do somefin for to start me. *An'* dey was a-waltzin' an' a-dancin'! *my!* but dey was havin' a time! an' I jist a-swellin' an' a-swellin' up! Pooty soon, 'long comes *sich* a spruce young nigger a-sailin' down de room wid a yaller wench roun' de wais'; an' roun' an' roun' an' roun' dey went, enough to make a body drunk to look at 'em; an' when dey got abreas' o' me, dey went to kin' o' balancin' aroun' fust on one leg an' den on t'other, an' smilin' at my big red turban, an' makin' fun, an' I ups an' says '*Git* along wid you!—rubbage!' De young man's face kin' o' changed, all of a sudden, for 'bout a second, but den he went to smilin' ag'in, same as he was befo'. Well, 'bout dis time, in comes some niggers dat played music and b'long' to de ban', an' dey *never* could git along widout puttin' on airs. An' de very fust air dey put on dat night, I lit into 'em! Dey laughed, an' dat made me wuss. De res' o' de niggers got to laughin', an' den my soul *alive* but I was hot! My eye was jist a-blazin'! I jist straightened myself up so—jist as I is now, plum to de ceilin', mos'—an' I digs my fists into my hips, an' I says, 'Look-a-heah!' I says, 'I want you niggers to understan' dat I wa'n't bawn in de mash to be fool' by trash! I's one o' de ole Blue Hen's Chickens, *I* is!' an' den I see dat young man stan' a-starin' an' stiff, lookin' kin' o' up at de ceilin' like he fo'got somefin, an' couldn't 'member it no mo'. Well, I jist march' on dem niggers— so, lookin' like a gen'l—an' dey jist cave' away befo' me an' out at de do'. An' as dis young man was a-goin' out, I heah him say to another nigger, 'Jim,' he says, 'you go 'long an' tell de cap'n I be on han' 'bout eight o'clock in de mawnin'; dey's somefin on my mine,' he says; 'I don't sleep no mo' dis night. You go 'long,' he says, 'an' leave me by my own se'f.'

"Dis was 'bout one o'clock in de mawnin'. Well, 'bout seven, I was up an' on han', gittin' de officers' breakfast. I was a-stoopin' down by de stove—jist so, same as if yo' foot was de stove—an' I'd opened de stove do' wid my right han'—so, pushin' it back, jist as I pushes yo' foot—an' I'd jist got de pan o' hot biscuits in my han' an' was 'bout to raise up, when I see a black face come aroun' under mine, an' de eyes a-lookin' up into mine, jist as I's a-lookin' up clost under yo' face now; an' I jist stopped *right dah,* an' never budged! jist gazed an' gazed so; an' de pan begin to tremble, an' all of a sudden I *knowed!* De pan drop' on de flo' an' I grab his lef' han' an' shove back his sleeve—jist so, as I's doin' to you—an' den I goes for his forehead an' push de hair back so, an' 'Boy!' I says, 'if you an't my Henry, what is you doin' wid dis welt on yo' wris' an' dat sk-yar on yo' forehead? De Lord God ob heaven be praise', I got my own ag'in!'

"Oh no, Misto C——, *I* hain't had no trouble. An' no *joy!*"

1874

THE McWILLIAMSES
AND THE BURGLAR ALARM

The conversation drifted smoothly and pleasantly along from weather to crops, from crops to literature, from literature to scandal, from scandal to religion; then took a random jump, and landed on the subject of burglar alarms. And now for the first time Mr. McWilliams showed feeling. Whenever I perceive this sign on this man's dial, I comprehend it, and lapse into silence, and give him opportunity to unload his heart. Said he, with but ill-controlled emotion:

I do not go one single cent on burglar alarms, Mr. Twain—not a single cent—and I will tell you why. When we were finishing our house, we found we had a little cash left over, on account of the plumber not knowing it. I was for enlightening the heathen with it, for I was always unaccountably down on the heathen somehow; but Mrs. McWilliams said no, let's have a burglar alarm. I agreed to this compromise. I will explain that whenever I want a thing, and Mrs. McWilliams wants another thing, and we decide upon the thing that Mrs.

McWilliams wants—as we always do—she calls that a compromise. Very well: the man came up from New York and put in the alarm, and charged three hundred and twenty-five dollars for it, and said we could sleep without uneasiness now. So we did for awhile—say a month. Then one night we smelled smoke, and I was advised to get up and see what the matter was. I lit a candle, and started toward the stairs, and met a burglar coming out of a room with a basket of tinware, which he had mistaken for solid silver in the dark. He was smoking a pipe. I said, "My friend, we do not allow smoking in this room." He said he was a stranger, and could not be expected to know the rules of the house: said he had been in many houses just as good as this one, and it had never been objected to before. He added that as far as his experience went, such rules had never been considered to apply to burglars, anyway.

I said: "Smoke along, then, if it is the custom, though I think that the conceding of a privilege to a burglar which is denied to a bishop is a conspicuous sign of the looseness of the times. But waiving all that, what business have you to be entering this house in this furtive and clandestine way, without ringing the burglar alarm?"

He looked confused and ashamed, and said, with embarrassment: "I beg a thousand pardons. I did not know you had a burglar alarm, else I would have rung it. I beg you will not mention it where my parents may hear of it, for they are old and feeble, and such a seemingly wanton breach of the hallowed conventionalities of our Christian civilization might all too rudely sunder the frail bridge which hangs darkling between the pale and evanescent present and the solemn great deeps of the eternities. May I trouble you for a match?"

I said: "Your sentiments do you honor, but if you will allow me to say it, metaphor is not your best hold. Spare your thigh; this kind light only on the box, and seldom there, in fact, if my experience may be trusted. But to return to business: how did you get in here?"

"Through a second-story window."

It was even so. I redeemed the tinware at pawnbroker's rates, less cost of advertising, bade the burglar good-night, closed the window after him, and retired to headquarters to report. Next morning we sent for the burglar-alarm man, and he came up and explained that the reason the alarm did not "go off" was that no part of the house but the first floor was attached to the alarm. This was simply idiotic; one might as well have no armor on at all in battle as to have it only on his legs. The expert now put the whole second story on the alarm, charged three hundred dollars for it, and went his way. By and by, one night, I found a burglar in the third story, about to start down a ladder with a lot of miscellaneous property. My first impulse was to crack his head with a billiard cue; but my second was to refrain from this attention, because he was between me and the cue rack. The second impulse was plainly the soundest, so I refrained, and proceeded to compromise. I redeemed the property at former rates, after deducting ten per cent for use of ladder, it being my ladder, and next day we sent down for the expert once more, and had the third story attached to the alarm, for three hundred dollars.

By this time the "annunciator" had grown to formidable dimensions. It had forty-seven tags on it, marked with the names of the various rooms and chimneys, and it occupied the space of an ordinary wardrobe. The gong was the size of a wash-bowl, and was placed above the head of our bed. There was a wire from the house to the coachman's quarters in the stable, and a noble gong alongside his pillow.

We should have been comfortable now but for one defect. Every morning at five the cook opened the kitchen door, in the way of business, and rip went that gong! The first time this happened I thought the last day was come sure. I didn't think it *in* bed—no, but out of it— for the first effect of that frightful gong is to hurl you across the house, and slam you against the wall, and then curl you up, and squirm you like a spider on a stove lid, till somebody shuts the kitchen door. In solid fact, there is no clamor that is even remotely comparable to the dire clamor which that gong makes. Well, this catastrophe happened every morning regularly at five o'clock, and lost us three hours sleep; for, mind you, when that thing wakes you, it doesn't merely wake you in spots; it wakes you all over, conscience and all, and you are good for eighteen hours of wide-awakeness subsequently—eighteen hours of the very most inconceivable wide-awakeness that you ever experienced in your life. A stranger died on our hands one time, and we vacated and left him in our room overnight. Did that stranger wait for the general judgment? *No,* sir; he got up at five the next morning in the most prompt and unostentatious way. I knew he would; I knew it mighty well. He collected his life-insurance, and lived happy ever after, for there was plenty of proof as to the perfect squareness of his death.

Well, we were gradually fading toward a better land, on account of the daily loss of sleep; so we finally had the expert up again, and he ran a wire to the outside of the door, and placed a switch there, whereby Thomas, the butler, always made one little mistake—he switched the alarm off at night when he went to bed, and switched it on again at daybreak in the morning, just in time for the cook to open the kitchen door, and enable that gong to slam us across the house, sometimes breaking a window with one or the other of us. At the end of a week we recognized that this switch business was a delusion and a snare. We also discovered that a band of burglars had been lodging in the house the whole time—not exactly to steal, for there wasn't much left now, but to hide from the police, for they were hot pressed, and they shrewdly judged that the detectives would never think of a tribe of burglars taking sanctuary in a house notoriously protected by the most imposing and elaborate burglar alarm in America.

Sent down for the expert again, and this time he struck a most dazzling idea—he fixed the thing so that opening the kitchen door would take off the alarm. It was a noble idea, and he charged accordingly. But you already foresee the result. I switched on the alarm every night at bed-time, no longer trusting on Thomas's frail memory; and as soon as the lights were out the burglars walked in at the kitchen door, thus taking the alarm off without waiting for the cook to do it in the morning. You see how aggravatingly we were situated. For months we couldn't have any company. Not a spare bed in the house; all occupied by burglars.

Finally, I got up a cure of my own. The expert answered the call, and ran another ground wire to the stable, and established a switch there, so that the coachman could put on and take off the alarm. That worked first rate, and a season of peace ensued, during which we got to inviting company once more and enjoying life.

But by and by the irrepressible alarm invented a new kink. One winter's night we were flung out of bed by the sudden music of that awful gong, and when we hobbled to the annunciator, turned up the gas, and saw the word "Nursery" exposed, Mrs. McWilliams fainted dead away, and I came precious near doing the same thing myself. I seized my shotgun, and stood timing the coachman whilst that appalling buzzing went on. I knew that his gong had flung him out, too, and that he would be along with his gun as soon as he could jump into his clothes. When I judged that the time was ripe, I crept to the room next the nursery, glanced through the window, and saw the dim outline of the coachman in the yard below, standing at present-arms and waiting for a chance. Then I hopped into the nursery and fired, and in the same instant the coachman fired at the red flash of my gun. Both of us were successful; I crippled a nurse, and he shot off all my back hair. We turned up the gas, and telephoned for a surgeon. There was not a sign of a burglar, and no window had been raised. One glass was absent, but that was where the coachman's charge had come through. Here was a fine mystery—a burglar alarm "going off" at midnight of its own accord, and not a burglar in the neighborhood!

The expert answered the usual call, and explained that it was a "False alarm." Said it was easily fixed. So he overhauled the nursery window, charged a remunerative figure for it, and departed.

What we suffered from false alarms for the next three years no stylographic pen can describe. During the next three months I always flew with my gun to the room indicated, and the coachman always sallied forth with his battery to support me. But there was never anything to shoot at—windows all tight and secure. We always sent down for the expert next day, and he fixed those particular windows so they would keep quiet a week or so, and always remembered to send us a bill about like this:

Wire	$2.15
Nipple	.75
Two hours' labor	1.50
Wax	.47
Tape	.34
Screws	.15
Recharging battery	.98
Three hours' labor	2.25
String	.02
Lard	.66
Pond's Extract	1.25
Springs at 50	2.00
Railroad fares	7.25
	$19.77

At length a perfectly natural thing came about—after we had answered three or four hundred false alarms—to wit, we stopped answering them. Yes, I simply rose up calmly, when slammed across the house by the alarm, calmly inspected the annunciator, took note of the room indicated, and then calmly disconnected that room from the alarm, and went back to bed as if nothing had happened. Moreover, I left that room off permanently, and did not send for the expert. Well, it goes without saying that in the course of time *all* the rooms were taken off, and the entire machine was out of service.

It was at this unprotected time that the heaviest calamity of all happened. The burglars walked in one night and carried off the burglar alarm! yes, sir, every hide and hair of it: ripped it out, tooth and nail; springs, bells, gongs, battery, and all; they took a hundred and fifty miles of copper wire; they just cleaned her out, bag and baggage, and never left us a vestige of her to swear at—swear by, I mean.

We had a time of it to get her back; but we accomplished it finally, for money. The alarm firm said that what we needed now was to have her put in right—with their new patent springs in the windows to make false alarms impossible, and their new patent clock attached to take off and put on the alarm morning and night without human assistance. That seemed a good scheme. They promised to have the whole thing finished in ten days. They began work, and we left for the summer. They worked a couple of days; then *they* left for the summer. After which the burglars moved in, and began *their* summer vacation. When we returned in the fall, the house was as empty as a beer closet in premises where painters have been at work. We refurnished, and then sent down to hurry up the expert. He came up and finished the job, and said: "Now this clock is set to put on the alarm every night at 10, and take it off every morning at 5:45. All you've got to do is to wind her up every week, and then leave her alone—she will take care of the alarm herself."

After that we had a most tranquil season during three months. The bill was prodigious, of course, and I had said I would not pay it until the new machinery had proved itself to be flawless. The time stipulated was three months. So I paid the bill, and the very next day the alarm went to buzzing like ten thousand bee swarms at ten o'clock in the morning. I turned the hands around twelve hours, according to instructions, and this took off the alarm; but there was another hitch at night, and I had to set her ahead twelve hours once more to get her to put the alarm on again. That sort of nonsense went on a week or two, then the expert came up and put in a new clock. He came up every three months during the next three years, and put in a new clock. But it was always a failure. His clocks all had the same perverse defect: they would put the alarm on in the daytime, and they would *not* put it on at night; and if you forced it on yourself, they *would* take it off again the minute your back was turned.

Now there is the history of that burglar alarm—everything just as it happened; nothing extenuated, and naught set down in malice. Yes, sir,—and when I had slept nine years with burglars, and maintained an expensive burglar alarm the whole time, for their protection, not mine, and at my sole cost—for not a d——d cent could I ever get *them* to contribute—I just said to Mrs. McWilliams that I had had enough of that kind of pie; so with her full consent I took the whole thing out and traded it off for a dog, and shot the dog. I don't know what *you* think about it, Mr. Twain; but *I* think those things are made solely in the interest of the burglars. Yes, sir, a burglar alarm combines in its person all that is objectionable about a fire, a riot, and a harem, and at the same time had none of the compensating advantages, of one sort or another, that customarily belong with that combination. Goodby: I get off here.

1882

THE STOLEN WHITE ELEPHANT*

The following curious history was related to me by a chance railway acquaintance. He was a gentleman more than seventy years of age, and his thoroughly good and gentle face and earnest and sincere manner imprinted the unmistakable stamp of truth upon every statement which fell from his lips. He said:

You know in what reverence the royal white elephant of Siam is held by the people of that country. You know it is sacred to kings, only kings may possess it, and that it is, indeed, in a measure even superior

* Left out of *A Tramp Abroad,* because it was feared that some of the particulars had been exaggerated, and that others were not true. Before these suspicions had been proven groundless, the book had gone to press.   M. T.

to kings, since it receives not merely honor but worship. Very well; five years ago, when the troubles concerning the frontier line arose between Great Britain and Siam, it was presently manifest that Siam had been in the wrong. Therefore every reparation was quickly made, and the British representative stated that he was satisfied and the past should be forgotten. This greatly relieved the King of Siam, and partly as a token of gratitude, but partly also, perhaps, to wipe out any little remaining vestige of unpleasantness which England might feel toward him, he wished to send the Queen a present—the sole sure way of propitiating an enemy, according to Oriental ideas. This present ought not only to be a royal one, but transcendently royal. Wherefore, what offering could be so meet as that of a white elephant? My position in the Indian civil service was such that I was deemed peculiarly worthy of the honor of conveying the present to her Majesty. A ship was fitted out for me and my servants and the officers and attendants of the elephant, and in due time I arrived in New York harbor and placed my royal charge in admirable quarters in Jersey City. It was necessary to remain awhile in order to recruit the animal's health before resuming the voyage.

All went well during a fortnight—then my calamities began. The white elephant was stolen! I was called up at dead of night and informed of this fearful misfortune. For some moments I was beside myself with terror and anxiety; I was helpless. Then I grew calmer and collected my faculties. I soon saw my course—for, indeed, there was but the one course for an intelligent man to pursue. Late as it was, I flew to New York and got a policeman to conduct me to the headquarters of the detective force. Fortunately I arrived in time, though the chief of the force, the celebrated Inspector Blunt, was just on the point of leaving for his home. He was a man of middle size and compact frame, and when he was thinking deeply he had a way of knitting his brows and tapping his forehead reflectively with his finger, which impressed you at once with the conviction that you stood in the presence of a person of no common order. The very sight of him gave me confidence and made me hopeful. I stated my errand. It did not flurry him in the least; it had no more visible effect upon his iron self-possession than if I had told him somebody had stolen my dog. He motioned me to a seat, and said, calmly:

"Allow me to think a moment, please."

So saying, he sat down at his office table and leaned his head upon his hand. Several clerks were at work at the other end of the room; the scratching of their pens was all the sound I heard during the next six or seven minutes. Meantime the inspector sat there, buried in thought. Finally he raised his head, and there was that in the firm lines of his face which showed me that his brain had done its work and his plan was made. Said he—and his voice was low and impressive:

"This is no ordinary case. Every step must be warily taken; each step must be made sure before the next is ventured. And secrecy must be observed—secrecy profound and absolute. Speak to no one about the matter, not even the reporters. I will take care of *them;* I will see that they get only what it may suit my ends to let them know." He touched a bell; a youth appeared. "Alaric, tell the reporters to remain for the present." The boy retired. "Now let us proceed to business— and systematically. Nothing can be accomplished in this trade of mine without strict and minute method."

He took a pen and some paper. "Now—name of the elephant?"

"Hassan Ben Ali Ben Selim Abdallah Mohammed Moisé Alhammal Jamsetjejeebhoy Dhuleep Sultan Ebu Bhudpoor."

"Very well. Given name?"

"Jumbo."

"Very well. Place of birth?"

"The capital city of Siam."

"Parents living?"

"No—dead."

"Had they any other issue besides this one?"

"None. He was an only child."

"Very well. These matters are sufficient under that head. Now please describe the elephant, and leave out no particular, however insignificant—that is, insignificant from *your* point of view. To men in my profession there *are* no insignificant particulars; they do not exist."

I described—he wrote. When I was done, he said:

"Now listen. If I have made any mistakes, correct me."

He read as follows:

"Height, 19 feet; length from apex of forehead to insertion of tail, 26 feet; length of trunk, 16 feet; length of tail, 6 feet; total length, including trunk and tail, 48 feet; length of tusks, 9½ feet; ears in keeping with these dimensions; footprint resembles the mark left when one upends a barrel in the snow; color of the elephant, a dull white; has a hole the size of a plate in each ear for the insertion of jewelry, and

possesses the habit in a remarkable degree of squirting water upon
spectators and of maltreating with his trunk not only such persons as
he is acquainted with, but even entire strangers; limps slightly with his
right hind leg, and has a small scar in his left armpit caused by a
former boil; had on, when stolen, a castle containing seats for fifteen
persons, and a gold-cloth saddle-blanket the size of an ordinary carpet."

There were no mistakes. The inspector touched the bell, handed the
description to Alaric, and said:

"Have fifty thousand copies of this printed at once and mailed to
every detective office and pawnbroker's shop on the continent." Alaric
retired. "There—so far, so good. Next, I must have a photograph of
the property."

I gave him one. He examined it critically, and said:

"It must do, since we can do no better; but he has his trunk curled
up and tucked into his mouth. That is unfortunate, and is calculated
to mislead, for of course he does not usually have it in that position."
He touched his bell.

"Alaric, have fifty thousand copies of this photograph made the first
thing in the morning, and mail them with the descriptive circulars."

Alaric retired to execute his orders. The inspector said:

"It will be necessary to offer a reward, of course. Now as to the
amount?"

"What sum would you suggest?"

"To *begin* with, I should say—well, twenty-five thousand dollars. It
is an intricate and difficult business; there are a thousand avenues of
escape and opportunities of concealment. These thieves have friends
and pals everywhere—"

"Bless me, do you know who they are?"

The wary face, practised in concealing the thoughts and feelings
within, gave me no token, nor yet the replying words, so quietly uttered:

"Never mind about that. I may, and I may not. We generally gather
a pretty shrewd inkling of who our man is by the manner of his work
and the size of the game he goes after. We are not dealing with a
pickpocket or a hall thief now, make up your mind to that. This
property was not 'lifted' by a novice. But, as I was saying, considering
the amount of travel which will have to be done, and the diligence
with which the thieves will cover up their traces as they move along,

twenty-five thousand may be too small a sum to offer, yet I think it worth while to start with that."

So we determined upon that figure as a beginning. Then this man, whom nothing escaped which could by any possibility be made to serve as a clue, said:

"There are cases in detective history to show that criminals have been detected through peculiarities in their appetites. Now, what does this elephant eat, and how much?"

"Well, as to *what* he eats—he will eat *anything*. He will eat a man, he will eat a Bible—he will eat anything *between* a man and a Bible."

"Good—very good, indeed, but too general. Details are necessary—details are the only valuable things in our trade. Very well—as to men. At one meal—or, if you prefer, during one day—how many men will he eat, if fresh?"

"He would not care whether they were fresh or not; at a single meal he would eat five ordinary men."

"Very good; five men; we will put that down. What nationalities would he prefer?"

"He is indifferent about nationalities. He prefers acquaintances, but is not prejudiced against strangers."

"Very good. Now, as to Bibles. How many Bibles would he eat at a meal?"

"He would eat an entire edition."

"It is hardly succinct enough. Do you mean the ordinary octavo, or the family illustrated?"

"I think he would be indifferent to illustrations; that is, I think he would not value illustrations above simple letterpress."

"No, you do not get my idea. I refer to bulk. The ordinary octavo Bible weighs about two pounds and a half, while the great quarto with the illustrations weighs ten or twelve. How many Doré Bibles would he eat at a meal?"

"If you knew this elephant, you could not ask. He would take what they had."

"Well, put it in dollars and cents, then. We must get at it somehow. The Doré costs a hundred dollars a copy, Russia leather, beveled."

"He would require about fifty thousand dollars' worth—say an edition of five hundred copies."

"Now that is more exact. I will put that down. Very well; he likes men and Bibles; so far, so good. What else will he eat? I want particulars."

"He will leave Bibles to eat bricks, he will leave bricks to eat bottles, he will leave bottles to eat clothing, he will leave clothing to eat cats, he will leave cats to eat oysters, he will leave oysters to eat ham, he will leave ham to eat sugar, he will leave sugar to eat pie, he will leave pie to eat potatoes, he will leave potatoes to eat bran, he will leave bran to eat hay, he will leave hay to eat oats, he will leave oats to eat rice, for he was mainly raised on it. There is nothing whatever that he will not eat but European butter, and he would eat that if he could taste it."

"Very good. General quantity at a meal—say about—"

"Well, anywhere from a quarter to half a ton."

"And he drinks—"

"Everything that is fluid. Milk, water, whisky, molasses, castor oil, camphene, carbolic acid—it is no use to go into particulars; whatever fluid occurs to you set it down. He will drink anything that is fluid, except European coffee."

"Very good. As to quantity?"

"Put it down five to fifteen barrels—his thirst varies; his other appetites do not."

"These things are unusual. They ought to furnish quite good clues toward tracing him."

He touched the bell.

"Alaric, summon Captain Burns."

Burns appeared. Inspector Blunt unfolded the whole matter to him, detail by detail. Then he said in the clear, decisive tones of a man whose plans are clearly defined in his head and who is accustomed to command:

"Captain Burns, detail Detectives Jones, Davis, Halsey, Bates, and Hackett to shadow the elephant."

"Yes, sir."

"Detail Detectives Moses, Dakin, Murphy, Rogers, Tupper, Higgins, and Batholomew to shadow the thieves."

"Yes, sir."

"Place a strong guard—a guard of thirty picked men, with a relief of thirty—over the place from whence the elephant was stolen, to keep strict watch there night and day, and allow none to approach—except reporters—without written authority from me."

"Yes, sir."

"Place detectives in plain clothes in the railway, steamship, and ferry depots, and upon all roadways leading out of Jersey City, with orders to search all suspicious persons."

"Yes, sir."

"Furnish all these men with photograph and accompanying description of the elephant, and instruct them to search all trains and outgoing ferryboats and other vessels."

"Yes, sir."

"If the elephant should be found, let him be seized, and the information forwarded to me by telegraph."

"Yes, sir."

"Let me be informed at once if any clues should be found—footprints of the animal, or anything of that kind."

"Yes, sir."

"Get an order commanding the harbor police to patrol the frontages vigilantly."

"Yes, sir."

"Despatch detectives in plain clothes over all the railways, north as far as Canada, west as far as Ohio, south as far as Washington."

"Yes, sir."

"Place experts in all the telegraph offices to listen to all messages; and let them require that all cipher despatches be interpreted to them."

"Yes, sir."

"Let all these things be done with the utmost secrecy—mind, the most impenetrable secrecy."

"Yes, sir."

"Report to me promptly at the usual hour."

"Yes, sir."

"Go!"

"Yes, sir."

He was gone.

Inspector Blunt was silent and thoughtful a moment, while the fire in his eye cooled down and faded out. Then he turned to me and said in a placid voice:

"I am not given to boasting, it is not my habit; but—we shall find the elephant."

I shook him warmly by the hand and thanked him; and I *felt* my thanks, too. The more I had seen of the man the more I liked him and the more I admired him and marveled over the mysterious wonders of his profession. Then we parted for the night, and I went home with a far happier heart than I had carried with me to his office.

2

Next morning it was all in the newspapers, in the minutest detail. It even had additions—consisting of Detective This, Detective That, and Detective The Other's "Theory" as to how the robbery was done, who the robbers were, and whither they had flown with their booty. There were eleven of these theories, and they covered all the possibilities; and this single fact shows what independent thinkers detectives are. No two theories were alike, or even much resembled each other, save in one striking particular, and in that one all the other eleven theories were absolutely agreed. That was, that although the rear of my building was torn out and the only door remained locked, the elephant had not been removed through the rent, but by some other (undiscovered) outlet. All agreed that the robbers had made that rent only to mislead the detectives. That never would have occurred to me or to any other layman, perhaps, but it had not deceived the detectives for a moment. Thus, what I had supposed was the only thing that had no mystery about it was in fact the very thing I had gone furthest astray in. The eleven theories all named the supposed robbers, but no two named the same robbers; the total number of suspected persons was thirty-seven. The various newspaper accounts all closed with the most important opinion of all—that of Chief Inspector Blunt. A portion of this statement read as follows:

The chief knows who the two principals are, namely, "Brick" Duffy and "Red" McFadden. Ten days before the robbery was achieved he was already aware that it was to be attempted, and had quietly proceeded to shadow these two noted villains; but unfortunately on the night in question their track was lost, and before it could be found again the bird was flown—that is, the elephant.

Duffy and McFadden are the boldest scoundrels in the profession; the chief has reasons for believing that they are the men who stole the stove out of the detective headquarters on a bitter night last winter—in conse-

quence of which the chief and every detective present were in the hands of the physicians before morning, some with frozen feet, others with frozen fingers, ears, and other members.

When I read the first half of that I was more astonished than ever at the wonderful sagacity of this strange man. He not only saw everything in the present with a clear eye, but even the future could not be hidden from him. I was soon at his office, and said I could not help wishing he had had those men arrested, and so prevented the trouble and loss; but his reply was simple and unanswerable:

"It is not our province to prevent crime, but to punish it. We cannot punish it until it is committed."

I remarked that the secrecy with which we had begun had been marred by the newspapers; not only all our facts but all our plans and purposes had been revealed; even all the suspected persons had been named; these would doubtless disguise themselves now, or go into hiding.

"Let them. They will find that when I am ready for them my hand will descend upon them, in their secret places, as unerringly as the hand of fate. As to the newspapers, we *must* keep in with them. Fame, reputation, constant public mention—these are the detective's bread and butter. He must publish his facts, else he will be supposed to have none; he must publish his theory, for nothing is so strange or striking as a detective's theory, or brings him so much wonderful respect; we must publish our plans, for these the journals insist upon having, and we could not deny them without offending. We must constantly show the public what we are doing, or they will believe we are doing nothing. It is much pleasanter to have a newspaper say, 'Inspector Blunt's ingenious and extraordinary theory is as follows,' than to have it say some harsh thing, or, worse still, some sarcastic one."

"I see the force of what you say. But I noticed that in one part of your remarks in the papers this morning you refused to reveal your opinion upon a certain minor point."

"Yes, we always do that; it has a good effect. Besides, I had not formed any opinion on that point, anyway."

I deposited a considerable sum of money with the inspector, to meet current expenses, and sat down to wait for news. We were expecting the telegrams to begin to arrive at any moment now. Meantime I reread the newspapers and also our descriptive circular, and observed that our twenty-five thousand dollars reward seemed to be offered only to detectives. I said I thought it ought to be offered to anybody who would catch the elephant. The inspector said:

"It is the detectives who will find the elephant, hence the reward will go to the right place. If other people found the animal, it would only be by watching the detectives and taking advantage of clues and indications stolen from them, and that would entitle the detectives to the reward, after all. The proper office of a reward is to stimulate the men who deliver up their time and their trained sagacities to this sort of work, and not to confer benefits upon chance citizens who stumble upon a capture without having earned the benefits by their own merits and labors."

This was reasonable enough, certainly. Now the telegraphic machine in the corner began to click, and the following despatch was the result:

> FLOWER STATION, N. Y., 7.30 A.M.
> HAVE GOT A CLUE. FOUND A SUCCESSION OF DEEP TRACKS ACROSS A FARM NEAR HERE. FOLLOWED THEM TWO MILES EAST WITHOUT RESULT; THINK ELEPHANT WENT WEST. SHALL NOW SHADOW HIM IN THAT DIRECTION.
> DARLEY, DETECTIVE

"Darley's one of the best men on the force," said the inspector. "We shall hear from him again before long."

Telegram No. 2 came:

> BARKER'S, N. J., 7.40 A.M.
> JUST ARRIVED. GLASS FACTORY BROKEN OPEN HERE DURING NIGHT, AND EIGHT HUNDRED BOTTLES TAKEN. ONLY WATER IN LARGE QUANTITY NEAR HERE IS FIVE MILES DISTANT. SHALL STRIKE FOR THERE. ELEPHANT WILL BE THIRSTY. BOTTLES WERE EMPTY.
> BAKER, DETECTIVE

"That promises well, too," said the inspector. "I told you the creature's appetites would not be bad clues."

Telegram No. 3:

> TAYLORVILLE, L. I., 8.15 A.M.
> A HAYSTACK NEAR HERE DISAPPEARED DURING NIGHT. PROBABLY EATEN. HAVE GOT A CLUE, AND AM OFF.
> HUBBARD, DETECTIVE

"How he does move around!" said the inspector. "I knew we had a difficult job on hand, but we shall catch him yet."

FLOWER STATION, N. Y., 9 A.M.

SHADOWED THE TRACKS THREE MILES WESTWARD. LARGE, DEEP, AND RAGGED. HAVE JUST MET A FARMER WHO SAYS THEY ARE NOT ELEPHANT TRACKS. SAYS THEY ARE HOLES WHERE HE DUG UP SAPLINGS FOR SHADE-TREES WHEN GROUND WAS FROZEN LAST WINTER. GIVE ME ORDERS HOW TO PROCEED.

DARLEY, DETECTIVE

"Aha! a confederate of the thieves! The thing grows warm," said the inspector.

He dictated the following telegram to Darley:

ARREST THE MAN AND FORCE HIM TO NAME HIS PALS. CON-TINUE TO FOLLOW THE TRACKS—TO THE PACIFIC, IF NEC-ESSARY.

CHIEF BLUNT

Next telegram:

CONEY POINT, PA., 8.45 A.M.

GAS OFFICE BROKEN OPEN HERE DURING NIGHT AND THREE MONTHS' UNPAID GAS BILLS TAKEN. HAVE GOT A CLUE AND AM AWAY.

MURPHY, DETECTIVE

"Heavens!" said the inspector; "would he eat gas bills?"

"Through ignorance—yes; but they cannot support life. At least, unassisted."

Now came this exciting telegram:

IRONVILLE, N. Y., 9.30 A.M.

JUST ARRIVED. THIS VILLAGE IN CONSTERNATION. ELE-PHANT PASSED THROUGH HERE AT FIVE THIS MORNING. SOME SAY HE WENT EAST, SOME SAY WEST, SOME NORTH, SOME SOUTH—BUT ALL SAY THEY DID NOT WAIT TO NO-TICE PARTICULARLY. HE KILLED A HORSE; HAVE SECURED A PIECE OF IT FOR A CLUE. KILLED IT WITH HIS TRUNK; FROM STYLE OF BLOW, THINK HE STRUCK IT LEFT-

HANDED. FROM POSITION IN WHICH HORSE LIES, THINK
ELEPHANT TRAVELED NORTHWARD ALONG LINE OF BERK-
LEY RAILWAY. HAS FOUR AND A HALF HOURS' START, BUT
I MOVE ON HIS TRACK AT ONCE.

HAWES, DETECTIVE

I uttered exclamations of joy. The inspector was as self-contained as
a graven image. He calmly touched his bell.

"Alaric, send Captain Burns here."

Burns appeared.

"How many men are ready for instant orders?"

"Ninety-six, sir."

"Send them north at once. Let them concentrate along the line of
the Berkley road north of Ironville."

"Yes, sir."

"Let them conduct their movements with the utmost secrecy. As
fast as others are at liberty, hold them for orders."

"Yes, sir."

"Go!"

"Yes, sir."

Presently came another telegram:

SAGE CORNERS, N. Y., 10.30.

JUST ARRIVED. ELEPHANT PASSED THROUGH HERE AT 8.15.
ALL ESCAPED FROM THE TOWN BUT A POLICEMAN. APPAR-
ENTLY ELEPHANT DID NOT STRIKE AT POLICEMAN, BUT AT
THE LAMP-POST. GOT BOTH, I HAVE SECURED A PORTION
OF THE POLICEMAN AS CLUE.

STUMM, DETECTIVE

"So the elephant has turned westward," said the inspector. "However, he will not escape, for my men are scattered all over that region."

The next telegram said:

GLOVER'S, 11.15.

JUST ARRIVED. VILLAGE DESERTED, EXCEPT SICK AND
AGED. ELEPHANT PASSED THROUGH THREE-QUARTERS OF
AN HOUR AGO. THE ANTITEMPERANCE MASS-MEETING WAS
IN SESSION; HE PUT HIS TRUNK IN AT A WINDOW AND
WASHED IT OUT WITH WATER FROM CISTERN. SOME SWAL-

LOWED IT—SINCE DEAD; SEVERAL DROWNED. DETEC-
TIVES CROSS AND O'SHAUGHNESSY WERE PASSING
THROUGH TOWN, BUT GOING SOUTH—SO MISSED ELE-
PHANT. WHOLE REGION FOR MANY MILES AROUND IN TER-
ROR—PEOPLE FLYING FROM THEIR HOMES. WHEREVER
THEY TURN THEY MEET ELEPHANT, AND MANY ARE
KILLED.

BRANT, DETECTIVE

I could have shed tears, this havoc so distressed me. But the inspector only said:

"You see—we are closing in on him. He feels our presence; he has
turned eastward again."

Yet further troublous news was in store for us. The telegraph
brought this:

HOGANSPORT, 12.19.
JUST ARRIVED. ELEPHANT PASSED THROUGH HALF AN
HOUR AGO, CREATING WILDEST FRIGHT AND EXCITEMENT.
ELEPHANT RAGED AROUND STREETS; TWO PLUMBERS GO-
ING BY, KILLED ONE—OTHER ESCAPED. REGRET GENERAL.

O'FLAHERTY, DETECTIVE

"Now he is right in the midst of my men," said the inspector.
"Nothing can save him."

A succession of telegrams came from detectives who were scattered
through New Jersey and Pennsylvania, and who were following clues
consisting of ravaged barns, factories, and Sunday-school libraries,
with high hopes—hopes amounting to certainties, indeed. The inspector said:

"I wish I could communicate with them and order them north, but
that is impossible. A detective only visits a telegraph office to send his
report; then he is off again, and you don't know where to put your
hand on him."

Now came this despatch:

BRIDGEPORT, CT., 12.15.
BARNUM OFFERS RATE OF $4,000 A YEAR FOR EXCLUSIVE
PRIVILEGE OF USING ELEPHANT AS TRAVELING ADVERTIS-
ING MEDIUM FROM NOW TILL DETECTIVES FIND HIM.

WANTS TO PASTE CIRCUS-POSTERS ON HIM. DESIRES IMME-
DIATE ANSWER.

                              BOGGS, DETECTIVE

"That is perfectly absurd!" I exclaimed.

"Of course it is," said the inspector. "Evidently Mr. Barnum, who
thinks he is so sharp, does not know me—but I know him."

Then he dictated this answer to the despatch:

MR. BARNUM'S OFFER DECLINED. MAKE IT $7,000 OR NOTHING.

                              CHIEF BLUNT

"There. We shall not have to wait long for an answer. Mr. Barnum
is not at home; he is in the telegraph office—it is his way when he has
business on hand. Inside of three—"

              DONE.—P. T. BARNUM

So interrupted the clicking telegraphic instrument. Before I could
make a comment upon this extraordinary episode, the following despatch carried my thoughts into another and very distressing channel:

              BOLIVIA, N. Y., 12.50.

ELEPHANT ARRIVED HERE FROM THE SOUTH AND PASSED
THROUGH TOWARD THE FOREST AT 11.50, DISPERSING A
FUNERAL ON THE WAY, AND DIMINISHING THE MOURNERS
BY TWO. CITIZENS FIRED SOME SMALL CANNON-BALLS
INTO HIM, AND THEN FLED. DETECTIVE BURKE AND I AR-
RIVED TEN MINUTES LATER, FROM THE NORTH, BUT MIS-
TOOK SOME EXCAVATIONS FOR FOOTPRINTS, AND SO LOST
A GOOD DEAL OF TIME; BUT AT LAST WE STRUCK THE
RIGHT TRAIL AND FOLLOWED IT TO THE WOODS. WE THEN
GOT DOWN ON OUR HANDS AND KNEES AND CONTINUED
TO KEEP A SHARP EYE ON THE TRACK, AND SO SHADOWED
IT INTO THE BRUSH. BURKE WAS IN ADVANCE. UNFORTU-
NATELY THE ANIMAL HAD STOPPED TO REST; THEREFORE,
BURKE HAVING HIS HEAD DOWN, INTENT UPON THE
TRACK, BUTTED UP AGAINST THE ELEPHANT'S HIND LEGS
BEFORE HE WAS AWARE OF HIS VICINITY. BURKE IN-
STANTLY AROSE TO HIS FEET, SEIZED THE TAIL, AND EX-
CLAIMED JOYFULLY, "I CLAIM THE RE—" BUT GOT NO
FURTHER, FOR A SINGLE BLOW OF THE HUGE TRUNK LAID

THE BRAVE FELLOW'S FRAGMENTS LOW IN DEATH. I FLED REARWARD, AND THE ELEPHANT TURNED AND SHADOWED ME TO THE EDGE OF THE WOOD, MAKING TREMENDOUS SPEED, AND I SHOULD INEVITABLY HAVE BEEN LOST, BUT THAT THE REMAINS OF THE FUNERAL PROVIDENTIALLY INTERVENED AGAIN AND DIVERTED HIS ATTENTION. I HAVE JUST LEARNED THAT NOTHING OF THAT FUNERAL IS NOW LEFT; BUT THIS IS NO LOSS, FOR THERE IS ABUNDANCE OF MATERIAL FOR ANOTHER. MEANTIME, THE ELEPHANT HAS DISAPPEARED AGAIN.

MULROONEY, DETECTIVE

We heard no news except from the diligent and confident detectives scattered about New Jersey, Pennsylvania, Delaware, and Virginia—who were all following fresh and encouraging clues—until shortly after 2 P.M., when this telegram came:

BAXTER CENTER, 2.15.

ELEPHANT BEEN HERE, PLASTERED OVER WITH CIRCUS-BILLS, AND BROKE UP A REVIVAL, STRIKING DOWN AND DAMAGING MANY WHO WERE ON THE POINT OF ENTERING UPON A BETTER LIFE. CITIZENS PENNED HIM UP AND ESTABLISHED A GUARD. WHEN DETECTIVE BROWN AND I ARRIVED, SOME TIME AFTER, WE ENTERED INCLOSURE AND PROCEEDED TO IDENTIFY ELEPHANT BY PHOTOGRAPH AND DESCRIPTION. ALL MARKS TALLIED EXACTLY EXCEPT ONE, WHICH WE COULD NOT SEE—THE BOIL-SCAR UNDER ARMPIT. TO MAKE SURE, BROWN CREPT UNDER TO LOOK, AND WAS IMMEDIATELY BRAINED—THAT IS, HEAD CRUSHED AND DESTROYED, THOUGH NOTHING ISSUED FROM DEBRIS. ALL FLED; SO DID ELEPHANT, STRIKING RIGHT AND LEFT WITH MUCH EFFECT. HAS ESCAPED, BUT LEFT BOLD BLOOD-TRACK FROM CANNON-WOUNDS. REDISCOVERY CERTAIN. HE BROKE SOUTHWARD, THROUGH A DENSE FOREST.

BRENT, DETECTIVE

That was the last telegram. At nightfall a fog shut down which was so dense that objects but three feet away could not be discerned. This lasted all night. The ferryboats and even the omnibuses had to stop running.

3

Next morning the papers were as full of detective theories as before; they had all our tragic facts in detail also, and a great many more which they had received from their telegraphic correspondents. Column after column was occupied, a third of its way down, with glaring head-lines, which it made my heart sick to read. Their general tone was like this:

THE WHITE ELEPHANT AT LARGE! HE MOVES UPON HIS FATAL MARCH! WHOLE VILLAGES DESERTED BY THEIR FRIGHT-STRICKEN OCCUPANTS! PALE TERROR GOES BEFORE HIM, DEATH AND DEVASTATION FOLLOW AFTER! AFTER THESE, THE DETECTIVES! BARNS DESTROYED, FACTORIES GUTTED, HARVESTS DEVOURED, PUBLIC ASSEMBLAGES DISPERSED, ACCOMPANIED BY SCENES OF CARNAGE IMPOSSIBLE TO DESCRIBE! THEORIES OF THIRTY-FOUR OF THE MOST DISTINGUISHED DETECTIVES ON THE FORCE! THEORY OF CHIEF BLUNT!

"There!" said Inspector Blunt, almost betrayed into excitement, "this is magnificent! This is the greatest windfall that any detective organization ever had. The fame of it will travel to the ends of the earth, and endure to the end of time, and my name with it."

But there was no joy for me. I felt as if I had committed all those red crimes, and that the elephant was only my irresponsible agent. And how the list had grown! In one place he had "interfered with an election and killed five repeaters." He had followed this act with the destruction of two poor fellows, named O'Donohue and McFlannigan, who had "found a refuge in the home of the oppressed of all lands only the day before, and were in the act of exercising for the first time the noble right of American citizens at the polls, when stricken down by the relentless hand of the Scourge of Siam." In another, he had "found a crazy sensation-preacher preparing his next season's heroic attacks on the dance, the theater, and other things which can't strike back, and had stepped on him." And in still another place he had "killed a lightning-rod agent." And so the list went on, growing redder and redder, and more and more heartbreaking. Sixty persons had been killed, and two hundred and forty wounded. All the accounts bore just testimony to the activity and devotion of the detectives, and all closed with the remark that "three hundred thousand citizens and four detectives saw the dread creature, and two of the latter he destroyed."

I dreaded to hear the telegraphic instrument begin to click again. By and by the messages began to pour in, but I was happily disappointed in their nature. It was soon apparent that all trace of the elephant was lost. The fog had enabled him to search out a good hiding-place unobserved. Telegrams from the most absurdly distant points reported that a dim vast mass had been glimpsed there through the fog at such and such an hour, and was "undoubtedly the elephant." This dim vast mass had been glimpsed in New Haven, in New Jersey, in Pennsylvania, in interior New York, in Brooklyn, and even in the city of New York itself! But in all cases the dim vast mass had vanished quickly and left no trace. Every detective of the large force scattered over this huge extent of country sent his hourly report, and each and every one of them had a clue, and was shadowing something, and was hot upon the heels of it.

But the day passed without other result.

The next day the same.

The next just the same.

The newspaper reports began to grow monotonous with facts that amounted to nothing, clues which led to nothing, and theories which had nearly exhausted the elements which surprise and delight and dazzle.

By advice of the inspector I doubled the reward.

Four more dull days followed. Then came a bitter blow to the poor, hard-working detectives—the journalists declined to print their theories, and coldly said, "Give us a rest."

Two weeks after the elephant's disappearance I raised the reward to seventy-five thousand dollars by the inspector's advice. It was a great sum, but I felt that I would rather sacrifice my whole private fortune than lose my credit with my government. Now that the detectives were in adversity, the newspapers turned upon them, and began to fling the most stinging sarcasms at them. This gave the minstrels an idea, and they dressed themselves as detectives and hunted the elephant on the stage in the most extravagant way. The caricaturists made pictures of detectives scanning the country with spyglasses, while the elephant, at their backs, stole apples out of their pockets. And they made all sorts of ridiculous pictures of the detective badge—you have seen that badge printed in gold on the back of detective novels, no doubt—it is a wide-staring eye, with the legend, "WE NEVER SLEEP." When detectives called for a drink, the would-be facetious barkeeper resurrected an obsolete form of expression and said, "Will you have an eye-opener?" All the air was thick with sarcasms.

But there was one man who moved calm, untouched, unaffected, through it all. It was that heart of oak, the chief inspector. His brave eye never drooped, his serene confidence never wavered. He always said:

"Let them rail on; he laughs best who laughs last."

My admiration for the man grew into a species of worship. I was at his side always. His office had become an unpleasant place to me, and now became daily more and more so. Yet if he could endure it I meant to do so also—at least, as long as I could. So I came regularly, and stayed—the only outsider who seemed to be capable of it. Everybody wondered how I could; and often it seemed to me that I must desert, but at such times I looked into that calm and apparently unconscious face, and held my ground.

About three weeks after the elephant's disappearance I was about to say, one morning, that I should *have* to strike my colors and retire, when the great detective arrested the thought by proposing one more superb and masterly move.

This was to compromise with the robbers. The fertility of this man's invention exceeded anything I have ever seen, and I have had a wide intercourse with the world's finest minds. He said he was confident he could compromise for one hundred thousand dollars and recover the elephant. I said I believed I could scrape the amount together, but what would become of the poor detectives who had worked so faithfully? He said:

"In compromises they always get half."

This removed my only objection. So the inspector wrote two notes, in this form:

DEAR MADAM—YOUR HUSBAND CAN MAKE A LARGE SUM OF MONEY (AND BE ENTIRELY PROTECTED FROM THE LAW) BY MAKING AN IMMEDIATE APPOINTMENT WITH ME.

CHIEF BLUNT

He sent one of these by his confidential messenger to the "reputed wife" of Brick Duffy, and the other to the reputed wife of Red McFadden.

Within the hour these offensive answers came:

YE OWLD FOOL: BRICK DUFFYS BIN DED 2 YERE.

BRIDGET MAHONEY

CHIEF BAT—RED MCFADDEN IS HUNG AND IN HEVING 18 MONTH. ANY ASS BUT A DETECTIVE KNOSE THAT.

MARY O'HOOLIGAN

"I had long suspected these facts," said the inspector; "this testimony proves the unerring accuracy of my instinct."

The moment one resource failed him he was ready with another. He immediately wrote an advertisement for the morning papers, and I kept a copy of it:

A.—xwblv. 242 N. Tjnd—fz328wmlg. Ozpo,—; 2 m! ogw. Mum.

He said that if the thief was alive this would bring him to the usual rendezvous. He further explained that the usual rendezvous was a place where all business affairs between detectives and criminals were conducted. This meeting would take place at twelve the next night.

We could do nothing till then, and I lost no time in getting out of the office, and was grateful indeed for the privilege.

At eleven the next night I brought one hundred thousand dollars in bank-notes and put them into the chief's hands, and shortly afterward he took his leave, with the brave old undimmed confidence in his eye. An almost intolerable hour dragged to a close; then I heard his welcome tread, and rose gasping and tottered to meet him. How his fine eyes flamed with triumph! He said:

"We've compromised! The jokers will sing a different tune to-morrow! Follow me!"

He took a lighted candle and strode down into the vast vaulted basement where sixty detectives always slept, and where a score were now playing cards to while the time. I followed close after him. He walked swiftly down to the dim and remote end of the place, and just as I succumbed to the pangs of suffocation and was swooning away he stumbled and fell over the outlying members of a mighty object, and I heard him exclaim as he went down:

"Our noble profession is vindicated. Here is your elephant!"

I was carried to the office above and restored with carbolic acid. The whole detective force swarmed in, and such another season of triumphant rejoicing ensued as I had never witnessed before. The reporters were called, baskets of champagne were opened, toasts were drunk, the handshakings and congratulations were continuous and enthusiastic. Naturally the chief was the hero of the hour, and his happiness was so complete and had been so patiently and worthily and bravely won that it made me happy to see it, though I stood there a homeless beggar, my priceless charge dead, and my position in my country's service lost to me through what would always seem my fatally careless execution of a great trust. Many an eloquent eye testified its deep admiration for the chief, and many a detective's voice murmured, "Look at him—just the king of the profession; only give him a clue, it's all he wants, and there ain't anything hid that he can't find." The dividing of the fifty thousand dollars made great pleasure; when it was finished the chief made a little speech while he put his share in his pocket, in which he said, "Enjoy it, boys, for you've earned it; and, more than that, you've earned for the detective profession undying fame."

A telegram arrived, which read:

> MONROE, MICH., 10 P.M.
> FIRST TIME I'VE STRUCK A TELEGRAPH OFFICE IN OVER THREE WEEKS. HAVE FOLLOWED THOSE FOOTPRINTS, HORSEBACK, THROUGH THE WOODS, A THOUSAND MILES TO HERE, AND THEY GET STRONGER AND BIGGER AND FRESHER EVERY DAY. DON'T WORRY—INSIDE OF ANOTHER WEEK I'LL HAVE THE ELEPHANT. THIS IS DEAD SURE.
>
> DARLEY, DETECTIVE

The chief ordered three cheers for "Darley, one of the finest minds on the force," and then commanded that he be telegraphed to come home and receive his share of the reward.

So ended that marvelous episode of the stolen elephant. The newspapers were pleasant with praises once more, the next day, with one contemptible exception. This sheet said, "Great is the detective! He may be a little slow in finding a little thing like a mislaid elephant—he may hunt him all day and sleep with his rotting carcass all night for three weeks, but he will find him at last—if he can get the man who mislaid him to show him the place!"

Poor Hassan was lost to me forever. The cannon-shots had wounded him fatally, he had crept to that unfriendly place in the fog, and there, surrounded by his enemies and in constant danger of detection, he had wasted away with hunger and suffering till death gave him peace.

The compromise cost me one hundred thousand dollars; my detective expenses were forty-two thousand dollars more; I never applied for a place again under my government; I am a ruined man and a wanderer on the earth—but my admiration for that man, whom I believe to be the greatest detective the world has ever produced, remains undimmed to this day, and will so remain unto the end.

1882

SKETCHES

SKETCHES

FIRST INTERVIEW WITH
ARTEMUS WARD

I had never seen him before. He brought letters of introduction from
mutual friends in San Francisco, and by invitation I breakfasted with
him. It was almost religion, there in the silver-mines, to precede such a
meal with whisky cocktails. Artemus, with the true cosmopolitan instinct, always deferred to the customs of the country he was in, and so
he ordered three of those abominations. Hingston was present. I said I
would rather not drink a whisky cocktail. I said it would go right to
my head, and confuse me so that I would be in a helpless tangle in ten
minutes. I did not want to act like a lunatic before strangers. But
Artemus gently insisted, and I drank the treasonable mixture under
protest, and felt all the time that I was doing a thing I might be sorry
for. In a minute or two I began to imagine that my ideas were clouded.
I waited in great anxiety for the conversation to open, with a sort of
vague hope that my understanding would prove clear, after all, and
my misgivings groundless.

Artemus dropped an unimportant remark or two, and then assumed
a look of superhuman earnestness, and made the following astounding
speech. He said:

"Now there is one thing I ought to ask you about before I forget it.
You have been here in Silverland—here in Nevada—two or three
years, and, of course, your position on the daily press has made it
necessary for you to go down in the mines and examine them carefully
in detail, and therefore you know all about the silver-mining business.
Now what I want to get at is—is, well, the way the deposits of ore are
made, you know. For instance. Now, as I understand it, the vein
which contains the silver is sandwiched in between casings of granite,

and runs along the ground, and sticks up like a curbstone. Well, take a vein forty feet thick, for example, or eighty, for that matter, or even a hundred—say you go down on it with a shaft, straight down, you know, or with what you call 'incline'—maybe you go down five hundred feet, or maybe you don't go down but two hundred—anyway, you go down, and all the time this vein grows narrower, when the casings come nearer or approach each other, you may say—that is, when they do approach, which, of course, they do not always do, particularly in cases where the nature of the formation is such that they stand apart wider than they otherwise would, and which geology has failed to account for, although everything in that science goes to prove that, all things being equal, it would if it did not, or would not certainly if it did, and then, of course, they are. Do not you think it is?"

I said to myself:

"Now I just knew how it would be—that whisky cocktail has done the business for me; I don't understand any more than a clam."

And then I said aloud:

"I—I—that is—if you don't mind, would you—would you say that over again? I ought—"

"Oh, certainly, certainly! You see I am very unfamiliar with the subject, and perhaps I don't present my case clearly, but I—"

"No, no—no, no—you state it plain enough, but that cocktail has muddled me a little. But I will—no, I do understand for that matter; but I would get the hang of it all the better if you went over it again—and I'll pay better attention this time."

He said, "Why, what I was after was this."

[Here he became even more fearfully impressive than ever, and emphasized each particular point by checking it off on his finger-ends.]

"This vein, or lode, or ledge, or whatever you call it, runs along between two layers of granite, just the same as if it were a sandwich. Very well. Now suppose you go down on that, say a thousand feet, or maybe twelve hundred (it don't really matter) before you drift, and then you start your drifts, some of them across the ledge, and others along the length of it, where the sulphurets—I believe they call them sulphurets, though why they should, considering that, so far as I can see, the main dependence of a miner does not so lie, as some suppose, but in which it cannot be successfully maintained, wherein the same should not continue, while part and parcel of the same ore not committed to either in the sense referred to, whereas, under different circumstances, the most inexperienced among us could not detect it if it were, or might overlook it if it did, or scorn the very idea of such a thing, even though it were palpably demonstrated as such. Am I not right?"

I said, sorrowfully: "I feel ashamed of myself, Mr. Ward. I know I ought to understand you perfectly well, but you see that treacherous whisky cocktail has got into my head, and now I cannot understand even the simplest proposition. I told you how it would be."

"Oh, don't mind it, don't mind it; the fault was my own, no doubt—though I did think it clear enough for—"

"Don't say a word. Clear! Why, you stated it as clear as the sun to anybody but an abject idiot; but it's that confounded cocktail that has played the mischief."

"No; now don't say that. I'll begin it all over again, and—"

"Don't now—for goodness' sake, don't do anything of the kind, because I tell you my head is in such a condition that I don't believe I could understand the most trifling question a man could ask me."

"Now don't you be afraid. I'll put it so plain this time that you can't help but get the hang of it. We will begin at the very beginning." [Leaning far across the table, with determined impressiveness wrought upon his every feature, and fingers prepared to keep tally of each point enumerated; and I, leaning forward with painful interest, resolved to comprehend or perish.] "You know the vein, the ledge, the thing that contains the metal, whereby it constitutes the medium between all other forces, whether of present or remote agencies, so brought to bear in favor of the former against the latter, or the latter against the former or all, or both, or compromising the relative differences existing within the radius whence culminate the several degrees of similarity to which—"

I said: "Oh, hang my wooden head, it ain't any use!—it ain't any use to try—I can't understand anything. The plainer you get it the more I can't get the hang of it."

I heard a suspicious noise behind me, and turned in time to see Hingston dodging behind a newspaper, and quaking with a gentle ecstasy of laughter. I looked at Ward again, and he had thrown off his dread solemnity and was laughing also. Then I saw that I had been sold—that I had been made a victim of a swindle in the way of a string of plausibly worded sentences that didn't mean anything under the sun. Artemus Ward was one of the best fellows in the world, and one of the most companionable. It has been said that he was not fluent in conversation, but, with the above experience in my mind, I differ.

1871

PUNCH, BROTHERS, PUNCH

Will the reader please to cast his eye over the following lines, and see if he can discover anything harmful in them?

> Conductor, when you receive a fare,
> Punch in the presence of the passenjare!
> A blue trip slip for an eight-cent fare,
> A buff trip slip for a six-cent fare,
> A pink trip slip for a three-cent fare,
> Punch in the presence of the passenjare!

> *Chorus*
> Punch, brothers! punch with care!
> Punch in the presence of the passenjare!

I came across these jingling rhymes in a newspaper, a little while ago, and read them a couple of times. They took instant and entire possession of me. All through breakfast they went waltzing through my brain; and when, at last, I rolled up my napkin, I could not tell whether I had eaten anything or not. I had carefully laid out my day's work the day before—a thrilling tragedy in the novel which I am writing. I went to my den to begin my deed of blood. I took up my pen, but all I could get it to say was, "Punch in the presence of the passenjare." I fought hard for an hour, but it was useless. My head kept humming, "A blue trip slip for an eight-cent fare, a buff trip slip for a six-cent fare," and so on and so on, without peace or respite. The day's work was ruined—I could see that plainly enough. I gave up and drifted down-town, and presently discovered that my feet were keeping time to that relentless jingle. When I could stand it no longer I altered my step. But it did no good; those rhymes accommodated themselves to the new step and went on harassing me just as before. I returned home, and suffered all the afternoon; suffered all through an unconscious and unrefreshing dinner; suffered, and cried, and jingled all through the evening; went to bed and rolled, tossed, and jingled right along, the same as ever; got up at midnight frantic, and tried to read; but there was nothing visible upon the whirling page except "Punch! punch in the presence of the passenjare." By sunrise I was out of my mind, and everybody marveled and was distressed at the idiotic burden of my ravings—"Punch! oh, punch! punch in the presence of the passenjare!"

Two days later, on Saturday morning, I arose, a tottering wreck, and went forth to fulfil an engagement with a valued friend, the Rev. Mr. ——, to walk to the Talcott Tower, ten miles distant. He stared at me, but asked no questions. We started. Mr. —— talked, talked, talked—as is his wont. I said nothing; I heard nothing. At the end of a mile, Mr. —— said:

"Mark, are you sick? I never saw a man look so haggard and worn and absent-minded. Say something, do!"

Drearily, without enthusiasm, I said: "Punch, brothers, punch with care! Punch in the presence of the passenjare!"

My friend eyed me blankly, looked perplexed, then said:

"I do not think I get your drift, Mark. There does not seem to be any relevancy in what you have said, certainly nothing sad; and yet—maybe it was the way you *said* the words—I never heard anything that sounded so pathetic. What is—"

But I heard no more. I was already far away with my pitiless, heartbreaking "blue trip slip for an eight-cent fare, buff trip slip for a six-cent fare, pink trip slip for a three-cent fare; punch in the presence of the passenjare." I do not know what occurred during the other nine miles. However, all of a sudden Mr. —— laid his hand on my shoulder and shouted:

"Oh, wake up! wake up! wake up! Don't sleep all day! Here we are at the Tower, man! I have talked myself deaf and dumb and blind, and never got a response. Just look at this magnificent autumn landscape! Look at it! look at it! Feast your eyes on it! You have traveled; you have seen boasted landscapes elsewhere. Come, now, deliver an honest opinion. What do you say to this?"

I sighed wearily, and murmured:

"A buff trip slip for a six-cent fare, a pink trip slip for a three-cent fare, punch in the presence of the passenjare."

Rev. Mr. —— stood there, very grave, full of concern, apparently, and looked long at me; then he said:

"Mark, there is something about this that I cannot understand. Those are about the same words you said before; there does not seem to be anything in them, and yet they nearly break my heart when you say them. Punch in the—how is it they go?"

I began at the beginning and repeated all the lines.

My friend's face lighted with interest. He said:

"Why, what a captivating jingle it is! It is almost music. It flows along so nicely. I have nearly caught the rhymes myself. Say them over just once more, and then I'll have them, sure."

I said them over. Then Mr. —— said them. He made one little mistake, which I corrected. The next time and the next he got them right. Now a great burden seemed to tumble from my shoulders. That torturing jingle departed out of my brain, and a grateful sense of rest and peace descended upon me. I was light-hearted enough to sing; and I did sing for half an hour, straight along, as we went jogging homeward. Then my freed tongue found blessed speech again, and the pent talk of many a weary hour began to gush and flow. It flowed on and on, joyously, jubilantly, until the fountain was empty and dry. As I wrung my friend's hand at parting, I said:

"Haven't we had a royal good time! But now I remember, you haven't said a word for two hours. Come, come, out with something!"

The Rev. Mr. —— turned a lack-luster eye upon me, drew a deep sigh, and said, without animation, without apparent consciousness:

"Punch, brothers, punch with care! Punch in the presence of the passenjare!"

A pang shot through me as I said to myself, "Poor fellow, poor fellow! *he* has got it, now."

I did not see Mr. —— for two or three days after that. Then, on Tuesday evening, he staggered into my presence and sank dejectedly into a seat. He was pale, worn; he was a wreck. He lifted his faded eyes to my face and said:

"Ah, Mark, it was a ruinous investment that I made in those heartless rhymes. They have ridden me like a nightmare, day and night, hour after hour, to this very moment. Since I saw you I have suffered the torments of the lost. Saturday evening I had a sudden call, by telegraph, and took the night train for Boston. The occasion was the death of a valued old friend who had requested that I should preach his funeral sermon. I took my seat in the cars and set myself to framing the discourse. But I never got beyond the opening paragraph; for then the train started and the car-wheels began their 'clack, clack—clack-clack-clack! clack-clack—clack-clack-clack!' and right away those odious rhymes fitted themselves to that accompaniment. For an hour I sat there and set a syllable of those rhymes to every separate and distinct clack the car-wheels made. Why, I was as fagged out, then, as if I had been chopping wood all day. My skull was splitting with headache. It seemed to me that I must go mad if I sat there any longer; so I undressed and went to bed. I stretched myself out in my berth, and—well, you know what the result was. The thing went right along, just the same. 'Clack-clack-clack, a blue trip slip, clack-clack-clack, for an eight-cent fare; clack-clack-clack, a buff trip slip, clack-clack-clack, for a six-cent fare, and so on, and so on, and so on—*punch* in the presence of the passenjare!' Sleep? Not a single wink! I was almost a lunatic when I got to Boston. Don't ask me about the funeral. I did the best I could, but every solemn individual sentence was meshed and tangled and woven in and out with 'Punch, brothers, punch with care, punch in the presence of the passenjare.' And the most distressing thing was that my *delivery* dropped into the undulating rhythm of those pulsing rhymes, and I could actually catch absent-minded people nodding *time* to the swing of it with their stupid heads. And, Mark, you may believe it or not, but before I got through the entire assemblage were placidly bobbing their heads in solemn unison, mourners, undertaker, and all. The moment I had finished, I fled to the anteroom in a state bordering on frenzy. Of course it would be my luck to find a sorrowing and aged maiden aunt of the deceased there, who had arrived from Springfield too late to get into the church. She began to sob, and said:

" 'Oh, oh, he is gone, he is gone, and I didn't see him before he died!'

" 'Yes!' I said, 'he *is* gone, he *is* gone, he *is* gone—oh, *will* this suffering never cease!'

" 'You loved him, then! Oh, you too loved him!'

" 'Loved him! Loved *who?*'

" 'Why, my poor George! my poor nephew!'

" 'Oh—*him!* Yes—oh, yes, yes. Certainly—certainly. Punch—punch—oh, this misery will kill me!'

" 'Bless you! bless you, sir, for these sweet words! *I,* too, suffer in this dear loss. Were you present during his last moments?'

" 'Yes. I—*whose* last moments?'

" '*His.* The dear departed's.'

" 'Yes! Oh, yes—yes—*yes!* I suppose so, I think so, *I* don't know! Oh, certainly—I was there—*I* was there!'

" 'Oh, what a privilege! what a precious privilege! And his last words—oh, tell me, tell me his last words! What did he say?'

" 'He said—he said—oh, my head, my head, my head! He said—he said—he never said *any*thing but Punch, punch, *punch* in the presence of the passenjare! Oh, leave me, madam! In the name of all that is generous, leave me to my madness, my misery, my despair!—a buff trip slip for a six-cent fare, a pink trip slip for a three-cent fare—endurance *can* no fur-ther go!—PUNCH in the presence of the passenjare!' "

My friend's hopeless eyes rested upon mine a pregnant minute, and then he said impressively:

"Mark, you do not say anything. You do not offer me any hope. But, ah me, it is just as well—it is just as well. You could not do me any good. The time has long gone by when words could comfort me. Something tells me that my tongue is doomed to wag forever to the jigger of that remorseless jingle. There—there it is coming on me again: a blue trip slip for an eight-cent fare, a buff trip slip for a—"

Thus murmuring faint and fainter, my friend sank into a peaceful trance and forgot his sufferings in a blessed respite.

How did I finally save him from an asylum? I took him to a neighboring university and made him discharge the burden of his persecuting rhymes into the eager ears of the poor, unthinking students. How is it with *them,* now? The result is too sad to tell. Why did I write this article? It was for a worthy, even a noble, purpose. It was to warn you, reader, if you should come across those merciless rhymes, to avoid them—avoid them as you would a pestilence!

1876

FENIMORE COOPER'S LITERARY OFFENSES

The Pathfinder and *The Deerslayer* stand at the head of Cooper's novels as artistic creations. There are others of his works which contain parts as perfect as are to be found in these, and scenes even more thrilling. Not one can be compared with either of them as a finished whole.

The defects in both of these tales are comparatively slight. They were pure works of art.—*Prof. Lounsbury.*

The five tales reveal an extraordinary fullness of invention.

. . . One of the very greatest characters in fiction, Natty Bumppo. . . .

The craft of the woodsman, the tricks of the trapper, all the delicate art of the forest, were familiar to Cooper from his youth up.—*Prof. Brander Matthews.*

Cooper is the greatest artist in the domain of romantic fiction yet produced by America.—*Wilkie Collins.*

It seems to me that it was far from right for the Professor of English Literature in Yale, the Professor of English Literature in Columbia, and Wilkie Collins to deliver opinions on Cooper's literature without having read some of it. It would have been much more decorous to keep silent and let persons talk who have read Cooper.

Cooper's art has some defects. In one place in *Deerslayer,* and in the restricted space of two-thirds of a page, Cooper has scored 114 offenses against literary art out of a possible 115. It breaks the record.

There are nineteen rules governing literary art in the domain of romantic fiction—some say twenty-two. In *Deerslayer* Cooper violated eighteen of them. These eighteen require:

1. That a tale shall accomplish something and arrive somewhere. But the *Deerslayer* tale accomplishes nothing and arrives in the air.

2. They require that the episodes of a tale shall be necessary parts of the tale, and shall help to develop it. But as the *Deerslayer* tale is

not a tale, and accomplishes nothing and arrives nowhere, the episodes have no rightful place in the work, since there was nothing for them to develop.

3. They require that the personages in a tale shall be alive, except in the case of corpses, and that always the reader shall be able to tell the corpses from the others. But this detail has often been overlooked in the *Deerslayer* tale.

4. They require that the personages in a tale, both dead and alive, shall exhibit a sufficient excuse for being there. But this detail also has been overlooked in the *Deerslayer* tale.

5. They require that when the personages of a tale deal in conversation, the talk shall sound like human talk, and be talk such as human beings would be likely to talk in the given circumstances, and have a discoverable meaning, also a discoverable purpose, and a show of relevancy, and remain in the neighborhood of the subject in hand, and be interesting to the reader, and help out the tale, and stop when the people cannot think of anything more to say. But this requirement has been ignored from the beginning of the *Deerslayer* tale to the end of it.

6. They require that when the author describes the character of a personage in his tale, the conduct and conversation of that personage shall justify said description. But this law gets little or no attention in the *Deerslayer* tale, as Natty Bumppo's case will amply prove.

7. They require that when a personage talks like an illustrated, gilt-edged, tree-calf, hand-tooled, seven-dollar Friendship's Offering in the beginning of a paragraph, he shall not talk like a negro minstrel in the end of it. But this rule is flung down and danced upon in the *Deerslayer* tale.

8. They require that crass stupidities shall not be played upon the reader as "the craft of the woodsman, the delicate art of the forest," by either the author or the people in the tale. But this rule is persistently violated in the *Deerslayer* tale.

9. They require that the personages of a tale shall confine themselves to possibilities and let miracles alone; or, if they venture a miracle, the author must so plausibly set it forth as to make it look possible and reasonable. But these rules are not respected in the *Deerslayer* tale.

10. They require that the author shall make the reader feel a deep interest in the personages of his tale and in their fate; and that he shall make the reader love the good people in the tale and hate the bad ones.

But the reader of the *Deerslayer* tale dislikes the good people in it, is indifferent to the others, and wishes they would all get drowned together.

11. They require that the characters in a tale shall be so clearly defined that the reader can tell beforehand what each will do in a given emergency. But in the *Deerslayer* tale this rule is vacated.

In addition to these large rules there are some little ones. These require that the author shall

12. *Say* what he is proposing to say, not merely come near it.

13. Use the right word, not its second cousin.

14. Eschew surplusage.

15. Not omit necessary details.

16. Avoid slovenliness of form.

17. Use good grammar.

18. Employ a simple and straightforward style.

Even these seven are coldly and persistently violated in the *Deerslayer* tale.

Cooper's gift in the way of invention was not a rich endowment; but such as it was he liked to work it, he was pleased with the effects, and indeed he did some quite sweet things with it. In his little box of stage-properties he kept six or eight cunning devices, tricks, artifices for his savages and woodsmen to deceive and circumvent each other with, and he was never so happy as when he was working these innocent things and seeing them go. A favorite one was to make a moccasined person tread in the tracks of the moccasined enemy, and thus hide his own trail. Cooper wore out barrels and barrels of moccasins in working that trick. Another stage-property that he pulled out of his box pretty frequently was his broken twig. He prized his broken twig above all the rest of his effects, and worked it the hardest. It is a restful chapter in any book of his when somebody doesn't step on a dry twig and alarm all the reds and whites for two hundred yards around. Every time a Cooper person is in peril, and absolute silence is worth four dollars a minute, he is sure to step on a dry twig. There may be a hundred handier things to step on, but that wouldn't satisfy Cooper. Cooper requires him to turn out and find a dry twig; and if he can't do it, go and borrow one. In fact, the Leatherstocking Series ought to have been called the Broken Twig Series.

I am sorry there is not room to put in a few dozen instances of the delicate art of the forest, as practised by Natty Bumppo and some of the other Cooperian experts. Perhaps we may venture two or three samples. Cooper was a sailor—a naval officer; yet he gravely tells us how a vessel, driving toward a lee shore in a gale, is steered for a particular spot by her skipper because he knows of an *undertow* there which will hold her back against the gale and save her. For just pure woodcraft, or sailorcraft, or whatever it is, isn't that neat? For several years Cooper was daily in the society of artillery, and he ought to have noticed that when a cannon-ball strikes the ground it either buries itself or skips a hundred feet or so; skips again a hundred feet or so— and so on, till finally it gets tired and rolls. Now in one place he loses some "females"—as he always calls women—in the edge of a wood near a plain at night in a fog, on purpose to give Bumppo a chance to show off the delicate art of the forest before the reader. These mislaid people are hunting for a fort. They hear a cannon-blast, and a cannon-ball presently comes rolling into the wood and stops at their feet. To the females this suggests nothing. The case is very different with the admirable Bumppo. I wish I may never know peace again if he doesn't strike out promptly and *follow the track* of that cannon-ball across the plain through the dense fog and find the fort. Isn't it a daisy? If Cooper had any real knowledge of Nature's ways of doing things, he had a most delicate art in concealing the fact. For instance: one of his acute Indian experts, Chingachgook (pronounced Chicago, I think), has lost the trail of a person he is tracking through the forest. Apparently that trail is hopelessly lost. Neither you nor I could ever have guessed out the way to find it. It was very different with Chicago. Chicago was not stumped for long. He turned a running stream out of its course, and there, in the slush in its old bed, were that person's moccasin tracks. The current did not wash them away, as it would have done in all other like cases—no, even the eternal laws of Nature have to vacate when Cooper wants to put up a delicate job of wood-craft on the reader.

We must be a little wary when Brander Matthews tells us that Cooper's books "reveal an extraordinary fullness of invention." As a rule, I am quite willing to accept Brander Matthews's literary judgments and applaud his lucid and graceful phrasing of them; but that particular statement needs to be taken with a few tons of salt. Bless your heart, Cooper hadn't any more invention than a horse; and I don't mean a high-class horse, either; I mean a clothes-horse. It would be very difficult to find a really clever "situation" in Cooper's books, and still more difficult to find one of any kind which he has failed to render absurd by his handling of it. Look at the episodes of "the caves"; and at the celebrated scuffle between Maqua and those others on the table-land a few days later; and at Hurry Harry's queer water-transit from the castle to the ark; and at Deerslayer's half-hour with his first corpse; and at the quarrel between Hurry Harry and Deerslayer later; and at—but choose for yourself; you can't go amiss.

If Cooper had been an observer his inventive faculty would have worked better; not more interestingly, but more rationally, more plausibly. Cooper's proudest creations in the way of "situations" suffer noticeably from the absence of the observer's protecting gift. Cooper's eye was splendidly inaccurate. Cooper seldom saw anything correctly. He saw nearly all things as through a glass eye, darkly. Of course a man who cannot see the commonest little every-day matters accurately is working at a disadvantage when he is constructing a "situation." In the *Deerslayer* tale Cooper has a stream which is fifty feet wide where it flows out of a lake; it presently narrows to twenty as it meanders along for no given reason, and yet when a stream acts like that it ought to be required to explain itself. Fourteen pages later the width of the brook's outlet from the lake has suddenly shrunk thirty feet, and become "the narrowest part of the stream." This shrinkage is not accounted for. The stream has bends in it, a sure indication that it has alluvial banks and cuts them; yet these bends are only thirty and fifty feet long. If Cooper had been a nice and punctilious observer he would have noticed that the bends were oftener nine hundred feet long than short of it.

Cooper made the exit of that stream fifty feet wide, in the first place, for no particular reason; in the second place, he narrowed it to less than twenty to accommodate some Indians. He bends a "sapling" to the form of an arch over this narrow passage, and conceals six Indians in its foliage. They are "laying" for a settler's scow or ark which is coming up the stream on its way to the lake; it is being hauled against the stiff current by a rope whose stationary end is anchored in the lake; its rate of progress cannot be more than a mile an hour. Cooper describes the ark, but pretty obscurely. In the matter of dimensions "it was little more than a modern canal-boat." Let us guess, then, that it was about one hundred and forty feet long. It was of "greater breadth than common." Let us guess, then, that it was about sixteen feet wide. This leviathan had been prowling down bends which were but a third as long as itself, and scraping between banks where it had only two feet of space to spare on each side. We cannot too much admire this miracle. A low-roofed log dwelling occupies "two-thirds of the ark's length"—a dwelling ninety feet long and sixteen feet wide, let us say— a kind of vestibule train. The dwelling has two rooms—each forty-five feet long and sixteen feet wide, let us guess. One of them is the bedroom of the Hutter girls, Judith and Hetty; the other is the parlor in the daytime, at night it is papa's bedchamber. The ark is arriving at the stream's exit now, whose width has been reduced to less than twenty feet to accommodate the Indians—say to eighteen. There is a foot to spare on each side of the boat. Did the Indians notice that there was going to be a tight squeeze there? Did they notice that they could make money by climbing down out of that arched sapling and just stepping aboard when the ark scraped by? No, other Indians would have noticed these things, but Cooper's Indians never notice anything. Cooper thinks they are marvelous creatures for noticing, but he was almost always in error about his Indians. There was seldom a sane one among them.

The ark is one hundred and forty-feet long; the dwelling is ninety feet long. The idea of the Indians is to drop softly and secretly from the arched sapling to the dwelling as the ark creeps along under it at the rate of a mile an hour, and butcher the family. It will take the ark a minute and a half to pass under. It will take the ninety-foot dwelling a minute to pass under. Now, then, what did the six Indians do? It would take you thirty years to guess, and even then you would have to give it up, I believe. Therefore, I will tell you what the Indians did. Their chief, a person of quite extraordinary intellect for a Cooper Indian, warily watched the canal-boat as it squeezed along under him, and when he had got his calculations fined down to exactly the right shade, as he judged, he let go and dropped. And *missed the house!* That is actually what he did. He missed the house, and landed in the stern of the scow. It was not much of a fall, yet it knocked him silly. He lay there unconscious. If the house had been ninety-seven feet long he would have made the trip. The fault was Cooper's, not his. The error lay in the construction of the house. Cooper was no architect.

There still remained in the roost five Indians. The boat has passed under and is now out of their reach. Let me explain what the five did —you would not be able to reason it out for yourself. No. 1 jumped for the boat, but fell in the water astern of it. Then No. 2 jumped for

the boat, but fell in the water still farther astern of it. Then No. 3
jumped for the boat, and fell a good way astern of it. Then No. 4
jumped for the boat, and fell in the water *away* astern. Then even No.
5 made a jump for the boat—for he was a Cooper Indian. In the
matter of intellect, the difference between a Cooper Indian and the
Indian that stands in front of the cigar-shop is not spacious. The scow
episode is really a sublime burst of invention; but it does not thrill,
because the inaccuracy of the details throws a sort of air of fictitious-
ness and general improbability over it. This comes of Cooper's inade-
quacy as an observer.

The reader will find some examples of Cooper's high talent for
inaccurate observation in the account of the shooting-match in *The
Pathfinder.*

A common wrought nail was driven lightly into the target,
its head having been first touched with paint.

The color of the paint is not stated—an important omission, but
Cooper deals freely in important omissions. No, after all, it was not an
important omission; for this nail-head is *a hundred yards from* the
marksmen, and could not be seen by them at that distance, no matter
what its color might be. How far can the best eyes see a common
house-fly? A hundred yards? It is quite impossible. Very well; eyes that
cannot see a house-fly that is a hundred yards away cannot see an
ordinary nail-head at that distance, for the size of the two objects is
the same. It takes a keen eye to see a fly or a nail-head at fifty yards—
one hundred and fifty feet. Can the reader do it?

The nail was lightly driven, its head painted, and game called. Then
the Cooper miracles began. The bullet of the first marksman chipped
an edge of the nail-head; the next man's bullet drove the nail a little
way into the target—and removed all the paint. Haven't the miracles
gone far enough now? Not to suit Cooper; for the purpose of this
whole scheme is to show off his prodigy, Deerslayer-Hawkeye-Long-
Rifle-Leatherstocking-Pathfinder-Bumppo before the ladies.

"Be all ready to clench it, boys!" cried out Pathfinder,
stepping into his friend's tracks the instant they were vacant.
"Never mind a new nail; I can see that, though the paint is
gone, and what I can see I can hit at a hundred yards,
though it were only a mosquito's eye. Be ready to clench!"

The rifle cracked, the bullet sped its way, and the head of the nail was buried in the wood, covered by the piece of flattened lead.

There, you see, is a man who could hunt flies with a rifle, and command a ducal salary in a Wild West show to-day if we had him back with us.

The recorded feat is certainly surprising just as it stands; but it is not surprising enough for Cooper. Cooper adds a touch. He has made Pathfinder do this miracle with another man's rifle; and not only that, but Pathfinder did not have even the advantage of loading it himself. He had everything against him, and yet he made that impossible shot; and not only made it, but did it with absolute confidence, saying, "Be ready to clench." Now a person like that would have undertaken that same feat with a brickbat, and with Cooper to help he would have achieved it, too.

Pathfinder showed off handsomely that day before the ladies. His very first feat a thing which no Wild West show can touch. He was standing with the group of marksmen, observing—a hundred yards from the target, mind; one Jasper raised his rifle and drove the center of the bull's-eye. Then the Quartermaster fired. The target exhibited no result this time. There was a laugh. "It's a dead miss," said Major Lundie. Pathfinder waited an impressive moment or two; then said, in that calm, indifferent, know-it-all way of his, "No, Major, he has covered Jasper's bullet, as will be seen if any one will take the trouble to examine the target."

Wasn't it remarkable! How *could* he see that little pellet fly through the air and enter that distant bullet-hole? Yet that is what he did; for nothing is impossible to a Cooper person. Did any of those people have any deep-seated doubts about this thing? No; for that would imply sanity, and these were all Cooper people.

The respect for Pathfinder's skill and for his *quickness and accuracy of sight* [the italics are mine] was so profound and general, that the instant he made this declaration the spectators began to distrust their own opinions, and a dozen rushed to the target in order to ascertain the fact. There, sure enough, it was found that the Quartermaster's bullet had gone through the hole made by Jasper's, and that, too, so accurately as to require a minute examination to be certain of the circumstance, which, however, was soon clearly established by discovering one bullet over the other in the stump against which the target was placed.

They made a "minute" examination; but never mind, how could they know that there were two bullets in that hole without digging the latest one out? for neither probe nor eyesight could prove the presence of any more than one bullet. Did they dig? No; as we shall see. It is the Pathfinder's turn now; he steps out before the ladies, takes aim, and fires.

But, alas! here is a disappointment; an incredible, an unimaginable disappointment—for the target's aspect is unchanged; there is nothing there but that same old bullet-hole!

> "If one dared to hint at such a thing," cried Major Duncan, "I should say that the Pathfinder has also missed the target!"

As nobody had missed it yet, the "also" was not necessary; but never mind about that, for the Pathfinder is going to speak.

> "No, no, Major," said he, confidently, "that *would* be a risky declaration. I didn't load the piece, and can't say what was in it; but if it was lead, you will find the bullet driving down those of the Quartermaster and Jasper, else is not my name Pathfinder."
>
> A shout from the target announced the truth of this assertion.

Is the miracle sufficient as it stands? Not for Cooper. The Pathfinder speaks again, as he "now slowly advances toward the stage occupied by the females":

> "That's not all, boys, that's not all; if you find the target touched at all, I'll own to a miss. The Quartermaster cut the wood, but you'll find no wood cut by that last messenger."

The miracle is at last complete. He knew—doubtless *saw*—at the distance of a hundred yards—that his bullet had passed into the hole *without fraying the edges*. There were now three bullets in that one hole—three bullets embedded processionally in the body of the stump back of the target. Everybody knew this—somehow or other—and yet nobody had dug any of them out to make sure. Cooper is not a close observer, but he is interesting. He is certainly always that, no matter what happens. And he is more interesting when he is not noticing what he is about than when he is. This is a considerable merit.

The conversations in the Cooper books have a curious sound in our modern ears. To believe that such talk really ever came out of people's mouths would be to believe that there was a time when time was of no value to a person who thought he had something to say; when it was the custom to spread a two-minute remark out to ten; when a man's mouth was a rolling-mill, and busied itself all day long in turning four-foot pigs of thought into thirty-foot bars of conversational railroad iron by attenuation; when subjects were seldom faithfully stuck to, but the talk wandered all around and arrived nowhere; when conversations consisted mainly of irrelevancies, with here and there a relevancy, a relevancy with an embarrassed look, as not being able to explain how it got there.

Cooper was certainly not a master in the construction of dialogue. Inaccurate observation defeated him here as it defeated him in so many other enterprises of his. He even failed to notice that the man who talks corrupt English six days in the week must and will talk it on the seventh, and can't help himself. In the *Deerslayer* story he lets Deerslayer talk the showiest kind of book-talk sometimes, and at other times the basest of base dialects. For instance, when some one asks him if he has a sweetheart, and if so, where she abides, this is his majestic answer:

> "She's in the forest—hanging from the boughs of the trees, in a soft rain—in the dew on the open grass—the clouds that float about in the blue heavens—the birds that sing in the woods—the sweet springs where I slake my thirst—and in all the other glorious gifts that come from God's Providence!"

And he preceded that, a little before, with this:

> "It consarns me as all things that touches a fri'nd consarns a fri'nd."

And this is another of his remarks:

> "If I was Injin born, now, I might tell of this, or carry in the scalp and boast of the expl'ite afore the whole tribe; or if my inimy had only been a bear"—[and so on].

We cannot imagine such a thing as a veteran Scotch Commander-in-Chief comporting himself in the field like a windy melodramatic actor, but Cooper could. On one occasion Alice and Cora were being chased by the French through a fog in the neighborhood of their father's fort:

> *"Point de quartier aux coquins!"* cried an eager pursuer, who seemed to direct the operations of the enemy.
>
> "Stand firm and be ready, my gallant 6oths!" suddenly exclaimed a voice above them; "wait to see the enemy; fire low, and sweep the glacis."
>
> "Father! father" exclaimed a piercing cry from out the mist. "it is I! Alice! thy own Elsie! spare, O! save your daughters!"
>
> "Hold!" shouted the former speaker, in the awful tones of parental agony, the sound reaching even to the woods, and rolling back in solemn echo. " 'Tis she! God has restored me my children! Throw open the sally-port; to the field, 6oths, to the field! pull not a trigger, lest ye kill my lambs! Drive off these dogs of France with your steel!"

Cooper's word-sense was singularly dull. When a person has a poor ear for music he will flat and sharp right along without knowing it. He keeps near the tune, but it is *not* the tune. When a person has a poor ear for words, the result is a literary flatting and sharping; you perceive what he is intending to say, but you also perceive that he doesn't *say* it. This is Cooper. He was not a word-musician. His ear was satisfied with the *approximate* word. I will furnish some circumstantial evidence in support of this charge. My instances are gathered from half a dozen pages of the tale called *Deerslayer*. He uses "Verbal" for "oral"; "precision" for "facility"; "phenomena" for "marvels"; "necessary" for "predetermined"; "unsophisticated" for "primitive"; "preparation" for "expectancy"; "rebuked" for "subdued"; "dependent on" for "resulting from"; "fact" for "condition"; "fact" for "conjecture"; "precaution" for "caution"; "explain" for "determine"; "mortified" for "disappointed"; "meretricious" for "factitious"; "materially" for "considerably"; "decreasing" for "deepening"; "increasing" for "disappearing"; "embedded" for "inclosed"; "treacherous" for "hostile"; "stood" for "stooped"; "softened" for "replaced"; "rejoined" for "remarked"; "situation" for "condition"; "different" for "differing"; "insensible" for "unsentient"; "brevity" for "celerity"; "distrusted" for "suspicious"; "mental imbecility" for "imbecility";

"eyes" for "sight"; "counteracting" for "opposing"; "funeral obsequies" for "obsequies."

There have been daring people in the world who claimed that
Cooper could write English, but they are all dead now—all dead but
Lounsbury. I don't remember that Lounsbury makes the claim in so
many words, still he makes it, for he says that *Deerslayer* is a "pure
work of art." Pure, in that connection, means faultless—faultless in all
details—and language is a detail. If Mr. Lounsbury had only compared Cooper's English with the English which he writes himself—but
it is plain that he didn't; and so it is likely that he imagines until this
day that Cooper's is as clean and compact as his own. Now I feel sure,
deep down in my heart, that Cooper wrote about the poorest English
that exists in our language, and that the English of *Deerslayer* is the
very worst that even Cooper ever wrote.

I may be mistaken, but it does seem to me that *Deerslayer* is not a
work of art in any sense; it does seem to me that it is destitute of every
detail that goes to the making of a work of art; in truth, it seems to me
that *Deerslayer* is just simply a literary *delirium tremens.*

A work of art? It has no invention; it has no order, system, sequence, or result; it has no lifelikeness, no thrill, no stir, no seeming of
reality; its characters are confusedly drawn, and by their acts and
words they prove that they are not the sort of people the author claims
that they are; its humor is pathetic; its pathos is funny; its conversations are—oh! indescribable; its love-scenes odious; its English a crime
against the language.

Counting these out, what is left is Art. I think we must all admit
that.

1895

INSTRUCTIONS IN ART
(With Illustrations by the Author)

The great trouble about painting a whole gallery of portraits at the
same time is, that the housemaid comes and dusts, and does not put

them back the way they were before, and so when the public flock to the studio and wish to know which is Howells and which is Depew and so on, you have to dissemble, and it is very embarrassing at first. Still, you know they are there, and this knowledge presently gives you more or less confidence, and you say sternly, *"This* is Howells," and watch the visitor's eye. If you see doubt there, you correct yourself and try another. In time you find one that will satisfy, and then you feel relief and joy, but you have suffered much in the meantime; and you know that this joy is only temporary, for the next inquirer will settle on another Howells of a quite different aspect, and one which you suspect is Edward VII or Cromwell, though you keep that to yourself, of course. It is much better to label a portrait when you first paint it, then there is no uncertainty in your mind and you can get bets out of the visitor and win them.

I believe I have had the most trouble with a portrait which I painted in installments—the head on one canvas and the bust on another.

The head on one canvas

The housemaid stood the bust up sideways, and now I don't know which way it goes. Some authorities think it belongs with the breastpin at the top, under the man's chin; others think it belongs the reverse way, on account of the collar, one of these saying, "A person can wear a breastpin on his stomach if he wants to, but he can't wear his collar anywhere he dern pleases." There is a certain amount of sense in that view of it. Still, there is no way to determine the matter for certain; when you join the installments, with the pin under the chin, that seems to be right; then when you reverse it and bring the collar under the chin it seems as right as ever; whichever way you fix it the lines come together snug and convincing, and either way you do it the portrait's face looks equally surprised and rejoiced, and as if it

wouldn't be satisfied to have it any way but just that one; in fact, even
if you take the bust away altogether the face seems surprised and
happy just the same—I have never seen an expression before, which
no vicissitudes could alter. I wish I could remember who it is. It looks
a little like Washington, but I do not think it can be Washington,
because he had as many ears on one side as the other. You can always
tell Washington by that; he was very particular about his ears, and
about having them arranged the same old way all the time.

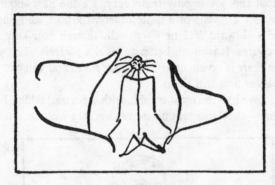

And the bust on another

By and by I shall get out of these confusions, and then it will be
plain sailing; but first-off the confusions were natural and not to be
avoided. My reputation came very suddenly and tumultuously when I
published my own portrait, and it turned my head a little, for indeed
there was never anything like it. In a single day I got orders from
sixty-two people not to paint their portraits, some of them the most
distinguished persons in the country—the President, the Cabinet, au-
thors, governors, admirals, candidates for office on the weak side—
almost everybody that was anybody, and it would really have turned
the head of nearly any beginner to get so much notice and have it
come with such a frenzy of cordiality. But I am growing calm and
settling down to business, now; and pretty soon I shall cease to be
flurried, and then when I do a portrait I shall be quite at myself and
able on the instant to tell it from the others and pick it out when
wanted.

I am living a new and exalted life of late. It steeps me in a sacred
rapture to see a portrait develop and take soul under my hand. First, I

throw off a study—just a mere study, a few apparently random lines—
and to look at it you would hardly ever suspect who it was going to be;
even I cannot tell, myself. Take this picture, for instance:

*First you think it's Dante; next you think it's Emer-
son; then you think it's Wayne Mac Veagh. Yet it isn't
any of them; it's the beginnings of Depew*

First you think it's Dante; next you think it's Emerson; then you
think it's Wayne Mac Veagh. Yet it isn't any of them; it's the beginnings of Depew. Now you wouldn't believe Depew could be devolved
out of that; yet the minute it is finished here you have him to the life,
and you say, yourself, "If that isn't Depew it isn't anybody."

Some would have painted him speaking, but he isn't always speaking, he has to stop and think sometimes.

That is a *genre* picture, as we say in the trade, and differs from the
encaustic and other schools in various ways, mainly technical, which
you wouldn't understand if I should explain them to you. But you will
get the idea as I go along, and little by little you will learn all that is

valuable about Art without knowing how it happened, and without
any sense of strain or effort, and then you will know what school a
picture belongs to, just at a glance, and whether it is an animal picture
or a landscape. It is then that the joy of life will begin for you.

When you come to examine my portraits of Mr. Joe Jefferson and
the rest, your eye will have become measurably educated by that time,
and you will recognize at once that no two of them are alike. I will
close the present chapter with an example of the nude, for your instruction.

This creation is different from any of the other works. The others
are from real life, but this is an example of still-life; so called because it
is a portrayal of a fancy only, a thing which has no actual and active
existence. The purpose of a still-life picture is to concrete to the eye
the spiritual, the intangible, a something which we feel, but cannot see
with the fleshy vision—such as joy, sorrow, resentment, and so on.
This is best achieved by the employment of that treatment which we
call the impressionist, in the trade. The present example is an impressionist picture, done in distemper, with a chiaroscuro motif modified
by monochromatic technique, so as to secure tenderness of feeling and
spirituality of expression. At a first glance it would seem to be a Botti-
celli, but it is not that; it is only a humble imitation of that great
master of longness and slimness and limbfulness.

The work is imagined from Greek story, and represents Proserpine
or Persepolis, or one of those other Bacchantes doing the solemnities
of welcome before the altar of Isis upon the arrival of the annual
shipload of Athenian youths in the island of Minos to be sacrificed in
appeasement of the Dordonian Cyclops.

The figure symbolizes solemn joy. It is severely Greek, therefore
does not call details of drapery or other factitious helps to its aid, but
depends wholly upon grace of action and symmetry of contour for its
effects. It is intended to be viewed from the south or southeast, and I
think that that is best; for while it expresses more and larger joy when
viewed from the east or the north, the features of the face are too
much foreshortened and wormy when viewed from that point. That
thing in the right hand is not a skillet; it is a tambourine.

This creation will be exhibited at the Paris Salon in June, and will
compete for the *Prix de Rome*.

That thing in the right hand is not a skillet; it is a tambou-rine

The portrait reproduces Mr. Joseph Jefferson,
the common friend of the human race

The above is a marine picture, and is intended to educate the eye in the important matters of perspective and foreshortening. The mountainous and bounding waves in the foreground, contrasted with the tranquil ship fading away as in a dream the other side of the fishing-pole, convey to us the idea of space and distance as no words could do. Such is the miracle wrought by that wondrous device, perspective.

The portrait reproduces Mr. Joseph Jefferson, the common friend of the human race. He is fishing, and is not catching anything. This is finely expressed by the moisture in the eye and the anguish of the mouth. The mouth is holding back words. The pole is bamboo, the line is foreshortened. This foreshortening, together with the smoothness of the water away out there where the cork is, gives a powerful impression of distance, and is another way of achieving a perspective effect.

We now come to the next portrait, which is either Mr. Howells or Mr. Laffan. I cannot tell which, because the label is lost. But it will do for both, because the features are Mr. Howells's, while the expression is Mr. Laffan's. This work will bear critical examination.

*Either Mr. Howells or Mr. Laffan. I
cannot tell which because the label
is lost*

The next picture is part of an animal, but I do not know the name of
it. It is not finished. The front end of it went around a corner before I
could get to it.

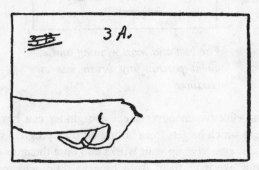

*The front end of it went around a corner be-
fore I could get to it*

We will conclude with the portrait of a lady in the style of Raphael. Originally I started it out for Queen Elizabeth, but was not able to do the lace hopper her head projects out of, therefore I tried to turn it into Pocahontas, but was again baffled, and was compelled to make further modifications, this time achieving success. By spiritualizing it and turning it into the noble mother of our race and throwing into the countenance the sacred joy which her first tailor-made outfit infuses into her spirit, I was enabled to add to my gallery the best and most winning and eloquent portrait my brush has ever produced.

The best and most winning and elo-quent portrait my brush has ever produced

The most effective encouragement a beginner can have is the encouragement which he gets from noting his own progress with an alert and persistent eye. Save up your works and date them; as the years go by, run your eye over them from time to time, and measure your advancing stride. This will thrill you, this will nerve you, this will inspire you as nothing else can.

It seems unbelievable that I have
climbed so high in thirty-one years

It has been my own course, and to it I owe the most that I am to-
day in Art. When I look back and examine my first effort and then
compare it with my latest, it seems unbelievable that I have climbed so
high in thirty-one years. Yet so it is. Practice—that is the secret. From
three to seven hours a day. It is all that is required. The results are
sure; whereas indolence achieves nothing great.

1903

Travel Books

The opening scene last night—the broadsword combat between two young amateurs and a famous Parthian gladiator who was sent here a prisoner—was very fine. The elder of the two young gentlemen handled his weapon with a grace that marked the possession of extraordinary talent. His feint of thrusting, followed instantly by a happily delivered blow which unhelmeted the Parthian, was received with hearty applause. He was not thoroughly up in the backhanded stroke, but it was very gratifying to his numerous friends to know that in time, practice would have overcome this defect. However, he was killed. His sisters, who were present, expressed considerable regret. His mother left the Coliseum. The other youth maintained the contest with such spirit as to call forth enthusiastic bursts of applause. When at last he fell a corpse, his aged mother ran screaming, with hair disheveled and tears streaming from her eyes, and swooned away just as her hands were clutching at the railings of the arena. She was promptly removed by the police. Under the circumstances the woman's conduct was pardonable, perhaps, but we suggest that such exhibitions interfere with the decorum which should be preserved during the performances, and are highly improper in the presence of the Emperor. The Parthian prisoner fought bravely and well; and well he might, for he was fighting for both life and liberty. His wife and children were there to nerve his arm with their love, and to remind him of the old home he should see again if he conquered. When his second assailant fell, the woman clasped her children to her breast and wept for joy. But it was only a transient happiness. The captive staggered toward her and she saw that the liberty he had earned was earned too late. He was wounded unto death. Thus the first act closed in a manner which was entirely satisfactory. The manager was called before the curtain and returned his thanks for the honor done him, in a speech which was replete with wit and humor, and closed by hoping that his humble efforts to afford cheerful and instructive entertainment would continue to meet with the approbation of the Roman public.

The star now appeared, and was received with vociferous applause and the simultaneous waving of sixty thousand handkerchiefs. Marcus Marcellus Valerian (stage-name—his real name is Smith) is a splendid specimen of physical development, and an artist of rare merit. His management of the battle-ax is wonderful. His gaiety and his playfulness are irresistible, in his comic parts, and yet they are inferior to his sublime conceptions in the grave realm of tragedy. When his ax was

THE INNOCENTS ABROAD

AN ANCIENT PLAYBILL

For me was reserved the high honor of discovering among the rubbish of the ruined Coliseum the only playbill of that establishment now extant. There was a suggestive smell of mint-drops about it still, a corner of it had evidently been chewed, and on the margin, in choice Latin, these words were written in a delicate female hand:

> Meet me on the Tarpeian Rock to-morrow evening, dear, at sharp seven. Mother will be absent on a visit to her friends in the Sabine Hills.
>
> CLAUDIA

Ah, where is that lucky youth to-day, and where the little hand that wrote those dainty lines? Dust and ashes these seventeen hundred years!

Thus reads the bill:

ROMAN COLISEUM
UNPARALLELED ATTRACTION!
NEW PROPERTIES! NEW LIONS! NEW GLADIATORS!
Engagement of the renowned
MARCUS MARCELLUS VALERIAN!
FOR SIX NIGHTS ONLY!

The management beg leave to offer to the public an entertainment surpassing in magnificence anything that has heretofore been attempted on any stage. No expense has been spared to make the opening season one which shall be wor-

thy the generous patronage which the management feel sure
will crown their efforts. The management beg leave to state
that they have succeeded in securing the services of a

GALAXY OF TALENT!

such as has not been beheld in Rome before.

The performance will commence this evening with a

GRAND BROADSWORD COMBAT!

between two young and promising amateurs and a celebrated
Parthian gladiator who has just arrived a prisoner from the
Camp of Verus.

This will be followed by a grand moral

BATTLE-AX ENGAGEMENT!

between the renowned Valerian (with one hand tied behind
him) and two gigantic savages from Britain.

After which the renowned Valerian (if he survive) will
fight with the broadsword,

LEFT HANDED!

against six Sophomores and a Freshman from the Gladia-
torial College!

A long series of brilliant engagements will follow, in
which the finest talent of the Empire will take part.

After which the celebrated Infant Prodigy known as

"THE YOUNG ACHILLES,"

will engage four tiger whelps in combat, armed with no other
weapon than his little spear!

The whole to conclude with a chaste and elegant

GENERAL SLAUGHTER!

In which thirteen African Lions and twenty-two Barbarian
Prisoners will war with each other until all are exterminated.

BOX OFFICE NOW OPEN

Dress Circle One Dollar; Children and servants half
price.

An efficient police force will be on hand to preserve order
and keep the wild beasts from leaping the railings and dis-
commoding the audience.

Doors open at 7; performance begins at 8.

POSITIVELY NO FREE LIST

Diodorus Job Press

It was as singular as it was gratifying that I was also so fortunate as
to find among the rubbish of the arena a stained and mutilated copy of
the *Roman Daily Battle-Ax*, containing a critique upon this very performance. It comes to hand too late by many centuries to rank as
news, and therefore I translate and publish it simply to show how very
little the general style and phraseology of dramatic criticism has altered in the ages that have dragged their slow length along since the
carriers laid this one damp and fresh before their Roman patrons:

THE OPENING SEASON.—COLISEUM.—Notwithstanding the i
clemency of the weather, quite a respectable number of the rank a
fashion of the city assembled last night to witness the debut up
metropolitan boards of the young tragedian who has of late been v
ning such golden opinions in the amphitheaters of the provinces. S
sixty thousand persons were present, and but for the fact that
streets were almost impassable, it is fair to presume that the h
would have been full. His august Majesty, the Emperor Aureliu
cupied the imperial box, and was the cynosure of all eyes. Many
trious nobles and generals of the Empire graced the occasio
their presence, and not the least among them was the young pa
lieutenant whose laurels, won in the ranks of the "Thunder
gion," are still so green upon his brow. The cheer which gre
entrance was heard beyond the Tiber!

The late repairs and decorations add both to the comeliness
comfort of the Coliseum. The new cushions are a great imp
upon the hard marble seats we have been so long accustome
present management deserve well of the public. They have
the Coliseum the gilding, the rich upholstery, and the unifor
icence which old Coliseum frequenters tell us Rome was
fifty years ago.

describing fiery circles about the heads of the bewildered barbarians, in exact time with his springing body and his prancing legs, the audience gave way to uncontrollable bursts of laughter; but when the back of his weapon broke the skull of one and almost in the same instant its edge clove the other's body in twain, the howl of enthusiastic applause that shook the building was the acknowledgment of a critical assemblage that he was a master of the noblest department of his profession. If he has a fault (and we are sorry to even intimate that he has), it is that of glancing at the audience, in the midst of the most exciting moments of the performance, as if seeking admiration. The pausing in a fight to bow when bouquets are thrown to him is also in bad taste. In the great left-handed combat he appeared to be looking at the audience half the time, instead of carving his adversaries; and when he had slain all the sophomores and was dallying with the freshman, he stooped and snatched a bouquet as it fell, and offered it to his adversary at a time when a blow was descending which promised favorably to be his death-warrant. Such levity is proper enough in the provinces, we make no doubt, but it ill suits the dignity of the metropolis. We trust our young friend will take these remarks in good part, for we mean them solely for his benefit. All who know us are aware that although we are at times justly severe upon tigers and martyrs, we never intentionally offend gladiators.

The Infant Prodigy performed wonders. He overcame his four tiger whelps with ease, and with no other hurt than the loss of a portion of his scalp. The General Slaughter was rendered with a faithfulness to details which reflects the highest credit upon the late participants in it.

Upon the whole, last night's performances shed honor not only upon the management but upon the city that encourages and sustains such wholesome and instructive entertainments. We would simply suggest that the practice of vulgar young boys in the gallery of shying peanuts and paper pellets at the tigers, and saying "Hi-yi!" and manifesting approbation or dissatisfaction by such observations as "Bully for the lion!" "Go it, Gladdy!" "Boots!" "Speech!" "Take a walk round the block!" and so on, are extremely reprehensible, when the Emperor is present, and ought to be stopped by the police. Several times last night when the supernumeraries entered the arena to drag out the bodies, the young ruffians in the gallery shouted, "Supe! supe!" and also, "Oh, what a coat!" and "Why don't you pad them shanks?"

and made use of various other remarks expressive of derision. These things are very annoying to the audience.

A matinée for the little folks is promised for this afternoon, on which occasion several martyrs will be eaten by the tigers. The regular performance will continue every night till further notice. Material change of program every evening. Benefit of Valerian, Tuesday, 29, if he lives.

I have been a dramatic critic myself, in my time, and I was often surprised to notice how much more I knew about Hamlet than Forrest did; and it gratifies me to observe, now, how much better my brethren of ancient times knew how a broadsword battle ought to be fought than the gladiators.

1869

THE INNOCENTS ABROAD

GUYING THE GUIDES

I used to worship the mighty genius of Michael Angelo—that man who was great in poetry, painting, sculpture, architecture—great in everything he undertook. But I do not want Michael Angelo for breakfast—for luncheon—for dinner—for tea—for supper—for between meals. I like a change, occasionally. In Genoa, he designed everything; in Milan he or his pupils designed everything; he designed the Lake of Como; in Padua, Verona, Venice, Bologna, who did we ever hear of, from guides, but Michael Angelo? In Florence, he painted everything, designed everything, nearly, and what he did not design he used to sit on a favorite stone and look at, and they showed us the stone. In Pisa he designed everything but the old shot-tower, and they would have attributed that to him if it had not been so awfully out of the perpendicular. He designed the piers of Leghorn and the custom-house regulations of Civita Vecchia. But, here—here it is frightful. He designed St. Peter's; he designed the Pope; he designed the Pantheon, the uniform of the Pope's soldiers, the Tiber, the Vatican, the Coliseum, the Capitol, the Tarpeian Rock, the Barberini Palace, St. John Lateran, the Campagna, the Appian Way, the Seven Hills, the Baths of Caracalla, the Claudian Aqueduct, the Cloaca Maxima—the eternal bore designed the Eternal City, and unless all men and books do lie, he painted everything in it! Dan said the other day to the guide, "Enough, enough, enough! Say no more! Lump the whole thing! Say that the Creator made Italy from designs by Michael Angelo!"

I never felt so fervently thankful, so soothed, so tranquil, so filled with a blessed peace, as I did yesterday when I learned that Michael Angelo was dead.

But we have taken it out of this guide. He has marched us through miles of pictures and sculpture in the vast corridors of the Vatican; and through miles of pictures and sculpture in twenty other palaces; he has shown us the great picture in the Sistine Chapel, and frescoes enough to fresco the heavens—pretty much all done by Michael Angelo. So with him we have played that game which has vanquished so many guides for us—imbecility and idiotic questions. These creatures never suspect—they have no idea of a sarcasm.

He shows us a figure and says: "Statoo brunzo." (Bronze statue.)

We look at it indifferently and the doctor asks: "By Michael Angelo?"

"No—not know who."

Then he shows us the ancient Roman Forum. The doctor asks: "Michael Angelo?"

A stare from the guide. "No—a thousan' year before he is born."

Then an Egyptian obelisk. Again: "Michael Angelo?"

"Oh, *mon dieu*, genteelmen! Zis is *two* thousan' year before he is born!"

He grows so tired of that unceasing question sometimes, that he dreads to show us anything at all. The wretch has tried all the ways he can think of to make us comprehend that Michael Angelo is only responsible for the creation of a *part* of the world, but somehow he has not succeeded yet. Relief for overtasked eyes and brain from study and sight-seeing is necessary, or we shall become idiotic sure enough. Therefore this guide must continue to suffer. If he does not enjoy it, so much the worse for him. We do.

In this place I may as well jot down a chapter concerning those

necessary nuisances, European guides. Many a man has wished in his
heart he could do without his guide; but knowing he could not, has
wished he could get some amusement out of him as a remuneration for
the affliction of his society. We accomplished this latter matter, and if
our experience can be made useful to others they are welcome to it.

Guides know about enough English to tangle everything up so that
a man can make neither head nor tail of it. They know their story by
heart—the history of every statue, painting, cathedral, or other wonder they show you. They know it and tell it as a parrot would—and if
you interrupt, and throw them off the track, they have to go back and
begin over again. All their lives long, they are employed in showing
strange things to foreigners and listening to their bursts of admiration.
It is human nature to take delight in exciting admiration. It is what
prompts children to say "smart" things, and do absurd ones, and in
other ways "show off" when company is present. It is what makes
gossips turn out in rain and storm to go and be the first to tell a
startling bit of news. Think, then, what a passion it becomes with a
guide, whose privilege it is, every day, to show to strangers wonders
that throw them into perfect ecstasies of admiration! He gets so that
he could not by any possibility live in a soberer atmosphere. After we
discovered this, we *never* went into ecstasies any more—we never admired anything—we never showed any but impassible faces and stupid
indifference in the presence of the sublimest wonders a guide had to
display. We had found their weak point. We have made good use of it
ever since. We have made some of those people savage, at times, but
we have never lost our own serenity.

The doctor asks the questions, generally, because he can keep his
countenance, and look more like an inspired idiot, and throw more
imbecility into the tone of his voice than any man that lives. It comes
natural to him.

The guides in Genoa are delighted to secure an American party,
because Americans so much wonder, and deal so much in sentiment
and emotion before any relic of Columbus. Our guide there fidgeted
about as if he had swallowed a spring mattress. He was full of animation—full of impatience. He said:

"Come wis me, genteelmen!—come! I show you ze letter-writing by
Christopher Colombo!—write it himself!—write it wis his own hand!
—come!"

He took us to the municipal palace. After much impressive fum-bling of keys and opening of locks, the stained and aged document was spread before us. The guide's eyes sparkled. He danced about us and tapped the parchment with his finger:

"What I tell you, genteelmen! Is it not so? See! handwriting Christopher Colombo!—write it himself!"

We looked indifferent—unconcerned. The doctor examined the document very deliberately, during a painful pause. Then he said, without any show of interest:

"Ah—Ferguson—what—what did you say was the name of the party who wrote this?"

"Christopher Colombo! ze great Christopher Colombo!"

Another deliberate examination.

"Ah—did he write it himself, or—or how?"

"He write it himself!—Christopher Colombo! he's own handwriting, write by himself!"

Then the doctor laid the document down and said:

"Why, I have seen boys in America only fourteen years old that could write better than that."

"But zis is ze great Christo—"

"I don't care who it is! It's the worst writing I ever saw. Now you mustn't think you can impose on us because we are strangers. We are not fools, by a good deal. If you have got any specimens of penmanship of real merit, trot them out!—and if you haven't, drive on!"

We drove on. The guide was considerably shaken up, but he made one more venture. He had something which he thought would overcome us. He said:

"Ah, genteelmen, you come wis me! I show you beautiful, oh, magnificent bust Christopher Colombo!—splendid, grand, magnificent!"

He brought us before the beautiful bust—for it *was* beautiful—and sprang back and struck an attitude:

"Ah, look, genteelmen!—beautiful, grand,—bust Christopher Colombo!—beautiful bust, beautiful pedestal!"

The doctor put up his eyeglass—procured for such occasions:

"Ah—what did you say this gentleman's name was?"

"Christopher Colombo!—ze great Christopher Colombo!"

"Christopher Colombo—the great Christopher Colombo. Well, what did *he* do?"

"Discover America!—discover America, oh, ze devil!"

"Discover America. No—that statement will hardly wash. We are

just from America ourselves. We heard nothing about it. Christopher
Colombo—pleasant name—is—is he dead?"

"Oh, *corpo di Baccho!*—three hundred year!"

"What did he die of?"

"I do not know!—I cannot tell."

"Smallpox, think?"

"I do not know, genteelmen!—I do not know *what* he die of!"

"Measles, likely?"

"Maybe—maybe—I do *not* know—I think he die of somethings."

"Parents living?"

"Im-posseeble!"

"Ah—which is the bust and which is the pedestal?"

"Santa Maria!—*zis* ze bust!—*zis* ze pedestal!"

"Ah, I see, I see—happy combination—very happy combination,
indeed. Is—is this the first time this gentleman was ever on a bust?"

That joke was lost on the foreigner—guides cannot master the subtleties of the American joke.

We have made it interesting for this Roman guide. Yesterday we
spent three or four hours in the Vatican again, that wonderful world of
curiosities. We came very near expressing interest, sometimes—even
admiration—it was very hard to keep from it. We succeeded though.
Nobody else ever did, in the Vatican museums. The guide was bewildered—nonplussed. He walked his legs off, nearly, hunting up extraordinary things, and exhausted all his ingenuity on us, but it was a
failure; we never showed any interest in anything. He had reserved
what he considered to be his greatest wonder till the last—a royal
Egyptian mummy, the best-preserved in the world, perhaps. He took
us there. He felt so sure, this time, that some of his old enthusiasm
came back to him:

"See, genteelmen!—Mummy! Mummy!"

The eyeglass came up as calmly, as deliberately as ever.

"Ah,—Ferguson—what did I understand you to say the gentleman's name was?"

"Name?—he got no name!—Mummy!—'Gyptian mummy!"

"Yes, yes. Born here?"

"No! 'Gyptian mummy!"

"Ah, just so. Frenchman, I presume?"

"No!—*not* Frenchman, not Roman!—born in Egypta!"

"Born in Egypta. Never heard of Egypta before. Foreign locality, likely. Mummy—mummy. How calm he is—how self-possessed. Is, ah—is he dead?"

"Oh, *sacré bleu*, been dead three thousan' year!"

The doctor turned on him savagely:

"Here, now, what do you mean by such conduct as this! Playing us for Chinamen because we are strangers and trying to learn! Trying to impose your vile second-hand carcasses on *us!*—thunder and lightning, I've a notion to—to—if you've got a nice *fresh* corpse, fetch him out!—or, by George, we'll brain you!"

We make it exceedingly interesting for this Frenchman. However, he has paid us back, partly, without knowing it. He came to the hotel this morning to ask if we were up, and he endeavored as well as he could to describe us, so that the landlord would know which persons he meant. He finished with the casual remark that we were lunatics. The observation was so innocent and so honest that it amounted to a very good thing for a guide to say.

There is one remark (already mentioned) which never yet has failed to disgust these guides. We use it always, when we can think of nothing else to say. After they have exhausted their enthusiasm pointing out to us and praising the beauties of some ancient bronze image or broken-legged statue, we look at it stupidly and in silence for five, ten, fifteen minutes—as long as we can hold out, in fact—and then ask:

"Is—is he dead?"

That conquers the serenest of them. It is not what they are looking for—especially a new guide. Our Roman Ferguson is the most patient, unsuspecting, long-suffering subject we have had yet. We shall be sorry to part with him. We have enjoyed his society very much. We trust he has enjoyed ours, but we are harassed with doubts.

1869

THE INNOCENTS ABROAD

THE TURKISH BATH

When I think how I have been swindled by books of Oriental travel, I want a tourist for breakfast. For years and years I have dreamed of the wonders of the Turkish bath; for years and years I have promised myself that I would yet enjoy one. Many and many a time, in fancy, I have lain in the marble bath, and breathed the slumbrous fragrance of Eastern spices that filled the air; then passed through a weird and complicated system of pulling and hauling, and drenching and scrubbing, by a gang of naked savages who loomed vast and vaguely through the steaming mists, like demons; then rested for a while on a divan fit for a king; then passed through another complex ordeal, and one more fearful than the first; and, finally, swathed in soft fabrics, been conveyed to a princely saloon and laid on a bed of eider down, where eunuchs, gorgeous of costume, fanned me while I drowsed and dreamed, or contentedly gazed at the rich hangings of the apartment, the soft carpets, the sumptuous furniture, the pictures, and drank delicious coffee, smoked the soothing narghili, and dropped, at the last, into tranquil repose, lulled by sensuous odors from unseen censers, by the gentle influence of the narghili's Persian tobacco, and by the music of fountains that counterfeited the pattering of summer rain.

That was the picture, just as I got it from incendiary books of travel. It was a poor, miserable imposture. The reality is no more like it than the Five Points are like the Garden of Eden. They received me in a great court, paved with marble slabs; around it were broad galleries, one above another, carpeted with seedy matting, railed with unpainted balustrades, and furnished with huge rickety chairs, cushioned with rusty old mattresses, indented with impressions left by the forms of nine successive generations of men who had reposed upon them. The place was vast, naked, dreary; its court a barn, its galleries stalls for human horses. The cadaverous, half nude varlets that served in the establishment had nothing of poetry in their appearance, nothing of romance, nothing of Oriental splendor. They shed no entrancing odors

—just the contrary. Their hungry eyes and their lank forms continually suggested one glaring, unsentimental fact—they wanted what they term in California "a square meal."

I went into one of the racks and undressed. An unclean starveling wrapped a gaudy table-cloth about his loins, and hung a white rag over my shoulders. If I had had a tub then, it would have come natural to me to take in washing. I was then conducted down stairs into the wet, slippery court, and the first things that attracted my attention were my heels. My fall excited no comment. They expected it, no doubt. It belonged in the list of softening, sensuous influences peculiar to this home of Eastern luxury. It was softening enough, certainly, but its application was not happy. They now gave me a pair of wooden clogs—benches in miniature, with leather straps over them to confine my feet (which they would have done, only I do not wear No. 13s). These things dangled uncomfortably by the straps when I lifted up my feet, and came down in awkward and unexpected places when I put them on the floor again, and sometimes turned sideways and wrenched my ankles out of joint. However, it was all Oriental luxury, and I did what I could to enjoy it.

They put me in another part of the barn and laid me on a stuffy sort of pallet, which was not made of cloth of gold, or Persian shawls, but was merely the unpretending sort of thing I have seen in the negro quarters of Arkansas. There was nothing whatever in this dim marble prison but five more of these biers. It was a very solemn place. I expected that the spiced odors of Araby were going to steal over my senses now, but they did not. A copper-colored skeleton, with a rag around him, brought me a glass decanter of water, with a lighted tobacco pipe in the top of it, and a pliant stem a yard long, with a brass mouth-piece to it.

It was the famous "narghili" of the East—the thing the Grand Turk smokes in the pictures. This began to look like luxury. I took one blast at it, and it was sufficient; the smoke went in a great volume down into my stomach, my lungs, even into the uttermost parts of my frame. I exploded one mighty cough, and it was as if Vesuvius had let go. For the next five minutes I smoked at every pore, like a frame house that is on fire on the inside. Not any more narghili for me. The smoke had a vile taste, and the taste of a thousand infidel tongues that remained on that brass mouthpiece was viler still. I was getting discouraged. Whenever, hereafter, I see the cross-legged Grand Turk smoking his narghili, in pretended bliss, on the outside of a paper of Connecticut tobacco, I shall know him for the shameless humbug he is.

This prison was filled with hot air. When I had got warmed up sufficiently to prepare me for a still warmer temperature, they took me where it was—into a marble room, wet, slippery and steamy, and laid me out on a raised platform in the centre. It was very warm. Presently my man sat me down by a tank of hot water, drenched me well, gloved his hand with a coarse mitten, and began to polish me all over with it. I began to smell disagreeably. The more he polished the worse I smelt. It was alarming. I said to him:

"I perceive that I am pretty far gone. It is plain that I ought to be buried without any unnecessary delay. Perhaps you had better go after my friends at once, because the weather is warm, and I can not 'keep' long."

He went on scrubbing, and paid no attention. I soon saw that he was reducing my size. He bore hard on his mitten, and from under it rolled little cylinders, like maccaroni. It could not be dirt, for it was too white. He pared me down in this way for a long time. Finally I said:

"It is a tedious process. It will take hours to trim me to the size you want me; I will wait; go and borrow a jack-plane."

He paid no attention at all.

After a while he brought a basin, some soap, and something that seemed to be the tail of a horse. He made up a prodigious quantity of soap-suds, deluged me with them from head to foot, without warning me to shut my eyes, and then swabbed me viciously with the horse-tail. Then he left me there, a snowy statue of lather, and went away. When I got tired of waiting I went and hunted him up. He was propped against the wall, in another room, asleep. I woke him. He was not disconcerted. He took me back and flooded me with hot water, then turbaned my head, swathed me with dry table-cloths, and conducted me to a latticed chicken-coop in one of the galleries, and pointed to one of those Arkansas beds. I mounted it, and vaguely expected the odors of Araby again. They did not come.

The blank, unornamented coop had nothing about it of that oriental voluptuousness one reads of so much. It was more suggestive of the county hospital than any thing else. The skinny servitor brought a narghili, and I got him to take it out again without wasting any time about it. Then he brought the world-renowned Turkish coffee that poets have sung so rapturously for many generations, and I seized upon it as the last hope that was left of my old dreams of Eastern luxury. It was another fraud. Of all the unchristian beverages that ever passed my lips, Turkish coffee is the worst. The cup is small, it is smeared with grounds; the coffee is black, thick, unsavory of smell, and execrable in taste. The bottom of the cup has a muddy sediment in it half an inch deep. This goes down your throat, and portions of it lodge by the way, and produce a tickling aggravation that keeps you barking and coughing for an hour.

Here endeth my experience of the celebrated Turkish bath, and here also endeth my dream of the bliss the mortal revels in who passes through it. It is a malignant swindle. The man who enjoys it is qualified to enjoy any thing that is repulsive to sight or sense, and he that can invest it with a charm of poetry is able to do the same with any thing else in the world that is tedious, and wretched, and dismal, and nasty.

1869

THE INNOCENTS ABROAD

THE BENTON HOUSE

Alexandria was too much like a European city to be novel, and we soon tired of it. We took the cars and came up here to ancient Cairo, which *is* an Oriental city and of the completest pattern. There is little about it to disabuse one's mind of the error if he should take it into his head that he was in the heart of Arabia. Stately camels and dromedaries, swarthy Egyptians, and likewise Turks and black Ethiopians, turbaned, sashed, and blazing in a rich variety of Oriental costumes of all shades of flashy colors, are what one sees on every hand crowding the narrow streets and the honeycombed bazars. We are stopping at Shepherd's Hotel, which is the worst on earth except the one I stopped at once in a small town in the United States. It is pleasant to read this sketch in my note-book, now, and know that I can stand Shepherd's

Hotel, sure, because I have been in one just like it in America and survived:

I stopped at the Benton House. It used to be a good hotel, but that proves nothing—I used to be a good boy, for that matter. Both of us have lost character of late years. The Benton is not a good hotel.

The Benton lacks a very great deal of being a good hotel. Perdition is full of better hotels than the Benton.

It was late at night when I got there, and I told the clerk I would like plenty of lights, because I wanted to read an hour or two. When I reached No. 15 with the porter (we came along a dim hall that was clad in ancient carpeting, faded, worn out in many places, and patched with old scraps of oilcloth—a hall that sank under one's feet, and creaked dismally to every footstep) he struck a light—two inches of sallow, sorrowful, consumptive tallow candle, that burned blue, and sputtered, and got discouraged and went out. The porter lit it again, and I asked if that was all the light the clerk sent. He said, "Oh no, I've got another one here," and he produced another couple of inches of tallow candle. I said, "Light them both—I'll have to have one to see the other by." He did it, but the result was drearier than darkness itself. He was a cheery, accommodating rascal. He said he would go "somewheres" and steal a lamp. I abetted and encouraged him in his criminal design. I heard the landlord get after him in the hall ten minutes afterward.

"Where are you going with that lamp?"

"Fifteen wants it, sir."

"Fifteen! why he's got a double lot of candles—does the man want to illuminate the house?—does he want to get up a torch-light procession?—what *is* he up to, anyhow?"

"He don't like them candles—says he wants a lamp."

"Why, what in the nation does—why I never heard of such a thing? What on earth can he want with that lamp?"

"Well, he only wants to read—that's what he says."

"Wants to read, does he?—ain't satisfied with a thousand candles, but has to have a lamp!—I do wonder what the devil that fellow wants that lamp for? Take him another candle, and then if—"

"But he wants the lamp—says he'll burn the d—d old house down if he don't get a lamp!" [A remark which I never made.]

"I'd like to see him at it once. Well, you take it along—but I swear it

beats *my* time, though—see if you can't find out what in the very
nation he *wants* with that lamp."

And he went off growling to himself and still wondering and wondering over the unaccountable conduct of No. 15. The lamp was a
good one, but it revealed some disagreeable things—a bed in the suburbs of a desert of room—a bed that had hills and valleys in it, and
you'd have to accommodate your body to the impression left in it by
the man that slept there last, before you could lie comfortably; a carpet that had seen better days; a melancholy washstand in a remote
corner, and a dejected pitcher on it sorrowing over a broken nose; a
looking-glass split across the center, which chopped your head off at
the chin and made you look like some dreadful unfinished monster or
other; the paper peeling in shreds from the walls.

I sighed and said: "This is charming; and now don't you think you
could get me something to read?"

The porter said, "Oh, certainly; the old man's got dead loads of
books"; and he was gone before I could tell him what sort of literature
I would rather have. And yet his countenance expressed the utmost
confidence in his ability to execute the commission with credit to himself. The old man made a descent on him.

"What are you going to do with that pile of books?"

"Fifteen wants 'em, sir."

"Fifteen, is it? He'll want a warming-pan, next—he'll want a nurse!
Take him everything there is in the house—take him the barkeeper—
take him the baggage-wagon—take him the chambermaid! Confound
me, I never saw anything like it. What did he say he wants with those
books?"

"Wants to read 'em, like enough; it ain't likely he wants to eat 'em, I
don't reckon."

"Wants to read 'em—wants to read 'em this time of night, the infernal lunatic! Well he can't have them."

"But he says he's mor'ly bound to have 'em: he says he'll just go
a-rairin' and a-chargin' through this house and raise more—well,
there's no tellin' what he won't do if he don't get 'em; because he's
drunk and crazy and desperate, and nothing'll soothe him down but
them cussed books." [I had not made any threats and was not in the
condition ascribed to me by the porter.]

"Well, go on; but I will be around when he goes to rairing and charging, and the first rair he makes I'll make him rair out of the window." And then the old gentleman went off growling as before.

The genius of that porter was something wonderful. He put an armful of books on the bed and said "Good night" as confidently as if he knew perfectly well that those books were exactly my style of reading-matter. And well he might. His selection covered the whole range of legitimate literature. It comprised *The Great Consummation,* by Rev. Dr. Cummings—theology; *Revised Statutes of the State of Missouri*—law; *The Complete Horse-Doctor*—medicine; *The Toilers of the Sea,* by Victor Hugo—romance; the works of William Shakespeare—poetry. I shall never cease to admire the tact and the intelligence of that gifted porter.

1869

THE INNOCENTS ABROAD

THE PYRAMID OF CHEOPS

We scrambled up the steep bank at the shabby town of Ghizeh, mounted the donkeys again, and scampered away. For four or five miles the route lay along a high embankment which they say is to be the bed of a railway the Sultan means to build for no other reason than that when the Empress of the French comes to visit him she can go to the Pyramids in comfort. This is true Oriental hospitality. I am very glad it is our privilege to have donkeys instead of cars.

At the distance of a few miles the Pyramids rising above the palms, looked very clean-cut, very grand and imposing, and very soft and filmy, as well. They swam in a rich haze that took from them all suggestions of unfeeling stone, and made them seem only the airy nothings of a dream—structures which might blossom into tiers of vague arches, or ornate colonnades, may be, and change and change again, into all graceful forms of architecture, while we looked, and then melt deliciously away and blend with the tremulous atmosphere.

At the end of the levee we left the mules and went in a sailboat across an arm of the Nile or an overflow, and landed where the sands of the Great Sahara left their embankment, as straight as a wall, along the verge of the alluvial plain of the river. A laborious walk in the flaming sun brought us to the foot of the great Pyramid of Cheops. It was a fairy vision no longer. It was a corrugated, unsightly mountain of stone. Each of its monstrous sides was a wide stairway which rose upward, step above step, narrowing as it went, till it tapered to a point far aloft in the air. Insect men and women—pilgrims from the *Quaker City*—were creeping about its dizzy perches, and one little black swarm were waving postage stamps from the airy summit—handkerchiefs will be understood.

Of course we were besieged by a rabble of muscular Egyptians and Arabs who wanted the contract of dragging us to the top—all tourists are. Of course you could not hear your own voice for the din that was around you. Of course the Sheiks said *they* were the only responsible parties; that all contracts must be made with them, all moneys paid over to them, and none exacted from us by any but themselves alone. Of course they contracted that the varlets who dragged us up should not mention bucksheesh once. For such is the usual routine. Of course we contracted with them, paid them, were delivered into the hands of the draggers, dragged up the Pyramids, and harried and be-deviled for bucksheesh from the foundation clear to the summit. We paid it, too, for we were purposely spread very far apart over the vast side of the Pyramid. There was no help near if we called, and the Herculeses who dragged us had a way of asking sweetly and flatteringly for bucksheesh, which was seductive, and of looking fierce and threatening to throw us down the precipice, which was persuasive and convincing.

Each step being full as high as a dinner-table; there being very, very many of the steps; an Arab having hold of each of our arms and springing upward from step to step and snatching us with them, forcing us to lift our feet as high as our breasts every time, and do it rapidly and keep it up till we were ready to faint, who shall say it is not lively, exhilarating, lacerating, muscle-straining, bone-wrenching and perfectly excruciating and exhausting pastime, climbing the Pyramids? I beseeched the varlets not to twist *all* my joints asunder; I iterated, reiterated, even *swore* to them that I did not wish to beat any body to the top; did all I could to convince them that if I got there the last of all I would feel blessed above men and grateful to them forever; I begged them, prayed them, pleaded with them to let me stop and rest a moment—only one little moment: and they only answered with some more frightful springs, and an unenlisted volunteer behind opened a bombardment of determined boosts with his head which threatened to batter my whole political economy to wreck and ruin.

Twice, for one minute, they let me rest while they extorted bucksheesh, and then continued their maniac flight up the Pyramid. They wished to beat the other parties. It was nothing to them that I, a stranger, must be sacrificed upon the altar of their unholy ambition. But in the midst of sorrow, joy blooms. Even in this dark hour I had a sweet consolation. For I knew that except these Mohammedans repented they would go straight to perdition some day. And *they* never repent—they never forsake their paganism. This thought calmed me, cheered me, and I sank down, limp and exhausted, upon the summit, but happy, *so* happy and serene within.

On the one hand, a mighty sea of yellow sand stretched away toward the ends of the earth, solemn, silent, shorn of vegetation, its solitude uncheered by any forms of creature life; on the other, the Eden of Egypt was spread below us—a broad green floor, cloven by the sinuous river, dotted with villages, its vast distances measured and marked by the diminishing stature of receding clusters of palms. It lay asleep in an enchanted atmosphere. There was no sound, no motion. Above the date-plumes in the middle distance, swelled a domed and pinnacled mass, glimmering through a tinted, exquisite mist; away toward the horizon a dozen shapely pyramids watched over ruined Memphis: and at our feet the bland impassible Sphynx looked out upon the picture from her throne in the sands as placidly and pensively as she had looked upon its like full fifty lagging centuries ago.

We suffered torture no pen can describe from the hungry appeals for bucksheesh that gleamed from Arab eyes and poured incessantly from Arab lips. Why try to call up the traditions of vanished Egyptian grandeur; why try to fancy Egypt following dead Rameses to his tomb in the Pyramid, or the long multitude of Israel departing over the desert yonder? Why try to think at all? The thing was impossible. One must bring his meditations cut and dried, or else cut and dry them afterward.

The traditional Arab proposed, in the traditional way, to run down Cheops, cross the eighth of a mile of sand intervening between it and the tall pyramid of Cephron, ascend to Cephron's summit and return to us on the top of Cheops—all in nine minutes by the watch, and the whole service to be rendered for a single dollar. In the first flush of irritation, I said let the Arab and his exploits go to the mischief. But stay. The upper third of Cephron was coated with dressed marble, smooth as glass. A blessed thought entered my brain. He must infallibly break his neck. Close the contract with dispatch, I said, and let him go. He started. We watched. He went bounding down the vast broadside, spring after spring, like an ibex. He grew small and smaller till he became a bobbing pigmy, away down toward the bottom—then disappeared. We turned and peered over the other side—forty seconds —eighty seconds—a hundred—happiness, he is dead already!—two minutes—and a quarter—"There he goes!" Too true—it was too true. He was very small, now. Gradually, but surely, he overcame the level ground. He began to spring and climb again. Up, up, up—at last he reached the smooth coating—now for it. But he clung to it with toes and fingers, like a fly. He crawled this way and that—away to the right, slanting upward—away to the left, still slanting upward—and stood at last, a black peg on the summit, and waved his pigmy scarf! Then he crept downward to the raw steps again, then picked up his agile heels and flew. We lost him presently. But presently again we saw him under us, mounting with undiminished energy. Shortly he bounded into our midst with a gallant war-whoop. Time, eight minutes, forty-one seconds. He had won. His bones were intact. It was a failure. I reflected. I said to myself, he is tired, and must grow dizzy. I will risk another dollar on him.

He started again. Made the trip again. Slipped on the smooth coating—I almost had him. But an infamous crevice saved him. He was with us once more—perfectly sound. Time, eight minutes, forty-six seconds.

I said to Dan, "Lend me a dollar—I can beat this game, yet."

Worse and worse. He won again. Time, eight minutes, forty-eight seconds. I was out of all patience, now. I was desperate.—Money was no longer of any consequence. I said, "Sirrah, I will give you a hundred dollars to jump off this pyramid head first. If you do not like the terms, name your bet. I scorn to stand on expenses now. I will stay right here and risk money on you as long as Dan has got a cent."

I was in a fair way to win, now, for it was a dazzling opportunity for an Arab. He pondered a moment, and would have done it, I think, but his mother arrived, then, and interfered. Her tears moved me—I never can look upon the tears of woman with indifference—and I said I would give her a hundred to jump off, too.

But it was a failure. The Arabs are too high-priced in Egypt. They put on airs unbecoming to such savages.

We descended, hot and out of humor. The dragoman lit candles, and we all entered a hole near the base of the pyramid, attended by a crazy rabble of Arabs who thrust their services upon us uninvited. They dragged us up a long inclined chute, and dripped candle-grease all over us. This chute was not more than twice as wide and high as a Saratoga trunk, and was walled, roofed and floored with solid blocks of Egyptian granite as wide as a wardrobe, twice as thick and three times as long. We kept on climbing, through the oppressive gloom, till I thought we ought to be nearing the top of the pyramid again, and then came to the "Queen's Chamber," and shortly to the Chamber of the King. These large apartments were tombs. The walls were built of monstrous masses of smoothed granite, neatly joined together. Some of them were nearly as large square as an ordinary parlor. A great stone sarcophagus like a bath-tub stood in the centre of the King's Chamber. Around it were gathered a picturesque group of Arab savages and soiled and tattered pilgrims, who held their candles aloft in the gloom while they chattered, and the winking blurs of light shed a dim glory down upon one of the irrepressible memento-seekers who was pecking at the venerable sarcophagus with his sacrilegious hammer.

We struggled out to the open air and the bright sunshine, and for the space of thirty minutes received ragged Arabs by couples, dozens and platoons, and paid them bucksheesh for services they swore and proved by each other that they had rendered, but which we had not been aware of before—and as each party was paid, they dropped into the rear of the procession and in due time arrived again with a newly-invented delinquent list for liquidation.

We lunched in the shade of the pyramid, and in the midst of this encroaching and unwelcome company, and then Dan and Jack and I started away for a walk. A howling swarm of beggars followed us—surrounded us—almost headed us off. A sheik, in flowing white bournous and gaudy head-gear, was with them. He wanted more bucksheesh. But we had adopted a new code—it was millions for defense, but not a cent for bucksheesh. I asked him if he could persuade the others to depart if we paid him. He said yes—for ten francs. We accepted the contract, and said—

"Now persuade your vassals to fall back."

He swung his long staff round his head and three Arabs bit the dust. He capered among the mob like a very maniac. His blows fell like hail, and wherever one fell a subject went down. We had to hurry to the rescue and tell him it was only necessary to damage them a little, he need not kill them.—In two minutes we were alone with the sheik, and remained so. The persuasive powers of this illiterate savage were re-markable.

1869

ROUGHING IT

WHEN THE BUFFALO CLIMBED A TREE

It did seem strange enough to see a town again after what appeared to us such a long acquaintance with deep, still, almost lifeless and house-less solitude! We tumbled out into the busy street feeling like meteoric people crumbled off the corner of some other world, and wakened up suddenly in this. For an hour we took as much interest in Overland City as if we had never seen a town before. The reason we had an hour to spare was because we had to change our stage (for a less sumptuous affair, called a "mud-wagon") and transfer our freight of mails.

Presently we got under way again. We came to the shallow, yellow, muddy South Platte, with its low banks and its scattering flat sand-bars and pygmy islands—a melancholy stream straggling through the center of the enormous flat plain, and only saved from being impossi-ble to find with the naked eye by its sentinel rank of scattering trees standing on either bank. The Platte was "up," they said—which made me wish I could see it when it was down, if it could look any sicker and sorrier. They said it was a dangerous stream to cross, now, be-cause its quicksands were liable to swallow up horses, coach, and passengers if an attempt was made to ford it. But the mails had to go, and we made the attempt. Once or twice in midstream the wheels sunk into the yielding sands so threateningly that we half believed we had dreaded and avoided the sea all our lives to be shipwrecked in a "mud-wagon" in the middle of a desert at last. But we dragged through and sped away toward the setting sun.

Next morning just before dawn, when about five hundred and fifty miles from St. Joseph, our mud-wagon broke down. We were to be delayed five or six hours, and therefore we took horses, by invitation, and joined a party who were just starting on a buffalo-hunt. It was noble sport galloping over the plain in the dewy freshness of the morning, but our part of the hunt ended in disaster and disgrace, for a wounded buffalo bull chased the passenger Bemis nearly two miles, and then he forsook his horse and took to a lone tree. He was very sullen about the matter for some twenty-four hours, but at last he began to soften little by little, and finally he said:

"Well, it was not funny, and there was no sense in those gawks making themselves so facetious over it. I tell you I was angry in earnest for a while. I should have shot that long gangly lubber they called Hank, if I could have done it without crippling six or seven other people—but of course I couldn't, the old 'Allen's so confounded comprehensive. I wish those loafers had been up in the tree; they wouldn't have wanted to laugh so. If I had had a horse worth a cent—but no, the minute he saw that buffalo bull wheel on him and give a bellow, he raised straight up in the air and stood on his heels. The saddle began to slip, and I took him round the neck and laid close to him, and began to pray. Then he came down and stood up on the other end awhile, and the bull actually stopped pawing sand and bellowing to contemplate the inhuman spectacle. Then the bull made a pass at him and uttered a bellow that sounded perfectly frightful, it was so close to me, and that seemed to literally prostrate my horse's reason, and make a raving distracted maniac of him, and I wish I may die if he didn't stand on his head for a quarter of a minute and shed tears. He was absolutely out of his mind—he was, as sure as truth itself, and he really didn't know what he was doing. Then the bull came charging at us, and my horse dropped down on all fours and took a fresh start—and then for the next ten minutes he would actually throw one handspring after another so fast that the bull began to get unsettled, too, and didn't know where to start in—and so he stood there sneezing, and shoveling dust over his back, and bellowing every now and then, and thinking he had got a fifteen-hundred-dollar circus horse for breakfast, certain. Well, I was first out on his neck—the horse's, not the bull's—and then underneath, and next on his rump, and sometimes head up, and sometimes heels—but I tell you it seemed solemn and awful to be ripping and tearing and carrying on so in the presence of death, as you might say. Pretty soon the bull made a snatch for us and brought away some of my horse's tail (I suppose, but do not know, being pretty busy at the time), but *something* made him hungry for solitude and suggested to him to get up and hunt for it. And then you ought to have seen that spider-legged old skeleton go! and you ought to have seen the bull cut out after him, too—head down, tongue out, tail up, bellowing like everything, and actually mowing down the weeds, and tearing up the earth, and boosting up the sand like a whirlwind! By George, it was a hot race! I and the saddle were back on the rump, and I had the bridle in my teeth and holding on to the pommel with both hands. First we left the dogs behind; then we passed a jackass-rabbit; then we overtook a coyote, and were gaining on an antelope when the rotten girths let go and threw me about thirty yards off to the left, and as the saddle went down over the horse's rump he gave it a lift with his heels that sent it more than four hundred yards up in the air, I wish I may die in a minute if he didn't. I fell at the foot of the only solitary tree there was in nine counties adjacent (as any creature could see with the naked eye), and the next second I had hold of the bark with four sets of nails and my teeth, and the next second after that I was astraddle of the main limb and blaspheming my luck in a way that made my breath smell of brimstone. I *had* the bull, now, if he did not think of *one* thing. But that one thing I dreaded. I dreaded it very seriously. There was a possibility that the bull might not think of it, but there were greater chances that he would. I made up my mind what I would do in case he did. It was a little over forty feet to the ground from where I sat. I cautiously unwound the lariat from the pommel of my saddle—"

"Your *saddle?* Did you take your saddle up in the tree with you?"

"Take it up in the tree with me? Why, how you talk! Of course I didn't. No man could do that. It *fell* in the tree when it came down."

"Oh—exactly."

"Certainly. I unwound the lariat, and fastened one end of it to the limb. It was the very best green rawhide, and capable of sustaining tons. I made a slip-noose in the other end, and then hung it down to see the length. It reached down twenty-two feet—half-way to the ground. I then loaded every barrel of the Allen with a double charge. I felt satisfied. I said to myself, if he never thinks of that one thing that I dread, all right—but if he does, all right anyhow—I am fixed for him. But don't you know that the very thing a man dreads is the thing that always happens? Indeed it is so. I watched the bull, now, with anxiety —anxiety which no one can conceive of who has not been in such a situation and felt that at any moment death might come. Presently a thought came into the bull's eye. I knew it! said I—if my nerve fails now, I am lost. Sure enough, it was just as I had dreaded, he started in to climb the tree—"

"What, the bull?"

"Of course—who else?"

"But a bull can't climb a tree."

"He can't, can't he? Since you know so much about it, did you ever see a bull try?"

"No! I never dreamt of such a thing."

"Well, then, what is the use of your talking that way, then? Because you never saw a thing done, is that any reason why it can't be done?"

"Well, all right—go on. What did you do?"

"The bull started up, and got along well for about ten feet, then slipped and slid back. I breathed easier. He tried it again—got up a little higher—slipped again. But he came at it once more, and this time he was careful. He got gradually higher and higher, and my spirits went down more and more. Up he came—an inch at a time— with his eyes hot, and his tongue hanging out. Higher and higher— hitched his foot over the stump of a limb, and looked up, as much as to say, 'You are my meat, friend.' Up again—higher and higher, and getting more excited the closer he got. He was within ten feet of me! I took a long breath—and then said I, 'It is now or never.' I had the coil of the lariat all ready; I paid it out slowly, till it hung right over his head; all of a sudden I let go of the slack and the slip-noose fell fairly round his neck! Quicker than lightning I out with the Allen and let him have it in the face. It was an awful roar, and must have scared the bull out of his senses. When the smoke cleared away, there he was, dangling in the air, twenty foot from the ground, and going out of one convulsion into another faster than you could count! I didn't stop to count, anyhow—I shinned down the tree and shot for home."

"Bemis, is all that true, just as you have stated it?"

"I wish I may rot in my tracks and die the death of a dog if it isn't."

"Well, we can't refuse to believe it, and we don't. But if there were some proofs—"

"Proofs! Did I bring back my lariat?"

"No."

"Did I bring back my horse?"

"No."

"Did you ever see the bull again?"

"No."

"Well, then, what more do you want? I never saw anybody as particular as you are about a little thing like that."

I made up my mind that if this man was not a liar he only missed it by the skin of his teeth.

1872

ROUGHING IT

A HUNDRED AND TEN TIN WHISTLES

It is a luscious country for thrilling evening stories about assassinations of intractable Gentiles. I cannot easily conceive of anything more cozy than the night in Salt Lake which we spent in a Gentile den, smoking pipes and listening to tales of how Burton galloped in among the pleading and defenseless "Morisites" and shot them down, men and women, like so many dogs. And how Bill Hickman, a Destroying Angel, shot Drown and Arnold dead for bringing suit against him for a debt. And how Porter Rockwell did this and that dreadful thing. And how heedless people often come to Utah and make remarks about Brigham, or polygamy, or some other sacred matter, and the very next morning at daylight such parties are sure to be found lying up some back alley, contentedly waiting for the hearse. And the next most interesting thing is to sit and listen to these Gentiles talk about polygamy; and how some portly old frog of an elder, or a bishop, marries a girl—likes her, marries her sister—likes her, marries another sister—

likes her, takes another—likes her, marries her mother—likes her, marries her father, grandfather, great grandfather, and then comes back hungry and asks for more. And how the pert young thing of eleven will chance to be the favorite wife, and her own venerable grandmother have to rank away down toward D 4 in their mutual husband's esteem, and have to sleep in the kitchen, as like as not. And how this dreadful sort of thing, this hiving together in one foul nest of mother and daughters, and the making a young daughter superior to her own mother in rank and authority, are things which Mormon women submit to because their religion teaches them that the more wives a man has on earth, and the more children he rears, the higher the place they will all have in the world to come—and the warmer, maybe, though they do not seem to say anything about that.

According to these Gentile friends of ours, Brigham Young's harem contains twenty or thirty wives. They said that some of them had grown old and gone out of active service, but were comfortably housed and cared for in the hennery—or the Lion House, as it is strangely named. Along with each wife were her children—fifty altogether. The house was perfectly quiet and orderly, when the children were still. They all took their meals in one room, and a happy and homelike sight it was pronounced to be. None of our party got an opportunity to take dinner with Mr. Young, but a Gentile by the name of Johnson professed to have enjoyed a sociable breakfast in the Lion House. He gave a preposterous account of the "calling of the roll," and other preliminaries, and the carnage that ensued when the buckwheat-cakes came in. But he embellished rather too much. He said that Mr. Young told him several smart sayings of certain of his "two-year-olds," observing with some pride that for many years he had been the heaviest contributor in that line to one of the Eastern magazines; and then he wanted to show Mr. Johnson one of the pets that had said the last good thing, but he could not find the child. He searched the faces of the children in detail, but could not decide which one it was. Finally, he gave it up with a sigh and said: "I thought I would know the little cub again, but I don't." Mr. Johnson said further, that Mr. Young observed that life was a sad, sad thing—"because the joy of every new marriage a man contracted was so apt to be blighted by the inopportune funeral of a less recent bride." And Mr. Johnson said that while he and Mr. Young were pleasantly conversing in private, one of the Mrs. Youngs came in and demanded a breastpin, remarking that she had found out that he had been giving a breastpin to No. 6, and *she,* for one, did not propose to let this partiality go on without making a satisfactory amount of trouble about it. Mr. Young reminded her that there was a stranger present. Mrs. Young said that if the state of things inside the house was not agreeable to the stranger, he could find room outside. Mr. Young promised the breastpin, and she went away. But in a minute or two another Mrs. Young came in and demanded a breastpin. Mr. Young began a remonstrance, but Mrs. Young cut him short. She said No. 6 had got one, and No. 11 was promised one, and it was "no use for him to try to impose on her—she hoped she knew her rights." He gave his promise, and she went. And presently three Mrs. Youngs entered in a body and opened on their husband a tempest of tears, abuse, and entreaty. They had heard all about No. 6, No. 11, and No. 14. Three more breastpins were promised. They were hardly gone when nine more Mrs. Youngs filed into the presence, and a new tempest burst forth and raged round about the prophet and his guest. Nine breastpins were promised, and the weird sisters filed out again. And in came eleven more, weeping and wailing and gnashing their teeth. Eleven promised breastpins purchased peace once more.

"That is a specimen," said Mr. Young. "You see how it is. You see what a life I lead. A man *can't* be wise all the time. In a heedless moment I gave my darling No. 6—excuse my calling her thus, as her other name has escaped me for the moment—a breastpin. It was only worth twenty-five dollars—that is, *apparently* that was its whole cost —but its ultimate cost was inevitably bound to be a good deal more. You yourself have seen it climb up to six hundred and fifty dollars— and alas, even that is not the end! For I have wives all over this territory of Utah. I have dozens of wives whose *numbers,* even, I do not know without looking in the family Bible. They are scattered far and wide among the mountains and valleys of my realm. And, mark you, every solitary one of them will hear of this wretched breastpin, and every last one of them will have one or die. No. 6's breastpin will cost me twenty-five hundred dollars before I see the end of it. And these creatures will compare these pins together, and if one is a shade finer than the rest, they will all be thrown on my hands, and I will have to order a new lot to keep peace in the family. Sir, you probably did not know it, but all the time you were present with my children your every movement was watched by vigilant servitors of mine. If you had offered to give a child a dime, or a stick of candy, or any trifle of the kind, you would have been snatched out of the house instantly, provided it could be done before your gift left your hand. Otherwise it would be absolutely necessary for you to make an exactly similar gift to all my children—and knowing by experience the importance of the thing, I would have stood by and seen to it myself that you did it, and did it thoroughly. Once a gentleman gave one of my children a tin whistle—a veritable invention of Satan, sir, and one which I have an unspeakable horror of, and so would you if you had eighty or ninety children in your house. But the deed was done—the man escaped. I knew what the result was going to be, and I thirsted for vengeance. I ordered out a flock of Destroying Angels, and they hunted the man far into the fastnesses of the Nevada mountains. But they never caught him. I am not cruel, sir—I am not vindictive except when sorely outraged—but if I had caught him, sir, so help me Joseph Smith, I would have locked him into the nursery till the brats whistled him to death. By the slaughtered body of St. Parley Pratt (whom God assoil!) there was never anything on this earth like it! *I* knew who gave the whistle to the child, but I could not make those jealous mothers believe me. They believed *I* did it, and the result was just what any man of reflection could have foreseen: I had to order a hundred and ten whistles—I think we had a hundred and ten children in the house then, but some of them are off at college now—I had to order a hundred and ten of those shrieking things, and I wish I may never speak another word if we didn't have to talk on our fingers entirely, from that time forth until the children got tired of the whistles. And if ever another man gives a whistle to a child of mine and I get my hands on him, I will hang him higher than Haman! That is the word with the bark on it! Shade of Nephi! *You* don't know anything about married life. I am rich, and everybody knows it. I am benevolent, and everybody takes advantage of it. I have a strong fatherly instinct, and all the foundlings are foisted on me. Every time a woman wants to do well by her darling, she puzzles her brain to cipher out some scheme for getting it into my hands. Why, sir, a woman came here once with a child of a curious lifeless sort of complexion (and so had the woman), and swore that the child was mine and she my wife—that I had married her at such-and-such a time in such-and-such a place, but she had forgotten her number, and of course I could not remember her name. Well, sir, she called my attention to the fact that the child looked like me, and really it did seem to resemble me—a common thing in the territory—and, to cut the story short, I put it in my nursery, and she left. And, by the ghost of Orson Hyde, when they came to wash the paint off that child it was an Injun! Bless my soul, you don't know anything about married life. It is a perfect dog's life, sir—a perfect dog's life. You can't economize. It isn't possible. I have tried keeping one set of bridal attire for all occasions. But it is of no use. First you'll marry a combination of calico and consumption that's as thin as a rail, and next you'll get a creature that's nothing more than the dropsy in disguise, and then you've got to eke out that bridal dress with an old balloon. That is the way it goes. And think of the wash-bill—(excuse these tears)—nine hundred and eighty-four pieces a week! No, sir, there is no such a thing as economy in a family like mine. Why, just the one item of cradles—think of it! And vermifuge! Soothing-syrup! Teething-rings! And 'papa's watches' for the babies to play with! And things to scratch the furniture with! And lucifer matches for them to eat, and pieces of glass to cut themselves with! The item of glass alone would support *your* family, I venture to say, sir. Let me scrimp and squeeze all I can, I still can't get ahead as fast as I feel I ought to, with my opportunities. Bless you, sir, at a time when I had seventy-two wives in this house, I groaned under the pressure of keeping thousands of dollars tied up in seventy-two bedsteads when the money ought to have been out at interest; and I just sold out the whole stock, sir, at a sacrifice, and built a bedstead seven feet long and ninety-six feet wide. But it was a failure, sir. I could *not* sleep. It appeared to me that the whole seventy-two women snored at once. The roar was deafening. And then the danger of it! That was what I was looking at. They would all draw in their breath at once, and you could actually see the walls of the house suck in—and then they would all exhale their breath at once, and you could see the walls swell out, and strain, and hear the rafters crack, and the shingles grind together. My friend, take an old man's advice and *don't* encumber yourself with a large family— mind, I tell you, don't do it. In a small family, and in a small family only, you will find that comfort and that peace of mind which are the best at last of the blessings this world is able to afford us, and for the lack of which no accumulation of wealth, and no acquisition of fame, power, and greatness can ever compensate us. Take my word for it, ten or eleven wives is all you need—never go over it."

Some instinct or other made me set this Johnson down as being unreliable. And yet he was a very entertaining person, and I doubt if

some of the information he gave us could have been acquired from any
other source. He was a pleasant contrast to those reticent Mormons.

1872

ROUGHING IT

THE ALKALI DESERT

At eight in the morning we reached the remnant and ruin of what had
been the important military station of "Camp Floyd," some forty-five
or fifty miles from Salt Lake City. At four P.M. we had doubled our
distance and were ninety or a hundred miles from Salt Lake. And now
we entered upon one of that species of deserts whose concentrated
hideousness shames the diffused and diluted horrors of Sahara—an
"alkali" desert. For sixty-eight miles there was but one break in it. I
do not remember that this was really a break; indeed it seems to me
that it was nothing but a watering depot in the midst of the stretch of
sixty-eight miles. If my memory serves me, there was no well or spring
at this place, but the water was hauled there by mule and ox teams
from the further side of the desert. There was a stage station there. It
was forty-five miles from the beginning of the desert, and twenty-three
from the end of it.

We plowed and dragged and groped along, the whole live-long
night, and at the end of this uncomfortable twelve hours we finished
the forty-five-mile part of the desert and got to the stage station where
the imported water was. The sun was just rising. It was easy enough to
cross a desert in the night while we were asleep; and it was pleasant to
reflect, in the morning, that we in actual person had encountered an
absolute desert and could always speak knowingly of deserts in presence of the ignorant thenceforward. And it was pleasant also to reflect
that this was not an obscure, back country desert, but a very celebrated one, the metropolis itself, as you may say. All this was very
well and very comfortable and satisfactory—but now we were to cross
a desert in daylight. This was fine—novel—romantic—dramatically

adventurous—*this,* indeed, was worth living for, worth traveling for! We would write home all about it.

This enthusiasm, this stern thirst for adventure, wilted under the sultry August sun and did not last above one hour. One poor little hour—and then we were ashamed that we had "gushed" so. The poetry was all in the anticipation—there is none in the reality. Imagine a vast, waveless ocean stricken dead and turned to ashes; imagine this solemn waste tufted with ash-dusted sage-bushes; imagine the lifeless silence and solitude that belong to such a place; imagine a coach, creeping like a bug through the midst of this shoreless level, and sending up tumbled volumes of dust as if it were a bug that went by steam; imagine this aching monotony of toiling and plowing kept up hour after hour, and the shore still as far away as ever, apparently; imagine team, driver, coach and passengers so deeply coated with ashes that they are all one colorless color; imagine ash-drifts roosting above moustaches and eyebrows like snow accumulations on boughs and bushes. This is the reality of it.

The sun beats down with dead, blistering, relentless malignity; the perspiration is welling from every pore in man and beast, but scarcely a sign of it finds its way to the surface—it is absorbed before it gets there; there is not the faintest breath of air stirring; there is not a merciful shred of cloud in all the brilliant firmament; there is not a living creature visible in any direction whither one searches the blank level that stretches its monotonous miles on every hand; there is not a sound—not a sigh—not a whisper—not a buzz, or a whir of wings, or distant pipe of bird—not even a sob from the lost souls that doubtless people that dead air. And so the occasional sneezing of the resting mules, and the champing of the bits, grate harshly on the grim stillness, not dissipating the spell but accenting it and making one feel more lonesome and forsaken than before.

The mules, under violent swearing, coaxing and whip-cracking, would make at stated intervals a "spurt," and drag the coach a hundred or may be two hundred yards, stirring up a billowy cloud of dust that rolled back, enveloping the vehicle to the wheel-tops or higher, and making it seem afloat in a fog. Then a rest followed, with the usual sneezing and bit-champing. Then another "spurt" of a hundred yards and another rest at the end of it. All day long we kept this up, without water for the mules and without ever changing the team. At least we kept it up ten hours, which, I take it, is a day, and a pretty honest one, in an alkali desert. It was from four in the morning till two in the afternoon. And it was so hot! and so close! and our water canteens went dry in the middle of the day and we got so thirsty! It was so stupid and tiresome and dull! and the tedious hours did lag and drag and limp along with such a cruel deliberation! It was so trying to give one's watch a good long undisturbed spell and then take it out and find that it had been fooling away the time and not trying to get ahead any! The alkali dust cut through our lips, it persecuted our eyes, it ate through the delicate membranes and made our noses bleed and *kept* them bleeding—and truly and seriously the romance all faded far away and disappeared, and left the desert trip nothing but a harsh reality—a thirsty, sweltering, longing, hateful reality!

Two miles and a quarter an hour for ten hours—that was what we accomplished. It was hard to bring the comprehension away down to such a snail-pace as that, when we had been used to making eight and ten miles an hour. When we reached the station on the farther verge of the desert, we were glad, for the first time, that the dictionary was along, because we never could have found language to tell how glad we were, in any sort of dictionary but an unabridged one with pictures in it. But there could not have been found in a whole library of dictionaries language sufficient to tell how tired those mules were after their twenty-three mile pull. To try to give the reader an idea of how *thirsty* they were, would be to "gild refined gold or paint the lily."

Somehow, now that it is there, the quotation does not seem to fit—but no matter, let it stay, anyhow. I think it is a graceful and attractive thing, and therefore have tried time and time again to work it in where it *would* fit, but could not succeed. These efforts have kept my mind distracted and ill at ease, and made my narrative seem broken and disjointed, in places. Under these circumstances it seems to me best to leave it in, as above, since this will afford at least a temporary respite from the wear and tear of trying to "lead up" to this really apt and beautiful quotation.

1872

ROUGHING IT

MR. ARKANSAS

There were two men in the company who caused me particular discomfort. One was a little Swede, about twenty-five years old, who knew only one song, and he was forever singing it. By day we were all crowded into one small, stifling barroom, and so there was no escaping this person's music. Through all the profanity, whisky-guzzling, "old sledge," and quarreling, his monotonous song meandered with never a variation in its tiresome sameness, and it seemed to me, at last, that I would be content to die, in order to be rid of the torture. The other man was a stalwart ruffian called "Arkansas," who carried two revolvers in his belt and a bowie-knife projecting from his boot, and who was always drunk and always suffering for a fight. But he was so feared, that nobody would accommodate him. He would try all manner of little wary ruses to entrap somebody into an offensive remark, and his face would light up now and then when he fancied he was fairly on the scent of a fight, but invariably his victim would elude his toils and then he would show a disappointment that was almost pathetic. The landlord, Johnson, was a meek, well-meaning fellow, and Arkansas fastened on him early, as a promising subject, and gave him no rest day or night, for a while. On the fourth morning, Arkansas got drunk and sat himself down to wait for an opportunity. Presently Johnson came in, just comfortably sociable with whisky, and said:

"I reckon the Pennsylvania 'lection—"

Arkansas raised his finger impressively and Johnson stopped. Arkansas rose unsteadily and confronted him. Said he:

"Wha-what do you know a-about Pennsylvania? Answer me that. Wha-what do you know 'bout Pennsylvania?"

"I was only goin' to say—"

"You was only goin' to *say*. *You* was! You was only goin' to say— *what* was you goin' to say? That's it! That's what *I* want to know. *I* want to know wha-what you (*'ic*) what you know about Pennsylvania, since you're makin' yourself so d—d free. Answer me that!"

"Mr. Arkansas, if you'd only let me—"

"Who's a-henderin' you? Don't you insinuate nothing agin me!—don't you do it. Don't you come in bullyin' around, and cussin' and goin' on like a lunatic—don't you do it. 'Coz *I* won't *stand* it. If fight's what you want, out with it! I'm your man! Out with it!"

Said Johnson, backing into a corner, Arkansas following, menacingly:

"Why, *I* never said nothing, Mr. Arkansas. You don't give a man no chance. I was only goin' to say that Pennsylvania was goin' to have an election next week—that was all—that was everything I was goin' to say—I wish I may never stir if it wasn't."

"Well then why d'n't you say it? What did you come swellin' around that way for, and tryin' to raise trouble?"

"Why, *I* didn't come swellin' around, Mr. Arkansas—I just—"

"I'm a liar am I! Ger-reat Caesar's ghost—"

"Oh, please, Mr. Arkansas, I never meant such a thing as that, I wish I may die if I did. All the boys will tell you that I've always spoke well of you, and respected you more'n any man in the house. Ask Smith. Ain't it so, Smith? Didn't I say, no longer ago than last night, that for a man that was a gentleman *all* the time and every way you took him, give me Arkansas? I'll leave it to any gentleman here if them warn't the very words I used. Come, now, Mr. Arkansas, le's take a drink—le's shake hands and take a drink. Come up—everybody! It's my treat. Come up, Bill, Tom, Bob, Scotty—come up. I want you all to take a drink with me and Arkansas—*old* Arkansas, I call him—bully old Arkansas. Gimme your hand ag'in. Look at him, boys—just take a *look* at him. Thar stands the whitest man in America!—and the man that denies it has got to fight *me*, that's all. Gimme that old flipper ag'in!"

They embraced, with drunken affection on the landlord's part and unresponsive toleration on the part of Arkansas, who, bribed by a drink, was disappointed of his prey once more. But the foolish landlord was so happy to have escaped butchery, that he went on talking when he ought to have marched himself out of danger. The consequence was that Arkansas shortly began to glower upon him dangerously, and presently said:

"Lan'lord, will you p-please make that remark over ag'in if you please?"

"I was a-sayin' to Scotty that my father was up'ards of eighty year old when he died."

"Was that *all* that you said?"

"Yes, that was all."

"Didn't say nothing but that?"

"No—nothing."

Then an uncomfortable silence.

Arkansas played with his glass a moment, lolling on his elbows on the counter. Then he meditatively scratched his left shin with his right boot, while the awkward silence continued. But presently he loafed away toward the stove, looking dissatisfied; roughly shouldered two or three men out of comfortable position; occupied it himself, gave a sleeping dog a kick that sent him howling under a bench, then spread his long legs and his blanket-coat tails apart and proceeded to warm his back. In a little while he fell to grumbling to himself, and soon he slouched back to the bar and said:

"Lan'lord, what's your idea for rakin' up old personalities and blowin' about your father? Ain't this company agreeable to you? Ain't it? If this company ain't agreeable to you, p'r'aps we'd better leave. Is that your idea? Is that what you're coming at?"

"Why, bless your soul, Arkansas, I warn't thinking of such a thing. My father and my mother—"

"Lan'lord, *don't* crowd a man! Don't do it. If nothing'll do you but a disturbance, out with it like a man *('ic)*—but *don't* rake up old bygones and fling 'em in the teeth of a passel of people that wants to be peaceable if they could git a chance. What's the matter with you this mornin', anyway? I never see a man carry on so."

"Arkansas, I reely didn't mean no harm, and I won't go on with it if it's onpleasant to you. I reckon my licker's got into my head, and what with the flood, and havin' so many to feed and look out for—"

"So *that's* what's a-ranklin' in your heart, is it? You want us to leave, do you? There's too many on us. You want us to pack up and swim. Is that it? Come!"

"Please be reasonable, Arkansas. Now *you* know that I ain't the man to—"

"Are you a-threatenin' me? Are you? By George, the man don't live that can skeer me! Don't you try to come that game, my chicken— 'cuz I can stand a good deal, but I won't stand that. Come out from behind that bar till I clean you! You want to drive us out, do you, you sneakin' underhanded hound! Come out from behind that bar! *I'll* learn you to bully and badger and browbeat a gentleman that's forever trying to befriend you and keep you out of trouble!"

"Please, Arkansas, please don't shoot! If there's got to be bloodshed—"

"Do you hear that, gentlemen? Do you hear him talk about bloodshed? So it's blood you want, is it, you ravin' desperado! You'd made up your mind to murder somebody this mornin'—I knowed it perfectly well. I'm the man, am I? It's me you're goin' to murder, is it? But you can't do it 'thout I get one chance first, you thievin' black-hearted, white-livered son of a nigger! Draw your weepon!"

With that, Arkansas began to shoot, and the landlord to clamber over benches, men, and every sort of obstacle in a frantic desire to escape. In the midst of the wild hubbub the landlord crashed through a glass door, and as Arkansas charged after him the landlord's wife suddenly appeared in the doorway and confronted the desperado with a pair of scissors! Her fury was magnificent. With head erect and flashing eye she stood a moment and then advanced, with her weapon raised. The astonished ruffian hesitated, and then fell back a step. She followed. She backed him step by step into the middle of the barroom, and then, while the wondering crowd closed up and gazed, she gave him such another tongue-lashing as never a cowed and shame-faced braggart got before, perhaps! As she finished and retired victorious, a roar of applause shook the house, and every man ordered "drinks for the crowd" in one and the same breath.

The lesson was entirely sufficient. The reign of terror was over, and the Arkansas domination broken for good. During the rest of the season of island captivity, there was one man who sat apart in a state of permanent humiliation, never mixing in any quarrel or uttering a boast, and never resenting the insults the once cringing crew now constantly leveled at him, and that man was Arkansas.

1872

ROUGHING IT

BUCK FANSHAW'S FUNERAL

Somebody has said that in order to know a community, one must observe the style of its funerals and know what manner of men they bury with most ceremony. I cannot say which class we buried with most eclat in our "flush times," the distinguished public benefactor or the distinguished rough—possibly the two chief grades or grand divisions of society honored their illustrious dead about equally; and hence, no doubt the philosopher I have quoted from would have needed to see two representative funerals in Virginia before forming his estimate of the people.

There was a grand time over Buck Fanshaw when he died. He was a representative citizen. He had "killed his man"—not in his own quarrel, it is true, but in defence of a stranger unfairly beset by numbers. He had kept a sumptuous saloon. He had been the proprietor of a dashing helpmeet whom he could have discarded without the formality of a divorce. He had held a high position in the fire department and been a very Warwick in politics. When he died there was great lamentation throughout the town, but especially in the vast bottom-stratum of society.

On the inquest it was shown that Buck Fanshaw, in the delirium of a wasting typhoid fever, had taken arsenic, shot himself through the body, cut his throat, and jumped out of a four-story window and broken his neck—and after due deliberation, the jury, sad and tearful, but with intelligence unblinded by its sorrow, brought in a verdict of death "by the visitation of God." What could the world do without juries?

Prodigious preparations were made for the funeral. All the vehicles in town were hired, all the saloons put in mourning, all the municipal and fire-company flags hung at half-mast, and all the firemen ordered to muster in uniform and bring their machines duly draped in black. Now—let us remark in parenthesis—as all the peoples of the earth had representative adventurers in the Silverland, and as each adventurer had brought the slang of his nation or his locality with him, the combination made the slang of Nevada the richest and the most infinitely varied and copious that had ever existed anywhere in the world, perhaps, except in the mines of California in the "early days." Slang was the language of Nevada. It was hard to preach a sermon without it, and be understood. Such phrases as "You bet!" "Oh, no, I reckon not!" "No Irish need apply," and a hundred others, became so common as to fall from the lips of a speaker unconsciously—and very often when they did not touch the subject under discussion and consequently failed to mean anything.

After Buck Fanshaw's inquest, a meeting of the short-haired brotherhood was held, for nothing can be done on the Pacific coast without a public meeting and an expression of sentiment. Regretful resolutions were passed and various committees appointed; among others, a committee of one was deputed to call on the minister, a fragile, gentle, spirituel new fledgling from an Eastern theological seminary, and as yet unacquainted with the ways of the mines. The committeeman, "Scotty" Briggs, made his visit; and in after days it was worth something to hear the minister tell about it. Scotty was a stalwart rough, whose customary suit, when on weighty official business, like committee work, was a fire helmet, flaming red flannel shirt, patent leather belt with spanner and revolver attached, coat hung over arm, and pants stuffed into boot tops. He formed something of a contrast to the pale theological student. It is fair to say of Scotty, however, in passing, that he had a warm heart, and a strong love for his friends, and never entered into a quarrel when he could reasonably keep out of it. Indeed, it was commonly said that whenever one of Scotty's fights was investigated, it always turned out that it had originally been no affair of his, but that out of native goodheartedness he had dropped in of his own accord to help the man who was getting the worst of it. He and Buck Fanshaw were bosom friends, for years, and had often taken adventurous "pot-luck" together. On one occasion, they had thrown off their coats and taken the weaker side in a fight among strangers, and after gaining a hard-earned victory, turned and found that the men they were helping had deserted early, and not only that, but had stolen their coats and made off with them! But to return to Scotty's visit to the minister. He was on a sorrowful mission, now, and his face was the picture of woe. Being admitted to the presence he sat down before the clergyman, placed his fire-hat on an unfinished manuscript sermon under the minister's nose, took from it a red silk handkerchief, wiped his brow and heaved a sigh of dismal impressiveness, explanatory of his business. He choked, and even shed tears; but with an effort he mastered his voice and said in lugubrious tones:

"Are you the duck that runs the gospel-mill next door?"

"Am I the—pardon me, I believe I do not understand?"

With another sigh and a half-sob, Scotty rejoined:

"Why you see we are in a bit of trouble, and the boys thought maybe you would give us a lift, if we'd tackle you—that is, if I've got the rights of it and you are the head clerk of the doxology-works next door."

"I am the shepherd in charge of the flock whose fold is next door."

"The which?"

"The spiritual adviser of the little company of believers whose sanctuary adjoins these premises."

Scotty scratched his head, reflected a moment, and then said:

"You ruther hold over me, pard. I reckon I can't call that hand. Ante and pass the buck."

"How? I beg pardon. What did I understand you to say?"

"Well, you've ruther got the bulge on me. Or maybe we've both got the bulge, somehow. You don't smoke me and I don't smoke you. You see, one of the boys has passed in his checks and we want to give him a good send-off, and so the thing I'm on now is to roust out somebody to jerk a little chin-music for us and waltz him through handsome."

"My friend, I seem to grow more and more bewildered. Your observations are wholly incomprehensible to me. Cannot you simplify them in some way? At first I thought perhaps I understood you, but I grope now. Would it not expedite matters if you restricted yourself to categorical statements of fact unencumbered with obstructing accumulations of metaphor and allegory?"

Another pause, and more reflection. Then, said Scotty:

"I'll have to pass, I judge."

"How?"

"You've raised me out, pard."

"I still fail to catch your meaning."

"Why, that last lead of yourn is too many for me—that's the idea. I can't neither trump nor follow suit."

The clergyman sank back in his chair perplexed. Scotty leaned his

head on his hand and gave himself up to thought. Presently his face
came up, sorrowful but confident.

"I've got it now, so's you can savvy," he said. "What we want is a
gospel-sharp. See?"

"A what?"

"Gospel-sharp. Parson."

"Oh! Why did you not say so before? I am a clergyman—a parson."

"Now you talk! You see my blind and straddle it like a man. Put it
there!"—extending a brawny paw, which closed over the minister's
small hand and gave it a shake indicative of fraternal sympathy and
fervent gratification.

"Now we're all right, pard. Let's start fresh. Don't you mind my
snuffling a little—becuz we're in a power of trouble. You see, one of
the boys has gone up the flume—"

"Gone where?"

"Up the flume—throwed up the sponge, you understand."

"Thrown up the sponge?"

"Yes—kicked the bucket—"

"Ah—has departed to that mysterious country from whose bourne
no traveler returns."

"Return! I reckon not. Why pard, he's *dead!*"

"Yes, I understand."

"Oh, you do? Well I thought maybe you might be getting tangled
some more. Yes, you see he's dead again—"

"*Again?* Why, has he ever been dead before?"

"Dead before? No! Do you reckon a man has got as many lives as a
cat? But you bet you he's awful dead now, poor old boy, and I wish I'd
never seen this day. I don't want no better friend than Buck Fanshaw.
I knowed him by the back; and when I know a man and like him, I
freeze to him—you hear *me.* Take him all round, pard, there never
was a bullier man in the mines. No man ever knowed Buck Fanshaw
to go back on a friend. But it's all up, you know, it's all up. It ain't no
use. They've scooped him."

"Scooped him?"

"Yes—death has. Well, well, well, we've got to give him up. Yes
indeed. It's a kind of a hard world, after all, *ain't* it? But pard, he was
a rustler! You ought to seen him get started once. He was a bully boy
with a glass eye! Just spit in his face and give him room according to
his strength, and it was just beautiful to see him peel and go in. He was

the worst son of a thief that ever drawed breath. Pard, he was *on* it! He was on it bigger than an Injun!"

"On it? On what?"

"On the shoot. On the shoulder. On the fight, you understand. *He* didn't give a continental for *any*body. *Beg* your pardon, friend, for coming so near a cuss-word—but you see I'm on an awful strain, in this palaver, on account of having to cramp down and draw everything so mild. But we've got to give him up. There ain't any getting around that, I don't reckon. Now if we can get you to help plant him—"

"Preach the funeral discourse? Assist at the obsequies?"

"Obs'quies is good. Yes. That's it—that's our little game. We are going to get the thing up regardless, you know. He was always nifty himself, and so you bet you his funeral ain't going to be no slouch—solid silver door-plate on his coffin, six plumes on the hearse, and a nigger on the box in a biled shirt and a plug hat—how's that for high? And we'll take care of *you,* pard. We'll fix you all right. There'll be a kerridge for you; and whatever you want, you just 'scape out and we'll 'tend to it. We've got a shebang fixed up for you to stand behind, in No. 1's house, and don't you be afraid. Just go in and toot your horn, if you don't sell a clam. Put Buck through as bully as you can, pard, for anybody that knowed him will tell you that he was one of the whitest men that was ever in the mines. You can't draw it too strong. He never could stand it to see things going wrong. He's done more to make this town quiet and peaceable than any man in it. I've seen him lick four Greasers in eleven minutes, myself. If a thing wanted regulating, *he* warn't a man to go browsing around after somebody to do it, but he would prance in and regulate it himself. He warn't a Catholic. Scasely. He was down on 'em. His word was, 'No Irish need apply!' But it didn't make no difference about that when it came down to what a man's rights was—and so, when some roughs jumped the Catholic bone-yard and started in to stake out town-lots in it he *went* for 'em! And he *cleaned* 'em, too! I was there, pard, and I seen it myself."

"That was very well indeed—at least the impulse was—whether the act was strictly defensible or not. Had deceased any religious convictions? That is to say, did he feel a dependence upon, or acknowledge allegiance to a higher power?"

More reflection.

"I reckon you've stumped me again, pard. Could you say it over once more, and say it slow?"

"Well, to simplify it somewhat, was he, or rather had he ever been connected with any organization sequestered from secular concerns and devoted to self-sacrifice in the interests of morality?"

"All down but nine—set 'em up on the other alley, pard."

"What did I understand you to say?"

"Why, you're most too many for me, you know. When you get in with your left I hunt grass every time. Every time you draw, you fill; but I don't seem to have any luck. Lets have a new deal."

"How? Begin again?"

"That's it."

"Very well. Was he a good man, and—"

"There—I see that; don't put up another chip till I look at my hand. A good man, says you? Pard, it ain't no name for it. He was the best man that ever—pard, you would have doted on that man. He could lam any galoot of his inches in America. It was him that put down the riot last election before it got a start; and everybody said he was the only man that could have done it. He waltzed in with a spanner in one hand and a trumpet in the other, and sent fourteen men home on a shutter in less than three minutes. He had that riot all broke up and prevented nice before anybody ever got a chance to strike a blow. He was always for peace, and he would *have* peace—he could not stand disturbances. Pard, he was a great loss to this town. It would please the boys if you could chip in something like that and do him justice. Here once when the Micks got to throwing stones through the Methodis' Sunday school windows, Buck Fanshaw, all of his own notion, shut up his saloon and took a couple of six-shooters and mounted guard over the Sunday school. Says he, 'No Irish need apply!' And they didn't. He was the bulliest man in the mountains, pard! He could run faster, jump higher, hit harder, and hold more tanglefoot whisky without spilling it than any man in seventeen counties. Put that in, pard—it'll please the boys more than anything you could say. And you can say, pard, that he never shook his mother."

"Never shook his mother?"

"That's it—any of the boys will tell you so."

"Well, but why *should* he shake her?"

"That's what *I* say—but some people does."

"Not people of any repute?"

"Well, some that averages pretty so-so."

"In my opinion the man that would offer personal violence to his own mother, ought to—"

"Cheese it, pard; you've banked your ball clean outside the string. What I was a drivin' at, was, that he never *throwed off* on his mother —don't you see? No indeedy. He give her a house to live in, and town lots, and plenty of money; and he looked after her and took care of her all the time; and when she was down with the small-pox I'm d—d if he didn't set up nights and nuss her himself! *Beg* your pardon for saying it, but it hopped out too quick for yours truly. You've treated me like a gentleman, pard, and I ain't the man to hurt your feelings intentional. I think you're white. I think you're a square man, pard. I like you, and I'll lick any man that don't. I'll lick him till he can't tell himself from a last year's corpse! Put it *there!*" [Another fraternal handshake—and exit.]

The obsequies were all that "the boys" could desire. Such a marvel of funeral pomp had never been seen in Virginia. The plumed hearse, the dirge-breathing brass bands, the closed marts of business, the flags drooping at half mast, the long, plodding procession of uniformed secret societies, military battalions and fire companies, draped engines, carriages of officials, and citizens in vehicles and on foot, attracted multitudes of spectators to the sidewalks, roofs and windows; and for years afterward, the degree of grandeur attained by any civic display in Virginia was determined by comparison with Buck Fanshaw's funeral.

Scotty Briggs, as a pall-bearer and a mourner, occupied a prominent place at the funeral, and when the sermon was finished and the last sentence of the prayer for the dead man's soul ascended, he responded, in a low voice, but with feeling:

"Amen. No Irish need apply."

As the bulk of the response was without apparent relevancy, it was probably nothing more than a humble tribute to the memory of the friend that was gone; for, as Scotty had once said, it was "his word."

Scotty Briggs, in after days, achieved the distinction of becoming the only convert to religion that was ever gathered from the Virginia roughs; and it transpired that the man who had it in him to espouse the quarrel of the weak out of inborn nobility of spirit was no mean timber whereof to construct a Christian. The making him one did not warp his generosity or diminish his courage; on the contrary it gave intelligent direction to the one and a broader field to the other. If his Sunday-school class progressed faster than the other classes, was it matter for wonder? I think not. He talked to his pioneer small-fry in a language they understood! It was my large privilege, a month before he died, to hear him tell the beautiful story of Joseph and his brethren to his class "without looking at the book." I leave it to the reader to fancy what it was like, as it fell, riddled with slang, from the lips of that grave, earnest teacher, and was listened to by his little learners with a consuming interest that showed that they were as unconscious as he was that any violence was being done to the sacred proprieties!

1872

ROUGHING IT

THE STORY OF THE OLD RAM

Every now and then, in these days, the boys used to tell me I ought to get one Jim Blaine to tell me the stirring story of his grandfather's old ram—but they always added that I must not mention the matter unless Jim was drunk at the time—just comfortably and sociably drunk. They kept this up until my curiosity was on the rack to hear the story. I got to haunting Blaine; but it was of no use, the boys always found fault with his condition; he was often moderately but never satisfactorily drunk. I never watched a man's condition with such absorbing interest, such anxious solicitude; I never so pined to see a man uncompromisingly drunk before. At last, one evening I hurried to his cabin, for I learned that this time his situation was such that even the most fastidious could find no fault with it—he was tranquilly, serenely, symmetrically drunk—not a hiccup to mar his voice, not a cloud upon his brain thick enough to obscure his memory. As I entered, he was sitting upon an empty powder-keg, with a clay pipe in one hand and the other raised to command silence. His face was round, red, and very serious; his throat was bare and his hair tumbled; in general appearance and costume he was a stalwart miner of the period. On the pine table stood a candle, and its dim light revealed "the boys" sitting here and there on bunks, candle-boxes, powder-kegs, etc. They said: "Sh—! Don't speak—he's going to commence."

THE STORY OF THE OLD RAM

I found a seat at once, and Blaine said:

"I don't reckon them times will ever come again. There never was a more bullier old ram than what he was. Grandfather fetched him from Illinois—got him of a man by the name of Yates—Bill Yates—maybe you might have heard of him; his father was a deacon—Baptist—and he was a rustler, too; a man had to get up ruther early to get the start of old Thankful Yates; it was him that put the Greens up to jining teams with my grandfather when he moved west. Seth Green was prob'ly the pick of the flock; he married a Wilkerson—Sarah Wilkerson—good cretur, she was—one of the likeliest heifers that was ever raised in old Stoddard, everybody said that knowed her. She could heft a bar'l of flour as easy as I can flirt a flapjack. And spin? Don't mention it! Independent? Humph! When Sile Hawkins come a browsing around her, she let him know that for all his tin he couldn't trot in harness alongside of *her*. You see, Sile Hawkins was—no, it warn't Sile Hawkins, after all—it was a galoot by the name of Filkins—I disremember his first name; but he *was* a stump—come into pra'r meeting drunk, one night, hooraying for Nixon, becuz he thought it was a primary; and old deacon Ferguson up and scooted him through the window and he lit on old Miss Jefferson's head, poor old filly. She was a good soul—had a glass eye and used to lend it to old Miss Wagner, that hadn't any, to receive company in; it warn't big enough, and when Miss Wagner warn't noticing, it would get twisted around in the socket, and look up, maybe, or out to one side, and every which way, while t' other one was looking as straight ahead as a spy-glass. Grown people didn't mind it, but it most always made the children cry, it was so sort of scary. She tried packing it in raw cotton, but it wouldn't work, somehow—the cotton would get loose and stick out and look so kind of awful that the children couldn't stand it no way. She was always dropping it out, and turning up her old dead-light on the company empty, and making them oncomfortable, becuz *she* never could tell when it hopped out, being blind on that side, you see. So somebody would have to hunch her and say, 'Your game eye has fetched loose, Miss Wagner dear'—and then all of them would have to sit and wait till she jammed it in again—wrong side before, as a general thing, and green as a bird's egg, being a bashful cretur and easy sot back before company. But being wrong side before warn't much difference, anyway, becuz her own eye was sky-blue and the glass one was yaller on the front side, so whichever way she turned it it didn't match nohow. Old Miss Wagner was considerable on the borrow, she was. When she had a quilting, or Dorcas S'iety at her house she gen'ally borrowed Miss Higgins's wooden leg to stump around on; it was considerable shorter than her other pin, but much *she* minded that. She said she couldn't abide crutches when she had company, becuz they were so slow; said when she had company and things had to be done, she wanted to get up and hump herself. She was as bald as a jug, and so she used to borrow Miss Jacops's wig—Miss Jacops was the coffin-peddler's wife—a ratty old buzzard, he was, that used to go roosting around where people was sick, waiting for 'em; and there that old rip would sit all day, in the shade, on a coffin that he judged would fit the can'idate; and if it was a slow customer and kind of uncertain, he'd fetch his rations and a blanket along and sleep in the coffin nights. He was anchored out that way, in frosty weather, for about three weeks, once, before old Robbins's place, waiting for him; and after that, for as much as two years, Jacops was not on speaking terms with the old man, on account of his disapp'inting him. He got one of his feet froze, and lost money, too, becuz old Robbins took a favorable turn and got well. The next time Robbins got sick, Jacops tried to make up with him, and varnished up the same old coffin and fetched it along; but old Robbins was too many for him; he had him in, and 'peared to be powerful weak; he bought the coffin for ten dollars and Jacops was to pay it back and twenty-five more besides if Robbins didn't like the coffin after he'd tried it. And then Robbins died, and at the funeral he bursted off the lid and riz up in his shroud and told the parson to let up on the performances, becuz he could *not* stand such a coffin as that. You see he had been in a trance once before, when he was young, and he took the chances on another, cal'lating that if he made the trip it was money in his pocket, and if he missed fire he couldn't lose a cent. And by George he sued Jacops for the rhino and got jedgment; and he set up the coffin in his back parlor and said he 'lowed to take his time, now. It was always an aggravation to Jacops, the way that miserable old thing acted. He moved back to Indiany pretty soon—went to Wellsville—Wellsville was the place the Hogadorns was from. Mighty fine family. Old Maryland stock. Old Squire Hogadorn could carry around more mixed licker, and cuss better than most any man I ever see. His second wife was the widder Billings—she that was Becky Martin; her dam was deacon Dunlap's first wife. Her oldest child, Maria, married a missionary and died in grace—et up by the savages. They et *him,* too, poor feller—biled him. It warn't the custom, so they say, but they explained to friends of his'n that went down there to bring away his things, that they'd tried missionaries every other way and never could get any good out of 'em—and so it annoyed all his relations to find out that that man's life was fooled away just out of a dern'd experiment, so to speak. But mind you, there ain't anything ever reely lost; everything that people can't understand and don't see the reason of does good if you only hold on and give it a fair shake; Prov'dence don't fire no blank ca'tridges, boys. That there missionary's substance, unbeknowns to himself, actu'ly converted every last one of them heathens that took a chance at the barbacue. Nothing ever fetched them but that. Don't tell *me* it was an accident that he was biled. There ain't no such a thing as an accident. When my uncle Lem was leaning up agin a scaffolding once, sick, or drunk, or suthin, an Irishman with a hod full of bricks fell on him out of the third story and broke the old man's back in two places. People said it was an accident. Much accident there was about that. He didn't know what he was there for, but he was there for a good object. If he hadn't been there the Irishman would have been killed. Nobody can ever make me believe anything different from that. Uncle Lem's dog was there. Why didn't the Irishman fall on the dog? Becuz the dog would a seen him a coming and stood from under. That's the reason the dog warn't appinted. A dog can't be depended on to carry out a special providence. Mark my words it was a put-up thing. Accidents don't happen, boys. Uncle Lem's dog—I wish you could a seen that dog. He was a reglar shepherd—or ruther he was part bull and part shepherd—splendid animal; belonged to parson Hagar before Uncle Lem got him. Parson Hagar belonged to the Western Reserve Hagars; prime family; his mother was a Watson; one of his sisters married a Wheeler; they settled in Morgan county, and he got nipped by the machinery in a carpet factory and went through in less than a quarter of a minute; his widder bought the piece of carpet that had his remains wove in, and people come a hundred mile to 'tend the funeral. There was fourteen yards in the piece. She wouldn't let them roll him up, but planted him just so—full length. The church was middling small where they preached the funeral, and they had to let one end of the coffin stick out of the window. They didn't bury him—they planted one end, and let him stand up, same as a monument. And they nailed a sign on it and put—put on—put on it—sacred to—the m-e-m-o-r-y—of fourteen y-a-r-d-s—of three-ply—car - - - pet—containing all that was—m-o-r-t-a-l—of—of—W-i-l-l-i-a-m—W-h-e—"

Jim Blaine had been growing gradually drowsy and drowsier—his head nodded, once, twice, three times—dropped peacefully upon his breast, and he fell tranquilly asleep. The tears were running down the boys' cheeks—they were suffocating with suppressed laughter—and had been from the start, though I had never noticed it. I perceived that I was "sold." I learned then that Jim Blaine's peculiarity was that whenever he reached a certain stage of intoxication, no human power could keep him from setting out, with impressive unction, to tell about a wonderful adventure which he had once had with his grandfather's old ram—and the mention of the ram in the first sentence was as far as any man had ever heard him get, concerning it. He always maundered off, interminably, from one thing to another, till his whisky got the best of him and he fell asleep. What the thing was that happened to him and his grandfather's old ram is a dark mystery to this day, for nobody has ever yet found out.

1872

A TRAMP ABROAD

THE LABORIOUS ANT

We followed the carriage-road, and had our usual luck; we traveled under a beating sun, and always saw the shade leave the shady places before we could get to them. In all our wanderings we seldom managed to strike a piece of road at its time for being shady. We had a particularly hot time of it on that particular afternoon, and with no comfort but what we could get out of the fact that the peasants at work away up on the steep mountainsides above our heads were even worse off than we were. By and by it became impossible to endure the intolerable glare and heat any longer; so we struck across the ravine and entered the deep cool twilight of the forest, to hunt for what the guide-book called the "old road."

We found an old road, and it proved eventually to be the right one, though we followed it at the time with the conviction that it was the wrong one. If it was the wrong one there could be no use in hurrying, therefore we did not hurry, but sat down frequently on the soft moss and enjoyed the restful quiet and shade of the forest solitudes. There had been distractions in the carriage-road—school-children, peasants, wagons, troops of pedestrianizing students from all over Germany— but we had the old road to ourselves.

Now and then, while we rested, we watched the laborious ant at his work. I found nothing new in him—certainly nothing to change my opinion of him. It seems to me that in the matter of intellect the ant must be a strangely overrated bird. During many summers, now, I have watched him, when I ought to have been in better business, and I have not yet come across a living ant that seemed to have any more sense than a dead one. I refer to the ordinary ant, of course; I have had no experience of those wonderful Swiss and African ones which vote, keep drilled armies, hold slaves, and dispute about religion. Those particular ants may be all that the naturalist paints them, but I am persuaded that the average ant is a sham. I admit his industry, of course; he is the hardest-working creature in the world—when any-body is looking—but his leatherheadedness is the point I make against him. He goes out foraging, he makes a capture, and then what does he do? Go home? No—he goes anywhere but home. He doesn't know where home is. His home may be only three feet away—no matter, he can't find it. He makes his capture, as I have said; it is generally something which can be of no sort of use to himself or anybody else; it is usually seven times bigger than it ought to be; he hunts out the awkwardest place to take hold of it; he lifts it bodily up in the air by main force, and starts; not toward home, but in the opposite direction; not calmly and wisely, but with a frantic haste which is wasteful of his strength; he fetches up against a pebble, and instead of going around it, he climbs over it backward dragging his booty after him, tumbles down on the other side, jumps up in a passion, kicks the dust off his clothes, moistens his hands, grabs his property viciously, yanks it this

way, then that, shoves it ahead of him a moment, turns tail and lugs it
after him another moment, gets madder and madder, then presently
hoists it into the air and goes tearing away in an entirely new direction; comes to a weed; it never occurs to him to go around it; no, he
must climb it; and he does climb it, dragging his worthless property to
the top—which is as bright a thing to do as it would be for me to carry
a sack of flour from Heidelberg to Paris by way of Strasburg steeple;
when he gets up there he finds that that is not the place; takes a
cursory glance at the scenery and either climbs down again or tumbles
down, and starts off once more—as usual, in a new direction. At the
end of half an hour, he fetches up within six inches of the place he
started from and lays his burden down; meantime he has been over all
the ground for two yards around, and climbed all the weeds and pebbles he came across. Now he wipes the sweat from his brow, strokes
his limbs, and then marches aimlessly off, in as violent a hurry as ever.
He traverses a good deal of zigzag country, and by and by stumbles on
his same booty again. He does not remember to have ever seen it
before; he looks around to see which is not the way home, grabs his
bundle and starts; he goes through the same adventures he had before;
finally stops to rest, and a friend comes along. Evidently the friend
remarks that a last year's grasshopper leg is a very noble acquisition,
and inquires where he got it. Evidently the proprietor does not remember exactly where he did get it, but thinks he got it "around here
somewhere." Evidently the friend contracts to help him freight it
home. Then, with a judgment peculiarly antic (pun not intentional),
they take hold of opposite ends of that grasshopper leg and begin to
tug with all their might in opposite directions. Presently they take a
rest and confer together. They decide that something is wrong, they
can't make out what. Then they go at it again, just as before. Same
result. Mutual recriminations follow. Evidently each accuses the other
of being an obstructionist. They warm up, and the dispute ends in a
fight. They lock themselves together and chew each other's jaws for a
while; then they roll and tumble on the ground till one loses a horn or
a leg and has to haul off for repairs. They make up and go to work
again in the same old insane way, but the crippled ant is at a disadvantage; tug as he may, the other one drags off the booty and him at the
end of it. Instead of giving up, he hangs on, and gets his shins bruised
against every obstruction that comes in the way. By and by, when that
grasshopper leg has been dragged all over the same old ground once

more, it is finally dumped at about the spot where it originally lay, the two perspiring ants inspect it thoughtfully and decide that dried grasshopper legs are a poor sort of property after all, and then each starts off in a different direction to see if he can't find an old nail or something else that is heavy enough to afford entertainment and at the same time valueless enough to make an ant want to own it.

There in the Black Forest, on the mountainside, I saw an ant go through with such a performance as this with a dead spider of fully ten times his own weight. The spider was not quite dead, but too far gone to resist. He had a round body the size of a pea. The little ant—observing that I was noticing—turned him on his back, sunk his fangs into his throat, lifted him into the air and started vigorously off with him, stumbling over little pebbles, stepping on the spider's legs and tripping himself up, dragging him backward, shoving him bodily ahead, dragging him up stones six inches high instead of going around them, climbing weeds twenty times his own height and jumping from their summits—and finally leaving him in the middle of the road to be confiscated by any other fool of an ant that wanted him. I measured the ground which this ass traversed, and arrived at the conclusion that what he had accomplished inside of twenty minutes would constitute some such job as this—relatively speaking—for a man; to wit: to strap two eight-hundred-pound horses together, carry them eighteen hundred feet, mainly over (not around) boulders averaging six feet high, and in the course of the journey climb up and jump from the top of one precipice like Niagara, and three steeples, each a hundred and twenty feet high; and then put the horses down, in an exposed place, without anybody to watch them, and go off to indulge in some other idiotic miracle for vanity's sake.

Science has recently discovered that the ant does not lay up anything for winter use. This will knock him out of literature, to some extent. He does not work, except when people are looking, and only then when the observer has a green, naturalistic look, and seems to be taking notes. This amounts to deception, and will injure him for the Sunday-schools. He has not judgment enough to know what is good to eat from what isn't. This amounts to ignorance, and will impair the world's respect for him. He cannot stroll around a stump and find his way home again. This amounts to idiocy, and once the damaging fact is established, thoughtful people will cease to look up to him, the sentimental will cease to fondle him. His vaunted industry is but a vanity and of no effect, since he never gets home with anything he starts with. This disposes of the last remnant of his reputation and wholly destroys his main usefulness as a moral agent, since it will make the sluggard hesitate to go to him any more. It is strange, beyond comprehension, that so manifest a humbug as the ant has been able to fool so many nations and keep it up so many ages without being found out.

1880

A TRAMP ABROAD

AMERICAN IN EUROPE

For some days we were content to enjoy looking at the blue Lake Lucerne and at the piled-up masses of snow-mountains that border it all around—an enticing spectacle, this last, for there is a strange and fascinating beauty and charm about a majestic snow-peak with the sun blazing upon it or the moonlight softly enriching it—but finally we concluded to try a bit of excursioning around on a steamboat, and a dash on foot at the Rigi. Very well, we had a delightful trip to Fluelen, on a breezy, sunny day. Everybody sat on the upper deck, on benches, under an awning; everybody talked, laughed, and exclaimed at the wonderful scenery; in truth, a trip on that lake is almost the perfection of pleasuring. The mountains were a never-ceasing marvel. Sometimes they rose straight up out of the lake, and towered aloft and overshadowed our pygmy steamer with their prodigious bulk in the most impressive way. Not snow-clad mountains, these, yet they climbed high enough toward the sky to meet the clouds and veil their foreheads in them. They were not barren and repulsive, but clothed in green, and restful and pleasant to the eye. And they were so almost straight-up-and-down, sometimes, that one could not imagine a man being able to keep his footing upon such a surface, yet there are paths, and the Swiss people go up and down them every day.

Sometimes one of these monster precipices had the slight inclination of the huge ship-houses in dockyards—then high aloft, toward the sky, it took a little stronger inclination, like that of a mansard roof— and perched on this dizzy mansard one's eye detected little things like martin boxes, and presently perceived that these were the dwellings of peasants—an airy place for a home, truly. And suppose a peasant should walk in his sleep, or his child should fall out of the front yard? —the friends would have a tedious long journey down out of those cloud-heights before they found the remains. And yet those far-away homes looked ever so seductive, they were so remote from the troubled world, they dozed in such an atmosphere of peace and dreams— surely no one who had learned to live up there would ever want to live on a meaner level.

We swept through the prettiest little curving arms of the lake, among these colossal green walls, enjoying new delights, always, as the stately panorama unfolded itself before us and rerolled and hid itself behind us; and now and then we had the thrilling surprise of bursting suddenly upon a tremendous white mass like the distant and dominating Jungfrau, or some kindred giant, looming head and shoulders above a tumbled waste of lesser Alps.

Once, while I was hungrily taking in one of these surprises, and doing my best to get all I possibly could of it while it should last, I was interrupted by a young and care-free voice:

"You're an American, I think—so'm I."

He was about eighteen, or possibly nineteen; slender and of medium height; open, frank, happy face; a restless but independent eye; a snub nose, which had the air of drawing back with a decent reserve from the silky new-born mustache below it until it should be introduced; a loosely hung jaw, calculated to work easily in the sockets. He wore a low-crowned, narrow-brimmed straw hat, with a broad blue ribbon around it which had a white anchor embroidered on it in front; nobby short-tailed coat, pantaloons, vest, all trim and neat and up with the fashion; red-striped stockings, very low-quarter patent-leather shoes, tied with black ribbon; blue ribbon around his neck, wide-open collar; tiny diamond studs; wrinkleless kids; projecting cuffs, fastened with large oxydized silver sleeve-buttons, bearing the device of a dog's face —English pug. He carried a slim cane, surmounted with an English pug's head with red glass eyes. Under his arm he carried a German grammar—Otto's. His hair was short, straight, and smooth, and presently when he turned his head a moment, I saw that it was nicely parted behind. He took a cigarette out of a dainty box, stuck it into a meerschaum holder which he carried in a morocco case, and reached for my cigar. While he was lighting, I said:

"Yes—I am an American."

"I knew it—I can always tell them. What ship did you come over in?"

"*Holsatia.*"

"We came in the *Batavia*—Cunard, you know. What kind of a passage did you have?"

"Tolerably rough."

"So did we. Captain said he'd hardly ever seen it rougher. Where are you from?"

"New England."

"So'm I. I'm from New Bloomfield. Anybody with you?"

"Yes—a friend."

"Our whole family's along. It's awful slow, going around alone—don't you think so?"

"Rather slow."

"Ever been over here before?"

"Yes."

"I haven't. My first trip. But we've been all around—Paris and everywhere. I'm to enter Harvard next year. Studying German all the time, now. Can't enter till I know German. I know considerable French—I get along pretty well in Paris, or anywhere where they speak French. What hotel are you stopping at?"

"Schweitzerhof."

"No! is that so? I never see you in the reception-room. I go to the reception-room a good deal of the time, because there's so many Americans there. I make lots of acquaintances. I know an American as soon as I see him—and so I speak to him and make his acquaintance. I like to be always making acquaintances—don't you?"

"Lord, yes!"

"You see it breaks up a trip like this, first rate. I never get bored on a trip like this, if I can make acquaintances and have somebody to talk to. But I think a trip like this would be an awful bore, if a body couldn't find anybody to get acquainted with and talk to on a trip like this. I'm fond of talking, ain't you?"

"Passionately."

"Have you felt bored, on this trip?"

"Not all the time, part of it."

"That's it!—you see you ought to go around and get acquainted, and talk. That's my way. That's the way I always do—I just go 'round, 'round, 'round, and talk, talk, talk—I never get bored. You been up the Rigi yet?"

"No."

"Going?"

"I think so."

"What hotel you going to stop at?"

"I don't know. Is there more than one?"

"Three. You stop at the Schreiber—you'll find it full of Americans. What ship did you say you came over in?"

"*City of Antwerp.*"

"German, I guess. You going to Geneva?"

"Yes."

"What hotel you going to stop at?"

"Hotel de l'Écu de Génève."

"Don't you do it! No Americans there! You stop at one of those big hotels over the bridge—they're packed full of Americans."

"But I want to practise my Arabic."

"Good gracious, do you speak Arabic?"

"Yes—well enough to get along."

"Why, hang it, you won't get along in Geneva—*they* don't speak Arabic, they speak French. What hotel are you stopping at here?"

"Hotel Pension-Beaurivage."

"Sho, you ought to stop at the Schweitzerhof. Didn't you know the Schweitzerhof was the best hotel in Switzerland?—look at your Baedeker."

"Yes, I know—but I had an idea there warn't any Americans there."

"No Americans! Why, bless your soul, it's just alive with them! I'm in the great reception-room most all the time. I make lots of acquaintances there. Not as many as I did at first, because now only the new ones stop in there—the others go right along through. Where are you from?"

"Arkansaw."

"Is that so? I'm from New England—New Bloomfield's my town when I'm at home. I'm having a mighty good time to-day, ain't you?"

"Divine."

"That's what I call it. I like this knocking around, loose and easy, and making acquaintances and talking. I know an American, soon as I see him; so I go and speak to him and make his acquaintance. I ain't ever bored, on a trip like this, if I can make new acquaintances and talk. I'm awful fond of talking when I can get hold of the right kind of a person, ain't you?"

"I prefer it to any other dissipation."

"That's my notion, too. Now some people like to take a book and sit down and read, and read, and read, or moon around yawping at the lake or these mountains and things, but that ain't my way; no, sir, if they like it, let 'em do it, I don't object; but as for me, talking's what *I* like. You been up the Rigi?"

"Yes."

"What hotel did you stop at?"

"Schreiber."

"That's the place!—I stopped there too. *Full* of Americans, *wasn't* it? It always is—always is. That's what they say. Everybody says that. What ship did you come over in?"

"*Ville de Paris.*"

"French, I reckon. What kind of a passage did . . . excuse me a minute, there's some Americans I haven't seen before."

And away he went. He went uninjured, too—I had the murderous impulse to harpoon him in the back with my alpenstock, but as I raised the weapon the disposition left me; I found I hadn't the heart to kill him, he was such a joyous, innocent, good-natured numbskull.

Half an hour later I was sitting on a bench inspecting, with strong interest, a noble monolith which we were skimming by—a monolith not shaped by man, but by Nature's free great hand—a massy pyramidal rock eighty feet high, devised by Nature ten million years ago against the day when a man worthy of it should need it for his monument. The time came at last, and now this grand remembrancer bears Schiller's name in huge letters upon its face. Curiously enough, this rock was not degraded or defiled in any way. It is said that two years ago a stranger let himself down from the top of it with ropes and pulleys, and painted all over it, in blue letters bigger than those in Schiller's name, these words:

"TRY SOZODONT;"
"BUY SUN STOVE POLISH;"

"HELMBOLD'S BUCHU;"
"TRY BENZALINE FOR THE BLOOD."

He was captured, and it turned out that he was an American. Upon his trial the judge said to him:

"You are from a land where any insolent that wants to is privileged to profane and insult Nature, and, through her, Nature's God, if by so doing he can put a sordid penny in his pocket. But here the case is different. Because you are a foreigner and ignorant, I will make your sentence light; if you were a native I would deal strenuously with you. Hear and obey:—You will immediately remove every trace of your offensive work from the Schiller monument; you pay a fine of ten thousand francs; you will suffer two years' imprisonment at hard labor; you will then be horsewhipped, tarred and feathered, deprived of your ears, ridden on a rail to the confines of the canton, and banished forever. The severest penalties are omitted in your case—not as a grace to you, but to that great republic which had the misfortune to give you birth."

The steamer's benches were ranged back to back across the deck. My back hair was mingling innocently with the back hair of a couple of ladies. Presently they were addressed by some one and I overheard this conversation:

"You are Americans, I think? So'm I."

"Yes—we are Americans."

"I knew it—I can always tell them. What ship did you come over in?"

"City of Chester."

"Oh, yes—Inman line. We came in the *Batavia*—Cunard, you know. What kind of a passage did you have?"

"Pretty fair."

"That was luck. We had it awful rough. Captain said he'd hardly ever seen it rougher. Where are you from?"

"New Jersey."

"So'm I. No—I didn't mean that; I'm from New England. New Bloomfield's my place. These your children?—belong to both of you?"

"Only to one of us; they are mine; my friend is not married."

"Single, I reckon? So'm I. Are you two ladies traveling alone?"

"No—my husband is with us."

"Our whole family's along. It's awful slow, going around alone—don't you think so?"

"I suppose it must be."

"Hi, there's Mount Pilatus coming in sight again. Named after Pontius Pilate, you know, that shot the apple off of William Tell's head. Guide-book tells all about it, they say. I didn't read it—an American told me. I don't read when I'm knocking around like this, having a good time. Did you ever see the chapel where William Tell used to preach?"

"I did not know he ever preached there."

"Oh, yes, he did. That American told me so. He don't ever shut up his guide-book. He knows more about this lake than the fishes in it. Besides, they *call* it 'Tell's Chapel'—you know that yourself. You ever been over here before?"

"Yes."

"I haven't. It's my first trip. But we've been all around—Paris and everywhere. I'm to enter Harvard next year. Studying German all the time now. Can't enter till I know German. This book's Otto's grammar. It's a mighty good book to get the *ich habe gehabt haben's* out of. But I don't really study when I'm knocking around this way. If the notion takes me, I just run over my little old *ich habe gehabt, du hast gehabt, er hat gehabt, wir haben gehabt, ihr haben gehabt, sie haben gehabt*—kind of 'Now-I-lay-me-down-to-sleep' fashion, you know, and after that, maybe I don't buckle to it again for three days. It's awful undermining to the intellect, German is; you want to take it in small doses, or first you know your brains all run together, and you feel them sloshing around in your head same as so much drawn butter. But French is different; *French* ain't anything. I ain't any more afraid of French than a tramp's afraid of pie; I can rattle off my little *j'ai, tu as, il a*, and the rest of it, just as easy as a-b-c. I get along pretty well in Paris, or anywhere where they speak French. What hotel are you stopping at?"

"The Schweitzerhof."

"No! is that so? I never see you in the big reception-room. I go in there a good deal of the time, because there's so many Americans there. I make lots of acquaintances. You been up the Rigi yet?"

"No."

"Going?"

"We think of it."

"What hotel you going to stop at?"

"I don't know."

"Well, then, you stop at the Schreiber—it's full of Americans. What ship did you come over in?"

"City of Chester."

"Oh, yes, I remember I asked you that before. But I always ask everybody what ship they came over in, and so sometimes I forget and ask again. You going to Geneva?"

"Yes."

"What hotel you going to stop at?"

"We expect to stop in a pension."

"I don't hardly believe you'll like that; there's very few Americans in the pensions. What hotel are you stopping at here?"

"The Schweitzerhof."

"Oh, yes, I asked you that before, too. But I always ask everybody what hotel they're stopping at, and so I've got my head all mixed up with hotels. But it makes talk, and I love to talk. It refreshes me up so —don't it you—on a trip like this?"

"Yes—sometimes."

"Well, it does me, too. As long as I'm talking I never feel bored— ain't that the way with you?"

"Yes—generally. But there are exceptions to the rule."

"Oh, of course. *I* don't care to talk to everybody, *myself.* If a person starts in to jabber-jabber-jabber about scenery, and history, and pictures, and all sorts of tiresome things, I get the fan-tods mighty soon. I say 'Well, I must be going now—hope I'll see you again'—and then I take a walk. Where you from?"

"New Jersey."

"Why, bother it all, I asked you *that* before, too. Have you seen the Lion of Lucerne?"

"Not yet."

"Nor I, either. But the man who told me about Mount Pilatus says it's one of the things to see. It's twenty-eight feet long. It don't seem reasonable, but he said so, anyway. He saw it yesterday; said it was dying, then, so I reckon it's dead by this time. But that ain't any matter, of course they'll stuff it. Did you say the children are yours— or *hers?*"

"Mine."

"Oh, so you did. Are you going up the . . . no, I asked you that."

What ship . . . no, I asked you that, too. What hotel are you . . .
no, you told me that. Let me see . . . um. . . . Oh, what kind of a
voy . . . no, we've been over that ground, too. Um . . . um . . .
well, I believe that is all. *Bonjour*—I am very glad to have made your
acquaintance, ladies. *Guten Tag.*"

1880

A TRAMP ABROAD

THE AWFUL GERMAN LANGUAGE

A little learning makes the whole world kin.
—*Proverbs xxxii, 7.*

I went often to look at the collection of curiosities in Heidelberg Castle, and one day I surprised the keeper of it with my German. I spoke
entirely in that language. He was greatly interested; and after I had
talked a while he said my German was very rare, possibly a "unique";
and wanted to add it to his museum.

If he had known what it had cost me to acquire my art, he would
also have known that it would break any collector to buy it. Harris
and I had been hard at work on our German during several weeks at
that time, and although we had made good progress, it had been
accomplished under great difficulty and annoyance, for three of our
teachers had died in the mean time. A person who has not studied
German can form no idea of what a perplexing language it is.

Surely there is not another language that is so slipshod and systemless, and so slippery and elusive to the grasp. One is washed about in
it, hither and thither, in a most helpless way; and when at last he
thinks he has captured a rule which offers firm ground to take a rest
on amid the general rage and turmoil of the ten parts of speech, he
turns over the page and reads, "Let the pupil make careful note of the
following *exceptions.*" He runs his eye down and finds that there are
more exceptions to the rule than instances of it. So overboard he goes
again, to hunt for another Ararat and find another quicksand. Such

has been, and continues to be, my experience. Every time I think I have got one of these four confusing "cases" where I am master of it, a seemingly insignificant preposition intrudes itself into my sentence, clothed with an awful and unsuspected power, and crumbles the ground from under me. For instance, my book inquires after a certain bird—(it is always inquiring after things which are of no sort of consequence to anybody): "Where is the bird?" Now the answer to this question—according to the book—is that the bird is waiting in the blacksmith shop on account of the rain. Of course no bird would do that, but then you must stick to the book. Very well, I begin to cipher out the German for that answer. I begin at the wrong end, necessarily, for that is the German idea. I say to myself, *Regen* (rain) is masculine —or maybe it is feminine—or possibly neuter—it is too much trouble to look now. Therefore, it is either *der* (the) Regen, or *die* (the) Regen, or *das* (the) Regen, according to which gender it may turn out to be when I look. In the interest of science, I will cipher it out on the hypothesis that it is masculine. Very well—then *the* rain is *der* Regen, if it is simply in the quiescent state of being *mentioned,* without enlargement or discussion—Nominative case; but if this rain is lying around, in a kind of a general way on the ground, it is then definitely located, it is *doing something*—that is, *resting* (which is one of the German grammar's ideas of doing something), and this throws the rain into the Dative case, and makes it *dem* Regen. However, this rain is not resting, but is doing something *actively*—it is falling—to interfere with the bird, likely—and this indicates *movement,* which has the effect of sliding it into the Accusative case and changing *dem* Regen into *den* Regen. Having completed the grammatical horoscope of this matter, I answer up confidently and state in German that the bird is staying in the blacksmith shop "wegen (on account of) *den* Regen." Then the teacher lets me softly down with the remark that whenever the word "wegen" drops into a sentence, it *always* throws that subject into the *Genitive* case, regardless of consequences—and that therefore this bird stayed in the blacksmith shop "wegen *des* Regens."

N.B.—I was informed, later, by a higher authority, that there was an "exception" which permits one to say "wegen *den* Regen" in certain peculiar and complex circumstances, but that this exception is not extended to anything *but* rain.

There are ten parts of speech, and they are all troublesome. An average sentence, in a German newspaper, is a sublime and impressive curiosity; it occupies a quarter of a column; it contains all the ten parts of speech—not in regular order, but mixed; it is built mainly of compound words constructed by the writer on the spot, and not to be found in any dictionary—six or seven words compacted into one, without joint or seam—that is, without hyphens; it treats of fourteen or fifteen different subjects, each inclosed in a parenthesis of its own, with here and there extra parentheses which reinclose three or four of the minor parentheses, making pens within pens: finally, all the parentheses and reparentheses are massed together between a couple of king-parentheses, one of which is placed in the first line of the majestic sentence and the other in the middle of the last line of it—*after which comes the* VERB, and you find out for the first time what the man has been talking about; and after the verb—merely by way of ornament, as far as I can make out—the writer shovels in *"haben sind gewesen gehabt haben geworden sein,"* or words to that effect, and the monument is finished. I suppose that this closing hurrah is in the nature of the flourish to a man's signature—not necessary, but pretty. German books are easy enough to read when you hold them before the looking-glass or stand on your head—so as to reverse the construction—but I think that to learn to read and understand a German newspaper is a thing which must always remain an impossibility to a foreigner.

Yet even the German books are not entirely free from attacks of the Parenthesis distemper—though they are usually so mild as to cover only a few lines, and therefore when you at last get down to the verb it carries some meaning to your mind because you are able to remember a good deal of what has gone before.

Now here is a sentence from a popular and excellent German novel —with a slight parenthesis in it. I will make a perfectly literal translation, and throw in the parenthesis-marks and some hyphens for the assistance of the reader—though in the original there are no parenthesis-marks or hyphens, and the reader is left to flounder through to the remote verb the best way he can:

"But when he, upon the street, the (in-satin-and-silk-covered-now-very-unconstrainedly-after-the-newest-fashion-dressed)   government counselor's wife *met,"* etc., etc.*

That is from *The Old Mamselle's Secret,* by Mrs. Marlitt. And that sentence is constructed upon the most approved German model. You

---

* *Wenn er aber auf der Strasse der in Sammt und Seide gehüllten jetz sehr ungenirt nach der neusten mode gekleideten Regierungsrathin begegnet.*

observe how far that verb is from the reader's base of operations; well, in a German newspaper they put their verb away over on the next page; and I have heard that sometimes after stringing along on exciting preliminaries and parentheses for a column or two, they get in a hurry and have to go to press without getting to the verb at all. Of course, then the reader is left in a very exhausted and ignorant state.

We have the Parenthesis disease in our literature, too; and one may see cases of it every day in our books and newspapers: but with us it is the mark and sign of an unpractised writer or a cloudy intellect, whereas with the Germans it is doubtless the mark and sign of a practised pen and of the presence of that sort of luminous intellectual fog which stands for clearness among these people. For surely it is *not* clearness—it necessarily can't be clearness. Even a jury would have penetration enough to discover that. A writer's ideas must be a good deal confused, a good deal out of line and sequence, when he starts out to say that a man met a counselor's wife in the street, and then right in the midst of this so simple undertaking halts these approaching people and makes them stand still until he jots down an inventory of the woman's dress. That is manifestly absurd. It reminds a person of those dentists who secure your instant and breathless interest in a tooth by taking a grip on it with the forceps, and then stand there and drawl through a tedious anecdote before they give the dreaded jerk. Parentheses in literature and dentistry are in bad taste.

The Germans have another kind of parenthesis, which they make by splitting a verb in two and putting half of it at the beginning of an exciting chapter and the *other half* at the end of it. Can any one conceive of anything more confusing than that? These things are called "separable verbs." The German grammar is blistered all over with separable verbs; and the wider the two portions of one of them are spread apart, the better the author of the crime is pleased with his performance. A favorite one is *reiste ab*—which means *departed*. Here is an example which I culled from a novel and reduced to English:

"The trunks being now ready, he DE-after kissing his mother and sisters, and once more pressing to his bosom his adored Gretchen, who, dressed in simple white muslin, with a single tuberose in the ample folds of her rich brown hair, had tottered feebly down the stairs, still pale from the terror and excitement of the past evening, but longing to lay her poor aching head yet once again upon the breast of him whom she loved more dearly than life itself, PARTED."

However, it is not well to dwell too much on the separable verbs. One is sure to lose his temper early; and if he sticks to the subject, and will not be warned, it will at last either soften his brain or petrify it. Personal pronouns and adjectives are a fruitful nuisance in this language, and should have been left out. For instance, the same sound, *sie,* means *you,* and it means *she,* and it means *her,* and it means *it,* and it means *they,* and it means *them.* Think of the ragged poverty of a language which has to make one word do the work of six—and a poor little weak thing of only three letters at that. But mainly, think of the exasperation of never knowing which of these meanings the speaker is trying to convey. This explains why, whenever a person says *sie* to me, I generally try to kill him, if a stranger.

Now observe the Adjective. Here was a case where simplicity would have been an advantage; therefore, for no other reason, the inventor of this language complicated it all he could. When we wish to speak of our "good friend or friends," in our enlightened tongue, we stick to the one form and have no trouble or hard feeling about it; but with the German tongue it is different. When a German gets his hands on an adjective, he declines it, and keeps on declining it until the common sense is all declined out of it. It is as bad as Latin. He says, for instance:

SINGULAR

Nominative—Mein gut*er* Freund, my good friend.
Genitive—Mein*es* gut*en* Freund*es,* of my good friend.
Dative—Mein*em* gut*en* Freund, to my good friend.
Accusative—Mein*en* gut*en* Freund, my good friend.

PLURAL

N.—Mein*e* gut*en* Freund*e,* my good friends.
G.—Mein*er* gut*en* Freund*e,* of my good friends.
D.—Mein*en* gut*en* Freund*en,* to my good friends.
A.—Mein*e* gut*en* Freund*e,* my good friends.

Now let the candidate for the asylum try to memorize those variations, and see how soon he will be elected. One might better go without friends in Germany than take all this trouble about them. I have shown what a bother it is to decline a good (male) friend; well this is only a third of the work, for there is a variety of new distortions of the adjective to be learned when the object is feminine, and still another when the object is neuter. Now there are more adjectives in this language than there are black cats in Switzerland, and they must all be as elaborately declined as the examples above suggested. Difficult?—troublesome?—these words cannot describe it. I heard a Californian student in Heidelberg say, in one of his calmest moods, that he would rather decline two drinks than one German adjective.

The inventor of the language seems to have taken pleasure in complicating it in every way he could think of. For instance, if one is casually referring to a house, *Haus,* or a horse, *Pferd,* or a dog, *Hund,* he spells these words as I have indicated; but if he is referring to them in the Dative case, he sticks on a foolish and unnecessary *e* and spells them *Hause, Pferde, Hunde.* So, as an added *e* often signifies the plural, as the *s* does with us, the new student is likely to go on for a month making twins out of a Dative dog before he discovers his mistake; and on the other hand, many a new student who could ill afford loss, has bought and paid for two dogs and only got one of them, because he ignorantly bought that dog in the Dative singular when he really supposed he was talking plural—which left the law on the seller's side, of course, by the strict rules of grammar, and therefore a suit for recovery could not lie.

In German, all the Nouns begin with a capital letter. Now that is a good idea; and a good idea, in this language, is necessarily conspicuous from its lonesomeness. I consider this capitalizing of nouns a good idea, because by reason of it you are almost always able to tell a noun the minute you see it. You fall into error occasionally, because you mistake the name of a person for the name of a thing, and waste a good deal of time trying to dig a meaning out of it. German names almost always do mean something, and this helps to deceive the student. I translated a passage one day, which said that "the infuriated tigress broke loose and utterly ate up the unfortunate fir forest" *(Tannenwald).* When I was girding up my loins to doubt this, I found out that Tannenwald in this instance was a man's name.

Every noun has a gender, and there is no sense or system in the distribution; so the gender of each must be learned separately and by heart. There is no other way. To do this one has to have a memory like a memorandum-book. In German, a young lady has no sex, while a turnip has. Think what overwrought reverence that shows for the turnip, and what callous disrespect for the girl. See how it looks in print—I translate this from a conversation in one of the best of the German Sunday-school books:

"*Gretchen.*—Wilhelm, where is the turnip?

"*Wilhelm.*—She has gone to the kitchen.

"*Gretchen.*—Where is the accomplished and beautiful English maiden?

"*Wilhelm.*—It has gone to the opera."

To continue with the German genders: a tree is male, its buds are female, its leaves are neuter; horses are sexless, dogs are male, cats are female—tomcats included, of course; a person's mouth, neck, bosom, elbows, fingers, nails, feet, and body are of the male sex, and his head is male or neuter according to the word selected to signify it, and *not* according to the sex of the individual who wears it—for in Germany all the women wear either male heads or sexless ones; a person's nose, lips, shoulders, breast, hands, and toes are of the female sex; and his hair, ears, eyes, chin, legs, knees, heart, and conscience haven't any sex at all. The inventor of the language probably got what he knew about a conscience from hearsay.

Now, by the above dissection, the reader will see that in Germany a man may *think* he is a man, but when he comes to look into the matter closely, he is bound to have his doubts; he finds that in sober truth he is a most ridiculous mixture; and if he ends by trying to comfort himself with the thought that he can at least depend on a third of this mess as being manly and masculine, the humiliating second thought will quickly remind him that in this respect he is no better off than any woman or cow in the land.

In the German it is true that by some oversight of the inventor of the language, a Woman is a female; but a Wife *(Weib)* is not—which is unfortunate. A Wife, here, has no sex; she is neuter; so, according to the grammar, a fish is *he,* his scales are *she,* but a fishwife is neither. To describe a wife as sexless may be called under-description; that is bad enough, but over-description is surely worse. A German speaks of an Englishman as the *Engländer;* to change the sex, he adds *inn,* and that stands for Englishwoman—*Engländerinn.* That seems descriptive enough, but still it is not exact enough for a German; so he precedes the word with that article which indicates that the creature to follow is feminine, and writes it down thus: "*die* Engländer*inn,* "—which means "the *she-Englishwoman.*" I consider that that person is over-described.

Well, after the student has learned the sex of a great number of nouns, he is still in a difficulty, because he finds it impossible to persuade his tongue to refer to things as *"he"* and *"she,"* and *"him"* and *"her,"* which it has been always accustomed to refer to as *"it."* When he even frames a German sentence in his mind, with the hims and hers in the right places, and then works up his courage to the utterance-point, it is no use—the moment he begins to speak his tongue flies the track and all those labored males and females come out as *"its."* And even when he is reading German to himself, he always calls those things *"it,"* whereas he ought to read in this way:

Tale of the Fishwife and its sad Fate*

It is a bleak Day. Hear the Rain, how he pours, and the Hail, how he rattles; and see the Snow, how he drifts along, and oh the Mud, how deep he is! Ah the poor Fishwife, it is stuck fast in the Mire; it has dropped its Basket of Fishes; and its Hands have been cut by the Scales as it seized some of the falling Creatures; and one Scale has even got into its Eye, and it cannot get her out. It opens its Mouth to cry for Help; but if any Sound comes out of him, alas he is drowned by the raging of the Storm. And now a Tomcat has got one of the Fishes and she will surely escape with him. No, she bites off a Fin, she holds her in her Mouth—will she swallow her? No, the Fishwife's brave Mother-dog deserts his Puppies and rescues the Fin—which he eats, himself, as his Reward. O, horror, the Lightning has struck the Fish-basket; he sets him on Fire; see the Flame, how she licks the doomed Utensil with her red and angry Tongue; now she attacks the helpless Fishwife's Foot—she burns him up, all but the big Toe, and even *she* is partly consumed; and still she spreads, still she waves her fiery Tongues; she attacks the Fishwife's Leg and destroys *it;* she attacks its Hand and destroys *her;* she attacks its poor worn Garment and destroys *her* also; she attacks its Body and consumes *him;* she wreathes herself about its Heart and *it* is consumed; next about its Breast, and in a Moment *she* is a Cinder; now she reaches its Neck—*he* goes; now its Chin—*it* goes; now its Nose—*she* goes. In another Moment, except Help come, the Fishwife will be no more. Time presses—is there none to succor and save? Yes! Joy, joy, with flying Feet the she-English-woman comes! But alas, the generous she-Female is too late: where now is the fated Fishwife? It has ceased from its Sufferings, it has gone

* I capitalize the nouns, in the German (and ancient English) fashion.

to a better Land; all that is left of it for its loved Ones to lament over, is this poor smoldering Ash-heap. Ah, woeful, woeful Ash-heap! Let us take him up tenderly, reverently, upon the lowly Shovel, and bear him to his long Rest, with the Prayer that when he rises again it will be in a Realm where he will have one good square responsible Sex, and have it all to himself, instead of having a mangy lot of assorted Sexes scattered all over him in Spots.

There, now, the reader can see for himself that this pronoun business is a very awkward thing for the unaccustomed tongue.

I suppose that in all languages the similarities of look and sound between words which have no similarity in meaning are a fruitful source of perplexity to the foreigner. It is so in our tongue, and it is notably the case in the German. Now there is that troublesome word *vermählt:* to me it has so close a resemblance—either real or fancied— to three or four other words, that I never know whether it means despised, painted, suspected, or married; until I look in the dictionary, and then I find it means the latter. There are lots of such words and they are a great torment. To increase the difficulty there are words which *seem* to resemble each other, and yet do not; but they make just as much trouble as if they did. For instance, there is the word *vermiethen* (to let, to lease, to hire); and the word *verheirathen* (another way of saying to *marry*). I heard of an Englishman who knocked at a man's door in Heidelberg and proposed, in the best German he could command, to *"verheirathen"* that house. Then there are some words which mean one thing when you emphasize the first syllable, but mean something very different if you throw the emphasis on the last syllable. For instance, there is a word which means a runaway, or the act of glancing through a book, according to the placing of the emphasis; and another word which signifies to *associate* with a man, or to *avoid* him, according to where you put the emphasis—and you can generally depend on putting it in the wrong place and getting into trouble.

There are some exceedingly useful words in this language. *Schlag,* for example; and *Zug.* There are three-quarters of a column of *Schlags* in the dictionary, and a column and a half of *Zugs.* The word *Schlag* means Blow, Stroke, Dash, Hit, Shock, Clap, Slap, Time, Bar, Coin, Stamp, Kind, Sort, Manner, Way, Apoplexy, Wood-cutting, Inclosure, Field, Forest-clearing. This is its simple and *exact* meaning—that is to say, its restricted, its fettered meaning; but there are ways by which you can set it free, so that it can soar away, as on the wings of the morning, and never be at rest. You can hang any word you please to its tail, and make it mean anything you want to. You can begin with *Schlag-ader,* which means artery, and you can hang on the whole dictionary, word by word, clear through the alphabet to *Schlag-wasser,* which means bilge-water—and including *Schlag-mutter,* which means mother-in-law.

Just the same with *Zug.* Strictly speaking, *Zug* means Pull, Tug, Draught, Procession, March, Progress, Flight, Direction, Expedition, Train, Caravan, Passage, Stroke, Touch, Line, Flourish, Trait of Character, Feature, Lineament, Chess-move, Organ-stop, Team, Whiff, Bias, Drawer, Propensity, Inhalation, Disposition: but that thing which it does *not* mean—when all its legitimate pennants have been hung on, has not been discovered yet.

One cannot overestimate the usefulness of *Schlag* and *Zug.* Armed just with these two, and the word *Also,* what cannot the foreigner on German soil accomplish? The German word *Also* is the equivalent of the English phrase "You know," and does not mean anything at all—in *talk,* though it sometimes does in print. Every time a German opens his mouth an *Also* falls out; and every time he shuts it he bites one in two that was trying to *get* out.

Now, the foreigner, equipped with these three noble words, is master of the situation. Let him talk right along, fearlessly; let him pour his indifferent German forth, and when he lacks for a word, let him heave a *Schlag* into the vacuum; all the chances are that it fits it like a plug, but if it doesn't let him promptly heave a *Zug* after it; the two together can hardly fail to bung the hole; but if, by a miracle, they *should* fail, let him simply say *Also!* and this will give him a moment's chance to think of the needful word. In Germany, when you load your conversational gun it is always best to throw in a *Schlag* or two and a *Zug* or two, because it doesn't make any difference how much the rest of the charge may scatter, you are bound to bag something with *them.* Then you blandly say *Also,* and load up again. Nothing gives such an air of grace and elegance and unconstraint to a German or an English conversation as to scatter it full of "Also's" or "You-knows."

In my note-book I find this entry:

July 1.—In the hospital yesterday, a word of thirteen syllables was successfully removed from a patient—a North German from near

Hamburg; but as most unfortunately the surgeons had opened him in the wrong place, under the impression that he contained a panorama, he died. The sad event has cast a gloom over the whole community.

That paragraph furnishes a text for a few remarks about one of the most curious and notable features of my subject—the length of German words. Some German words are so long that they have a perspective. Observe these examples:

Freundschaftsbezeigungen.

Dilettantenaufdringlichkeiten.

Stadtverordnetenversammlungen.

These things are not words, they are alphabetical processions. And they are not rare; one can open a German newspaper any time and see them marching majestically across the page—and if he has any imagination he can see the banners and hear the music, too. They impart a martial thrill to the meekest subject. I take a great interest in these curiosities. Whenever I come across a good one, I stuff it and put it in my museum. In this way I have made quite a valuable collection. When I get duplicates, I exchange with other collectors, and thus increase the variety of my stock. Here are some specimens which I lately bought at an auction sale of the effects of a bankrupt bric-à-brac hunter:

Generalstaatsverordnetenversammlungen.

Alterthumswissenschaften.

Kinderbewahrungsanstalten.

Unabhaengigkeitserklaerungen.

Wiedererstellungsbestrebungen.

Waffenstillstandsunterhandlungen.

Of course when one of these grand mountain ranges goes stretching across the printed page, it adorns and ennobles that literary landscape —but at the same time it is a great distress to the new student, for it blocks up his way; he cannot crawl under it, or climb over it, or tunnel through it. So he resorts to the dictionary for help, but there is no help there. The dictionary must draw the line somewhere—so it leaves this sort of words out. And it is right, because these long things are hardly legitimate words, but are rather combinations of words, and the inventor of them ought to have been killed. They are compound words with the hyphens left out. The various words used in building them are in the dictionary, but in a very scattered condition; so you can hunt the materials out, one by one, and get at the meaning at last, but it is a tedious and harassing business. I have tried this process upon some of the above examples. *"Freundschaftsbezeigungen"* seems to be "Friendship demonstrations," which is only a foolish and clumsy way of saying "demonstrations of friendship." *"Unabhaengigkeitserklaerungen"* seems to be "Independencedeclarations," which is no improvement upon "Declarations of Independence," so far as I can see. *"General-staatsverordnetenversammlungen"* seems to be "Generalstates-representativesmeetings," as nearly as I can get at it—a mere rhythmical, gushy euphuism for "meetings of the legislature," I judge. We used to have a good deal of this sort of crime in our literature, but it has gone out now. We used to speak of a thing as a "never-to-be-forgotten" circumstance, instead of cramping it into the simple and sufficient word "memorable" and then going calmly about our business as if nothing had happened. In those days we were not content to embalm the thing and bury it decently, we wanted to build a monument over it.

But in our newspapers the compounding-disease lingers a little to the present day, but with the hyphens left out, in the German fashion. This is the shape it takes: instead of saying "Mr. Simmons, clerk of the county and district courts, was in town yesterday," the new form puts it thus: "Clerk of the County and District Courts Simmons was in town yesterday." This saves neither time nor ink, and has an awkward sound besides. One often sees a remark like this in our papers: *"Mrs.* Assistant District Attorney Johnson returned to her city residence yesterday for the season." That is a case of really unjustifiable compounding; because it not only saves no time or trouble, but confers a title on Mrs. Johnson which she has no right to. But these little instances are trifles indeed, contrasted with the ponderous and dismal German system of piling jumbled compounds together. I wish to submit the following local item, from a Mannheim journal, by way of illustration:

"In the daybeforeyesterdayshortlyaftereleveno'clock Night, the inthistownstandingtavern called 'The Wagoner' was downburnt. When the fire to the onthedownburninghouseresting Stork's Nest reached, flew the parent Storks away. But when the bytheraging, firesurrounded Nest *itself* caught Fire, straightway plunged the quickreturning Mother-stork into the Flames and died, her wings over her young ones outspread."

Even the cumbersome German construction is not able to take the pathos out of that picture—indeed, it somehow seems to strengthen it. This item is dated away back yonder months ago. I could have used it sooner, but I was waiting to hear from the Father-stork. I am still waiting.

"Also!" If I have not shown that the German is a difficult language, I have at least intended to do it. I have heard of an American student who was asked how he was getting along with his German, and who answered promptly: "I am not getting along at all. I have worked at it hard for three level months, and all I have got to show for it is one solitary German phrase—*'Zwei glas'* " (two glasses of beer). He paused a moment, reflectively; then added with feeling: "But I've got that *solid!*"

And if I have not also shown that German is a harassing and infuriating study, my execution has been at fault, and not my intent. I heard lately of a worn and sorely tried American student who used to fly to a certain German word for relief when he could bear up under his aggravations no longer—the only word in the whole language whose sound was sweet and precious to his ear and healing to his lacerated spirit. This was the word *Damit*. It was only the *sound* that helped him, not the meaning;* and so, at last, when he learned that the emphasis was not on the first syllable, his only stay and support was gone, and he faded away and died.

I think that a description of any loud, stirring, tumultuous episode must be tamer in German than in English. Our descriptive words of this character have such a deep, strong, resonant sound, while their German equivalents do seem so thin and mild and energyless. Boom, burst, crash, roar, storm, bellow, blow, thunder, explosion; howl, cry, shout, yell, groan; battle, hell. These are magnificent words; they have a force and magnitude of sound befitting the things which they describe. But their German equivalents would be ever so nice to sing the children to sleep with, or else my awe-inspiring ears were made for display and not for superior usefulness in analyzing sounds. Would any man want to die in a battle which was called by so tame a term as a *Schlacht?* Or would not a consumptive feel too much bundled up, who was about to go out, in a shirt-collar and a seal-ring, into a storm which the bird-song word *Gewitter* was employed to describe? And observe the strongest of the several German equivalents for explosion

---

* It merely means, in its general sense, *"herewith."*

—*Ausbruch*. Our word Toothbrush is more powerful than that. It seems to me that the Germans could do worse than import it into their language to describe particularly tremendous explosions with. The German word for hell—Hölle—sounds more like *helly* than anything else; therefore, how necessarily chipper, frivolous, and unimpressive it is. If a man were told in German to go there, could he really rise to the dignity of feeling insulted?

Having pointed out, in detail, the several vices of this language, I now come to the brief and pleasant task of pointing out its virtues. The capitalizing of the nouns I have already mentioned. But far before this virtue stands another—that of spelling a word according to the sound of it. After one short lesson in the alphabet, the student can tell how any German word is pronounced without having to ask; whereas in our language if a student should inquire of us. "What does B, O, W, spell?" we should be obliged to reply, "Nobody can tell what it spells when you set it off by itself; you can only tell by referring to the context and finding out what it signifies—whether it is a thing to shoot arrows with, or a nod of one's head, or the forward end of a boat."

There are some German words which are singularly and powerfully effective. For instance, those which describe lowly, peaceful, and affectionate home life; those which deal with love, in any and all forms, from mere kindly feeling and honest good will toward the passing stranger, clear up to courtship; those which deal with outdoor Nature, in its softest and loveliest aspects—with meadows and forests, and birds and flowers, the fragrance and sunshine of summer, and the moonlight of peaceful winter nights; in a word, those which deal with any and all forms of rest, repose, and peace; those also which deal with the creatures and marvels of fairyland; and lastly and chiefly, in those words which express pathos, is the language surpassingly rich and effective. There are German songs which can make a stranger to the language cry. That shows that the *sound* of the words is correct—it interprets the meanings with truth and with exactness; and so the ear is informed, and through the ear, the heart.

The Germans do not seem to be afraid to repeat a word when it is the right one. They repeat it several times, if they choose. That is wise. But in English, when we have used a word a couple of times in a paragraph, we imagine we are growing tautological, and so we are weak enough to exchange it for some other word which only approximates exactness, to escape what we wrongly fancy is a greater blemish. Repetition may be bad, but surely inexactness is worse.

There are people in the world who will take a great deal of trouble to point out the faults in a religion or a language, and then go blandly about their business without suggesting any remedy. I am not that kind of a person. I have shown that the German language needs reforming. Very well, I am ready to reform it. At least I am ready to make the proper suggestions. Such a course as this might be immodest in another; but I have devoted upward of nine full weeks, first and last, to a careful and critical study of this tongue, and thus have acquired a confidence in my ability to reform it which no mere superficial culture could have conferred upon me.

In the first place, I would leave out the Dative case. It confuses the plurals; and, besides, nobody ever knows when he is in the Dative case, except he discover it by accident—and then he does not know when or where it was that he got into it, or how long he has been in it, or how he is ever going to get out of it again. The Dative case is but an ornamental folly—it is better to discard it.

In the next place, I would move the Verb further up to the front. You may load up with ever so good a Verb, but I notice that you never really bring down a subject with it at the present German range—you only cripple it. So I insist that this important part of speech should be brought forward to a position where it may be easily seen with the naked eye.

Thirdly, I would import some strong words from the English tongue—to swear with, and also to use in describing all sorts of vigorous things in a vigorous way.*

Fourthly, I would reorganize the sexes, and distribute them according to the will of the Creator. This as a tribute of respect, if nothing else.

---

* *"Verdammt,"* and its variations and enlargements, are words which have plenty of meaning, but the *sounds* are so mild and ineffectual that German ladies can use them without sin. German ladies who could not be induced to commit a sin by any persuasion or compulsion, promptly rip out one of these harmless little words when they tear their dresses or don't like the soup. It sounds about as wicked as our "My gracious." German ladies are constantly saying, *"Ach! Gott!" "Mein Gott!" "Gott in Himmel!" "Herr Gott!" "Der Herr Jesus!"* etc. They think our ladies have the same custom, perhaps; for I once heard a gentle and lovely old German lady say to a sweet young American girl: "The two languages are so alike—how pleasant that is; we say *'Ach! Gott!'* you say 'Goddam.' "

Fifthly, I would do away with those great long compounded words; or require the speaker to deliver them in sections, with intermissions for refreshments. To wholly do away with them would be best, for ideas are more easily received and digested when they come one at a time than when they come in bulk. Intellectual food is like any other; it is pleasanter and more beneficial to take it with a spoon than with a shovel.

Sixthly, I would require a speaker to stop when he is done, and not hang a string of those useless *"haben sind gewesen gehabt haben geworden seins"* to the end of his oration. This sort of gewgaws un-dignify a speech, instead of adding a grace. They are, therefore, an offense, and should be discarded.

Seventhly, I would discard the Parenthesis. Also the reparent. is, the re-reparenthesis, and the re-re-re-re-re-reparentheses, and likewise the final wide-reaching all-inclosing king-parenthesis. I would require every individual, be he high or low, to unfold a plain straightforward tale, or else coil it and sit on it and hold his peace. Infractions of this law should be punishable with death.

And eighthly, and last, I would retain *Zug* and *Schlag,* with their pendants, and discard the rest of the vocabulary. This would simplify the language.

I have now named what I regard as the most necessary and impor-tant changes. These are perhaps all I could be expected to name for nothing; but there are other suggestions which I can and will make in case my proposed application shall result in my being formally em-ployed by the government in the work of reforming the language.

My philological studies have satisfied me that a gifted person ought to learn English (barring spelling and pronouncing) in thirty hours, French in thirty days, and German in thirty years. It seems manifest, then, that the latter tongue ought to be trimmed down and repaired. If it is to remain as it is, it ought to be gently and reverently set aside among the dead languages, for only the dead have time to learn it.

A FOURTH OF JULY ORATION IN THE GERMAN TONGUE,

DELIVERED

AT A BANQUET OF THE ANGLO-AMERICAN CLUB OF STUDENTS

BY THE AUTHOR OF THIS BOOK

GENTLEMEN: Since I arrived, a month ago, in this old wonderland, this vast garden of Germany, my English tongue has so often proved a useless piece of baggage to me, and so troublesome to carry around, in a country where they haven't the checking system for luggage, that I finally set to work, last week, and learned the German language. Also! Es freut mich dass dies so ist, denn es muss, in ein hauptsächlich degree, höflich sein, dass man auf ein occasion like this, sein Rede in die Sprache des Landes worin he boards, aussprechen soll. Dafür habe ich, aus reinische Verlegenheit—no, Vergangenheit—no, I mean Höflichkeit—aus reinische Höflichkeit habe ich resolved to tackle this business in the German language, um Gottes willen! Also! Sie müssen sprechen freundlich sein, und verzeih mich die interlarding von ein oder zwei englischer Worte, hie und da, denn ich finde dass die deutsche is not a copious language, and so when you've really got anything to say, you've got to draw on a language that can stand the strain.

Wenn aber man kann nicht meinem Rede verstehen, so werde ich ihm später dasselbe übersetz, wenn er solche Dienst verlangen wollen haben werden sollen sein hätte. (I don't know what wollen haben werden sollen sein hätte means, but I notice they always put it at the end of a German sentence—merely for general literary gorgeousness, I suppose.)

This is a great and justly honored day—a day which is worthy of the veneration in which it is held by the true patriots of all climes and nationalities—a day which offers a fruitful theme for thought and speech; und meinem Freunde—no, meinen Freunden—meines Freundes—well, take your choice, they're all the same price; I don't know which one is right—also! ich habe gehabt haben worden gewesen sein, as Goethe says in his Paradise Lost—ich—ich—that is to say—ich—but let us change cars.

Also! Die Anblick so viele Grossbrittanischer und Amerikanischer hier zusammengetroffen in Bruderliche concord, ist zwar a welcome and inspiriting spectacle. And what has moved you to it? Can the terse German tongue rise to the expression of this impulse? Is it Freundschaftsbezeigungenstadtverordnetenversammlungenfamilien-eigenthümlichkeiten? Nein, o nein! This is a crisp and noble word, but it fails to pierce the marrow of the impulse which has gathered this friendly meeting and produced diese Anblick—eine Anblick welche ist gut zu sehen—gut für die Augen in a foreign land and a far country—eine Anblick solche als in die gewöhnliche Heidelberger phrase nennt man ein "schönes Aussicht!" Ja, freilich natürlich wahrscheinlich ebensowohl! Also! Die Aussicht auf dem Königsstuhl mehr grösserer ist, aber geistlische sprechend nicht so schön, lob' Gott! Because sie sind hier zusammengetroffen, in Bruderlichem concord, ein grossen Tag zu feiern, whose high benefits were not for one land and one locality only, but have conferred a measure of good upon all lands that know liberty to-day, and love it. Hundert Jahre vorüber, waren die Engländer und die Amerikaner Feinde; aber heute sind sie herzlichen Freunde, Gott sei Dank! May this good-fellowship endure; may these banners here blended in amity so remain; may they never any more wave over opposing hosts, or be stained with blood which was kindred, is kindred, and always will be kindred, until a line drawn upon a map shall be able to say: "*This* bars the ancestral blood from flowing in the veins of the descendant!"

1880

LIFE ON THE MISSISSIPPI

THE BOYS' AMBITION

When I was a boy, there was but one permanent ambition among my comrades in our village* on the west bank of the Mississippi River. That was, to be a steamboatman. We had transient ambitions of other sorts, but they were only transient. When a circus came and went, it left us all burning to become clowns; the first negro minstrel show that came to our section left us all suffering to try that kind of life; now and then we had a hope that if we lived and were good, God would permit us to be pirates. These ambitions faded out, each in its turn; but the ambition to be a streamboatman always remained.

Once a day a cheap, gaudy packet arrived upward from St. Louis, and another downward from Keokuk. Before these events, the day was glorious with expectancy; after them, the day was a dead and empty thing. Not only the boys, but the whole village, felt this. After

* Hannibal, Missouri.—M. T.

all these years I can picture that old time to myself now, just as it was
then: the white town drowsing in the sunshine of a summer's morning;
the streets empty, or pretty nearly so; one or two clerks sitting in front
of the Water Street stores, with their splint-bottomed chairs tilted back
against the wall, chins on breasts, hats slouched over their faces,
asleep—with shingle-shavings enough around to show what broke
them down; a sow and a litter of pigs loafing along the sidewalk, doing
a good business in watermelon rinds and seeds; two or three lonely
little freight piles scattered about the "levee;" a pile of "skids" on the
slope of the stone-paved wharf, and the fragrant town drunkard asleep
in the shadow of them; two or three wood flats at the head of the
wharf, but nobody to listen to the peaceful lapping of the wavelets
against them; the great Mississippi, the majestic, the magnificent Mississippi, rolling its mile-wide tide along, shining in the sun; the dense
forest away on the other side; the "point" above the town, and the
"point" below, bounding the river-glimpse and turning it into a sort of
sea, and withal a very still and brilliant and lonely one. Presently a
film of dark smoke appears above one of those remote "points;" instantly a negro drayman, famous for his quick eye and prodigious
voice, lifts up the cry "S-t-e-a-m-boat a-comin'!" and the scene
changes! The town drunkard stirs, the clerks wake up, a furious clatter
of drays follows, every house and store pours out a human contribution, and all in a twinkling the dead town is alive and moving. Drays,
carts, men, boys, all go hurrying from many quarters to a common
centre, the wharf. Assembled there, the people fasten their eyes upon
the coming boat as upon a wonder they are seeing for the first time.
And the boat *is* rather a handsome sight, too. She is long and sharp
and trim and pretty; she has two tall, fancy-topped chimneys, with a
gilded device of some kind swung between them; a fanciful pilot-
house, all glass and "gingerbread," perched on top of the "texas" deck
behind them; the paddle-boxes are gorgeous with a picture or with
gilded rays above the boat's name; the boiler deck, the hurricane deck,
and the texas deck are fenced and ornamented with clean white railings; there is a flag gallantly flying from the jack-staff; the furnace
doors are open and the fires glaring bravely; the upper decks are black
with passengers; the captain stands by the big bell, calm, imposing, the
envy of all; great volumes of the blackest smoke are rolling and tumbling out of the chimneys—a husbanded grandeur created with a bit of
pitch pine just before arriving at a town; the crew are grouped on the

forecastle; the broad stage is run far out over the port bow, and an
envied deck-hand stands picturesquely on the end of it with a coil of
rope in his hand; the pent steam is screaming through the gauge-
cocks; the captain lifts his hand, a bell rings, the wheels stop; then they
turn back, churning the water to foam, and the steamer is at rest.
Then such a scramble as there is to get aboard, and to get ashore, and
to take in freight and to discharge freight, all at one and the same
time; and such yelling and cursing as the mates facilitate it all with!
Ten minutes later the steamer is under way again, with no flag on the
jack-staff and no black smoke issuing from the chimneys. After ten
more minutes the town is dead again, and the town drunkard asleep
by the skids once more.

My father was a justice of the peace, and I supposed he possessed
the power of life and death over all men and could hang anybody that
offended him. This was distinction enough for me as a general thing;
but the desire to be a steamboatman kept intruding, nevertheless. I
first wanted to be a cabin-boy, so that I could come out with a white
apron on and shake a table-cloth over the side, where all my old
comrades could see me; later I thought I would rather be the deck-
hand who stood on the end of the stage-plank with the coil of rope in
his hand, because he was particularly conspicuous. But these were
only day-dreams,—they were too heavenly to be contemplated as real
possibilities. By and by one of our boys went away. He was not heard
of for a long time. At last he turned up as apprentice engineer or
"striker" on a steamboat. This thing shook the bottom out of all my
Sunday-school teachings. That boy had been notoriously worldly, and
I just the reverse; yet he was exalted to this eminence, and I left in
obscurity and misery. There was nothing generous about this fellow in
his greatness. He would always manage to have a rusty bolt to scrub
while his boat tarried at our town, and he would sit on the inside
guard and scrub it, where we could all see him and envy him and
loathe him. And whenever his boat was laid up he would come home
and swell around the town in his blackest and greasiest clothes, so that
nobody could help remembering that he was a steamboatman; and he
used all sorts of steamboat technicalities in his talk, as if he were so
used to them that he forgot common people could not understand
them. He would speak of the "labboard" side of a horse in an easy,
natural way that would make one wish he was dead. And he was
always talking about "St. Looy" like an old citizen; he would refer

casually to occasions when he "was coming down Fourth Street," or when he was "passing by the Planter's House," or when there was a fire and he took a turn on the brakes of "the old Big Missouri;" and then he would go on and lie about how many towns the size of ours were burned down there that day. Two or three of the boys had long been persons of consideration among us because they had been to St. Louis once and had a vague general knowledge of its wonders, but the day of their glory was over now. They lapsed into a humble silence, and learned to disappear when the ruthless "cub"-engineer approached. This fellow had money, too, and hair oil. Also an ignorant silver watch and a showy brass watch chain. He wore a leather belt and used no suspenders. If ever a youth was cordially admired and hated by his comrades, this one was. No girl could withstand his charms. He "cut out" every boy in the village. When his boat blew up at last, it diffused a tranquil contentment among us such as we had not known for months. But when he came home the next week, alive, renowned, and appeared in church all battered up and bandaged, a shining hero, stared at and wondered over by everybody, it seemed to us that the partiality of Providence for an undeserving reptile had reached a point where it was open to criticism.

This creature's career could produce but one result, and it speedily followed. Boy after boy managed to get on the river. The minister's son became an engineer. The doctor's and the post-master's sons became "mud clerks;" the wholesale liquor dealer's son became a bar-keeper on a boat; four sons of the chief merchant, and two sons of the county judge, became pilots. Pilot was the grandest position of all. The pilot, even in those days of trivial wages, had a princely salary—from a hundred and fifty to two hundred and fifty dollars a month, and no board to pay. Two months of his wages would pay a preacher's salary for a year. Now some of us were left disconsolate. We could not get on the river—at least our parents would not let us.

So by and by I ran away. I said I never would come home again till I was a pilot and could come in glory. But somehow I could not manage it. I went meekly aboard a few of the boats that lay packed together like sardines at the long St. Louis wharf, and very humbly inquired for the pilots, but got only a cold shoulder and short words from mates and clerks. I had to make the best of this sort of treatment for the time being, but I had comforting day-dreams of a future when

I should be a great and honored pilot, with plenty of money, and could kill some of these mates and clerks and pay for them.

Months afterward the hope within me struggled to a reluctant death, and I found myself without an ambition. But I was ashamed to go home. I was in Cincinnati, and I set to work to map out a new career. I had been reading about the recent exploration of the river Amazon by an expedition sent out by our government. It was said that the expedition, owing to difficulties, had not thoroughly explored a part of the country lying about the head-waters, some four thousand miles from the mouth of the river. It was only about fifteen hundred miles from Cincinnati to New Orleans, where I could doubtless get a ship. I had thirty dollars left; I would go and complete the exploration of the Amazon. This was all the thought I gave to the subject. I never was great in matters of detail. I packed my valise, and took passage on an ancient tub called the "Paul Jones," for New Orleans. For the sum of sixteen dollars I had the scarred and tarnished splendors of "her" main saloon principally to myself, for she was not a creature to attract the eye of wiser travellers.

When we presently got under way and went poking down the broad Ohio, I became a new being, and the subject of my own admiration. I was a traveller! A word never had tasted so good in my mouth before. I had an exultant sense of being bound for mysterious lands and distant climes which I never have felt in so uplifting a degree since. I was in such a glorified condition that all ignoble feelings departed out of me, and I was able to look down and pity the untravelled with a compassion that had hardly a trace of contempt in it. Still, when we stopped at villages and wood-yards, I could not help lolling carelessly upon the railings of the boiler deck to enjoy the envy of the country boys on the bank. If they did not seem to discover me, I presently sneezed to attract their attention, or moved to a position where they could not help seeing me. And as soon as I knew they saw me I gaped and stretched, and gave other signs of being mightily bored with travelling.

I kept my hat off all the time, and stayed where the wind and the sun could strike me, because I wanted to get the bronzed and weather-beaten look of an old traveller. Before the second day was half gone, I experienced a joy which filled me with the purest gratitude; for I saw that the skin had begun to blister and peel off my face and neck. I wished that the boys and girls at home could see me now.

We reached Louisville in time—at least the neighborhood of it. We stuck hard and fast on the rocks in the middle of the river, and lay there four days. I was now beginning to feel a strong sense of being a part of the boat's family, a sort of infant son to the captain and younger brother to the officers. There is no estimating the pride I took in this grandeur, or the affection that began to swell and grow in me for those people. I could not know how the lordly steamboatman scorns that sort of presumption in a mere landsman. I particularly longed to acquire the least trifle of notice from the big stormy mate, and I was on the alert for an opportunity to do him a service to that end. It came at last. The riotous powwow of setting a spar was going on down on the forecastle, and I went down there and stood around in the way—or mostly skipping out of it—till the mate suddenly roared a general order for somebody to bring him a capstan bar. I sprang to his side and said: "Tell me where it is—I'll fetch it!"

If a rag-picker had offered to do a diplomatic service for the Emperor of Russia, the monarch could not have been more astounded than the mate was. He even stopped swearing. He stood and stared down at me. It took him ten seconds to scrape his disjointed remains together again. Then he said impressively: "Well, if this don't beat hell!" and turned to his work with the air of a man who had been confronted with a problem too abstruse for solution.

I crept away, and courted solitude for the rest of the day. I did not go to dinner; I stayed away from supper until everybody else had finished. I did not feel so much like a member of the boat's family now as before. However, my spirits returned, in instalments, as we pursued our way down the river. I was sorry I hated the mate so, because it was not in (young) human nature not to admire him. He was huge and muscular, his face was bearded and whiskered all over; he had a red woman and a blue woman tattooed on his right arm,—one on each side of a blue anchor with a red rope to it; and in the matter of profanity he was sublime. When he was getting out cargo at a landing, I was always where I could see and hear. He felt all the majesty of his great position, and made the world feel it, too. When he gave even the simplest order, he discharged it like a blast of lightning, and sent a long, reverberating peal of profanity thundering after it. I could not help contrasting the way in which the average landsman would give an order, with the mate's way of doing it. If the landsman should wish the gang-plank moved a foot farther forward, he would probably say: "James, or William, one of you push that plank forward, please;" but put the mate in his place, and he would roar out: "Here, now, start that gang-plank for'ard! Lively, now! *What'*re you about! Snatch it! *snatch* it! There! there! Aft again! aft again! Don't you hear me? Dash it to dash! are you going to *sleep* over it! *'Vast* heaving. 'Vast heaving, I tell you! Going to heave it clear astern? WHERE're you going with that barrel! *for'ard* with it 'fore I make you swallow it, you dash-dash-dash-*dashed* split between a tired mud-turtle and a crippled hearse-horse!"

I wished I could talk like that.

When the soreness of my adventure with the mate had somewhat worn off, I began timidly to make up to the humblest official connected with the boat—the night watchman. He snubbed my advances at first, but I presently ventured to offer him a new chalk pipe, and that softened him. So he allowed me to sit with him by the big bell on the hurricane deck, and in time he melted into conversation. He could not well have helped it, I hung with such homage on his words and so plainly showed that I felt honored by his notice. He told me the names of dim capes and shadowy islands as we glided by them in the solemnity of the night, under the winking stars, and by and by got to talking about himself. He seemed over-sentimental for a man whose salary was six dollars a week—or rather he might have seemed so to an older person than I. But I drank in his words hungrily, and with a faith that might have moved mountains if it had been applied judiciously. What was it to me that he was soiled and seedy and fragrant with gin? What was it to me that his grammar was bad, his construction worse, and his profanity so void of art that it was an element of weakness rather than strength in his conversation? He was a wronged man, a man who had seen trouble, and that was enough for me. As he mellowed into his plaintive history his tears dripped upon the lantern in his lap, and I cried, too, from sympathy. He said he was the son of an English nobleman—either an earl or an alderman, he could not remember which, but believed was both; his father, the nobleman, loved him, but his mother hated him from the cradle; and so while he was still a little boy he was sent to "one of them old, ancient colleges"—he couldn't remember which; and by and by his father died and his mother seized the property and "shook" him, as he phrased it. After his mother shook him, members of the nobility with whom he was acquainted used their influence to get him the position of "loblolly-boy in a ship;" and from that point my watchman threw off all trammels of date and locality and branched out into a narrative that bristled all along with incredible adventures; a narrative that was so reeking with bloodshed and so crammed with hair-breadth escapes and the most engaging and unconscious personal villainies, that I sat speechless, enjoying, shuddering, wondering, worshipping.

It was a sore blight to find out afterwards that he was a low, vulgar, ignorant, sentimental, half-witted humbug, an untravelled native of the wilds of Illinois, who had absorbed wildcat literature and appropriated its marvels, until in time he had woven odds and ends of the mess into this yarn, and then gone on telling it to fledglings like me, until he had come to believe it himself.

1883

LIFE ON THE MISSISSIPPI

THE HOUSE BEAUTIFUL

We took passage in a Cincinnati boat for New Orleans; or on a Cincinnati boat—either is correct; the former is the eastern form of putting it, the latter the western.

Mr. Dickens declined to agree that the Mississippi steamboats were "magnificent," or that they were "floating palaces,"—terms which had always been applied to them; terms which did not over-express the admiration with which the people viewed them.

Mr. Dickens's position was unassailable, possibly; the people's position was certainly unassailable. If Mr. Dickens was comparing these boats with the crown jewels; or with the Taj, or with the Matterhorn; or with some other priceless or wonderful thing which he had seen, they were not magnificent—he was right. The people compared them with what *they* had seen; and, thus measured, thus judged, the boats were magnificent—the term was the correct one, it was not at all too

strong. The people were as right as was Mr. Dickens. The steamboats
were finer than anything on shore; compared with superior dwel-
linghouses and first class hotels in the Valley, they were indubitably
magnificent, they were "palaces." To a few people living in New Orleans and St. Louis, they were not magnificent, perhaps; not palaces;
but to the great majority of those populations, and to the entire populations spread over both banks between Baton Rouge and St. Louis,
they were palaces; they tallied with the citizen's dream of what magnificence was, and satisfied it.

Every town and village along that vast stretch of double river-
frontage had a best dwelling, finest dwelling, mansion,—the home of
its wealthiest and most conspicuous citizen. It is easy to describe it:
large grassy yard, with paling fence painted white—in fair repair;
brick walk from gate to door; big, square, two-story "frame" house,
painted white and porticoed like a Grecian temple—with this difference, that the imposing fluted columns and Corinthian capitals were a
pathetic sham, being made of white pine, and painted; iron knocker;
brass door knob—discolored, for lack of polishing. Within, an un-
carpeted hall, of planed boards; opening out of it, a parlor, fifteen feet
by fifteen—in some instances five or ten feet larger; ingrain carpet;
mahogany centre-table; lamp on it, with green-paper shade—standing
on a gridiron, so to speak, made of high-colored yarns, by the young
ladies of the house, and called a lamp-mat; several books, piled and
disposed, with cast-iron exactness, according to an inherited and un-
changeable plan; among them, Tupper, much pencilled; also, "Friendship's Offering," and "Affection's Wreath," with their sappy inanities
illustrated in die-away mezzotints; also, Ossian; "Alonzo and Me-
lissa;" maybe "Ivanhoe;" also "Album," full of original "poetry" of
the Thou-hast-wounded-the-spirit-that-loved-thee breed; two or three
goody-goody works—"Shepherd of Salisbury Plain," etc.; current
number of the chaste and innocuous Godey's "Lady's Book," with
painted fashion-plate of wax-figure women with mouths all alike—lips
and eyelids the same size—each five-foot woman with a two-inch
wedge sticking from under her dress and letting-on to be half of her
foot. Polished air-tight stove (new and deadly invention), with pipe
passing through a board which closes up the discarded good old fireplace. On each end of the wooden mantel, over the fireplace, a large
basket of peaches and other fruits, natural size, all done in plaster,
rudely, or in wax, and painted to resemble the originals—which they

don't. Over middle of mantel, engraving—Washington Crossing the
Delaware; on the wall by the door, copy of it done in thunder-and-
lightning crewels by one of the young ladies—work of art which
would have made Washington hesitate about crossing, if he could have
foreseen what advantage was going to be taken of it. Piano—kettle in
disguise—with music, bound and unbound, piled on it, and on a stand
near by: Battle of Prague; Bird Waltz; Arkansas Traveller; Rosin the
Bow; Marseilles Hymn; On a Lone Barren Isle (St. Helena); The Last
Link is Broken; She wore a Wreath of Roses the Night when last we
met; Go, forget me, Why should Sorrow o'er that Brow a Shadow
fling; Hours there were to Memory Dearer; Long, Long Ago; Days of
Absence; A Life on the Ocean Wave, a Home on the Rolling Deep;
Bird at Sea; and spread open on the rack, where the plaintive singer
has left it, *Ro*-holl on, silver *moo*-hoon, guide the *trav*-el-lerr his *way*,
etc. Tilted pensively against the piano, a guitar—guitar capable of
playing the Spanish Fandango by itself, if you give it a start. Frantic
work of art on the wall—pious motto, done on the premises, sometimes in colored yarns, sometimes in faded grasses: progenitor of the
"God Bless Our Home" of modern commerce. Framed in black
mouldings on the wall, other works of art, conceived and committed
on the premises, by the young ladies; being grim black-and-white cray-
ons; landscapes, mostly: lake, solitary sail-boat, petrified clouds, pre-
geological trees on shore, anthracite precipice; name of criminal conspicuous in the corner. Lithograph, Napoleon Crossing the Alps. Lithograph, The Grave at St. Helena. Steel-plates, Trumbull's Battle of
Bunker Hill, and the Sally from Gibraltar. Copper-plates, Moses Smit-
ing the Rock, and Return of the Prodigal Son. In big gilt frame, slan-
der of the family in oil: papa holding a book ("Constitution of the
United States"); guitar leaning against mamma, blue ribbons fluttering
from its neck; the young ladies, as children, in slippers and scalloped
pantelettes, one embracing toy horse, the other beguiling kitten with
ball of yarn, and both simpering up at mamma, who simpers back.
These persons all fresh, raw, and red—apparently skinned. Opposite,
in gilt frame, grandpa and grandma, at thirty and twenty-two, stiff,
old-fashioned, high-collared, puff-sleeved, glaring pallidly out from a
background of solid Egyptian night. Under a glass French clock dome,
large bouquet of stiff flowers done in corpsy white wax. Pyramidal
what-not in the corner, the shelves occupied chiefly with bric-a-brac of
the period, disposed with an eye to best effect: shell, with the Lord's

Prayer carved on it; another shell—of the long-oval sort, narrow, straight orifice, three inches long, running from end to end—portrait of Washington carved on it; not well done; the shell had Washington's mouth, originally—artist should have built to that. These two are memorials of the long-ago bridal trip to New Orleans and the French Market. Other bric-a-brac: Californian "specimens"—quartz, with gold wart adhering; old Guinea-gold locket, with circlet of ancestral hair in it; Indian arrow-heads, of flint; pair of bead moccasins, from uncle who crossed the Plains; three "alum" baskets of various colors —being skeleton-frame of wire, clothed-on with cubes of crystallized alum in the rock-candy style—works of art which were achieved by the young ladies; their doubles and duplicates to be found upon all what-nots in the land; convention of desiccated bugs and butterflies pinned to a card; painted toy-dog, seated upon bellows-attachment— drops its under jaw and squeaks when pressed upon; sugar-candy rabbit—limbs and features merged together, not strongly defined; pewter presidential-campaign medal; miniature card-board wood-saw-yer, to be attached to the stove-pipe and operated by the heat; small Napoleon, done in wax; spread-open daguerreotypes of dim children, parents, cousins, aunts, and friends, in all attitudes but customary ones; no templed portico at back, and manufactured landscape stretching away in the distance—that came in later, with the photograph; all these vague figures lavishly chained and ringed—metal indicated and secured from doubt by stripes and splashes of vivid gold bronze; all of them too much combed, too much fixed up; and all of them uncomfortable in inflexible Sunday-clothes of a pattern which the spectator cannot realize could ever have been in fashion; husband and wife generally grouped together—husband sitting, wife standing, with hand on his shoulder—and both preserving, all these fading years, some traceable effect of the daguerreotypist's brisk "Now smile, if you please!" Bracketed over what-not—place of special sacredness— an outrage in water-color, done by the young niece that came on a visit long ago, and died. Pity, too; for she might have repented of this in time. Horse-hair chairs, horse-hair sofa which keeps sliding from under you. Window shades, of oil stuff, with milk-maids and ruined castles stencilled on them in fierce colors. Lambrequins dependent from gaudy boxings of beaten tin, gilded. Bedrooms with rag carpets; bedsteads of the "corded" sort, with a sag in the middle, the cords needing tightening; snuffy feather-bed—not aired often enough; cane-seat chairs, splint-bottomed rocker; looking-glass on wall, school-slate size, veneered frame; inherited bureau; wash-bowl and pitcher, possibly—but not certainly; brass candlestick, tallow candle, snuffers. Nothing else in the room. Not a bathroom in the house; and no visitor likely to come along who has ever seen one.

That was the residence of the principal citizen, all the way from the suburbs of New Orleans to the edge of St. Louis. When he stepped aboard a big fine steamboat, he entered a new and marvellous world: chimney-tops cut to counterfeit a spraying crown of plumes—and maybe painted red; pilot-house, hurricane deck, boiler-deck guards, all garnished with white wooden filigree-work of fanciful patterns; gilt acorns topping the derricks; gilt deer-horns over the big bell; gaudy symbolical picture on the paddle-box, possibly; big roomy boiler-deck, painted blue, and furnished with Windsor arm-chairs; inside, a far receding snow-white "cabin;" porcelain knob and oil-picture on every state-room door; curving patterns of filigree-work touched up with gilding, stretching overhead all down the converging vista; big chandeliers every little way, each an April shower of glittering glass-drops; lovely rainbow-light falling everywhere from the colored glazing of the skylights; the whole a long-drawn, resplendent tunnel, a bewildering and soul-satisfying spectacle! in the ladies' cabin a pink and white Wilton carpet, as soft as mush, and glorified with a ravishing pattern of gigantic flowers. Then the Bridal Chamber—the animal that invented that idea was still alive and unhanged, at that day—Bridal Chamber whose pretentious flummery was necessarily overawing to the now tottering intellect of that hosannahing citizen. Every state-room had its couple of cosy clean bunks, and perhaps a looking-glass and a snug closet; and sometimes there was even a wash-bowl and pitcher, and part of a towel which could be told from mosquito netting by an expert—though generally these things were absent, and the shirt-sleeved passengers cleansed themselves at a long row of stationary bowls in the barber shop, where were also public towels, public combs, and public soap.

Take the steamboat which I have just described, and you have her in her highest and finest, and most pleasing, and comfortable, and satisfactory estate. Now cake her over with a layer of ancient and obdurate dirt, and you have the Cincinnati steamer awhile ago referred to. Not all over—only inside; for she was ably officered in all departments except the steward's.

But wash that boat and repaint her, and she would be about the counterpart of the most complimented boat of the old flush times: for the steamboat architecture of the West has undergone no change; neither has steamboat furniture and ornamentation undergone any.

1883

LIFE ON THE MISSISSIPPI

THE ART OF INHUMATION

About the same time I encountered a man in the street whom I had not seen for six or seven years; and something like this talk followed. I said:

"But you used to look sad and oldish; you don't now. Where did you get all this youth and bubbling cheerfulness? Give me the address."

He chuckled blithely, took off his shining tile, pointed to a notched pink circlet of paper pasted into its crown, with something lettered on it, and went on chuckling while I read, "J. B., UNDERTAKER." Then he clapped his hat on, gave it an irreverent tilt to leeward, and cried out:

"That's what's the matter! It used to be rough times with me when you knew me—insurance-agency business, you know; mighty irregular. Big fire, all right—brisk trade for ten days while people scared; after that, dull policy business till next fire. Town like this don't have fires often enough—a fellow strikes so many dull weeks in a row that he gets discouraged. But you bet you, *this* is the business! People don't wait for examples to *die*. No, sir, they drop off right along—there ain't any dull spots in the undertaker line. I just started in with two or three little old coffins and a hired hearse, and *now* look at the thing! I've worked up a business here that would satisfy any man, don't care who he is. Five years ago, lodged in an attic; live in a swell house now, with a mansard roof, and all the modern inconveniences."

"Does a coffin pay so well? Is there much profit on a coffin?"

"*Go*-way! How you talk!" Then, with a confidential wink, a dropping of the voice, and an impressive laying of his hand on my arm: "Look here; there's one thing in this world which isn't ever cheap. That's a coffin. There's one thing in this world which a person don't ever try to jew you down on. That's a coffin. There's one thing in this world which a person don't say—'I'll look around a little, and if I find I can't do better I'll come back and take it.' That's a coffin. There's one thing in this world which a person won't take in pine if he can go walnut; and won't take in walnut if he can go mahogany; and won't take in mahogany if he can go an iron casket with silver door-plate and bronze handles. That's a coffin. And there's one thing in this world which you don't have to worry around after a person to get him to pay for. And *that's* a coffin. Undertaking?—why it's the dead-surest business in Christendom, and the nobbiest.

"Why, just look at it. A rich man won't have anything but your very best; and you can just pile it on, too—pile it on and sock it to him—he won't ever holler. And you take in a poor man, and if you work him right he'll bust himself on a single lay-out. Or especially a woman. F'r instance: Mrs. O'Flaherty comes in—widow—wiping her eyes and kind of moaning. Unhandkerchiefs one eye, bats it around tearfully over the stock; says:

" 'And fhat might ye ask for that wan?'

" 'Thirty-nine dollars, madam,' says I.

" 'It's a foine big price, sure, but Pat shall be buried like a gintleman, as he was, if I have to work me fingers off for it. I'll have that wan, sor.'

" 'Yes, madam,' says I, 'and it is a very good one, too; not costly, to be sure, but in this life we must cut our garments to our cloth, as the saying is.' And as she starts out, I heave in, kind of casually, 'This one with the white satin lining is a beauty, but I am afraid—well, sixty-five dollars *is* a rather—rather—but no matter, I felt obliged to say to Mrs. O'Shaughnessy—'

" 'D'ye mane to soy that Bridget O'Shaughnessy bought the mate to that joo-ul box to ship that dhrunken divil to Purgatory in?'

" 'Yes, madam.'

" 'Then Pat shall go to heaven in the twin to it, if it takes the last rap the O'Flahertys can raise; and moind you, stick on some extras, too, and I'll give ye another dollar.'

"And as I lay in with the livery stables, of course I don't forget to mention that Mrs. O'Shaughnessy hired fifty-four dollars' worth of hacks and flung as much style into Dennis's funeral as if he had been a duke or an assassin. And of course she sails in and goes the O'Shaughnessy about four hacks and an omnibus better. That *used* to be, but that's all played now; that is, in this particular town. The Irish got to piling up hacks so, on their funerals, that a funeral left them ragged and hungry for two years afterward; so the priest pitched in and broke it all up. He don't allow them to have but two hacks now, and sometimes only one."

"Well," said I, "if you are so light-hearted and jolly in ordinary times, what *must* you be in an epidemic?"

He shook his head.

"No, you're off, there. We don't like to see an epidemic. An epidemic don't pay. Well, of course I don't mean that, exactly; but it don't pay in proportion to the regular thing. Don't it occur to you why?"

"No."

"Think."

"I can't imagine. What is it?"

"It's just two things."

"Well, what *are* they?"

"One's Embamming."

"And what's the other?"

"Ice."

"How is that?"

"Well, in ordinary times, a person dies, and we lay him up in ice; one day, two days, maybe three, to wait for friends to come. Takes a lot of it—melts fast. We charge jewelry rates for that ice, and war prices for attendance. Well, don't you know, when there's an epidemic, they rush 'em to the cemetery the minute the breath's out. No market for ice in an epidemic. Same with Embamming. You take a family that's able to embam, and you've got a soft thing. You can mention sixteen different ways to do it—though there *ain't* only one or two ways, when you come down to the bottom facts of it—and they'll take the highest-priced way, every time. It's human nature—human nature in grief. It don't reason, you see. Time being, it don't care a d——n. All it wants is physical immortality for deceased, and they're willing to pay for it. All you've got to do is to just be ca'm and stack it up—they'll stand the racket. Why, man, you can take a defunct that you couldn't *give* away; and get your embamming traps around you and go to work; and in a couple of hours he is worth a cool six hundred—that's what *he's* worth. There ain't anything equal to it but trading rats for diamonds in time of famine. Well, don't you see, when there's an epidemic, people don't wait to embam. No, indeed they don't; and it hurts the business like hellth, as we say—hurts it like hell-th, *health*, see?—our little joke in the trade. Well, I must be going. Give me a call whenever you need any—I mean, when you're going by, some time."

In his joyful high spirits, he did the exaggerating himself, if any had been done. I have not enlarged on him.

With the above brief references to inhumation, let us leave the subject. As for me, I hope to be cremated. I made that remark to my pastor once, who said, with what he seemed to think was an impressive manner:

"I wouldn't worry about that, if I had your chances."

Much he knew about it—the family all so opposed to it.

1883

NOVELS

PAP

Well, three or four months run along, and it was well into the winter, now. I had been to school most all the time, and could spell, and read, and write just a little, and could say the multiplication table up to six times seven is thirty-five, and I don't reckon I could ever get any further than that if I was to live forever. I don't take no stock in mathematics, anyway.

At first I hated the school, but by-and-by I got so I could stand it. Whenever I got uncommon tired I played hookey, and the hiding I got next day done me good and cheered me up. So the longer I went to school the easier it got to be. I was getting sort of used to the widow's ways, too, and they warn't so raspy on me. Living in a house, and sleeping in a bed, pulled on me pretty tight, mostly, but before the cold weather I used to slide out and sleep in the woods, sometimes, and so that was a rest to me. I liked the old ways best, but I was getting so I liked the new ones, too, a little bit. The widow said I was coming along slow but sure, and doing very satisfactory. She said she warn't ashamed of me.

One morning I happened to turn over the salt-cellar at breakfast. I reached for some of it as quick as I could, to throw over my left shoulder and keep off the bad luck, but Miss Watson was in ahead of me, and crossed me off. She says, "Take your hands away, Huckleberry—what a mess you are always making." The widow put in a good word for me, but that warn't going to keep off the bad luck, I knowed that well enough. I started out, after breakfast, feeling worried and shaky, and wondering where it was going to fall on me, and what it was going to be. There is ways to keep off some kinds of bad luck, but this wasn't one of them kind; so I never tried to do anything, but just poked along low-spirited and on the watch-out.

I went down the front garden and clumb over the stile, where you

go through the high board fence. There was an inch of new snow on
the ground, and I seen somebody's tracks. They had come up from the
quarry and stood around the stile a while, and then went on around
the garden fence. It was funny they hadn't come in, after standing
around so. I couldn't make it out. It was very curious, somehow. I was
going to follow around, but I stooped down to look at the tracks first.
I didn't notice anything at first, but next I did. There was a cross in
the left boot-heel made with big nails, to keep off the devil.

I was up in a second and shinning down the hill. I looked over my
shoulder every now and then, but I didn't see nobody. I was at Judge
Thatcher's as quick as I could get there. He said:

"Why, my boy, you are all out of breath. Did you come for your
interest?"

"No sir," I says; "is there some for me?"

"Oh, yes, a half-yearly is in, last night. Over a hundred and fifty
dollars. Quite a fortune for you. You better let me invest it along with
your six thousand, because if you take it you'll spend it."

"No sir," I says, "I don't want to spend it. I don't want it at all—
nor the six thousand, nuther. I want you to take it; I want to give it to
you—the six thousand and all."

He looked surprised. He couldn't seem to make it out. He says:

"Why, what can you mean, my boy?"

I says, "Don't you ask me no questions about it, please. You'll take
it—won't you?"

He says:

"Well I'm puzzled. Is something the matter?"

"Please take it," says I, "and don't ask me nothing—then I won't
have to tell no lies."

He studied a while, and then he says:

"Oho-o. I think I see. You want to *sell* all your property to me—not
give it. That's the correct idea."

Then he wrote something on a paper and read it over, and says:

"There—you see it says 'for a consideration.' That means I have
bought it of you and paid you for it. Here's a dollar for you. Now, you
sign it."

So I signed it, and left.

Miss Watson's nigger, Jim, had a hair-ball as big as your fist, which
had been took out of the fourth stomach of an ox, and he used to do

magic with it. He said there was a spirit inside of it, and it knowed everything. So I went to him that night and told him pap was here again, for I found his tracks in the snow. What I wanted to know, was, what he was going to do, and was he going to stay? Jim got out his hair-ball, and said something over it, and then he held it up and dropped it on the floor. It fell pretty solid, and only rolled about an inch. Jim tried it again, and then another time, and it acted just the same. Jim got down on his knees and put his ear against it and listened. But it warn't no use; he said it wouldn't talk. He said sometimes it wouldn't talk without money. I told him I had an old slick counterfeit quarter that warn't no good because the brass showed through the silver a little, and it wouldn't pass nohow, even if the brass didn't show, because it was so slick it felt greasy, and so that would tell on it every time. (I reckoned I wouldn't say nothing about the dollar I got from the judge.) I said it was pretty bad money, but maybe the hair-ball would take it, because maybe it wouldn't know the difference. Jim smelt it, and bit it, and rubbed it, and said he would manage so the hair-ball would think it was good. He said he would split open a raw Irish potato and stick the quarter in between and keep it there all night, and next morning you couldn't see no brass, and it wouldn't feel greasy no more, and so anybody in town would take it in a minute, let alone a hair-ball. Well, I knowed a potato would do that, before, but I had forgot it.

Jim put the quarter under the hair-ball and got down and listened again. This time he said the hair-ball was all right. He said it would tell my whole fortune if I wanted it to. I says, go on. So the hair-ball talked to Jim, and Jim told it to me. He says:

"Yo' ole father doan' know, yit, what's he's a-gwyne to do. Sometimes he spec he'll go 'way, en den agin he spec he'll stay. De bes' way is to res' easy en let de ole man take his own way. Dey's two angels hoverin' roun' 'bout him. One uv 'em is white en shiny, en 'tother one is black. De white one gits him to go right, a little while, den de black one sail in en bust it all up. A body can't tell, yit, which one gwyne to fetch him at de las'. But you is all right. You gwyne to have considable trouble in yo' life, en considable joy. Sometimes you gwyne to git hurt, en sometimes you gwyne to git sick; but every time you's gwyne to git well agin. Dey's two gals flyin' 'bout you in yo' life. One uv 'em's light en 'tother one is dark. One is rich en 'tother is po'. You's gwyne to marry de po' one fust en de rich one by-en-by. You wants to keep 'way fum de water as much as you kin, en don't run no resk, 'kase it's down in de bills dat you's gwyne to git hung."

When I lit my candle and went up to my room that night, there set pap, his own self!

I had shut the door to. Then I turned around, and there he was. I used to be scared of him all the time, he tanned me so much. I reckoned I was scared now, too; but in a minute I see I was mistaken. That is, after the first jolt, as you may say, when my breath sort of hitched —he being so unexpected; but right away after, I see I warn't scared of him worth bothering about.

He was most fifty, and he looked it. His hair was long and tangled and greasy, and hung down, and you could see his eyes shining through like he was behind vines. It was all black, no gray; so was his long, mixed-up whiskers. There warn't no color in his face, where his face showed; it was white; not like another man's white, but a white to make a body sick, a white to make a body's flesh crawl—a tree-toad white, a fish-belly white. As for his clothes—just rags, that was all. He had one ankle resting on 'tother knee; the boot on that foot was busted, and two of his toes stuck through, and he worked them now and then. His hat was laying on the floor; an old black slouch with the top caved in, like a lid.

I stood a-looking at him; he set there a-looking at me, with his chair tilted back a little. I set the candle down. I noticed the window was up; so he had clumb in by the shed. He kept a-looking me all over. By-and-by he says:

"Starchy clothes—very. You think you're a good deal of a big-bug, *don't* you?"

"Maybe I am, maybe I ain't," I says.

"Don't you give me none o' your lip," says he. "You've put on considerble many frills since I been away. I'll take you down a peg before I get done with you. You're educated, too, they say; can read and write. You think you're better'n your father, now, don't you, because he can't? I'll take it out of you. Who told you you might meddle with such hifalut'n foolishness, hey?—who told you you could?"

"The widow. She told me."

"The widow, hey?—and who told the widow she could put in her shovel about a thing that ain't none of her business?"

"Nobody never told her."

"Well, I'll learn her how to meddle. And looky here—you drop that school, you hear? I'll learn people to bring up a boy to put on airs over his own father and let on to be better'n what *he* is. You lemme catch you fooling around that school again, you hear? Your mother couldn't read, and she couldn't write, nuther, before she died. None of the family couldn't, before *they* died. *I* can't; and here you're a-swelling yourself up like this. I ain't the man to stand it—you hear? Say—lemme hear you read."

I took up a book and begun something about General Washington and the wars. When I'd read about a half a minute, he fetched the book a whack with his hand and knocked it across the house. He says:

"It's so. You can do it. I had my doubts when you told me. Now looky here; you stop that putting on frills. I won't have it. I'll lay for you, my smarty; and if I catch you about that school I'll tan you good. First you know you'll get religion, too. I never see such a son."

He took up a little blue and yaller picture of some cows and a boy, and says:

"What's this?"

"It's something they give me for learning my lessons good."

He tore it up, and says—

"I'll give you something better—I'll give you a cowhide."

He set there a-mumbling and a-growling a minute, and then he says—

"*Ain't* you a sweet-scented dandy, though? A bed; and bedclothes; and a look'n-glass; and a piece of carpet on the floor—and your own father got to sleep with the hogs in the tanyard. I never see such a son. I bet I'll take some o' these frills out o' you before I'm done with you. Why there ain't no end to your airs—they say you're rich. Hey?—how's that?"

"They lie—that's how."

"Looky here—mind how you talk to me; I'm a-standing about all I can stand, now—so don't gimme no sass. I've been in town two days, and I hain't heard nothing but about you bein' rich. I heard about it away down the river, too. That's why I come. You git me that money to-morrow—I want it."

"I hain't got no money."

"It's a lie. Judge Thatcher's got it. You git it. I want it."

"I hain't got no money, I tell you. You ask Judge Thatcher; he'll tell you the same."

"All right. I'll ask him; and I'll make him pungle, too, or I'll know the reason why. Say—how much you got in your pocket? I want it."

"I hain't got only a dollar, and I want that to——"

"It don't make no difference what you want it for—you just shell it out."

He took it and bit it to see if it was good, and then he said he was going down town to get some whisky; said he hadn't had a drink all day. When he had got out on the shed, he put his head in again, and cussed me for putting on frills and trying to be better than him; and when I reckoned he was gone, he come back and put his head in again, and told me to mind about that school, because he was going to lay for me and lick me if I didn't drop that.

Next day he was drunk, and he went to Judge Thatcher's and bully-ragged him and tried to make him give up the money, but he couldn't, and then he swore he'd make the law force him.

The judge and the widow went to law to get the court to take me away from him and let one of them be my guardian; but it was a new judge that had just come, and he didn't know the old man; so he said courts mustn't interfere and separate families if they could help it; said he'd druther not take a child away from its father. So Judge Thatcher and the widow had to quit on the business.

That pleased the old man till he couldn't rest. He said he'd cowhide me till I was black and blue if I didn't raise some money for him. I borrowed three dollars from Judge Thatcher, and pap took it and got drunk and went a-blowing around and cussing and whooping and carrying on; and he kept it up all over town, with a tin pan, till most midnight; then they jailed him, and next day they had him before court, and jailed him again for a week. But he said *he* was satisfied; said he was boss of his son, and he'd make it warm for *him*.

When he got out the new judge said he was agoing to make a man of him. So he took him to his own house, and dressed him up clean and nice, and had him to breakfast and dinner and supper with the family, and was just old pie to him, so to speak. And after supper he talked to him about temperance and such things till the old man cried, and said he'd been a fool, and fooled away his life; but now he was agoing to turn over a new leaf and be a man nobody wouldn't be ashamed of, and he hoped the judge would help him and not look down on him.

The judge said he could hug him for them words; so *he* cried, and his wife she cried again; pap said he'd been a man that had always been misunderstood before, and the judge said he believed it. The old man said that what a man wanted that was down, was sympathy; and the judge said it was so; so they cried again. And when it was bedtime, the old man rose up and held out his hand, and says:

"Look at it gentlemen, and ladies all; take ahold of it; shake it. There's a hand that was the hand of a hog; but it ain't so no more; it's the hand of a man that's started in on a new life, and 'll die before he'll go back. You mark them words—don't forget I said them. It's a clean hand now; shake it—don't be afeard."

So they shook it, one after the other, all around, and cried. The judge's wife she kissed it. Then the old man he signed a pledge—made his mark. The judge said it was the holiest time on record, or something like that. Then they tucked the old man into a beautiful room, which was the spare room, and in the night sometime he got powerful thirsty and clumb out onto the porch-roof and slid down a stanchion and traded his new coat for a jug of forty-rod, and clumb back again and had a good old time; and towards daylight he crawled out again, drunk as a fiddler, and rolled off the porch and broke his left arm in two places and was most froze to death when somebody found him after sun-up. And when they come to look at that spare room, they had to take soundings before they could navigate it.

The judge he felt kind of sore. He said he reckoned a body could reform the ole man with a shot-gun, maybe, but he didn't know no other way.

1885

TRASH

We judged that three nights more would fetch us to Cairo, at the bottom of Illinois, where the Ohio River comes in, and that was what we was after. We would sell the raft and get on a steamboat and go way up the Ohio amongst the free States, and then be out of trouble.

Well, the second night a fog begun to come on, and we made for a tow-head to tie to, for it wouldn't do to try to run in fog; but when I paddled ahead in the canoe, with the line, to make fast, there warn't anything but little saplings to tie to. I passed the line around one of them right on the edge of the cut bank, but there was a stiff current, and the raft come booming down so lively she tore it out by the roots and away she went. I see the fog closing down, and it made me so sick and scared I couldn't budge for most a half a minute it seemed to me —and then there warn't no raft in sight; you couldn't see twenty yards. I jumped into the canoe and run back to the stern and grabbed the paddle and set her back a stroke. But she didn't come. I was in such a hurry I hadn't untied her. I got up and tried to untie her, but I was so excited my hands shook so I couldn't hardly do anything with them.

As soon as I got started I took out after the raft, hot and heavy, right down the tow-head. That was all right as far as it went, but the tow-head warn't sixty yards long, and the minute I flew by the foot of it I shot out into the solid white fog, and hadn't no more idea which way I was going than a dead man.

Thinks I, it won't do to paddle; first I know I'll run into the bank or a tow-head or something; I got to set still and float, and yet it's mighty fidgety business to have to hold your hands still at such a time. I whooped and listened. Away down there, somewheres, I hears a small whoop, and up comes my spirits. I went tearing after it, listening sharp to hear it again. The next time it come, I see I warn't heading for it but heading away to the right of it. And the next time, I was heading away to the left of it—and not gaining on it much, either, for I was flying around, this way and that and 'tother, but it was going straight ahead all the time.

I did wish the fool would think to beat a tin pan, and beat it all the time, but he never did, and it was the still places between the whoops that was making the trouble for me. Well, I fought along, and directly I hears the whoop *behind* me. I was tangled good, now. That was somebody else's whoop, or else I was turned around.

I throwed the paddle down. I heard the whoop again; it was behind me yet, but in a different place; it kept coming, and kept changing its place, and I kept answering, till by-and-by it was in front of me again and I knowed the current had swung the canoe's head down stream and I was all right, if that was Jim and not some other raftsman hollering. I couldn't tell nothing about voices in a fog, for nothing don't look natural nor sound natural in a fog.

The whooping went on, and in about a minute I come a booming down on a cut bank with smoky ghosts of big trees on it, and the current threw me off to the left and shot by, amongst a lot of snags that fairly roared, the current was tearing by them so swift.

In another second or two it was solid white and still again. I set perfectly still, then, listening to my heart thump, and I reckon I didn't draw a breath while it thumped a hundred.

I just give up, then. I knowed what the matter was. That cut bank was an island, and Jim had gone down 'tother side of it. It warn't no tow-head, that you could float by in ten minutes. It had the big timber of a regular island; it might be five or six mile long and more than a half a mile wide.

I kept quiet, with my ears cocked, about fifteen minutes, I reckon. I was floating along, of course, four or five mile an hour; but you don't ever think of that. No, you *feel* like you are laying dead still on the water; and if a little glimpse of a snag slips by, you don't think to yourself how fast *you're* going, but you catch your breath and think, my! how that snag's tearing along. If you think it ain't dismal and lonesome out in a fog that way, by yourself, in the night, you try it once—you'll see.

Next, for about a half an hour, I whoops now and then; at last I hears the answer a long ways off, and tries to follow it, but I couldn't do it, and directly I judged I'd got into a nest of tow-heads, for I had little dim glimpses of them on both sides of me, sometimes just a narrow channel between; and some that I couldn't see, I knowed was

there, because I'd hear the wash of the current against the old dead
brush and trash that hung over the banks. Well, I warn't long losing
the whoops, down amongst the tow-heads; and I only tried to chase
them a little while, anyway, because it was worse than chasing a Jack-
o-lantern. You never knowed a sound dodge around so, and swap
places so quick and so much.

I had to claw away from the bank pretty lively, four or fives times,
to keep from knocking the islands out of the river; and so I judged the
raft must be butting into the bank every now and then, or else it would
get further ahead and clear out of hearing—it was floating a little
faster than what I was.

Well, I seemed to be in the open river again, by-and-by, but I
couldn't hear no sign of a whoop nowheres. I reckoned Jim had
fetched up on a snag, maybe, and it was all up with him. I was good
and tired, so I laid down in the canoe and said I wouldn't bother no
more. I didn't want to go to sleep, of course; but I was so sleepy I
couldn't help it; so I thought I would take just one little cat-nap.

But I reckon it was more than a cat-nap, for when I waked up the
stars was shining bright, the fog was all gone, and I was spinning
down a big bend stern first. First I didn't know where I was; I thought
I was dreaming; and when things begun to come back to me, they
seemed to come up dim out of last week.

It was a monstrous big river here, with the tallest and the thickest
kind of timber on both banks; just a solid wall, as well as I could see,
by the stars. I looked away down stream, and seen a black speck on
the water. I took out after it; but when I got to it it warn't nothing but
a couple of saw-logs made fast together. Then I see another speck, and
chased that; then another, and this time I was right. It was the raft.

When I got to it Jim was setting there with his head down between
his knees, asleep, with his right arm hanging over the steering oar. The
other oar was smashed off, and the raft was littered up with leaves and
branches and dirt. So she'd had a rough time.

I made fast and laid down under Jim's nose on the raft, and begun
to gap, and stretch my fists out against Jim, and says:

"Hello, Jim, have I been asleep? Why didn't you stir me up?"

"Goodness gracious, is dat you, Huck? En you ain' dead—you ain'
drownded—you's back agin? It's too good for true, honey, it's too
good for true. Lemme look at you, chile, lemme feel o' you. No, you

ain' dead! you's back agin, 'live en soun', jis de same ole Huck—de same ole Huck, thanks to goodness!"

"What's the matter with you, Jim? You been a drinking?"

"Drinkin'? Has I ben a drinkin'? Has I had a chance to be a drinkin'?"

"Well, then, what makes you talk so wild?"

"How does I talk wild?"

"*How?* why, hain't you been talking about my coming back, and all that stuff, as if I'd been gone away?"

"Huck—Huck Finn, you look me in de eye; look me in de eye. *Hain't* you ben gone away?"

"Gone away? Why, what in the nation do you mean? *I* hain't been gone anywheres. Where would I go to?"

"Well, looky here, boss, dey's sumf'n wrong, dey is. Is I *me,* or who *is* I? Is I heah, or whah *is* I? Now dat's what I wants to know?"

"Well, I think you're here, plain enough, but I think you're a tangleheaded old fool, Jim."

"I is, is I? Well you answer me dis. Didn't you tote out de line in de canoe, fer to make fas' to de tow-head?"

"No, I didn't. What tow-head? I hain't seen no tow-head."

"You hain't seen no tow-head? Looky here—didn't de line pull loose en de raf' go a hummin' down de river, en leave you en de canoe behine in de fog?"

"What fog?"

"Why *de* fog. De fog dat's ben aroun' all night. En didn't you whoop, en didn't I whoop, tell we got mix' up in de islands en one un us got los' en 'tother one was jis' as good as los', 'kase he didn' know whah he wuz? En didn't I bust up agin a lot er dem islands en have a turrible time en mos' git drownded? Now ain' dat so, boss—ain't it so? You answer me dat."

"Well, this is too many for me, Jim. I hain't seen no fog, nor no islands, nor no troubles, nor nothing. I been setting here talking with you all night till you went to sleep about ten minutes ago, and I reckon I done the same. You couldn't a got drunk in that time, so of course you've been dreaming."

"Dad fetch it, how is I gwyne to dream all dat in ten minutes?"

"Well, hang it all, you did dream it, because there didn't any of it happen."

"But Huck, it's all jis' as plain to me as——"

"It don't make no difference how plain it is, there ain't nothing in it. I know, because I've been here all the time."

Jim didn't say nothing for about five minutes, but set there studying over it. Then he says:

"Well, den, I reck'n I did dream it, Huck; but dog my cats ef it ain't de powerfullest dream I ever see. En I hain't ever had no dream b'fo' dat's tired me like dis one."

"Oh, well, that's all right, because a dream does tire a body like everything, sometimes. But this one was a staving dream—tell me all about it, Jim."

So Jim went to work and told me the whole thing right through, just as it happened, only he painted it up considerable. Then he said he must start in and " 'terpret" it, because it was sent for a warning. He said the first tow-head stood for a man that would try to do us some good, but the current was another man that would get us away from him. The whoops was warnings that would come to us every now and then, and if we didn't try hard to make out to understand them they'd just take us into bad luck, 'stead of keeping us out of it. The lot of tow-heads was troubles we was going to get into with quarrelsome people and all kinds of mean folks, but if we minded our business and didn't talk back and aggravate them, we would pull through and get out of the fog and into the big clear river, which was the free States, and wouldn't have no more trouble.

It had clouded up pretty dark just after I got onto the raft, but it was clearing up again, now.

"Oh, well, that's all interpreted well enough, as far as it goes, Jim," I says; "but what does *these* things stand for?"

It was the leaves and rubbish on the raft, and the smashed oar. You could see them first-rate, now.

Jim looked at the trash, and then looked at me, and back at the trash again. He had got the dream fixed so strong in his head that he couldn't seem to shake it loose and get the facts back into its place again, right away. But when he did get the thing straightened around, he looked at me steady, without ever smiling, and says:

"What do dey stan' for? I's gwyne to tell you. When I got all wore out wid work, en wid de callin' for you, en went to sleep, my heart wuz mos' broke bekase you wuz los', en I didn' k'yer no mo' what become er me en de raf'. En when I wake up en fine you back agin', all safe en soun', de tears come en I could a got down on my knees en kiss' yo' foot I's so thankful. En all you wuz thinkin 'bout wuz how you could make a fool uv ole Jim wid a lie. Dat truck dah is *trash;* en trash is what people is dat puts dirt on de head er dey fren's en makes 'em ashamed."

Then he got up slow, and walked to the wigwam, and went in there, without saying anything but that. But that was enough. It made me feel so mean I could almost kissed *his* foot to get him to take it back.

It was fifteen minutes before I could work myself up to go and humble myself to a nigger—but I done it, and I warn't ever sorry for it afterwards, neither. I didn't do him no more mean tricks, and I wouldn't done that one if I'd a knowed it would make him feel that way.

1885

ADVENTURES OF HUCKLEBERRY FINN

KEELBOAT TALK AND MANNERS

This chapter was originally lifted from the work-in-progress which became *Adventures of Huckleberry Finn* and published in *Life on the Mississippi* (1883). Clemens didn't restore it to the novel. I did in my edition of the novel (1985).—C.N.

By way of illustrating keelboat talk and manners, and that now departed and hardly remembered raft life, I will throw in, in this place, a chapter from a book which I have been working at, by fits and starts, during the past five or six years, and may possibly finish in the course of five or six more. The book is a story which details some passages in the life of an ignorant village boy, Huck Finn, son of the town drunkard of my time out West, there. He has run away from his persecuting father, and from a persecuting good widow who wishes to make a nice, truth-telling, respectable boy of him; and with him a slave of the widow's has also escaped. They have found a fragment of a lumberraft (it is high water and dead summer-time), and are floating down the river by night, and hiding in the willows by day—bound for Cairo, whence the negro will seek freedom in the heart of the free states. But, in a fog, they pass Cairo without knowing it. By and by they begin to suspect the truth, and Huck Finn is persuaded to end the dismal suspense by swimming down to a huge raft which they have seen in the distance ahead of them, creeping aboard under cover of the darkness, and gathering the needed information by eavesdropping:

But you know a young person can't wait very well when he is impatient to find a thing out. We talked it over, and by and by Jim said it was such a black night, now, that it wouldn't be no risk to swim down to the big raft and crawl aboard and listen—they would talk about Cairo, because they would be calculating to go ashore there for a spree, maybe; or anyway they would send boats ashore to buy whisky or fresh meat or something. Jim had a wonderful level head, for a nigger: he could most always start a good plan when you wanted one.

I stood up and shook my rags off and jumped into the river, and struck out for the raft's light. By and by, when I got down nearly to her, I eased up and went slow and cautious. But everything was all right—nobody at the sweeps. So I swung down along the raft till I was most abreast the camp-fire in the middle, then I crawled aboard and inched along and got in among some bundles of shingles on the weather side of the fire. There was thirteen men there—they was the watch on deck of course. And a mighty rough-looking lot, too. They had a jug, and tin cups, and they kept the jug moving. One man was singing—roaring, you may say; and it wasn't a nice song—for a parlor, anyway. He roared through his nose, and strung out the last word of every line very long. When he was done they all fetched a kind of Injun war-whoop, and then another was sung. It begun:

> "There was a woman in our towdn,
>   In our towdn did dwed'l [dwell],
>   She loved her husband dear-i-lee,
>   But another man twyste as wed'l.
>
> "Singing too, riloo, riloo, riloo,
>   Ri-too, riloo, rilay- - - e,
>   She loved her husband dear-i-lee,
>   But another man twyste as wed'l."

And so on—fourteen verses. It was kind of poor, and when he was going to start on the next verse one of them said it was the tune the old cow died on; and another one said: "Oh, give us a rest!" And another one told him to take a walk. They made fun of him till he got mad and jumped up and begun to cuss the crowd, and said he could lam any thief in the lot.

They was all about to make a break for him, but the biggest man there jumped up and says:

"Set whar you are, gentlemen. Leave him to me; he's my meat."

Then he jumped up in the air three times, and cracked his heels together every time. He flung off a buckskin coat that was all hung with fringes, and says, "You lay thar tell the chawin-up's done"; and flung his hat down, which was all over ribbons, and says, "You lay thar tell his sufferin's is over."

Then he jumped up in the air and cracked his heels together again, and shouted out:

"Whoo-oop! I'm the old original iron-jawed, brass-mounted, copper-bellied corpse-maker from the wilds of Arkansaw! Look at me! I'm the man they call Sudden Death and General Desolation! Sired by a hurricane, dam'd by an earthquake, half-brother to the cholera, nearly related to the smallpox on the mother's side! Look at me! I take nineteen alligators and a bar'l of whisky for breakfast when I'm in robust health, and a bushel of rattlesnakes and a dead body when I'm ailing. I split the everlasting rocks with my glance, and I squench the thunder when I speak! Whoo-oop! Stand back and give me room according to my strength! Blood's my natural drink, and the wails of the dying is music to my ear. Cast your eye on me, gentlemen! and lay low and hold your breath, for I'm 'bout to turn myself loose!"

All the time he was getting this off, he was shaking his head and looking fierce, and kind of swelling around in a little circle, tucking up his wristbands, and now and then straightening up and beating his breast with his fist, saying, "Look at me, gentlemen!" When he got through, he jumped up and cracked his heels together three times, and let off a roaring "Whoo-oop! I'm the bloodiest son of a wildcat that lives!"

Then the man that had started the row tilted his old slouch hat down over his right eye; then he bent stooping forward, with his back sagged and his south end sticking out far, and his fists a-shoving out and drawing in in front of him, and so went around in a little circle

about three times, swelling himself up and breathing hard. Then he
straightened, and jumped up and cracked his heels together three
times before he lit again (that made them cheer), and he began to
shout like this:

"Whoo-oop! bow your neck and spread, for the kingdom of sorrow's a-coming! Hold me down to the earth, for I feel my powers a-
working! whoo-oop! I'm a child of sin, *don't* let me get a start! Smoked
glass, here, for all! Don't attempt to look at me with the naked eye,
gentlemen! When I'm playful I use the meridians of longitude and
parallels of latitude for a seine, and drag the Atlantic Ocean for
whales! I scratch my head with the lightning and purr myself to sleep
with the thunder! When I'm cold, I bile the Gulf of Mexico and bathe
in it; when I'm hot I fan myself with an equinoctial storm; when I'm
thirsty I reach up and suck a cloud dry like a sponge; when I range the
earth hungry, famine follows in my tracks! Whoo-oop! Bow your neck
and spread! I put my hand on the sun's face and make it night in the
earth; I bite a piece out of the moon and hurry the seasons; I shake
myself and crumble the mountains! Contemplate me through leather
—*don't* use the naked eye! I'm the man with a petrified heart and
biler-iron bowels! The massacre of isolated communities is the pastime
of my idle moments, the destruction of nationalities the serious business of my life! The boundless vastness of the great American desert is
my inclosed property, and I bury my dead on my own premises!" He
jumped up and cracked his heels together three times before he lit
(they cheered him again), and as he come down he shouted out:
"Whoo-oop! bow your neck and spread, for the Pet Child of Calamity's a-coming!"

Then the other one went to swelling around and blowing again—the
first one—the one they called Bob; next, the Child of Calamity
chipped in again, bigger than ever; then they both got at it at the same
time, swelling round and round each other and punching their fists
most into each other's faces, and whooping and jawing like Injuns;
then Bob called the Child names, and the Child called him names
back again; next, Bob called him a heap rougher names, and the Child
come back at him with the very worst kind of language; next, Bob
knocked the Child's hat off, and the Child picked it up and kicked
Bob's ribbony hat about six foot; Bob went and got it and said never
mind, this warn't going to be the last of this thing, because he was a
man that never forgot and never forgive, and so the Child better look

out, for there was a time a-coming, just as sure as he was a living man, that he would have to answer to him with the best blood in his body. The Child said no man was willinger than he for that time to come, and he would give Bob fair warning, *now,* never to cross his path again, for he could never rest till he had waded in his blood, for such was his nature, though he was sparing him now on account of his family, if he had one.

Both of them was edging away in different directions, growling and shaking their heads and going on about what they was going to do; but a little black-whiskered chap skipped up and says:

"Come back here, you couple of chicken-livered cowards, and I'll thrash the two of ye!"

And he done it, too. He snatched them, he jerked them this way and that, he booted them around, he knocked them sprawling faster than they could get up. Why, it warn't two minutes till they begged like dogs—and how the other lot did yell and laugh and clap their hands all the way through, and shout, "Sail in, Corpse-Maker!" "Hi! at him again, Child of Calamity!" "Bully for you, little Davy!" Well, it was a perfect pow-wow for a while. Bob and the Child had red noses and black eyes when they got through. Little Davy made them own up that they was sneaks and cowards and not fit to eat with a dog or drink with a nigger; then Bob and the Child shook hands with each other, very solemn, and said they had always respected each other and was willing to let bygones be bygones. So then they washed their faces in the river; and just then there was a loud order to stand by for a crossing, and some of them went forward to man the sweeps there, and the rest went aft to handle the after sweeps.

I lay still and waited for fifteen minutes, and had a smoke out of a pipe that one of them left in reach; then the crossing was finished, and they stumped back and had a drink around and went to talking and singing again. Next they got out an old fiddle, and one played, and another patted juba, and the rest turned themselves loose on a regular old-fashioned keelboat breakdown. They couldn't keep that up very long without getting winded, so by and by they settled around the jug again.

They sung "Jolly, Jolly Raftsman's the Life for Me," with a rousing chorus, and then they got to talking about differences betwixt hogs, and their different kind of habits; and next about women and their different ways; and next about the best ways to put out houses that

was afire; and next about what ought to be done with the Injuns; and
next about what a king had to do, and how much he got; and next
about how to make cats fight; and next about what to do when a man
has fits; and next about differences betwixt clear-water rivers and
muddy-water ones. The man they called Ed said the muddy Mississippi water was wholesomer to drink than the clear water of the Ohio;
he said if you let a pint of this yaller Mississippi water settle, you
would have about a half to three-quarters of an inch of mud in the
bottom, according to the stage of the river, and then it warn't no
better than Ohio water—what you wanted to do was to keep it stirred
up—and when the river was low, keep mud on hand to put in and
thicken the water up the way it ought to be.

The Child of Calamity said that was so; he said there was nutri-
tiousness in the mud, and a man that drunk Mississippi water could
grow corn in his stomach if he wanted to. He says:

"You look at the graveyards; that tells the tale. Trees won't grow
worth shucks in a Cincinnati graveyard, but in a Sent Louis graveyard
they grow upwards of eight hundred foot high. It's all on account of
the water the people drunk before they laid up. A Cincinnati corpse
don't richen a soil any."

And they talked about how Ohio water didn't like to mix with
Mississippi water. Ed said if you take the Mississippi on a rise when
the Ohio is low, you'll find a wide band of clear water all the way
down the east side of the Mississippi for a hundred mile or more, and
the minute you get out a quarter of a mile from shore and pass the
line, it is all thick and yaller the rest of the way across. Then they
talked about how to keep tobacco from getting moldy, and from that
they went into ghosts and told about a lot that other folks had seen;
but Ed says:

"Why don't you tell something that you've seen yourselves? Now
let me have a say. Five years ago I was on a raft as big as this, and
right along here it was a bright moonshiny night, and I was on watch
and boss of the stabboard oar forrard, and one of my pards was a man
named Dick Allbright, and he come along to where I was sitting,
forrard—gaping and stretching, he was—and stooped down on the
edge of the raft and washed his face in the river, and come and set
down by me and got out his pipe, and had just got it filled, when he
looks up and says:

" 'Why looky-here,' he says, 'ain't that Buck Miller's place, over yander in the bend?'

" 'Yes,' says I, 'it is—why?' He laid his pipe down and leaned his head on his hand, and says:

" 'I thought we'd be furder down.' I says:

" 'I thought it, too, when I went off watch'—we was standing six hours on and six off—'but the boys told me,' I says, 'that the raft didn't seem to hardly move, for the last hour,' says I, 'though she's a-slipping along all right now,' says I. He give a kind of a groan, and says:

" 'I've seed a raft act so before, along here,' he says, ' 'pears to me the current has most quit above the head of this bend durin' the last two years,' he says.

"Well, he raised up two or three times, and looked away off and around on the water. That started me at it, too. A body is always doing what he sees somebody else doing, though there mayn't be no sense in it. Pretty soon I see a black something floating on the water away off to stabboard and quartering behind us. I see he was looking at it, too. I says:

" 'What's that?' He says, sort of pettish:

" ' 'Tain't nothing but an old empty bar'l.'

" 'An empty bar'l!" says I, 'why,' says I, 'a spy-glass is a fool to *your* eyes. How can you tell it's an empty bar'l?' He says:

" 'I don't know; I reckon it ain't a bar'l, but I thought it might be,' says he.

" 'Yes,' I says, 'so it might be, and it might be anything else, too; a body can't tell nothing about it, such a distance as that,' I says.

"We hadn't nothing else to do, so we kept on watching it. By and by I says:

" 'Why, looky-here, Dick Allbright, that thing's a-gaining on us, I believe.'

"He never said nothing. The thing gained and gained, and I judged it must be a dog that was about tired out. Well, we swung down into the crossing, and the thing floated across the bright streak of the moonshine, and by George, it *was* a bar'l. Says I:

" 'Dick Allbright, what made you think that thing was a bar'l, when it was half a mile off?' says I. Says he:

" 'I don't know.' Says I:

" 'You tell me, Dick Allbright.' Says he:

" 'Well, I knowed it was a bar'l; I've seen it before; lots has seen it; they says it's a ha'nted bar'l.'

"I called the rest of the watch, and they come and stood there, and I told them what Dick said. It floated right along abreast, now, and didn't gain any more. It was about twenty foot off. Some was for having it aboard, but the rest didn't want to. Dick Allbright said rafts that had fooled with it had got bad luck by it. The captain of the watch said he didn't believe in it. He said he reckoned the bar'l gained on us because it was in a little better current than what we was. He said it would leave by and by.

"So then we went to talking about other things, and we had a song, and then a breakdown; and after that the captain of the watch called for another song; but it was clouding up now, and the bar'l stuck right thar in the same place, and the song didn't seem to have much warmup to it, somehow, and so they didn't finish it, and there warn't any cheers, but it sort of dropped flat, and nobody said anything for a minute. Then everybody tried to talk at once, and one chap got off a joke, but it warn't no use, they didn't laugh, and even the chap that made the joke didn't laugh at it, which ain't usual. We all just settled down glum, and watched the bar'l, and was oneasy and oncomfortable. Well, sir, it shut down black and still, and then the wind began to moan around, and next the lightning began to play and the thunder to grumble. And pretty soon there was a regular storm, and in the middle of it a man that was running aft stumbled and fell and sprained his ankle so that he had to lay up. This made the boys shake their heads. And every time the lightning come, there was that bar'l, with the blue lights winking around it. We was always on the lookout for it. But by and by, toward dawn, she was gone. When the day come we couldn't see her anywhere, and we warn't sorry, either.

"But next night about half past nine, when there was songs and high jinks going on, here she comes again, and took her old roost on the stabboard side. There warn't no more high jinks. Everybody got solemn; nobody talked; you couldn't get anybody to do anything but set around moody and look at the bar'l. It begun to cloud up again. When the watch changed, the off watch stayed up, 'stead of turning in. The storm ripped and roared around all night, and in the middle of it another man tripped and sprained his ankle, and had to knock off. The bar'l left toward day, and nobody see it go.

"Everybody was sober and down in the mouth all day. I don't mean the kind of sober that comes of leaving liquor alone—not that. They was quiet, but they all drunk more than usual—not together, but each man sidled off and took it private, by himself.

"After dark the off watch didn't turn in; nobody sung, nobody talked; the boys didn't scatter around, neither; they sort of huddled together, forrard; and for two hours they set there, perfectly still, looking steady in the one direction, and heaving a sigh once in a while. And then, here comes the bar'l again. She took up her old place. She stayed there all night; nobody turned in. The storm come on again, after midnight. It got awful dark; the rain poured down; hail, too; the thunder boomed and roared and bellowed; the wind blowed a hurricane; and the lightning spread over everything in big sheets of glare, and showed the whole raft as plain as day; and the river lashed up white as milk as far as you could see for miles, and there was that bar'l jiggering along, same as ever. The captain ordered the watch to man the after sweeps for a crossing, and nobody would go—no more sprained ankles for them, they said. They wouldn't even *walk* aft. Well, then, just then the sky split wide open, with a crash, and the lightning killed two men of the after watch, and crippled two more. Crippled them how, say you? Why, *sprained their ankles!*

"The bar'l left in the dark betwixt lightnings, toward dawn. Well, not a body eat a bite at breakfast that morning. After that the men loafed around, in twos and threes, and talked low together. But none of them herded with Dick Allbright. They all give him the cold shake. If he come around where any of the men was, they split up and sidled away. They wouldn't man the sweeps with him. The captain had all the skiffs hauled up on the raft, alongside of his wigwam, and wouldn't let the dead men be took ashore to be planted; he didn't believe a man that got ashore would come back; and he was right.

"After night come, you could see pretty plain that there was going to be trouble if that bar'l come again; there was such a muttering going on. A good many wanted to kill Dick Allbright, because he'd seen the bar'l on other trips, and that had an ugly look. Some wanted to put him ashore. Some said: 'Let's all go ashore in a pile, if the bar'l comes again.'

"This kind of whispers was still going on, the men being bunched together forrard watching for the bar'l, when lo and behold you! here she comes again. Down she comes, slow and steady, and settles into her old tracks. You could 'a' heard a pin drop. Then up comes the captain, and says:

" 'Boys, don't be a pack of children and fools; I don't want this bar'l to be dogging us all the way to Orleans, and *you* don't: Well, then, how's the best way to stop it? Burn it up—that's the way. I'm going to fetch it aboard,' he says. And before anybody could say a word, in he went.

"He swum to it, and as he come pushing it to the raft, the men spread to one side. But the old man got it aboard and busted in the head, and there was a baby in it! Yes, sir; a stark-naked baby. It was Dick Allbright's baby; he owned up and said so.

" 'Yes,' he says, a-leaning over it, 'yes, it is my own lamented darling, my poor lost Charles William Allbright deceased,' says he—for he could curl his tongue around the bulliest words in the language when he was a mind to, and lay them before you without a jint started anywheres. Yes, he said, he used to live up at the head of this bend, and one night he choked his child, which was crying, not intending to kill it—which was prob'ly a lie—and then he was scared, and buried it in a bar'l, before his wife got home, and off he went, and struck the northern trail and went to rafting; and this was the third year that the bar'l had chased him. He said the bad luck always begun light, and lasted till four men was killed, and then the bar'l didn't come any more after that. He said if the men would stand it one more night— and was a-going on like that—but the men had got enough. They started to get out a boat to take him ashore and lynch him, but he grabbed the little child all of a sudden and jumped overboard with it, hugged up to his breast and shedding tears, and we never see him again in this life, poor old suffering soul, nor Charles William neither."

"*Who* was shedding tears?" says Bob; "was it Allbright or the baby?"

"Why, Allbright, of course; didn't I tell you the baby was dead? Been dead three years—how could it cry?"

"Well, never mind how it could cry—how could it *keep* all that time?" says Davy. "You answer me that."

"I don't know how it done it," says Ed. "It done it, though—that's all I know about it."

"Say—what did they do with the bar'l?" says the Child of Calamity.

"Why, they hove it overboard, and it sunk like a chunk of lead."

"Edward, did the child look like it was choked?" says one.

"Did it have its hair parted?" says another.

"What was the brand on that bar'l, Eddy?" says a fellow they called Bill.

"Have you got the papers for them statistics, Edmund?" says Jimmy.

"Say, Edwin, was you one of the men that was killed by the lightning?" says Davy.

"Him? Oh, no! he was both of 'em," says Bob. Then they all hawhawed.

"Say, Edward, don't you reckon you'd better take a pill? You look bad—don't you feel pale?" says the Child of Calamity.

"Oh, come, now, Eddy," says Jimmy, "show up; you must 'a' kept part of that bar'l to prove the thing by. Show us the bung-hole—*do*—and we'll all believe you."

"Say, boys," says Bill, "less divide it up. Thar's thirteen of us. I can swaller a thirteenth of the yarn, if you can worry down the rest."

Ed got up mad and said they could all go to some place which he ripped out pretty savage, and then walked off aft, cussing to himself, and they yelling and jeering at him, and roaring and laughing so you could hear them a mile.

"Boys, we'll split a watermelon on that," says the Child of Calamity; and he came rummaging around in the dark amongst the shingle bundles where I was, and put his hand on me. I was warm and soft and naked; so he says "Ouch!" and jumped back.

"Fetch a lantern or a chunk of fire here, boys—there's a snake here as big as a cow!"

So they run there with a lantern, and crowded up and looked in on me.

"Come out of that, you beggar!" says one.

"Who are you?" says another.

"What are you after here? Speak up prompt, or overboard you go."

"Snake him out, boys. Snatch him out by the heels."

I began to beg, and crept out amongst them trembling. They looked me over, wondering, and the Child of Calamity says:

"A cussed thief! Lend a hand and less heave him overboard!"

"No," says Big Bob, "less get out the paint-pot and paint him a skyblue all over from head to heel, and *then* heave him over."

"Good! that's it. Go for the paint, Jimmy."

When the paint come, and Bob took the brush and was just going to begin, the others laughing and rubbing their hands, I begun to cry, and that sort of worked on Davy, and he says:

" 'Vast there. He's nothing but a cub. I'll paint the man that teches him!"

So I looked around on them, and some of them grumbled and growled, and Bob put down the paint, and the others didn't take it up.

"Come here to the fire, and less see what you're up to here," says Davy. "Now set down there and give an account of yourself. How long have you been aboard here?"

"Not over a quarter of a minute, sir," says I.

"How did you get dry so quick?"

"I don't know, sir. I'm always that way, mostly."

"Oh, you are, are you? What's your name?"

I warn't going to tell my name. I didn't know what to say, so I just says:

"Charles William Allbright, sir."

Then they roared—the whole crowd; and I was mighty glad I said that, because, maybe, laughing would get them in a better humor.

When they got done laughing, Davy says:

"It won't hardly do, Charles William. You couldn't have growed this much in five year, and you was a baby when you come out of the bar'l, you know, and dead at that. Come, now, tell a straight story, and nobody'll hurt you, if you ain't up to anything wrong. What *is* your name?"

"Aleck Hopkins, sir. Aleck James Hopkins."

"Well, Aleck, where did you come from, here?"

"From a trading-scow. She lays up the bend yonder. I was born on her. Pap has traded up and down here all his life; and he told me to swim off here, because when you went by he said he would like to get some of you to speak to a Mr. Jonas Turner, in Cairo, and tell him—"

"Oh, come!"

"Yes, sir, it's as true as the world. Pap he says—"

"Oh, your grandmother!"

They all laughed, and I tried again to talk, but they broke in on me and stopped me.

"Now, looky-here," says Davy; "you're scared, and so you talk wild. Honest, now, do you live in a scow, or is it a lie?"

"Yes, sir, in a trading-scow. She lays up at the head of the bend. But I warn't born in her. It's our first trip."

"Now you're talking! What did you come aboard here for? To steal?"

"No, sir, I didn't. It was only to get a ride on the raft. All boys does that."

"Well, I know that. But what did you hide for?"

"Sometimes they drive the boys off."

"So they do. They might steal. Looky-here; if we let you off this time, will you keep out of these kind of scrapes hereafter?"

" 'Deed I will, boss. You try me."

"All right, then. You ain't but little ways from shore. Overboard with you, and don't you make a fool of yourself another time this way. Blast it, boy, some raftsmen would rawhide you till you were black and blue!"

I didn't wait to kiss good-by, but went overboard and broke for shore. When Jim come along by and by, the big raft was away out of sight around the point. I swum out and got aboard, and was mighty glad to see home again.

ADVENTURES OF HUCKLEBERRY FINN

GOING THE WHOLE HOG

I went to the raft, and set down in the wigwam to think. But I couldn't come to nothing. I thought till I wore my head sore, but I couldn't see no way out of the trouble. After all this long journey, and after all we'd done for them scoundrels, here was it all come to nothing, everything all busted up and ruined, because they could have the heart to serve Jim such a trick as that, and make him a slave again all his life, and amongst strangers, too, for forty dirty dollars.

Once I said to myself it would be a thousand times better for Jim to be a slave at home where his family was, as long as he'd *got* to be a slave, and so I'd better write a letter to Tom Sawyer and tell him to tell

Miss Watson where he was. But I soon give up that notion, for two things: she'd be mad and disgusted at his rascality and ungratefulness for leaving her, and so she'd sell him straight down the river again; and if she didn't, everybody naturally despises an ungrateful nigger, and they'd make Jim feel it all the time, and so he'd feel ornery and disgraced. And then think of *me!* It would get all around, that Huck Finn helped a nigger to get his freedom; and if I was to ever see anybody from that town again, I'd be ready to get down and lick his boots for shame. That's just the way: a person does a low-down thing, and then he don't want to take no consequences of it. Thinks as long as he can hide it, it ain't no disgrace. That was my fix exactly. The more I studied about this, the more my conscience went to grinding me, and the more wicked and low-down and ornery I got to feeling. And at last, when it hit me all of a sudden that here was the plain hand of Providence slapping me in the face and letting me know my wickedness was being watched all the time from up there in heaven, whilst I was stealing a poor old woman's nigger that hadn't ever done me no harm, and now was showing me there's One that's always on the lookout, and ain't agoing to allow no such miserable doings to go only just so fur and no further, I most dropped in my tracks I was so scared. Well, I tried the best I could to kinder soften it up somehow for myself, by saying I was brung up wicked, and so I warn't so much to blame; but something inside of me kept saying, "There was the Sunday school, you could a gone to it; and if you'd a done it they'd a learnt you, there, that people that acts as I'd been acting about that nigger goes to everlasting fire."

It made me shiver. And I about made up my mind to pray; and see if I couldn't try to quit being the kind of a boy I was, and be better. So I kneeled down. But the words wouldn't come. Why wouldn't they? It warn't no use to try and hide it from Him. Nor from *me,* neither. I knowed very well why they wouldn't come. It was because my heart warn't right; it was because I warn't square; it was because I was playing double. I was letting *on* to give up sin, but away inside of me I was holding on to the biggest one of all. I was trying to make my mouth *say* I would do the right thing and the clean thing, and go and write to that nigger's owner and tell where he was; but deep down in me I knowed it was a lie—and He knowed it. You can't pray a lie—I found that out.

So I was full of trouble, full as I could be; and didn't know what to do. At last I had an idea; and I says, I'll go and write the letter—and *then* see if I can pray. Why, it was astonishing, the way I felt as light as a feather, right straight off, and my troubles all gone. So I got a piece of paper and a pencil, all glad and excited, and set down and wrote:

> Miss Watson your runaway nigger Jim is down here two mile below Pikesville and Mr. Phelps has got him and he will give him up for the reward if you send.
>
> HUCK FINN.

I felt good and all washed clean of sin for the first time I had ever felt so in my life, and I knowed I could pray now. But I didn't do it straight off, but laid the paper down and set there thinking—thinking how good it was all this happened so, and how near I come to being lost and going to hell. And went on thinking. And got to thinking over our trip down the river; and I see Jim before me, all the time, in the day, and in the night-time, sometimes moonlight, sometimes storms, and we a floating along, talking, and singing, and laughing. But somehow I couldn't seem to strike no places to harden me against him, but only the other kind. I'd see him standing my watch on top of his'n, stead of calling me, so I could go on sleeping; and see him how glad he was when I come back out of the fog; and when I come to him again in the swamp, up there where the feud was; and such-like times; and would always call me honey, and pet me, and do everything he could think of for me, and how good he always was; and at last I struck the time I saved him by telling the men we had small-pox aboard, and he was so grateful, and said I was the best friend old Jim ever had in the world, and the *only* one he's got now; and then I happened to look around, and see that paper.

It was a close place. I took it up, and held it in my hand. I was a trembling, because I'd got to decide, forever, betwixt two things, and I knowed it. I studied a minute, sort of holding my breath, and then says to myself:

"All right, then, I'll *go* to hell"—and tore it up.

It was awful thoughts, and awful words, but they was said. And I let them stay said; and never thought no more about reforming. I shoved the whole thing out of my head; and said I would take up wickedness again, which was in my line, being brung up to it, and the other warn't. And for a starter, I would go to work and steal Jim out of slavery again; and if I could think up anything worse, I would do that, too; because as long as I was in, and in for good, I might as well go the whole hog.

1885

A CONNECTICUT YANKEE IN
KING ARTHUR'S COURT

KING ARTHUR'S COURT

The moment I got a chance I slipped aside privately and touched an ancient common looking man on the shoulder and said, in an insinuating, confidential way—

"Friend, do me a kindness. Do you belong to the asylum, or are you just here on a visit or something like that?"

He looked me over stupidly, and said—

"Marry, fair sir, me seemeth—"

"That will do," I said; "I reckon you are a patient."

I moved away, cogitating, and at the same time keeping an eye out for any chance passenger in his right mind that might come along and give me some light. I judged I had found one, presently; so I drew him aside and said in his ear—

"If I could see the head keeper a minute—only just a minute—"

"Prithee do not let me."

"Let you *what?*"

"*Hinder* me, then, if the word please thee better." Then he went on to say he was an under-cook and could not stop to gossip, though he would like it another time; for it would comfort his very liver to know where I got my clothes. As he started away he pointed and said yonder was one who was idle enough for my purpose, and was seeking me besides, no doubt. This was an airy slim boy in shrimp-colored tights that made him look like a forked carrot; the rest of his gear was blue silk and dainty laces and ruffles; and he had long yellow curls, and wore a plumed pink satin cap tilted complacently over his ear. By his look, he was good-natured; by his gait, he was satisfied with himself. He was pretty enough to frame. He arrived, looked me over with a smiling and impudent curiosity; said he had come for me, and informed me that he was a page.

"Go 'long," I said; "you ain't more than a paragraph."

It was pretty severe, but I was nettled. However, it never phazed him; he didn't appear to know he was hurt. He began to talk and laugh, in happy, thoughtless, boyish fashion, as we walked along, and made himself old friends with me at once; asked me all sorts of questions about myself and about my clothes, but never waited for an answer—always chattered straight ahead, as if he didn't know he had asked a question and wasn't expecting any reply, until at last he happened to mention that he was born in the beginning of the year 513.

It made the cold chills creep over me! I stopped, and said, a little faintly:

"Maybe I didn't hear you just right. Say it again—and say it slow. What year was it?"

"513."

"513! You don't look it! Come, my boy, I am a stranger and friendless: be honest and honorable with me. Are you in your right mind?"

He said he was.

"Are these other people in their right minds?"

He said they were.

"And this isn't an asylum? I mean, it isn't a place where they cure crazy people?"

He said it wasn't.

"Well, then," I said, "either I am a lunatic, or something just as awful has happened. Now tell me, honest and true, where am I?"

"IN KING ARTHUR'S COURT."

I waited a minute, to let that idea shudder its way home, and then said:

"And according to your notions, what year is it now?"

"528—nineteenth of June."

I felt a mournful sinking at the heart, and muttered: "I shall never see my friends again—never, never again. They will not be born for more than thirteen hundred years yet."

I seemed to believe the boy, I didn't know why. *Something* in me seemed to believe him—my consciousness, as you may say; but my reason didn't. My reason straightway began to clamor; that was natural. I didn't know how to go about satisfying it, because I knew that the testimony of men wouldn't serve—my reason would say they were lunatics, and throw out their evidence. But all of a sudden I stumbled on the very thing, just by luck. I knew that the only total eclipse of the sun in the first half of the sixth century occurred on the 21st of June, A.D. 528, O. S., and began at 3 minutes after 12 noon. I also knew that no total eclipse of the sun was due in what to *me* was the present year —*i. e.,* 1879. So, if I could keep my anxiety and curiosity from eating the heart out of me for forty-eight hours, I should then find out for certain whether this boy was telling me the truth or not.

Wherefore, being a practical Connecticut man, I now shoved this whole problem clear out of my mind till its appointed day and hour should come, in order that I might turn all my attention to the circumstances of the present moment, and be alert and ready to make the most out of them that could be made. One thing at a time, is my motto —and just play that thing for all it is worth, even if it's only two pair and a jack. I made up my mind to two things; if it was still the nineteenth century and I was among lunatics and couldn't get away, I would presently boss that asylum or know the reason why; and if on the other hand it was really the sixth century, all right, I didn't want any softer thing: I would boss the whole country inside of three months; for I judged I would have the start of the best-educated man in the kingdom by a matter of thirteen hundred years and upwards. I'm not a man to waste time after my mind's made up and there's work on hand; so I said to the page—

"Now, Clarence, my boy—if that might happen to be your name— I'll get you to post me up a little if you don't mind. What is the name of that apparition that brought me here?"

"My master and thine? That is the good knight and great lord Sir Kay the Seneschal, foster brother to our liege the king."

"Very good; go on, tell me everything."

He made a long story of it; but the part that had immediate interest for me was this. He said I was Sir Kay's prisoner, and that in the due course of custom I would be flung into a dungeon and left there on scant commons until my friends ransomed me—unless I chanced to rot, first. I saw that the last chance had the best show, but I didn't waste any bother about that; time was too precious. The page said, further, that dinner was about ended in the great hall by this time, and that as soon as the sociability and the heavy drinking should begin, Sir

Kay would have me in and exhibit me before King Arthur and his illustrious knights seated at the Table Round, and would brag about his exploit in capturing me, and would probably exaggerate the facts a little, but it wouldn't be good form for me to correct him, and not over safe, either; and when I was done being exhibited, then ho for the dungeon; but he, Clarence, would find a way to come and see me every now and then, and cheer me up, and help me get word to my friends.

Get word to my friends! I thanked him; I couldn't do less; and about this time a lackey came to say I was wanted; so Clarence led me in and took me off to one side and sat down by me.

Well, it was a curious kind of spectacle, and interesting. It was an immense place, and rather naked—yes, and full of loud contrasts. It was very, very lofty; so lofty that the banners depending from the arched beams and girders away up there floated in a sort of twilight; there was a stone-railed gallery at each end, high up, with musicians in the one, and women, clothed in stunning colors, in the other. The floor was of big stone flags laid in black and white squares, rather battered by age and use, and needing repair. As to ornament, there wasn't any, strictly speaking; though on the walls hung some huge tapestries which were probably taxed as works of art; battle-pieces, they were, with horses shaped like those which children cut out of paper or create in gingerbread; with men on them in scale armor whose scales are represented by round holes—so that the man's coat looks as if it had been done with a biscuit-punch. There was a fireplace big enough to camp in; and its projecting sides and hood, of carved and pillared stone-work, had the look of a cathedral door. Along the walls stood men-at-arms, in breastplate and morion, with halberds for their only weapon—rigid as statues; and that is what they looked like.

In the middle of this groined and vaulted public square was an oaken table which they called the Table Round. It was as large as a circus ring; and around it sat a great company of men dressed in such various and splendid colors that it hurt one's eyes to look at them. They wore their plumed hats, right along, except that whenever one addressed himself directly to the king, he lifted his hat a trifle just as he was beginning his remark.

Mainly they were drinking—from entire ox horns; but a few were still munching bread or gnawing beef bones. There was about an average of two dogs to one man; and these sat in expectant attitudes till a spent bone was flung to them, and then they went for it by brigades and divisions, with a rush, and there ensued a fight which filled the prospect with a tumultuous chaos of plunging heads and bodies and flashing tails, and the storm of howlings and barkings deafened all speech for the time; but that was no matter, for the dog-fight was always a bigger interest anyway; the men rose, sometimes, to observe it the better and bet on it, and the ladies and the musicians stretched themselves out over their balusters with the same object; and all broke into delighted ejaculations from time to time. In the end, the winning dog stretched himself out comfortably with his bone between his paws, and proceeded to growl over it, and gnaw it, and grease the floor with it, just as fifty others were already doing; and the rest of the court resumed their previous industries and entertainments.

As a rule the speech and behavior of these people were gracious and courtly; and I noticed that they were good and serious listeners when anybody was telling anything—I mean in a dog-fightless interval. And plainly, too, they were a childlike and innocent lot; telling lies of the stateliest pattern with a most gentle and winning naivety, and ready and willing to listen to anybody else's lie, and believe it, too. It was hard to associate them with anything cruel or dreadful; and yet they dealt in tales of blood and suffering with a guileless relish that made me almost forget to shudder.

I was not the only prisoner present. There were twenty or more. Poor devils, many of them were maimed, hacked, carved, in a frightful way; and their hair, their faces, their clothing, were caked with black and stiffened drenchings of blood. They were suffering sharp physical pain, of course; and weariness, and hunger and thirst, no doubt; and at least none had given them the comfort of a wash, or even the poor charity of a lotion for their wounds; yet you never heard them utter a moan or a groan, or saw them show any sign of restlessness, or any disposition to complain. The thought was forced upon me: "The rascals—*they* have served other people so in their day; it being their own turn, now, they were not expecting any better treatment than this; so their philosophical bearing is not an outcome of mental training, intellectual fortitude, reasoning; it is mere animal training; they are white Indians."

Mainly the Round Table talk was monologues—narrative accounts of the adventures in which these prisoners were captured and their friends and backers killed and stripped of their steeds and armor. As a

general thing—as far as I could make out—these murderous adventures were not forays undertaken to avenge injuries, nor to settle old
disputes or sudden fallings out; no, as a rule they were simply duels
between strangers—duels between people who had never even been
introduced to each other, and between whom existed no cause of offense whatever. Many a time I had seen a couple of boys, strangers,
meet by chance, and say simultaneously, "I can lick you," and go at it
on the spot; but I had always imagined until now, that that sort of
thing belonged to children only, and was a sign and mark of child-
hood; but here were these big boobies sticking to it and taking pride in
it clear up into full age and beyond. Yet there was something very
engaging about these great simple-hearted creatures, something attractive and lovable. There did not seem to be brains enough in the entire
nursery, so to speak, to bait a fish-hook with; but you didn't seem to
mind that, after a little, because you soon saw that brains were not
needed in a society like that, and, indeed would have marred it, hin-
dered it, spoiled its symmetry—perhaps rendered its existence impossible.

There was a fine manliness observable in almost every face; and in
some a certain loftiness and sweetness that rebuked your belittling
criticisms and stilled them. A most noble benignity and purity reposed
in the countenance of him they called Sir Galahad, and likewise in the
king's also; and there was majesty and greatness in the giant frame and
high bearing of Sir Launcelot of the Lake.

There was presently an incident which centred the general interest
upon this Sir Launcelot. At a sign from a sort of master of ceremonies,
six or eight of the prisoners rose and came forward in a body and knelt
on the floor and lifted up their hands toward the ladies' gallery and
begged the grace of a word with the queen. The most conspicuously
situated lady in that massed flower-bed of feminine show and finery
inclined her head by way of assent, and then the spokesman of the
prisoners delivered himself and his fellows into her hands for free
pardon, ransom, captivity or death, as she in her good pleasure might
elect; and this, as he said, he was doing by command of Sir Kay the
Seneschal, whose prisoners they were, he having vanquished them by
his single might and prowess in sturdy conflict in the field.

Surprise and astonishment flashed from face to face all over the
house; the queen's gratified smile faded out at the name of Sir Kay,

and she looked disappointed; and the page whispered in my ear with
an accent and manner expressive of extravagant derision—

"Sir *Kay,* forsooth! Oh, call me pet names, dearest, call me a marine!
In twice a thousand years shall the unholy invention of man labor at
odds to beget the fellow to this majestic lie!"

Every eye was fastened with severe inquiry upon Sir Kay. But he
was equal to the occasion. He got up and played his hand like a major
—and took every trick. He said he would state the case, exactly according to the facts; he would tell the simple straightforward tale,
without comment of his own; "and then," said he, "if ye find glory and
honor due, ye will give it unto him who is the mightiest man of his
hands that ever bare shield or strake with sword in the ranks of Christian battle—even him that sitteth there!" and he pointed to Sir Launcelot. Ah, he fetched them; it was a rattling good stroke. Then he went
on and told how Sir Launcelot, seeking adventures, some brief time
gone by, killed seven giants at one sweep of his sword, and set a
hundred and forty-two captive maidens free; and then went further,
still seeking adventures, and found him (Sir Kay) fighting a desperate
fight against nine foreign knights, and straightway took the battle
solely into his own hands, and conquered the nine; and that night Sir
Launcelot rose quietly, and dressed him in Sir Kay's armor and took
Sir Kay's horse and gat him away into distant lands, and vanquished
sixteen knights in one pitched battle and thirty-four in another; and all
these and the former nine he made to swear that about Whitsuntide
they would ride to Arthur's court and yield them to Queen Guenever's
hands as captives of Sir Kay the Seneschal, spoil of his knightly prowess; and now here were these half dozen, and the rest would be along
as soon as they might be healed of their desperate wounds.

Well, it was touching to see the queen blush and smile, and look
embarrassed and happy, and fling furtive glances at Sir Launcelot that
would have got him shot in Arkansas, to a dead certainty.

Everybody praised the valor and magnanimity of Sir Launcelot; and
as for me, I was perfectly amazed, that one man, all by himself, should
have been able to beat down and capture such battalions of practiced
fighters. I said as much to Clarence; but this mocking featherhead
only said—

"An Sir Kay had had time to get another skin of sour wine into
him, ye had seen the accompt doubled."

I looked at the boy in sorrow; and as I looked I saw the cloud of a deep despondency settle upon his countenance. I followed the direction of his eye, and saw that a very old and white-bearded man, clothed in a flowing black gown, had risen and was standing at the table upon unsteady legs, and feebly swaying his ancient head and surveying the company with his watery and wandering eye. The same suffering look that was in the page's face was observable in all the faces around—the look of dumb creatures who know that they must endure and make no moan.

"Marry, we shall have it again," sighed the boy; "that same old weary tale that he hath told a thousand times in the same words, and that he *will* tell till he dieth, every time he hath gotten his barrel full and feeleth his exaggeration-mill a-working. Would God I had died or I saw this day!"

"Who is it?"

"Merlin, the mighty liar and magician, perdition singe him for the weariness he worketh with his one tale! But that men fear him for that he hath the storms and the lightnings and all the devils that be in hell at his beck and call, they would have dug his entrails out these many years ago to get at that tale and squelch it. He telleth it always in the third person, making believe he is too modest to glorify himself—maledictions light upon him, misfortune be his dole! Good friend, prithee call me for evensong."

The boy nestled himself upon my shoulder and pretended to go to sleep. The old man began his tale; and presently the lad was asleep in reality; so also were the dogs, and the court, the lackeys, and the files of men-at-arms. The droning voice droned on; a soft snoring arose on all sides and supported it like a deep and subdued accompaniment of wind instruments. Some heads were bowed upon folded arms, some lay back with open mouths that issued unconscious music; the flies buzzed and bit, unmolested, the rats swarmed softly out from a hundred holes, and pattered about, and made themselves at home everywhere; and one of them sat up like a squirrel on the king's head and held a bit of cheese in its hands and nibbled it, and dribbled the crumbs in the king's face with naïve and impudent irreverence. It was a tranquil scene, and restful to the weary eye and the jaded spirit.

1889

THE BOSS

To be vested with enormous authority is a fine thing; but to have the on-looking world consent to it is a finer. The tower episode solidified my power, and made it impregnable. If any were perchance disposed to be jealous and critical before that, they experienced a change of heart, now. There was not any one in the kingdom who would have considered it good judgment to meddle with my matters.

I was fast getting adjusted to my situation and circumstances. For a time, I used to wake up, mornings, and smile at my "dream," and listen for the Colt's factory whistle; but that sort of thing played itself out, gradually, and at last I was fully able to realize that I was actually living in the sixth century, and in Arthur's court, not a lunatic asylum. After that, I was just as much at home in that century as I could have been in any other; and as for preference, I wouldn't have traded it for the twentieth. Look at the opportunities here for a man of knowledge, brains, pluck and enterprise to sail in and grow up with the country. The grandest field that ever was; and all my own; not a competitor; not a man who wasn't a baby to me in acquirements and capacities; whereas, what would I amount to in the twentieth century? I should be foreman of a factory, that is about all; and could drag a seine downstreet any day and catch a hundred better men than myself.

What a jump I had made! I couldn't keep from thinking about it, and contemplating it, just as one does who has struck oil. There was nothing back of me that could approach it, unless it might be Joseph's case; and Joseph's only approached it, it didn't equal it, quite. For it stands to reason that as Joseph's splendid financial ingenuities advantaged nobody but the king, the general public must have regarded him with a good deal of disfavor, whereas I had done my entire public a kindness in sparing the sun, and was popular by reason of it.

I was no shadow of a king; I was the substance; the king himself was the shadow. My power was colossal; and it was not a mere name, as such things have generally been, it was the genuine article. I stood here, at the very spring and source of the second great period of the world's history; and could see the trickling stream of that history gather, and deepen and broaden, and roll its mighty tides down the far centuries; and I could note the upspringing of adventurers like myself in the shelter of its long array of thrones: De Montforts, Gavestons, Mortimers, Villierses; the war-making, campaign-directing wantons of France, and Charles the Second's sceptre-wielding drabs; but nowhere in the procession was my full-sized fellow visible. I was a Unique; and glad to know that that fact could not be dislodged or challenged for thirteen centuries and a half, for sure.

Yes, in power I was equal to the king. At the same time there was another power that was a trifle stronger than both of us put together. That was the Church. I do not wish to disguise that fact. I couldn't, if I wanted to. But never mind about that, now; it will show up, in its proper place, later on. It didn't cause me any trouble in the beginning —at least any of consequence.

Well, it was a curious country, and full of interest. And the people! They were the quaintest and simplest and trustingest race; why, they were nothing but rabbits. It was pitiful for a person born in a wholesome free atmosphere to listen to their humble and hearty outpourings of loyalty toward their king and Church and nobility; as if they had any more occasion to love and honor king and Church and noble than a slave has to love and honor the lash, or a dog has to love and honor the stranger that kicks him! Why, dear me, *any* kind of royalty, howsoever modified, *any* kind of aristocracy, howsoever pruned, is rightly an insult; but if you are born and brought up under that sort of arrangement you probably never find it out for yourself, and don't believe it when somebody else tells you. It is enough to make a body ashamed of his race to think of the sort of froth that has always occupied its thrones without shadow of right or reason, and the seventh-rate people that have always figured as its aristocracies—a company of monarchs and nobles who, as a rule, would have achieved only poverty and obscurity if left, like their betters, to their own exertions.

The most of King Arthur's British nation were slaves, pure and simple, and bore that name, and wore the iron collar on their necks; and the rest were slaves in fact, but without the name; they imagined themselves men and freemen, and called themselves so. The truth was, the nation as a body was in the world for one object, and one only: to grovel before king and Church and noble; to slave for them, sweat blood for them, starve that they might be fed, work that they might play, drink misery to the dregs that they might be happy, go naked that they might wear silks and jewels, pay taxes that they might be spared from paying them, be familiar all their lives with the degrading language and postures of adulation that they might walk in pride and think themselves the gods of this world. And for all this, the thanks they got were cuffs and contempt; and so poor-spirited were they that they took even this sort of attention as an honor.

Inherited ideas are a curious thing, and interesting to observe and examine. I had mine, the king and his people had theirs. In both cases they flowed in ruts worn deep by time and habit, and the man who should have proposed to divert them by reason and argument would have had a long contract on his hands. For instance, those people had inherited the idea that all men without title and a long pedigree, whether they had great natural gifts and acquirements or hadn't, were creatures of no more consideration than so many animals, bugs, insects; whereas I had inherited the idea that human daws who can consent to masquerade in the peacock-shams of inherited dignities and unearned titles, are of no good but to be laughed at. The way I was looked upon was odd, but it was natural. You know how the keeper and the public regard the elephant in the menagerie: well, that is the idea. They are full of admiration of his vast bulk and his prodigious strength; they speak with pride of the fact that he can do a hundred marvels which are far and away beyond their own powers; and they speak with the same pride of the fact that in his wrath he is able to drive a thousand men before him. But does that make him one of *them?* No; the raggedest tramp in the pit would smile at the idea. He couldn't comprehend it; couldn't take it in; couldn't in any remote way conceive of it. Well, to the king, the nobles, and all the nation, down to the very slaves and tramps, I was just that kind of an elephant, and nothing more. I was admired, also feared; but it was as an animal is admired and feared. The animal is not reverenced, neither was I; I was not even respected. I had no pedigree, no inherited title; so in the king's and nobles' eyes I was mere dirt; the people regarded me with wonder and awe, but there was no reverence mixed with it; through the force of inherited ideas they were not able to conceive of anything being entitled to that except pedigree and lordship. There you see the hand of that awful power, the Roman Catholic Church. In two or three little centuries it had converted a nation of men to a nation of worms. Before the day of the Church's supremacy in the world, men were men, and held their heads up, and had a man's pride and spirit and independence; and what of greatness and position a person got, he got mainly by achievement, not by birth. But then the Church came to the front, with an axe to grind; and she was wise, subtle, and knew more than one way to skin a cat—or a nation; she invented "divine right of kings," and propped it all around, brick by brick, with the Beatitudes—wrenching them from their good purpose to make them fortify an evil one; she preached (to the commoner,) humility, obedience to superiors, the beauty of self-sacrifice; she preached (to the commoner,) meekness under insult; preached (still to the commoner, always to the commoner,) patience, meanness of spirit, nonresistance under oppression; and she introduced heritable ranks and aristocracies, and taught all the Christian populations of the earth to bow down to them and worship them. Even down to my birth-century that poison was still in the blood of Christendom, and the best of English commoners was still content to see his inferiors impudently continuing to hold a number of positions, such as lordships and the throne, to which the grotesque laws of his country did not allow him to aspire; in fact he was not merely contented with this strange condition of things, he was even able to persuade himself that he was proud of it. It seems to show that there isn't anything you can't stand, if you are only born and bred to it. Of course that taint, that reverence for rank and title, had been in our American blood, too—I know that; but when I left America it had disappeared—at least to all intents and purposes. The remnant of it was restricted to the dudes and dudesses. When a disease has worked its way down to that level, it may fairly be said to be out of the system.

But to return to my anomalous position in King Arthur's kingdom. Here I was, a giant among pigmies, a man among children, a master intelligence among intellectual moles: by all rational measurement the one and only actually great man in that whole British world; and yet there and then, just as in the remote England of my birth-time, the sheep-witted earl who could claim long descent from a king's leman, acquired at second-hand from the slums of London, was a better man than I was. Such a personage was fawned upon in Arthur's realm and reverently looked up to by everybody, even though his dispositions were as mean as his intelligence, and his morals as base as his lineage. There were times when *he* could sit down in the king's presence, but I couldn't. I could have got a title easily enough, and that would have raised me a large step in everybody's eyes; even in the king's, the giver of it. But I didn't ask for it; and I declined it when it was offered. I couldn't have enjoyed such a thing with my notions; and it wouldn't have been fair, anyway, because as far back as I could go, our tribe had always been short of the bar sinister. I couldn't have felt really and satisfactorily fine and proud and set-up over any title except one that should come from the nation itself, the only legitimate source; and such an one I hoped to win; and in the course of years of honest and honorable endeavor, I did win it and did wear it with a high and clean pride. This title fell casually from the lips of a blacksmith, one day, in a village, was caught up as a happy thought and tossed from mouth to mouth with a laugh and an affirmative vote; in ten days it had swept the kingdom, and was become as familiar as the king's name. I was never known by any other designation afterwards, whether in the nation's talk or in grave debate upon matters of state at the council-board of the sovereign. This title, translated into modern speech, would be THE BOSS. Elected by the nation. That suited me. And it was a pretty high title. There were very few THE'S, and I was one of them. If you spoke of the duke, or the earl, or the bishop, how could anybody tell which one you meant? But if you spoke of The King or The Queen or The Boss, it was different.

Well, I liked the king, and *as* king I respected him—respected the office; at least respected it as much as I was capable of respecting any unearned supremacy; but as *men* I looked down upon him and his nobles—privately. And he and they liked me, and respected my office; but as an animal, without birth or sham title, they looked down upon me—and were not particularly private about it, either. I didn't charge for my opinion about them, and they didn't charge for their opinion about me: the account was square, the books balanced, everybody was satisfied.

1889

A CONNECTICUT YANKEE IN
KING ARTHUR'S COURT

THE YANKEE IN SEARCH
OF ADVENTURES

There never was such a country for wandering liars; and they were of both sexes. Hardly a month went by without one of these tramps arriving; and generally loaded with a tale about some princess or other wanting help to get her out of some far-away castle where she was held in captivity by a lawless scoundrel, usually a giant. Now you would think that the first thing the king would do after listening to such a novelette from an entire stranger, would be to ask for credentials—yes, and a pointer or two as to locality of castle, best route to it, and so on. But nobody ever thought of so simple and common-sense a thing as that. No, everybody swallowed these people's lies whole, and never asked a question of any sort or about anything. Well, one day when I was not around, one of these people came along—it was a she one, this time—and told a tale of the usual pattern. Her mistress was a captive in a vast and gloomy castle, along with forty-four other young and beautiful girls, pretty much all of them princesses; they had been languishing in that cruel captivity for twenty-six years; the masters of the castle were three stupendous brothers, each with four arms and one eye—the eye in the centre of the forehead, and as big as a fruit. Sort of fruit not mentioned; their usual slovenliness in statistics.

Would you believe it? The king and the whole Round Table were in raptures over this preposterous opportunity for adventure. Every knight of the Table jumped for the chance, and begged for it; but to their vexation and chagrin the king conferred it upon me, who had not asked for it at all.

By an effort, I contained my joy when Clarence brought me the news. But he—he could not contain his. His mouth gushed delight and gratitude in a steady discharge—delight in my good fortune, gratitude to the king for this splendid mark of his favor for me. He could keep neither his legs nor his body still, but pirouetted about the place in an airy ecstasy of happiness.

On my side, I could have cursed the kindness that conferred upon me this benefaction, but I kept my vexation under the surface for policy's sake, and did what I could to let on to be glad. Indeed, I *said* I was glad. And in a way it was true; I was as glad as a person is when he is scalped.

Well, one must make the best of things, and not waste time with useless fretting, but get down to business and see what can be done. In all lies there is wheat among the chaff; I must get at the wheat in this case: so I sent for the girl and she came. She was a comely enough creature, and soft and modest, but if signs went for anything, she didn't know as much as a lady's watch. I said—

"My dear, have you been questioned as to particulars?"

She said she hadn't.

"Well, I didn't expect you had, but I thought I would ask to make sure; it's the way I've been raised. Now you mustn't take it unkindly if I remind you that as we don't know you, we must go a little slow. You may be all right, of course, and we'll hope that you are; but to take it for granted isn't business. *You* understand that. I'm obliged to ask you a few questions; just answer up fair and square, and don't be afraid. Where do you live, when you are at home?"

"In the land of Moder, fair sir."

"Land of Moder. I don't remember hearing of it before. Parents living?"

"As to that, I know not if they be yet on live, sith it is many years that I have lain shut up in the castle."

"Your name, please?"

"I hight the Demoiselle Alisande la Carteloise, an it please you."

"Do you know anybody here who can identify you?"

"That were not likely, fair lord, I being come hither now for the first time."

"Have you brought any letters—any documents—any proofs that you are trustworthy and truthful?"

"Of a surety, no; and wherefore should I? Have I not a tongue, and cannot I say all that myself?"

"But *your* saying it, you know, and somebody else's saying it, is different."

"Different? How might that be? I fear me I do not understand."

"Don't *understand?* Land of—why, you see—you see—why, great Scott, can't you understand a little thing like that? Can't you understand the difference between your—*why* do you look so innocent and idiotic!"

"I? In truth I know not, but an it were the will of God."

"Yes, yes, I reckon that's about the size of it. Don't mind my seeming excited; I'm not. Let us change the subject. Now as to this castle, with forty-five princesses in it, and three ogres at the head of it, tell me —where is this harem?"

"Harem?"

"The *castle,* you understand; where is the castle?"

"Oh, as to that, it is great, and strong, and well beseen, and lieth in a far country. Yes, it is many leagues."

"How many?"

"Ah, fair sir, it were woundily hard to tell, they are so many, and do so lap the one upon the other, and being made all in the same image and tincted with the same color, one may not know the one league from its fellow, nor how to count them except they be taken apart, and ye wit well it were God's work to do that, being not within man's capacity; for ye will note—"

"Hold on, hold on, never mind about the distance; *whereabouts* does the castle lie? What's the direction from here?"

"Ah, please you sir, it hath no direction from here; by reason that the road lieth not straight, but turneth evermore; wherefore the direction of its place abideth not, but is sometime under the one sky and anon under another, whereso if ye be minded that it is in the east, and wend thitherward, ye shall observe that the way of the road doth yet again turn upon itself by the space of half a circle, and this marvel happing again and yet again and still again, it will grieve you that you had thought by vanities of the mind to thwart and bring to naught the will of Him that giveth not a castle a direction from a place except it pleaseth Him, and if it please Him not, will the rather that even all castles and all directions thereunto vanish out of the earth, leaving the places wherein they tarried desolate and vacant, so warning His creatures that where He will He will, and where He will not He—"

"Oh, that's all right, that's all right, give us a rest; never mind about the direction, *hang* the direction—I beg pardon, I beg a thousand pardons, I am not well to-day; pay no attention when I soliloquize, it is an old habit, an old, bad habit, and hard to get rid of when one's digestion is all disordered with eating food that was raised forever and ever before he was born; good land! a man can't keep his functions regular on spring chickens thirteen hundred years old. But come— never mind about that; let's—have you got such a thing as a map of that region about you? Now a good map—"

"Is it peradventure that manner of thing which of late the unbelievers have brought from over the great seas, which, being boiled in oil, and an onion and salt added thereto, doth—"

"What, a map? What are you talking about? Don't you know what a map is? There, there, never mind, don't explain. I hate explanations; they fog a thing up so that you can't tell anything about it. Run along, dear; good-day; show her the way, Clarence."

Oh, well, it was reasonably plain, now, why these donkeys didn't prospect these liars for details. It may be that this girl had a fact in her somewhere, but I don't believe you could have sluiced it out with a hydraulic; nor got it with the earlier forms of blasting, even; it was a case for dynamite. Why, she was a perfect ass; and yet the king and his knights had listened to her as if she had been a leaf out of the gospel. It kind of sizes up the whole party. And think of the simple ways of this court: this wandering wench hadn't any more trouble to get access to the king in his palace than she would have had to get into the poorhouse in my day and country. In fact he was glad to see her, glad to hear her tale; with that adventure of hers to offer, she was as welcome as a corpse is to a coroner.

Just as I was ending-up these reflections, Clarence came back. I remarked upon the barren result of my efforts with the girl; hadn't got hold of a single point that could help me to find the castle. The youth looked a little surprised, or puzzled, or something, and intimated that he had been wondering to himself what I had wanted to ask the girl all those questions for.

"Why, great guns," I said, "don't I want to find the castle? And how else would I go about it?"

"La, sweet your worship, one may lightly answer that, I ween. She will go with thee. They always do. She will ride with thee."

"Ride with me? Nonsense!"

"But of a truth she will. She will ride with thee. Thou shalt see."

"What? She browse around the hills and scour the woods with me —alone—and I as good as engaged to be married? Why, it's scandalous. Think how it would look."

My, the dear face that rose before me! The boy was eager to know all about this tender matter. I swore him to secrecy and then whispered her name—"Puss Flanagan." He looked disappointed, and said he didn't remember the countess. How natural it was for the little courtier to give her a rank. He asked me where she lived.

"In East Har—" I came to myself and stopped, a little confused; then I said, "Never mind, now; I'll tell you sometime."

And might he see her? Would I let him see her some day?

It was but a little thing to promise—thirteen hundred years or so— and he so eager; so I said Yes. But I sighed; I couldn't help it. And yet there was no sense in sighing, for she wasn't born yet. But that is the way we are made: we don't reason, where we feel; we just feel.

My expedition was all the talk that day and that night, and the boys were very good to me, and made much of me, and seemed to have forgotten their vexation and disappointment, and come to be as anxious for me to hive those ogres and set those ripe old virgins loose as if it were themselves that had the contract. Well, they *were* good children —but just children, that is all. And they gave me no end of points about how to scout for giants, and how to scoop them in; and they told me all sorts of charms against enchantments, and gave me salves and other rubbish to put on my wounds. But it never occurred to one of them to reflect that if I was such a wonderful necromancer as I was pretending to be, I ought not to need salves or instructions, or charms against enchantments, and least of all, arms and armor, on a foray of any kind—even against fire-spouting dragons, and devils hot from perdition, let alone such poor adversaries as these I was after, these commonplace ogres of the back settlements.

I was to have an early breakfast, and start at dawn, for that was the usual way; but I had the demon's own time with my armor, and this delayed me a little. It is troublesome to get into, and there is so much detail. First you wrap a layer or two of blanket around your body, for a sort of cushion and to keep off the cold iron; then you put on your sleeves and shirt of chain-mail—these are made of small steel links woven together, and they form a fabric so flexible that if you toss your shirt onto the floor, it slumps into a pile like a peck of wet fish-net; it is very heavy and is nearly the uncomfortablest material in the world for a night-shirt, yet plenty used it for that—tax collectors, and reformers, and one-horse kings with a defective title, and those sorts of people; then you put on your shoes—flat-boats roofed over with interleaving bands of steel—and screw your clumsy spurs into the heels. Next you buckle your greaves on your legs, and your cuisses on your thighs; then come your backplate and your breastplate, and you begin to feel crowded; then you hitch onto the breastplate the half-petticoat of broad overlapping bands of steel which hangs down in front but is scolloped out behind so you can sit down, and isn't any real improvement on an inverted coal scuttle, either for looks or for wear, or to wipe your hands on; next you belt on your sword; then you put your stovepipe joints onto your arms, your iron gauntlets onto your hands, your iron rat-trap onto your head, with a rag of steel web hitched onto it to hang over the back of your neck—and there you are, snug as a candle in a candle-mould. This is no time to dance. Well, a man that is packed away like that, is a nut that isn't worth the cracking, there is so little of the meat, when you get down to it, by comparison with the shell.

The boys helped me, or I never could have got in. Just as we finished, Sir Bedivere happened in, and I saw that as like as not I hadn't chosen the most convenient outfit for a long trip. How stately he looked; and tall and broad and grand. He had on his head a conical steel casque that only came down to his ears, and for visor had only a narrow steel bar that extended down to his upper lip and protected his nose; and all the rest of him, from neck to heel, was flexible chain-mail, trowsers and all. But pretty much all of him was hidden under his outside garment, which of course was of chain-mail, as I said, and hung straight from his shoulders to his ancles; and from his middle to the bottom, both before and behind, was divided, so that he could ride and let the skirts hang down on each side. He was going grailing, and it was just the outfit for it, too. I would have given a good deal for that ulster, but it was too late now to be fooling around. The sun was just up, the king and the court were all on hand to see me off and wish me luck; so it wouldn't be etiquette for me to tarry. You don't get on your horse yourself; no, if you tried it you would get disappointed. They carry you out, just as they carry a sun-struck man to the drug store, and put you on, and help get you to rights, and fix your feet in the stirrups; and all the while you do feel so strange and stuffy and like somebody else—like somebody that has been married on a sudden, or struck by lightning, or something like that, and hasn't quite fetched around, yet, and is sort of numb, and can't just get his bearings. Then they stood up the mast they called a spear, in its socket by my left foot, and I gripped it with my hand; lastly they hung my shield around my neck, and I was all complete and ready to up anchor and get to sea. Everybody was as good to me as they could be, and a maid of honor gave me the stirrup-cup her own self. There was nothing more to do, now, but for that damsel to get up behind me on a pillion, which she did, and put an arm or so around me to hold on.

And so we started; and everybody gave us a good-bye and waved their handkerchiefs or helmets. And everybody we met, going down the hill and through the village was respectful to us, except some shabby little boys on the outskirts. They said—

"Oh, what a guy!" And hove clods at us.

In my experience boys are the same in all ages. They don't respect anything, they don't care for anything or anybody. They say "Go up, baldhead" to the prophet going his unoffending way in the gray of antiquity; they sass me in the holy gloom of the Middle Ages; and I had seen them act the same way in Buchanan's administration; I remember, because I was there and helped. The prophet had his bears and settled with his boys; and I wanted to get down and settle with mine, but it wouldn't answer, because I couldn't have got up again. I hate a country without a derrick.

1889

ESSAYS

AIX, THE PARADISE OF
THE RHEUMATICS

Aix-les-Bains. Certainly this is an enchanting place. It is a strong word, but I think the facts justify it. True, there is a rabble of nobilities, big and little, here all the time, and often a king or two; but as these behave quite nicely and also keep mainly to themselves, they are little or no annoyance. And then a king makes the best advertisement there is, and the cheapest. All he costs is a reception at the station by the mayor and the police in their Sunday uniforms, shop-front decorations along the route from station to hotel, brass band at the hotel, fireworks in the evening, free bath in the morning. This is the whole expense; and in return for it he goes away from here with the broad of his back metaphorically stenciled over with display ads., which shout to all nations of the world, assisted by the telegraph:

RHEUMATISM ROUTED AT AIX-LES-BAINS!
GOUT ADMONISHED, NERVES BRACED UP!
ALL DISEASES WELCOMED, AND SATISFACTION GIVEN OR
THE MONEY RETURNED AT THE DOOR!

We leave nature's noble cliffs and crags undefiled and uninsulted by the advertiser's paint brush. We use the back of a king, which is better and properer and more effective, too, for the cliffs stay still and few see it, but the king moves across the fields of the world and is visible from all points, like a constellation. We are out of kings this week, but one will be along soon—possibly His Satanic Majesty of Russia. There's a colossus for you! A mysterious and terrible form that towers up into unsearchable space and casts a shadow across the universe like a planet in eclipse. There will be but one absorbing spectacle in this world when we stencil him and start him out.

This is an old valley, this of Aix, both in the history of man and in the geological records of its rocks. Its little lake of Bourget carries the human history back to the lake dwellers, furnishing seven groups of their habitations, and Dr. William Wakefield says in his interesting local guide that the mountains round about furnish "Geographically, a veritable epitome of the globe." The stratified chapters of the earth's history are clearly and permanently written on the sides of the roaring bulk of the Dent du Chat, but many of the layers of race, religion, and government which in turn have flourished and perished here between the lake dweller of several thousand years ago and the French republican of to-day, are ill defined and uninforming by comparison. There are several varieties of pagans. They went their way, one after the other, down into night and oblivion, leaving no account of themselves, no memorials. The Romans arrived 2,300 years ago, other parts of France are rich with remembrances of their eight centuries of occupation, but not many are here. Other pagans followed the Romans. By and by Christianity arrived, some 400 years after the time of Christ. The long procession of races, languages, religions, and dynasties demolished one another's records—it is man's way always.

As a result, nothing is left of the handiwork of the remoter inhabitants of the region except the constructions of the lake dwellers and some Roman odds and ends. There is part of a small Roman temple, there is part of a Roman bath, there is a graceful and battered Roman arch. It stands on a turfy level over the way from the present great bath house, is surrounded by magnolia trees, and is both a picturesque and suggestive object. It has stood there some 1,600 years. Its nearest neighbor, not twenty steps away, is a Catholic church. They are symbols of the two chief eras in the history of Aix. Yes, and of the European world. I judge that the venerable arch is held in reverent esteem by everybody, and that this esteem is its sufficient protection from insult, for it is the only public structure I have yet seen in France which lacks the sign, "It is forbidden to post bills here." Its neighbor the church has that sign on more than one of its sides, and other signs, too, forbidding certain other sorts of desecration.

The arch's nearest neighbor—just at its elbow, like the church—is the telegraph office. So there you have the three great eras bunched together—the era of War, the era of Theology, the era of Business.

You pass under the arch, and the buried Caesars seem to rise from the dust of the centuries and flit before you; you pass by that old battered church, and are in touch with the Middle Ages, and with another step you can put down ten francs and shake hands with Oshkosh under the Atlantic.

It is curious to think what changes the last of the three symbols stand for; changes in men's ways and thoughts, changes in material civilization, changes in the Deity—or in men's conception of the Deity, if that is an exacter way of putting it. The second of the symbols arrived in the earth at a time when the Deity's possessions consisted of a small sky freckled with mustard-seed stars, and under it a patch of landed estate not so big as the holdings of the Tsar to-day, and all His time was taken up in trying to keep a handful of Jews in some sort of order—exactly the same number of them that the Tsar has lately been dealing with in a more abrupt and far less loving and long-suffering way. At a later time—a time within all old men's memories—the Deity was otherwise engaged. He was dreaming His eternities away on His Great White Throne, steeped in the soft bliss of hymns of praise wafted aloft without ceasing from choirs of ransomed souls, Presbyterians and the rest. This was a Deity proper enough to the size and conditions of things, no doubt a provincial Deity with provincial tastes. The change since has been inconceivably vast. His empire has been unimaginably enlarged. To-day He is a Master of a universe made up of myriads upon myriads of gigantic suns, and among them, lost in that limitless sea of light, floats that atom. His earth, which once seemed so good and satisfactory and cost so many days of patient labor to build, is a mere cork adrift in the waters of a shoreless Atlantic. This is a business era, and no doubt he is governing His huge empire now, not by dreaming the time away in the buzz of hymning choirs, with occasional explosions of arbitrary power disproportioned to the size of the annoyance, but by applying laws of a sort proper and necessary to the sane and successful management of a complex and prodigious establishment, and by seeing to it that the exact and constant operation of these laws is not interfered with for the accommodation of any individual or political or religious faction or nation.

Mighty has been the advance of the nations and the liberalization of thought. A result of it is a changed Deity, a Deity of a dignity and sublimity proportioned to the majesty of His office and the magnitude of His empire, a Deity who has been freed from a hundred fretting chains and will in time be freed from the rest by the several ecclesiastical bodies who have these matters in charge. It was, without doubt, a mistake and a step backward when the Presbyterian Synods of America lately decided, by vote, to leave Him still embarrassed with the dogma of infant damnation. Situated as we are, we cannot at present know with how much of anxiety He watched the balloting, nor with how much of grieved disappointment He observed the result.

Well, all these eras above spoken of are modern, they are of last week, they are of yesterday, they are of this morning, so to speak. The springs, the healing waters that gush up from under this hillside village, indeed are ancient. They, indeed, are a genuine antiquity; they antedate all those fresh human matters by processions of centuries; they were born with the fossils of the Dent du Chat, and they have been always abundant. They furnished a million gallons a day to wash the lake dwellers with, the same to wash the Caesars with, no less to wash Balzac with, and have not diminished on my account. A million gallons a day for how many days? Figures cannot set forth the number. The delivery, in the aggregate, has amounted to an Atlantic. And there is still an Atlantic down in there. By Doctor Wakefield's calculation the Atlantic is three-quarters of a mile down in the earth. The calculation is based upon the temperature of the water, which is 114 degrees to 117 degrees Fahrenheit, the natural law being that below a certain depth heat augments at the rate of one degree for every sixty feet of descent.

Aix is handsome, and is handsomely situated, too, on its hill slope, with its stately prospect of mountain range and plain spread out before it and about it. The streets are mainly narrow, and steep and crooked and interesting, and offer considerable variety in the way of names; on the corner of one of them you read this: "Rue du Puits d'Enfer" ("Pit of Hell Street"). Some of the sidewalks are only eighteen inches wide; they are for the cats, probably. There is a pleasant park, and there are spacious and beautiful grounds connected with the two great pleasure resorts, the Cercle and the Villa des Fleurs. The town consists of big hotels, little hotels, and *pensions.* The season lasts about six months, beginning with May. When it is at its height there are thousands of visitors here, and in the course of the season as many as 20,000 in the aggregate come and go.

These are not all here for the baths; some come for the gambling facilities and some for the climate. It is a climate where the field

strawberry flourishes through the spring, summer, and fall. It is hot in
the summer, and hot in earnest; but that is only in the daytime; it is
not hot at night. The English season is May and June; they get a good
deal of rain then, and they like that. The Americans take July, and the
French take August. By the 1st of July the open-air music and the
evening concerts and operas and plays are fairly under way, and from
that time onward the rush of pleasure has a steadily increasing boom.
It is said that in August the great grounds and the gambling rooms are
crowded all the time and no end of ostensible fun going on.

It is a good place for rest and sleep and general recuperation of
forces. The book of Doctor Wakefield says there is something about
this atmosphere which is the deadly enemy of insomnia, and I think
this must be true, for if I am any judge, this town is at times the
noisiest one in Europe, and yet a body gets more sleep here than he
would at home, I don't care where his home is. Now, we are living at a
most comfortable and satisfactory *pension,* with a garden of shade
trees and flowers and shrubs, and a convincing air of quiet and repose.
But just across the narrow street is the little market square, and at the
corner of that is the church that is neighbor to the Roman arch, and
that narrow street, and that billiard table of a market place, and that
church are able, on a bet, to turn out more noise to a cubic yard at the
wrong time than any other similar combination in the earth or out of
it. In the street you have the skull-bursting thunder of the passing
hack, a volume of sound not producible by six hacks anywhere else; on
the hack is a lunatic with a whip which he cracks to notify the public
to get out of his way. This crack is as keen and sharp and penetrating
and ear-splitting as a pistol shot at close range, and the lunatic delivers
it in volleys, not single shots. You think you will not be able to live till
he gets by, and when he does get by he leaves only a vacancy for the
bandit who sells *Le Petit Journal* to fill with his strange and awful yell.
He arrives with the early morning and the market people, and there is
a dog that arrives at about the same time and barks steadily at nothing
till he dies, and they fetch another dog just like him. The bark of this
breed is the twin of the whip volley, and stabs like a knife. By and by,
what is left of you the church bell gets. There are many bells, and
apparently six or seven thousand town clocks, and as they are all five
minutes apart—probably by law—there are no intervals. Some of
them are striking all the time—at least, after you go to bed they are.
There is one clock that strikes the hour and then strikes it over again

to see if it was right. Then for evenings and Sundays there is a chime—a chime that starts in pleasantly and musically, then suddenly breaks into a frantic roar, and boom, and crash of warring sounds that makes you think Paris is up and the Revolution come again. And yet, as I have said, one sleeps here—sleeps like the dead. Once he gets his grip on his sleep, neither hack, nor whip, nor news fiend, nor dog, nor bell cyclone, nor all of them together, can wrench it loose or mar its deep and tranquil continuity. Yes, there is indeed something in this air that is death to insomnia.

The buildings of the Cercle and the Villa des Fleurs are huge in size, and each has a theater in it, and a great restaurant, also conveniences for gambling and general and variegated entertainment.

They stand in ornamental grounds of great extent and beauty. The multitudes of fashionable folk sit at refreshment tables in the open air, afternoons, and listen to the music, and it is there that they mainly go to break the Sabbath.

To get the privilege of entering these grounds and buildings you buy a ticket for a few francs, which is good for the whole season. You are then free to go and come at all hours, attend the plays and concerts free, except on special occasions, gamble, buy refreshments, and make yourself symmetrically comfortable.

Nothing could be handier than those two little theaters. The curtain doesn't rise until 8.30; then between the acts one can idle for half an hour in the other departments of the building, damaging his appetite in the restaurants or his pocketbook in the baccarat room. The singers and actors are from Paris, and their performance is beyond praise.

I was never in a fashionable gambling hell until I came here. I had read several millions of descriptions of such places, but the reality was new to me. I very much wanted to see this animal, especially the new historic game of baccarat, and this was a good place, for Aix ranks next to Monte Carlo for high play and plenty of it. But the result was what I might have expected—the interest of the looker-on perishes with the novelty of the spectacle; that is to say, in a few minutes. A permanent and intense interest is acquirable in baccarat, or in any other game, but you have to buy it. You don't get it by standing around and looking on.

The baccarat table is covered with green cloth and is marked off in divisions with chalk or something. The banker sits in the middle, the croupier opposite. The customers fill all the chairs at the table, and the rest of the crowd are massed at their back and leaning over them to deposit chips or gold coins. Constantly money and chips are flung upon the table, and the game seems to consist in the croupier's reaching for these things with a flexible sculling oar, and raking them home. It appeared to be a rational enough game for him, and if I could have borrowed his oar I would have stayed, but I didn't see where the entertainment of the others came in. This was because I saw without perceiving, and observed without understanding. For the widow and the orphan and the others do win money there. Once an old gray mother in Israel or elsewhere pulled out, and I heard her say to her daughter or her granddaughter as they passed me, "There, I've won six louis, and I'm going to quit while I'm ahead." Also there was this statistic. A friend pointed to a young man with the dead stub of a cigar in his mouth, which he kept munching nervously all the time and pitching hundred-dollar chips on the board while two sweet young girls reached down over his shoulders to deposit modest little gold pieces, and said: "He's only funning, now; wasting a few hundred to pass the time—waiting for the gold room to open, you know, which won't be till after midnight—then you'll see him bet! He won £14,000 there last night. They don't bet anything there but big money."

The thing I chiefly missed was the haggard people with the intense eye, the hunted look, the desperate mien, candidates for suicide and the pauper's grave. They are in the description, as a rule, but they were off duty that night. All the gamblers, male and female, old and young, looked abnormally cheerful and prosperous.

However, all the nations were there, clothed richly and speaking all the languages. Some of the women were painted, and were evidently shaky as to character. These items tallied with the descriptions well enough.

The etiquette of the place was difficult to master. In the brilliant and populous halls and corridors you don't smoke, and you wear your hat, no matter how many ladies are in the thick throng of drifting humanity, but the moment you cross the sacred threshold and enter the gambling hell, off the hat must come, and everybody lights his cigar and goes to suffocating the ladies.

But what I came here for five weeks ago was the baths. My right arm was disabled with rheumatism. To sit at home in America and guess out the European bath best fitted for a particular ailment or combination of ailments, it is not possible, and it would not be a good idea to experiment in that way, anyhow. There are a great many curative baths on the Continent, and some are good for one disease and bad for another. So it is necessary to let your physician name a bath for you. As a rule, Americans go to Europe to get this advice, and South Americans go to Paris for it. Now and then an economist chooses his bath himself and does a thousand miles of railroading to get to it, and then the local physicians tell him he has come to the wrong place. He sees that he has lost time and money and strength and almost the minute he realizes this he loses his temper. I had the rheumatism and was advised to go to Aix, not so much because I had that disease as because I had the promise of certain others. What they were was not explained to me, but they are either in the following menu or I have been sent to the wrong place. Doctor Wakefield's book says:

> We know that the class of maladies benefited by the water and baths at Aix are those due to defect of nourishment, debility of the nervous system, or to a gouty, rheumatic, herpetic, or scrofulous diathesis—all diseases extremely debilitating, and requiring a tonic, and not depressing action of the remedy. This it seems to find here, as recorded experience and daily action can testify. According to the line of treatment followed particularly with due regard to the temperature, the action of the Aix waters can be made sedative, exciting, derivative, or alterative and tonic.

The "Establishment" is the property of France, and all the officers and servants are employees of the French government. The bathhouse is a huge and massive pile of white marble masonry, and looks more like a temple than anything else. It has several floors and each is full of bath cabinets. There is every kind of bath—for the nose, the ears, the throat, vapor baths, swimming baths, and all people's favorite, the douche. It is a good building to get lost in, when you are not familiar with it. From early morning until nearly noon people are streaming in and streaming out without halt. The majority come afoot, but great numbers are brought in sedan chairs, a sufficiently ugly contrivance whose cover is a steep little tent made of striped canvas. You see nothing of the patient in this diving bell as the bearers tramp along, except a glimpse of his ankles bound together and swathed around with blankets or towels to that generous degree that the result suggests a sore piano leg. By attention and practice the pallbearers have got so that they can keep out of step all the time—and they do it. As a consequence their veiled churn goes rocking, tilting, swaying along like a bell buoy in a ground swell. It makes the oldest sailor homesick to look at that spectacle.

The "course" is usually fifteen douche baths and five tub baths. You take the douche three days in succession, then knock off and take a tub. You keep up this distribution through the course. If one course does not cure you, you take another one after an interval. You seek a local physician and he examines your case and prescribes the kind of bath required for it, with various other particulars; then you buy your course tickets and pay for them in advance—nine dollars. With the tickets you get a memorandum book with your dates and hours all set down on it. The doctor takes you into the bath the first morning and gives some instructions to the two *doucheurs* who are to handle you through the course. The *pourboires* are about ten cents to each of the men for each bath, payable at the end of the course. Also at the end of the course you pay three or four francs to the superintendent of your department of the bathhouse. These are useful particulars to know, and are not to be found in the books. A servant of your hotel carries your towels and sheet to the bath daily and brings them away again. They are the property of the hotel; the French government doesn't furnish these things.

You meet all kinds of people at a place like this, and if you give them a chance they will submerge you under their circumstances, for they are either very glad or very sorry they came, and they want to spread their feelings out and enjoy them. One of these said to me:

"It's great, these baths. I didn't come here for my health; I only came to find out if there was anything the matter with me. The doctor told me if there was the symptoms would soon appear. After the first douche I had sharp pains in all my muscles. The doctor said it was different varieties of rheumatism, and the best varieties there were, too. After my second bath I had aches in my bones, and skull and around. The doctor said it was different varieties of neuralgia, and the best in the market, anybody would tell me so. I got many new kinds of pains out of my third douche. These were in my joints. The doctor said it was gout, complicated with heart disease, and encouraged me to go on. Then we had the fourth douche, and I came out on a stretcher that time, and fetched with me one vast, diversified undulat-

ing continental kind of pain, with horizons to it, and zones, and parallels of latitude, and meridians of longitude, and isothermal belts, and
variations of the compass—oh, everything tidy, and right up to the
latest developments, you know. The doctor said it was inflammation of
the soul, and just the very thing. Well, I went right on gathering them
in, toothache, liver complaint, softening of the brain, nostalgia, bron-
chitis, osteology, fits, Coleoptera, hydrangea, Cyclopaedia Britannica,
delirium tremens, and a lot of other things that I've got down on my
list that I'll show you, and you can keep it if you like and tally off the
bric-à-brac as you lay it in.

"The doctor said I was a grand proof of what these baths could do;
said I had come here as innocent of disease as a grindstone, and inside
of three weeks these baths had sluiced out of me every important
ailment known to medical science, along with considerable more that
were entirely new and patentable. Why, he wanted to exhibit me in his
bay window!"

There seem to be a good many liars this year. I began to take the
baths and found them most enjoyable; so enjoyable that if I hadn't had
a disease I would have borrowed one, just to have a pretext for going
on. They took me into a stone-floored basin about fourteen feet square,
which had enough strange-looking pipes and things in it to make it
look like a torture chamber. The two half-naked men seated me on a
pine stool and kept a couple of warm-water jets as thick as one's wrist
playing upon me while they kneaded me, stroked me, twisted me, and
applied all the other details of the scientific massage to me for seven or
eight minutes. Then they stood me up and played a powerful jet upon
me all around for another minute. The cool shower bath came next,
and the thing was over. I came out of the bathhouse a few minutes
later feeling younger and fresher and finer than I have felt since I was
a boy. The spring and cheer and delight of this exaltation lasted three
hours, and the same uplifting effect has followed the twenty douches
which I have taken since.

After my first douche I went to the chemist's on the corner, as per
instructions, and asked for half a glass of Challe water. It comes from
a spring sixteen miles from here. It was furnished to me, but, perceiving that there was something the matter with it, I offered to wait till
they could get some that was fresh, but they said it always smelled
that way. They said the reason that this was so much ranker than the
sulphur water of the bath was that this contained thirty-two times as

much sulphur as that. It is true, but in my opinion that water comes from a cemetery, and not a fresh cemetery, either. History says that one of the early Roman generals lost an army down there somewhere. If he could come back now I think this water would help him find it again. However, I drank the Challe, and have drunk it once or twice every day since. I suppose it is all right, but I wish I knew what was the matter with those Romans.

My first baths developed plenty of pain, but the subsequent ones removed almost all of it. I have got back the use of my arm these last few days, and I am going away now.

There are many beautiful drives about Aix, many interesting places to visit, and much pleasure to be found in paddling around the little Lake Bourget on the small steamers, but the excursion which satisfied me best was a trip to Annecy and its neighborhood. You go to Annecy in an hour by rail, through a garden land that has not had its equal for beauty perhaps since Eden; and certainly not Eden was cultivated as this garden is. The charm and loveliness of the whole region are bewildering. Picturesque rocks, forest-clothed hills, slopes richly bright in the cleanest and greenest grass, fields of grain without freck or flaw, dainty of color and as shiny and shimmery as silk, old gray mansions and towers, half buried in foliage and sunny eminences, deep chasms with precipitous walls, and a swift stream of pale-blue water between, with now and then a tumbling cascade, and always noble mountains in view, with vagrant white clouds curling about their summits.

Then at the end of an hour you come to Annecy and rattle through its old crooked lanes, built solidly up with curious old houses that are a dream of the Middle Ages, and presently you come to the main object of your trip—Lake Annecy. It is a revelation; it is a miracle. It brings the tears to a body's eyes, it affects you just as all things that you instantly recognize as perfect affect you—perfect music, perfect eloquence, perfect art, perfect joy, perfect grief. It stretches itself out there in a caressing sunlight, and away toward its border of majestic mountains, a crisped and radiant plain of water of the divinest blue that can be imagined. All the blues are there, from the faintest shoal-water suggestion of the color, detectable only in the shadow of some overhanging object, all the way through, a little blue and a little bluer still, and again a shade bluer, till you strike the deep, rich Mediterranean splendor which breaks the heart in your bosom, it is so beautiful.

And the mountains, as you skim along on the steamboat, how

stately their forms, how noble their proportions, how green their velvet slopes, how soft the mottlings of the sun and shadow that play
about the rocky ramparts that crown them, how opaline the vast up-
heavals of snow banked against the sky in the remotenesses beyond—
Mont Blanc and the others—how shall anybody describe? Why, not
even the painter can quite do it, and the most the pen can do is to
suggest.

Up the lake there is an old abbey—Tallories—relic of the Middle
Ages. We stopped there; stepped from the sparkling water and the
rush and boom and fret and fever of the nineteenth century into the
solemnity and the silence and the soft gloom and the brooding mystery of a remote antiquity. The stone step at the water's edge had the
traces of a worn-out inscription on it; the wide flight of stone steps
that led up to the front door was polished smooth by the passing feet
of forgotten centuries, and there was not an unbroken stone among
them all. Within the pile was the old square cloister with covered
arcade all around it where the monks of the ancient times used to sit
and meditate, and now and then welcome to their hospitalities the
wandering knight with his tin breeches on, and in the middle of the
square court (open to the sky) was a stone well curb, cracked and slick
with age and use, and all about it were weeds, and among the weeds
moldy brickbats that the Crusaders used to throw at one another. A
passage at the further side of the cloister led to another weedy and
roofless little inclosure beyond where there was a ruined wall clothed
to the top with masses of ivy, and flanking it was a battered and
picturesque arch. All over the building there were comfortable rooms
and comfortable beds and clean plank floors with no carpets on them.
In one room upstairs were half a dozen portraits, dimming relics of
the vanished centuries—portraits of abbots who used to be as grand as
princes in their old day, and very rich, and much worshiped and very
bold; and in the next room there were a howling chromo and an
electric bell. Downstairs there was an ancient wood carving with a
Latin word commanding silence, and there was a spang-new piano
close by. Two elderly French women, with the kindest and honestest
and sincerest faces, have the abbey now, and they board and lodge
people who are tired of the roar of cities and want to be where the
dead silence and serenity and peace of this old nest will heal their
blistered spirits and patch up their ragged minds. They fed us well,

they slept us well, and I wish I could have stayed there a few years and got a solid rest.

1891

WHAT PAUL BOURGET* THINKS OF US

He reports the American joke correctly. In Boston they ask, How much does he know? in New York, How much is he worth? in Philadelphia, Who were his parents? And when an alien observer turns his telescope upon us—advertisedly in our own special interest—a natural apprehension moves us to ask, What is the diameter of his reflector?

I take a great interest in M. Bourget's chapters, for I know by the newspapers that there are several Americans who are expecting to get a whole education out of them; several who foresaw, and also foretold, that our long night was over, and a light almost divine about to break upon the land.

His utterances concerning us are bound to be weighty and well timed. He gives us an object-lesson which should be thoughtfully and profitably studied.

These well-considered and important verdicts were of a nature to restore public confidence, which had been disquieted by questionings as to whether so young a teacher would be qualified to take so large a class as seventy million, distributed over so extensive a school-house as America, and pull it through without assistance.

I was even disquieted myself, although I am of a cold, calm temperament, and not easily disturbed. I feared for my country. And I was not wholly tranquilized by the verdicts rendered as above. It seemed to me that there was still room for doubt. In fact, in looking the ground over I became more disturbed than I was before. Many worrying questions came up in my mind. Two were prominent. Where had the teacher gotten his equipment? What was his method?

* Paul Bourget (1852–1935), French novelist, critic, poet, journalist. Admitted to the French Academy in 1894.

He had gotten his equipment in France.

Then as to his method! I saw by his own intimations that he was an Observer, and had a System—that used by naturalists and other scientists. The naturalist collects many bugs and reptiles and butterflies and studies their ways a long time patiently. By this means he is presently able to group these creatures into families and subdivisions of families by nice shadings of differences observable in their characters. Then he labels all those shaded bugs and things with nicely descriptive group names, and is now happy, for his great work is completed, and as a result he intimately knows every bug and shade of a bug there, inside and out. It may be true, but a person who was not a naturalist would feel safer about it if he had the opinion of the bug. I think it is a pleasant System, but subject to error.

The Observer of Peoples has to be a Classifier, a Grouper, a Deducer, a Generalizer, a Psychologizer; and, first and last, a Thinker. He has to be all these, and when he is at home, observing his own folk, he is often able to prove competency. But history has shown that when he is abroad observing unfamiliar peoples the chances are heavily against him. He is then a naturalist observing a bug, with no more than a naturalist's chance of being able to tell the bug anything new about itself, and no more than a naturalist's chance of being able to teach it any new ways which it will prefer to its own.

To return to that first question. M. Bourget, as teacher, would simply be France teaching America. It seemed to me that the outlook was dark—almost Egyptian, in fact. What would the new teacher, representing France, teach us? Railroading? No. France knows nothing valuable about railroading. Steamshipping? No. France has no superiorities over us in that matter. Steamboating? No. French steamboating is still of Fulton's date—1809. Postal service? No. France is a back number there. Telegraphy? No, we taught her that ourselves. Journalism? No. Magazining? No, that is our own specialty. Government? No; Liberty, Equality, Fraternity, Nobility, Democracy, Adultery—the system is too variegated for our climate. Religion? No, not variegated enough for our climate. Morals? No, we cannot rob the poor to enrich ourselves. Novel-writing? No. M. Bourget and the others know only one plan, and when that is expurgated there is nothing left of the book.

I wish I could think what he is going to teach us. Can it be Deportment? But he experimented in that at Newport and failed to give satisfaction, except to a few. Those few are pleased. They are enjoying their joy as well as they can. They confess their happiness to the interviewer. They feel pretty striped, but they remember with reverent recognition that they had sugar between the cuts. True, sugar with sand in it, but sugar. And true, they had some trouble to tell which was sugar and which was sand, because the sugar itself looked just like the sand, and also had a gravelly taste; still, they knew that the sugar was there, and would have been very good sugar indeed if it had been screened. Yes, they are pleased; not noisily so, but pleased; invaded, or streaked, as one may say, with little recurrent shivers of joy—subdued joy, so to speak, not the overdone kind. And they commune together, these, and massage each other with comforting sayings, in a sweet spirit of resignation and thankfulness, mixing these elements in the same proportions as the sugar and the sand, as a memorial, and saying, the one to the other, and to the interviewer: "It was severe—yes, it was bitterly severe; but oh, how true it was; and it will do us so much good!"

If it isn't Deportment, what is left? It was at this point that I seemed to get on the right track at last. M. Bourget would teach us to know ourselves; that was it: he would reveal us to ourselves. That would be an education. He would explain us to ourselves. Then we should understand ourselves; and after that be able to go on more intelligently.

It seemed a doubtful scheme. He could explain *us* to *himself*—that would be easy. That would be the same as the naturalist explaining the bug to himself. But to explain the bug to the bug—that is quite a different matter. The bug may not know himself perfectly, but he knows himself better than the naturalist can know him, at any rate.

A foreigner can photograph the exteriors of a nation, but I think that that is as far as he can get. I think that no foreigner can report its interior—its soul, its life, its speech, its thought. I think that a knowledge of these things is acquirable in only one way—not two or four or six—*absorption;* years and years of unconscious absorption; years and years of intercourse with the life concerned; of living it, indeed; sharing personally in its shames and prides, its joys and griefs, its loves and hates, its prosperities and reverses, its shows and shabbinesses, its deep patriotism, its whirlwinds of political passion, its adoration—of flag, and heroic dead, and the glory of the national name. Observation? Of what real value is it? One learns peoples through the heart, not the eyes or the intellect.

There is only one expert who is qualified to examine the souls and the life of a people and make a valuable report—the native novelist. This expert is so rare that the most populous country can never have fifteen conspicuously and confessedly competent ones in stock at one time. This native specialist is not qualified to begin work until he has been absorbing during twenty-five years. How much of his competency is derived from conscious "observation"? The amount is so slight that it counts for next to nothing in the equipment. Almost the whole capital of the novelist is the slow accumulation of *un*conscious observation—absorption. The native expert's intentional observation of manners, speech, character, and ways of life can have value, for the native knows what they mean without having to cipher out the meaning. But I should be astonished to see a foreigner get at the right meanings, catch the elusive shades of these subtle things. Even the native novelist becomes a foreigner, with a foreigner's limitations, when he steps from the state whose life is familiar to him into a state whose life he has not lived. Bret Harte got his California and his Californians by unconscious absorption, and put both of them into his tales alive. But when he came from the Pacific to the Atlantic and tried to do Newport life from study—conscious observation—his failure was absolutely monumental. Newport is a disastrous place for the unacclimated observer, evidently.

To return to novel-building. Does the native novelist try to generalize the nation? No, he lays plainly before you the ways and speech and life of a few people grouped in a certain place—his own place—and that is one book. In time he and his brethren will report to you the life and the people of the whole nation—the life of a group in a New England village; in a New York village; in a Texan village; in an Oregon village; in villages in fifty states and territories; then the farm-life in fifty states and territories; a hundred patches of life and groups of people in a dozen widely separated cities. And the Indians will be attended to; and the cowboys; and the gold and silver miners; and the negroes; and the Idiots and Congressmen; and the Irish, the Germans, the Italians, the Swedes, the French, the Chinamen, the Greasers; and the Catholics, the Methodists, the Presbyterians, the Congregationalists, the Baptists, the Spiritualists, the Mormons, the Shakers, the Quakers, the Jews, the Campbellites, the infidels, the Christian Scientists, the Mind-Curists, the Faith-Curists, the train-robbers, the White Caps, the Moonshiners. And when a thousand able novels have been written, *there* you have the soul of the people, the life of the people, the speech of the people; and not anywhere else can these be had. And the shadings of character, manners, feelings, ambitions, will be infinite.

The nature of a people is always of a similar shade in its vices and its virtues, in its frivolities and in its labor. *It is this physiognomy which it is necessary to discover,* and every document is good, from the hall of a casino to the church, from the foibles of a fashionable woman to the suggestions of a revolutionary leader. I am therefore quite sure that this *American soul,* the principal interest and the great object of my voyage, appears behind the records of Newport for those who choose to see it.—*M. Paul Bourget.*

[The italics are mine.] It is a large contract which he has undertaken. "Records" is a pretty poor word there, but I think the use of it is due to hasty translation. In the original the word is *fastes.* I think M. Bourget meant to suggest that he expected to find the great "American soul" secreted behind the *ostentations* of Newport; and that he was going to get it out and examine it, and generalize it, and psychologize it, and make it reveal to him its hidden vast mystery: "the nature of the people" of the United States of America. We have been accused of being a nation addicted to inventing wild schemes. I trust that we shall be allowed to retire to second place now.

There isn't a single human characteristic that can be safely labeled "American." There isn't a single human ambition, or religious trend, or drift of thought, or peculiarity of education, or code of principles, or breed of folly, or style of conversation, or preference for a particular subject for discussion, or form of legs or trunk or head or face or expression or complexion, or gait, or dress, or manners, or disposition, or any other human detail, inside or outside, that can rationally be generalized as "American."

Whenever you have found what seems to be an "American" peculiarity, you have only to cross a frontier or two, or go down or up in the social scale, and you perceive that it has disappeared. And you can cross the Atlantic and find it again. There may be a Newport religious drift, or sporting drift, or conversational style or complexion, or cut of face, but there are entire empires in America, north, south, east, and west, where you could not find your duplicates. It is the same with everything else which one might propose to call "American." M. Bourget thinks he has found the American Coquette. If he had really found her he would also have found, I am sure, that she was not new, that she exists in other lands in the same forms, and with the same frivolous heart and the same ways and impulses. I think this because I have seen our coquette; I have seen her in life; better still, I have seen her in our novels, and seen her twin in foreign novels. I wish M. Bourget had seen ours. He thought he saw her. And so he applied his System to her. She was a Species. So he gathered a number of samples of what seemed to be her, and put them under his glass, and divided them into groups which he calls "types," and labeled them in his usual scientific way with "formulas"—brief, sharp descriptive flashes that make a person blink, sometimes, they are so sudden and vivid. As a rule they are pretty far-fetched, but that is not an important matter; they surprise, they compel admiration, and I notice by some of the comments which his efforts have called forth that they deceive the unwary. Here are a few of the coquette variants which he has grouped and labeled:

THE COLLECTOR.
THE EQUILIBREE.
THE PROFESSIONAL BEAUTY.
THE BLUFFER.
THE GIRL-BOY.

If he had stopped with describing these characters we should have been obliged to believe that they exist; that they exist, and that he has seen them and spoken with them. But he did not stop there; he went further and furnished to us light-throwing samples of their behavior, and also light-throwing samples of their speeches. He entered those things in his note-book without suspicion, he takes them out and delivers them to the world with a candor and simplicity which show that he believed them genuine. They throw altogether too much light. They reveal to the native the origin of his find. I suppose he knows how he came to make that novel and captivating discovery, by this time. If he does not, any American can tell him—any American to whom he will show his anecdotes. It was "put up" on him, as we say. It was a jest— to be plain, it was a series of frauds. To my mind it was a poor sort of jest, witless and contemptible. The players of it have their reward, such as it is; they have exhibited the fact that whatever they may be they are not ladies. M. Bourget did not discover a type of coquette; he merely discovered a type of practical joker. One may say *the* type of practical joker, for these people are exactly alike all over the world. Their equipment is always the same: a vulgar mind, a puerile wit, a cruel disposition as a rule, and always the spirit of treachery.

In his Chapter IV. M. Bourget has two or three columns gravely devoted to the collating and examining and psychologizing of these sorry little frauds. One is not moved to laugh. There is nothing funny in the situation; it is only pathetic. The stranger gave those people his confidence, and they dishonorably treated him in return.

But one must be allowed to suspect that M. Bourget was a little to blame himself. Even a practical joker has some little judgment. He has to exercise some degree of sagacity in selecting his prey if he would save himself from getting into trouble. In my time I have seldom seen such daring things marketed at any price as these conscienceless folk have worked off at par on this confiding observer. It compels the conviction that there was something about him that bred in those speculators a quite unusual sense of safety, and encouraged them to strain their powers in his behalf. They seem to have satisfied themselves that all he wanted was "significant" facts, and that he was not accustomed to examine the source whence they proceeded. It is plain that there was a sort of conspiracy against him almost from the start— a conspiracy to freight him up with all the strange extravagances those people's decayed brains could invent.

The lengths to which they went are next to incredible. They told him things which surely would have excited any one else's suspicion, but they did not excite his. Consider this:

There is not in all the United States an entirely nude statue.

If an angel should come down and say such a thing about heaven, a reasonably cautious observer would take that angel's number and inquire a little further before he added it to his catch. What does the present observer do? Adds it. Adds it at once. Adds it, and labels it with this innocent comment:

This small fact is strangely significant.

It does seem to me that this kind of observing is defective.

Here is another curiosity which some liberal person made him a present of. I should think it ought to have disturbed the deep slumber of his suspicion a little, but it didn't. It was a note from a fog-horn for strenuousness, it seems to me, but the doomed voyager did not catch it. If he had but caught it, it would have saved him from several disasters:

> If the American knows that you are traveling to take notes, he is interested in it, and at the same time rejoices in it, as in a tribute.

Again, this is defective observation. It is human to like to be praised; one can even notice it in the French. But it is not human to like to be ridiculed, even when it comes in the form of a "tribute." I think a little psychologizing ought to have come in there. Something like this: A dog does not like to be ridiculed, a redskin does not like to be ridiculed, a negro does not like to be ridiculed, a Chinaman does not like to be ridiculed; let us deduce from these significant facts this formula: the American's grade being higher than these, and the chain of argument stretching unbroken all the way up to him, there is room for suspicion that the person who said the American likes to be ridiculed, and regards it as a tribute, is not a capable observer.

I feel persuaded that in the matter of psychologizing, a professional is too apt to yield to the fascinations of the loftier regions of that great art, to the neglect of its lowlier walks. Every now and then, at half-hour intervals, M. Bourget collects a hatful of airy inaccuracies and dissolves them in a panful of assorted abstractions, and runs the charge into a mold and turns you out a compact principle which will explain an American girl, or an American woman, or why new people yearn for old things, or any other impossible riddle which a person wants answered.

It seems to be conceded that there are a few human peculiarities that can be generalized and located here and there in the world and named by the name of the nation where they are found. I wonder what they are. Perhaps one of them is temperament. One speaks of French vivacity and German gravity and English stubbornness. There is no American temperament. The nearest that one can come at it is to say there are two—the composed Northern and the impetuous Southern; and both are found in other countries. Morals? Purity of women may fairly be called universal with us, but that is the case in some other countries. We have no monopoly of it; it cannot be named American. I think that there is but a single specialty with us, only one thing that can be called by the wide name "American." That is the national devotion to ice-water. All Germans drink beer, but the British nation drinks beer, too; so neither of those peoples is *the* beer-drinking nation. I suppose we do stand alone in having a drink that nobody likes but ourselves. When we have been a month in Europe we lose our craving for it, and we finally tell the hotel folk that they needn't provide it any more. Yet we hardly touch our native shore again, winter or summer, before we are eager for it. The reasons for this state of things have not been psychologized yet. I drop the hint and say no more.

It is my belief that there are some "national" traits and things scattered about the world that are mere superstitions, frauds that have lived so long that they have the solid look of facts. One of them is the dogma that the French are the only chaste people in the world. Ever since I arrived in France this last time I have been accumulating doubts about that; and before I leave this sunny land again I will gather in a few random statistics and psychologize the plausibilities out of it. If people are to come over to America and find fault with our girls and our women, and psychologize every little thing they do, and try to teach them how to behave, and how to cultivate themselves up to where one cannot tell them from the French model, I intend to find out whether those missionaries are qualified or not. A nation ought always to examine into this detail before engaging the teacher for good. This last one has let fall a remark which renewed those doubts of mine when I read it:

> In our high Parisian existence, for instance, we find applied to arts and luxury, and to debauchery, all the powers and all the weaknesses of the French soul.

You see, it amounts to a trade with the French soul; a profession; a science; the serious business of life, so to speak, in our high Parisian existence. I do not quite like the look of it. I question if it can be taught with profit in our country, except, of course, to those pathetic, neglected minds that are waiting there so yearningly for the education which M. Bourget is going to furnish them from the serene summits of our high Parisian life.

I spoke a moment ago of the existence of some superstitions that have been parading the world as facts this long time. For instance, consider the Dollar. The world seems to think that the love of money is "American"; and that the mad desire to get suddenly rich is "American." I believe that both of these things are merely and broadly human, not American monopolies at all. The love of money is natural to all nations, for money is a good and strong friend. I think that this love has existed everywhere, ever since the Bible called it the root of all evil.

I think that the reason why we Americans seem to be so addicted to trying to get rich suddenly is merely because the *opportunity* to make promising efforts in that direction has offered itself to us with a frequency out of all proportion to the European experience. For eighty years this opportunity has been offering itself in one new town or region after another straight westward, step by step, all the way from the Atlantic coast to the Pacific. When a mechanic could buy ten town lots on tolerably long credit for ten months' savings out of his wages, and reasonably expect to sell them in a couple of years for ten times what he gave for them, it was human for him to try the venture, and he did it no matter what his nationality was. He would have done it in Europe or China if he had had the same chance.

In the flush times in the silver regions a cook or any other humble worker stood a very good chance to get rich out of a trifle of money risked in a stock deal; and that person promptly took that risk, no matter what his or her nationality might be. I was there, and saw it.

But these opportunities have not been plenty in our Southern states; so there you have a prodigious region where the rush for sudden wealth is almost an unknown thing—and has been, from the beginning.

Europe has offered few opportunities for poor Tom, Dick, and Harry; but when she has offered one, there has been no noticeable difference between European eagerness and American. England saw this in the wild days of the Railroad King; France saw it in 1720—time of Law and the Mississippi Bubble. I am sure I have never seen in the gold and silver mines any madness, fury, frenzy to get suddenly rich which was even remotely comparable to that which raged in France in the Bubble day. If I had a cyclopedia here I could turn to that memorable case, and satisfy nearly anybody that the hunger for the sudden dollar is no more "American" than it is French. And if I could furnish an American opportunity to staid Germany, I think I could wake her up like a house afire.

But I must return to the Generalizations, Psychologizings, Deductions. When M. Bourget is exploiting these arts, it is then that he is peculiarly and particularly himself. His ways are wholly original when he encounters a trait or a custom which is new to him. Another person would merely examine the find, verify it, estimate its value, and let it go; but that is not sufficient for M. Bourget: he always wants to know *why* that thing exists, he wants to know how it came to happen; and he will not let go of it until he has found out. And in every instance he will find that reason where no one but himself would have thought of looking for it. He does not seem to care for a reason that is not picturesquely located; one might almost say picturesquely and impossibly located.

He found out that in America men do not try to hunt down young married women. At once, as usual, he wanted to know *why*. Any one could have told him. He could have divined it by the lights thrown by the novels of the country. But no, he preferred to find out for himself. He has a trustfulness as regards men and facts which is fine and unusual; he is not particular about the source of a fact, he is not particular about the character and standing of the fact itself; but when it comes to pounding out the reason for the existence of the fact, he will trust no one but himself.

In the present instance here was his fact: American young married women are not pursued by the corrupter; and here was the question: What is it that protects her?

It seems quite unlikely that that problem could have offered difficulties to any but a trained philosopher. Nearly any person would have said to M. Bourget: "Oh, that is very simple. It is very seldom in America that a marriage is made on a commercial basis; our marriages, from the beginning, have been made for love; and where love is there is no room for the corrupter."

Now, it is interesting to see the formidable way in which M. Bourget went at that poor, humble little thing. He moved upon it in column —three columns—and with artillery.

"Two reasons of a very different kind explain"—that fact.

And now that I have got so far, I am almost afraid to say what his two reasons are, lest I be charged with inventing them. But I will not retreat now; I will condense them and print them, giving my word that I am honest and not trying to deceive any one.

1. Young married women are protected from the approaches of the seducer in New England and vicinity by the diluted remains of a prudence created by a Puritan law of two hundred years ago, which for a while punished adultery with death.

2. And young married women of the other forty or fifty states are protected by laws which afford extraordinary facilities for divorce.

If I have not lost my mind I have accurately conveyed those two Vesuvian irruptions of philosophy. But the reader can consult Chapter IV. of *Outre-Mer*, and decide for himself. Let us examine this paralyzing Deduction or Explanation by the light of a few sane facts.

1. This universality of "protection" has existed in our country *from the beginning;* before the death-penalty existed in New England, and during all the generations that have dragged by since it was annulled.

2. Extraordinary facilities for divorce are of such recent creation that any middle-aged American can remember a time when such things had not yet been thought of.

Let us suppose that the first easy divorce law went into effect forty years ago, and got noised around and fairly started in business thirty-five years ago, when we had, say, 25,000,000 of white population. Let us suppose that among 5,000,000 of them the young married women were "protected" by the surviving shudder of that ancient Puritan scare—what is M. Bourget going to do about those who lived among the 20,000,000? They were clean in their morals, they were pure, yet there was no easy divorce law to protect them.

Awhile ago I said that M. Bourget's method of truth-seeking—hunting for it in out-of-the-way places—was new; but that was an error. I remember that when Leverrier discovered the Milky Way, he and the other astronomers began to theorize about it in substantially the same fashion which M. Bourget employs in his reasonings about American social facts and their origin. Leverrier advanced the hypothesis that the Milky Way was caused by gaseous protoplasmic emanations from the field of Waterloo, which, ascending to an altitude determinable by their own specific gravity, became luminous through the development and exposure—by the natural processes of animal decay —of the phosphorus contained in them.

This theory was warmly complimented by Ptolemy, who, however, after much thought and research, decided that he could not accept it as final. His own theory was that the Milky Way was an emigration of lightning-bugs; and he supported and reinforced this theorem by the well-known fact that the locusts do like that in Egypt.

Giordano Bruno also was outspoken in his praises of Leverrier's important contribution to astronomical science, and was at first inclined to regard it as conclusive; but later, conceiving it to be erroneous, he pronounced against it, and advanced the hypothesis that the Milky Way was a detachment or corps of stars which became arrested and held in *suspenso suspensorum* by refraction of gravitation while on the march to join their several constellations; a proposition for which he was afterward burned at the stake in Jacksonville, Illinois.

These were all brilliant and picturesque theories, and each was received with enthusiasm by the scientific world; but when a New England farmer, who was not a thinker, but only a plain sort of person who tried to account for large facts in simple ways, came out with the opinion that the Milky Way was just common, ordinary stars, and was put where it was because God "wanted to hev it so," the admirable idea fell perfectly flat.

As a literary artist, M. Bourget is as fresh and striking as he is as a scientific one. He says, "Above all, I do not believe much in anecdotes." Why? "In history they are all false"—a sufficiently broad statement—"in literature all libelous"—also a sufficiently sweeping statement, coming from a critic who notes that we are a people who are peculiarly extravagant in our language—"and when it is a matter of social life, almost all biased." It seems to amount to stultification, almost. He has built two or three breeds of American coquettes out of anecdotes—mainly "biased" ones, I suppose; and, as they occur "in literature," furnished by his pen, they must be "all libelous." Or did he mean not *in* literature or anecdotes *about* literature or literary people? I am not able to answer that. Perhaps the original would be clearer, but I have only the translation of this instalment by me. I think the remark had an intention; also that this intention was booked for the trip; but that either in the hurry of the remark's departure it got left, or in the confusion of changing cars at the translator's frontier it got side-tracked.

"But on the other hand I believe in statistics; and those on divorces appear to me to be most conclusive." And he sets himself the task of explaining—in a couple of columns—the process by which Easy-Divorce conceived, invented, originated, developed, and perfected an empire-embracing condition of sexual purity in the States. *In forty years.* No, he doesn't state the interval. With all his passion for statistics he forgot to ask how long it took to produce this gigantic miracle.

I have followed his pleasant but devious trail through those columns, but I was not able to get hold of his argument and find out what it was. I was not even able to find out where it left off. It seemed to gradually dissolve and flow off into other matters. I followed it with interest, for I was anxious to learn how easy-divorce eradicated adultery in America, but I was disappointed; I have no idea yet how it did it. I only know it didn't. But that is not valuable; I knew it before.

Well, humor is the great thing, the saving thing, after all. The minute it crops up, all our hardnesses yield, all our irritations and resentments flit away, and a sunny spirit takes their place. And so, when M. Bourget said that bright thing about our grandfathers, I broke all up. I remember exploding its American countermine once, under that grand hero, Napoleon. He was only First Consul then, and I was Consul-General—for the United States, of course; but we were very intimate, notwithstanding the difference in rank, for I waived that. One day something offered the opening, and he said:

"Well, General, I suppose life can never get entirely dull to an American, because whenever he can't strike up any other way to put in his time he can always get away with a few years trying to find out who his grandfather was!"

I fairly shouted, for I had never heard it sound better; and then I was back at him as quick as a flash:

"Right, your Excellency! But I reckon a Frenchman's got *his* little stand-by for a dull time, too; because when all other interests fail he can turn in and see if he can't find out who his father was!"

Well, you should have heard him just whoop, and cackle, and carry on! He reached up and hit me one on the shoulder, and says:

"Land, but it's good! It's im-mensely good! I'George, I never heard it said so good in my life before! Say it again."

So I said it again, and he said his again, and I said mine again, and then he did, and then I did, and then he did, and we kept on doing it, and doing it, and I *never* had such a good time, and he said the same. In my opinion there isn't anything that is as killing as one of those dear old ripe pensioners if you know how to snatch it out in a kind of a fresh sort of original way.

But I wish M. Bourget had read more of our novels before he came. It is the only way to thoroughly understand a people. When I found I was coming to Paris, I read *La Terre.* *

1895

* A novel by Zola. Bourget wrote a novel called *La Terre promise.*

TO THE PERSON SITTING IN DARKNESS*

Christmas will dawn in the United States over a people full of hope
and aspiration and good cheer. Such a condition means contentment
and happiness. The carping grumbler who may here and there go
forth will find few to listen to him. The majority will wonder what is
the matter with him and pass on.—*New York Tribune,* on Christmas
Eve.

From the *Sun,* of New York:

> The purpose of this article is not to describe the terrible
> offenses against humanity committed in the name of Politics
> in some of the most notorious East Side districts. *They could
> not be described, even verbally.* But it is the intention to let
> the great mass of more or less careless citizens of this beauti-
> ful metropolis of the New World get some conception of the
> havoc and ruin wrought to man, woman, and child in the
> most densely populated and least-known section of the city.
> Name, date, and place can be supplied to those of little faith
> —or to any man who feels himself aggrieved. It is a plain
> statement of record and observation, written without license
> and without garnish.
>
> Imagine, if you can, a section of the city territory com-
> pletely dominated by one man, without whose permission
> neither legitimate nor illegitimate business can be conducted;
> *where illegitimate business is encouraged and legitimate busi-
> ness discouraged;* where the respectable residents have to
> fasten their doors and windows summer nights and sit in
> their rooms with asphyxiating air and 100-degree tempera-
> ture, rather than try to catch the faint whiff of breeze in their
> natural breathing places, the stoops of their homes; *where
> naked women dance by night in the streets, and unsexed men
> prowl like vultures through the darkness on "business"* not

* This essay and the essay following it appeared first in the *North American Review.*—
C.N.

only permitted but encouraged by the police; *where the education of infants begins with the knowledge of prostitution* and the training of little girls is training in the arts of Phryne; where *American* girls brought up with the refinements of *American* homes are imported from small towns up-state, Massachusetts, Connecticut, and New Jersey, and kept as virtually prisoners as if they were locked up behind jail bars until they have lost all semblance of womanhood; *where small boys are taught to solicit for the women of disorderly houses;* where there is an organized society of young men *whose sole business in life is to corrupt young girls and turn them over to bawdy houses;* where men walking with their wives along the street are openly insulted; *where children that have adult diseases are the chief patrons of the hospitals and dispensaries;* where it is the rule, rather than the exception, that *murder, rape, robbery, and theft go unpunished*—in short where the Premium of the most awful forms of Vice is the Profit of the politicians.

The following news from China appeared in the *Sun,* of New York, on Christmas Eve. The italics are mine:

The Rev. Mr. Ament, of the American Board of Foreign Missions, has returned from a trip which he made for the purpose of collecting indemnities for damages done by Boxers. *Everywhere he went he compelled the Chinese to pay.* He says that all his native Christians are now provided for. He had 700 of them under his charge, and 300 were killed. He has *collected 300 taels for each of these murders,* and has *compelled full payment for all the property belonging to Christians* that was destroyed. He also assessed *fines* amounting to THIRTEEN TIMES the amount of the indemnity. *This money will be used for the propagation of the Gospel.*

Mr. Ament declares that the compensation he has collected is *moderate* when compared with the amount secured by the Catholics, who demand, in addition to money, *head for head.* They collect 500 taels for each murder of a Catholic. In the Wenchiu country, 680 Catholics were killed, and for this the European Catholics here demand 750,000 strings of cash and 680 *heads.*

In the course of a conversation, Mr. Ament referred to the attitude of the missionaries toward the Chinese. He said:

"I deny emphatically that the missionaries are *vindictive,* that they *generally* looted, or that they have done anything *since* the siege that *the circumstances did not demand.* I criticize the Americans. *The soft hand of the Americans is not as good as the mailed fist of the Germans.* If you deal with the Chinese with a soft hand they will take advantage of it.

"The statement that the French government will return the loot taken by the French soldiers is the source of the greatest amusement here. The French soldiers were more systematic looters than the Germans, and it is a fact that today *Catholic Christians,* carrying French flags and armed with modern guns, *are looting villages* in the Province of Chili."

By happy luck, we get all these glad tidings on Christmas Eve—just in time to enable us to celebrate the day with proper gayety and enthusiasm. Our spirits soar, and we find we can even make jokes: Taels, I win, Heads you lose.

Our Reverend Ament is the right man in the right place. What we want of our missionaries out there is, not that they shall merely represent in their acts and persons the grace and gentleness and charity and loving-kindness of our religion, but that they shall also represent the American spirit. The oldest Americans are the Pawnees. Macallum's History says:

When a white Boxer kills a Pawnee and destroys his property, the other Pawnees do not trouble to seek *him* out, they kill any white person that comes along; also they make some white village pay deceased's heirs the full cash value of deceased, together with full cash value of the property destroyed; they also make the village pay, in addition, *thirteen times* the value of that property into a fund for the dissemination of the Pawnee religion, which they regard as the best of all religions for the softening and humanizing of the heart of man. It is their idea that it is only fair and right that the innocent should be made to suffer for the guilty, and that it

is better that ninety and nine innocent should suffer than
that one guilty person should escape.

Our Reverend Ament is justifiably jealous of those enterprising
Catholics, who not only get big money for each lost convert, but get
"head for head" besides. But he should soothe himself with the reflections that the entirety of their exactions are for their own pockets,
whereas he, less selfishly, devotes only 300 taels per head to that service, and gives the whole vast thirteen repetitions of the property-
indemnity to the service of propagating the Gospel. His magnanimity
has won him the approval of his nation, and will get him a monument.
Let him be content with these rewards. We all hold him dear for
manfully defending his fellow missionaries from exaggerated charges
which were beginning to distress us, but which his testimony has so
considerably modified that we can now contemplate them without
noticeable pain. For now we know that, even before the siege, the
missionaries were not "generally" out looting, and that, "since the
siege," they have acted quite handsomely, except when "circumstances" crowded them. I am arranging for the monument. Subscrip-
tions for it can be sent to the American Board; designs for it can be
sent to me. Designs must allegorically set forth the Thirteen Redupli-
cations of the Indemnity, and the Object for which they were exacted;
as Ornaments, the designs must exhibit 680 Heads, so disposed as to
give a pleasing and pretty effect; for the Catholics have done nicely,
and are entitled to notice in the monument. Mottos may be suggested,
if any shall be discovered that will satisfactorily cover the ground.

Mr. Ament's financial feat of squeezing a thirteenfold indemnity out
of the pauper peasants to square other people's offences, thus con-
demning them and their women and innocent little children to inevitable starvation and lingering death, in order that the blood money so
acquired might be *used for the propagation of the Gospel,* does not
flutter my serenity; although the act and the words, taken together,
concrete a blasphemy so hideous and so colossal that, without doubt,
its mate is not findable in the history of this or of any other age. Yet, if
a layman had done that thing and justified it with those words, I
should have shuddered, I know. Or, if I had done the thing and said
the words myself— However, the thought is unthinkable, irreverent as
some imperfectly informed people think me. Sometimes an ordained

minister sets out to be blasphemous. When this happens, the layman is out of the running; he stands no chance.

We have Mr. Ament's impassioned assurance that the missionaries are not "vindictive." Let us hope and pray that they will never become so, but will remain in the almost morbidly fair and just and gentle temper which is affording so much satisfaction to their brother and champion to-day.

The following is from the New York *Tribune* of Christmas Eve. It comes from that journal's Tokyo correspondent. It has a strange and impudent sound, but the Japanese are but partially civilized as yet. When they become wholly civilized they will not talk so:

> The missionary question, of course, occupies a foremost place in the discussion. It is now felt as essential that the Western Powers take cognizance of the sentiment here, that religious invasions of Oriental countries by powerful Western organizations are tantamount to filibustering expeditions, and should not only be discountenanced, but that stern measures should be adopted for their suppression. The feeling here is that the missionary organizations constitute a constant menace to peaceful international relations.

Shall we? That is, shall we go on conferring our Civilization upon the peoples that sit in darkness, or shall we give those poor things a rest? Shall we bang right ahead in our old-time, loud, pious way, and commit the new century to the game; or shall we sober up and sit down and think it over first? Would it not be prudent to get our Civilization tools together, and see how much stock is left on hand in the way of Glass Beads and Theology, and Maxim Guns and Hymn Books, and Trade Gin and Torches of Progress and Enlightenment (patent adjustable ones, good to fire villages with, upon occasion), and balance the books, and arrive at the profit and loss, so that we may intelligently decide whether to continue the business or sell out the property and start a new Civilization Scheme on the proceeds?

Extending the Blessings of Civilization to our Brother who Sits in Darkness has been a good trade and has paid well, on the whole; and there is money in it yet, if carefully worked—but not enough, in my judgment, to make any considerable risk advisable. The people that Sit in Darkness are getting to be too scarce—too scarce and too shy. And such darkness as is now left is really of but an indifferent quality, and not dark enough for the game. The most of those People that Sit in Darkness have been furnished with more light than was good for them or profitable for us. We have been injudicious.

The Blessings-of-Civilization Trust, wisely and cautiously administered, is a Daisy. There is more money in it, more territory, more sovereignty, and other kinds of emolument, than there is in any other game that is played. But Christendom has been playing it badly of late years, and must certainly suffer by it, in my opinion. She has been so eager to get every stake that appeared on the green cloth, that the People who Sit in Darkness have noticed it—they have noticed it, and have begun to show alarm. They have become suspicious of the Blessings of Civilization. More—they have begun to examine them. This is not well. The Blessings of Civilization are all right, and a good commercial property; there could not be a better, in a dim light. In the right kind of a light, and at a proper distance, with the goods a little out of focus, they furnish this desirable exhibit to the Gentlemen who Sit in Darkness:

LOVE,	LAW AND ORDER,
JUSTICE,	LIBERTY,
GENTLENESS,	EQUALITY,
CHRISTIANITY,	HONORABLE DEALING,
PROTECTION TO THE WEAK,	MERCY,
TEMPERANCE,	EDUCATION,

—and so on.

There. Is it good? Sir, it is pie. It will bring into camp any idiot that sits in darkness anywhere. But not if we adulterate it. It is proper to be emphatic upon that point. This brand is strictly for Export—apparently. *Apparently.* Privately and confidentially, it is nothing of the kind. Privately and confidentially, it is merely an outside cover, gay and pretty and attractive, displaying the special patterns of our Civilization which we reserve for Home Consumption, while *inside* the bale is the Actual Thing that the Customer Sitting in Darkness buys with his blood and tears and land and liberty. That Actual Thing is, indeed, Civilization, but it is only for Export. Is there a difference between the two brands? In some of the details, yes.

We all know that the Business is being ruined. The reason is not far to seek. It is because our Mr. McKinley, and Mr. Chamberlain, and the Kaiser, and the Tsar and the French have been exporting the Actual Thing *with the outside cover left off.* This is bad for the Game.

It shows that these new players of it are not sufficiently acquainted with it.

It is a distress to look on and note the mismoves, they are so strange and so awkward. Mr. Chamberlain manufactures a war of materials so inadequate and so fanciful that they make the boxes grieve and the gallery laugh, and he tries hard to persuade himself that it isn't purely a private raid for cash, but has a sort of dim, vague respectability about it somewhere, if he could only find the spot; and that, by and by, he can scour the flag clean again after he has finished dragging it through the mud, and make it shine and flash in the vault of heaven once more as it had shone and flashed there a thousand years in the world's respect until he laid his unfaithful hand upon it. It is bad play —bad. For it exposes the Actual Thing to Them that Sit in Darkness, and they say: "What! Christian against Christian? And only for money? Is *this* a case of magnanimity, forbearance, love, gentleness, mercy, protection of the weak—this strange and overshowy onslaught of an elephant upon a nest of field mice, on the pretext that the mice had squeaked an insolence at him—conduct which "no self-respecting government could allow to pass unavenged"? as Mr. Chamberlain said. Was that a good pretext in a small case, when it had not been a good pretext in a large one?—for only recently Russia had affronted the elephant three times and survived alive and unsmitten. Is this Civilization and Progress? Is it something better than we already possess? These harryings and burnings and desert-makings in the Transvaal—is this an improvement on our darkness? Is it, perhaps, possible that there are two kinds of Civilization—one for home consumption and one for the heathen market?

Then They that Sit in Darkness are troubled, and shake their heads; and they read this extract from a letter of a British private, recounting his exploits in one of Methuen's victories, some days before the affair of Magersfontein, and they are troubled again:

> We tore up the hill and into the intrenchments, and the Boers saw we had them; so they dropped their guns and went down on their knees and put up their hands clasped, and begged for mercy. And we gave it them—*with the long spoon.*

The long spoon is the bayonet. See *Lloyd's Weekly,* London, of those days. The same number—and the same column—contained some

quite unconscious satire in the form of shocked and bitter upbraidings
of the Boers for their brutalities and inhumanities!

Next, to our heavy damage, the Kaiser went to playing the game
without first mastering it. He lost a couple of missionaries in a riot in
Shantung, and in his account he made an overcharge for them. China
had to pay a hundred thousand dollars apiece for them, in money;
twelve miles of territory, containing several millions of inhabitants and
worth twenty million dollars; and to build a monument, and also a
Christian church; whereas the people of China could have been depended upon to remember the missionaries without the help of these
expensive memorials. This was all bad play. Bad, because it would not,
and could not and will not now or ever, deceive the Person Sitting in
Darkness. He knows that it was an overcharge. He knows that a
missionary is like any other man: he is worth merely what you can
supply his place for, and no more. He is useful, but so is a doctor, so is
a sheriff, so is an editor; but a just Emperor does not charge war prices
for such. A diligent, intelligent, but obscure missionary, and a diligent,
intelligent country editor are worth much, and we know it; but they
are not worth the earth. We esteem such an editor, and we are sorry to
see him go; but, when he goes, we should consider twelve miles of
territory, and a church, and a fortune, overcompensation for his loss. I
mean, if he was a Chinese editor, and we had to settle for him. It is no
proper figure for an editor or a missionary; one can get shop-worn
kings for less. It was bad play on the Kaiser's part. It got this property, true; but it *produced the Chinese revolt,* the indignant uprising of
China's traduced patriots, the Boxers. The results have been expensive
to Germany, and to the other Disseminators of Progress and the
Blessings of Civilization. The Kasier's claim was paid, yet it was bad
play, for it could not fail to have an evil effect upon Persons Sitting in
Darkness in China. They would muse upon the event, and be likely to
say: "Civilization is gracious and beautiful, for such is its reputation;
but can we afford it? There are rich Chinamen, perhaps they can
afford it; but this tax is not laid upon them, it is laid upon the peasants
of Shantung; it is they that must pay this mighty sum, and their wages
are but four cents a day. Is this a better civilization than ours, and
holier and higher and nobler? Is not this rapacity? Is not this extor-
tion? Would Germany charge America two hundred thousand dollars
for two missionaries, and shake the mailed fist in her face, and send
warships, and send soldiers, and say: 'Seize twelve miles of territory,

worth twenty millions of dollars, as additional pay for the missionaries; and make those peasants build a monument to the missionaries, and a costly Christian church to remember them by?' And later would Germany say to her soldiers: 'March through America and slay, *giving no quarter;* make the German face there, as has been our Hun-face here, a terror for a thousand years; march through the Great Republic and slay, slay, slay, carving a road for our offended religion through its heart and bowels?' Would Germany do like this to America, to England, to France, to Russia? Or only to China, the helpless—imitating the elephant's assault upon the field mice? Had we better invest in this Civilization—this Civilization which called Napoleon a buccaneer for carrying off Venice's bronze horses, but which steals our ancient astronomical instruments from our walls, and goes looting like common bandits—that is, all the alien soldiers except America's; and (Americans again excepted) storms frightened villages and cables the result to glad journals at home every day: 'Chinese losses, 450 killed; ours, *one officer and two men wounded.* Shall proceed against neighboring village to-morrow, where a *massacre* is reported.' Can we afford Civilization?"

And next Russia must go and play the game injudiciously. She affronts England once or twice—with the Person Sitting in Darkness observing and noting; by moral assistance of France and Germany, she robs Japan of her hard-earned spoil, all swimming in Chinese blood—Port Arthur—with the Person again observing and noting; then she seizes Manchuria, raids its villages, and chokes its great river with the swollen corpses of countless massacred peasants—that astonished Person still observing and noting. And perhaps he is saying to himself: "It is yet *another* Civilized Power, with its banner of the Prince of Peace in one hand and its loot basket and its butcher knife in the other. Is there no salvation for us but to adopt Civilization and lift ourselves down to its level?"

And by and by comes America, and our Master of the Game plays it badly—plays it as Mr. Chamberlain was playing it in South Africa. It was a mistake to do that; also, it was one which was quite unlooked for in a Master who was playing it so well in Cuba. In Cuba, he was playing the usual and regular *American* game, and it was winning, for there is no way to beat it. The Master, contemplating Cuba, said: "Here is an oppressed and friendless little nation which is willing to fight to be free; we go partners, and put up the strength of seventy

million sympathizers and the resources of the United States: play!"
Nothing but Europe combined could call that hand: and Europe cannot combine on anything. There, in Cuba, he was following our great
traditions in a way which made us very proud of him, and proud of
the deep dissatisfaction which his play was provoking in continental
Europe. Moved by a high inspiration, he threw out those stirring
words which proclaimed that forcible annexation would be "criminal
aggression"; and in that utterance fired another "shot heard round the
world." The memory of that fine saying will be outlived by the remembrance of no act of his but one—that he forgot it within the twelve-
month, and its honorable gospel along with it.

For, presently, came the Philippine temptation. It was strong; it was
too strong, and he made that bad mistake: he played the European
game, the Chamberlain game. It was a pity; it was a great pity, that
error; that one grievous error, that irrevocable error. For it was the
very place and time to play the American game again. And at no cost.
Rich winnings to be gathered in, too; rich and permanent; indestructi-
ble; a fortune transmissible forever to the children of the flag. Not
land, not money, not dominion—no, something worth many times
more than that dross: our share, the spectacle of a nation of long
harassed and persecuted slaves set free through our influence; our
posterity's share, the golden memory of that fair deed. The game was
in our hands. If it had been played according to the American rules,
Dewey would have sailed away from Manila as soon as he had destroyed the Spanish fleet—after putting up a sign on shore guarantee-
ing foreign property and life against damage by the Filipinos, and
warning the Powers that interference with the emancipated patriots
would be regarded as an act unfriendly to the United States. The
Powers cannot combine, in even a bad cause, and the sign would not
have been molested.

Dewey could have gone about his affairs elsewhere, and left the
competent Filipino army to starve out the little Spanish garrison and
send it home, and the Filipino citizens to set up the form of government they might prefer, and deal with the friars and their doubtful
acquisitions according to Filipino ideas of fairness and justice—ideas
which have since been tested and found to be of as high an order as
any that prevail in Europe or America.

But we played the Chamberlain game, and lost the chance to add
another Cuba and another honorable deed to our good record.

The more we examine the mistake, the more clearly we perceive that it is going to be bad for the Business. The Person Sitting in Darkness is almost sure to say: "There is something curious about this —curious and unaccountable. There must be two Americans; one that sets the captive free, and one that takes a once-captive's new freedom away from him, and picks a quarrel with him with nothing to found it on; then kills him to get his land."

The truth is, the Person Sitting in Darkness *is* saying things like that; and for the sake of the Business we must persuade him to look at the Philippine matter in another and healthier way. We must arrange his opinions for him. I believe it can be done; for Mr. Chamberlain has arranged England's opinion of the South African matter, and done it most cleverly and successfully. He presented the facts—some of the facts—and showed those confiding people what the facts meant. He did it statistically, which is a good way. He used the formula: "Twice 2 are 14, and 2 from 9 leaves 35." Figures are effective; figures will convince the elect.

Now, my plan is a still bolder one than Mr. Chamberlain's, though apparently a copy of it. Let us be franker than Mr. Chamberlain; let us audaciously present the whole of the facts, shirking none, then explain them according to Mr. Chamberlain's formula. This daring truthfulness will astonish and dazzle the Person Sitting in Darkness, and he will take the Explanation down before his mental vision has had time to get back into focus. Let us say to him:

"Our case is simple. On the 1st of May, Dewey destroyed the Spanish fleet. This left the Archipelago in the hands of its proper and rightful owners, the Filipino nation. Their army numbered 30,000 men, and they were competent to whip out or starve out the little Spanish garrison; then the people could set up a government of their own devising. Our traditions required that Dewey should now set up his warning sign, and go away. But the Master of the Game happened to think of another plan—the European plan. He acted upon it. This was, to send out an army—ostensibly to help the native patriots put the finishing touch upon their long and plucky struggle for independence, but really to take their land away from them and keep it. That is, in the interest of Progress and Civilization. The plan developed, stage by stage, and quite satisfactorily. We entered into a military alliance with the trusting Filipinos, and they hemmed in Manila on the land side, and by their valuable help the place, with its garrison of

8,000 or 10,000 Spaniards, was captured—a thing which we could not have accomplished unaided at that time. We got their help by—by ingenuity. We knew they were fighting for their independence, and that they had been at it for two years. We knew they supposed that we also were fighting in their worthy cause—just as we had helped the Cubans fight for Cuban independence—and we allowed them to go on thinking so. *Until Manila was ours and we could get along without them.* Then we showed our hand. Of course, they were surprised—that was natural; surprised and disappointed; disappointed and grieved. To them it looked un-American; uncharacteristic; foreign to our established traditions. And this was natural, too; for we were only playing the American Game in public—in private it was the European. It was neatly done, very neatly, and it bewildered them. They could not understand it; for we had been so friendly—so affectionate, even—with those simple-minded patriots! We, our own selves, had brought back out of exile their leader, their hero, their hope, their Washington—Aguinaldo; brought him in a warship, in high honor, under the sacred shelter and hospitality of the flag; brought him back and restored him to his people, and got their moving and eloquent gratitude for it. Yes, we had been so friendly to them, and had heartened them up in so many ways! We had lent them guns and ammunition; advised with them; exchanged pleasant courtesies with them; placed our sick and wounded in their kindly care; intrusted our Spanish prisoners to their humane and honest hands; fought shoulder to shoulder with them against "the common enemy" (our own phrase); praised their courage, praised their gallantry, praised their mercifulness, praised their fine and honorable conduct; borrowed their trenches, borrowed strong positions which they had previously captured from the Spaniards; petted them, lied to them—officially proclaiming that our land and naval forces came to give them their freedom and displace the bad Spanish Government—fooled them, used them until we needed them no longer; then derided the sucked orange and threw it away. We kept the positions which we had beguiled them of; by and by, we moved a force forward and overlapped patriot ground—a clever thought, for we needed trouble, and this would produce it. A Filipino soldier, crossing the ground, where no one had a right to forbid him, was shot by our sentry. The badgered patriots resented this with arms, without waiting to know whether Aguinaldo, who was absent, would approve or not. Aguinaldo did not approve;

but that availed nothing. What we wanted, in the interest of Progress and Civilization, was the Archipelago, unencumbered by patriots struggling for independence; and War was what we needed. We clinched our opportunity. It is Mr. Chamberlain's case over again—at least in its motive and intention; and we played the game as adroitly as he played it himself."

At this point in our frank statement of fact to the Person Sitting in Darkness, we should throw in a little trade taffy about the Blessings of Civilization—for a change, and for the refreshment of his spirit—then go on with our tale:

"We and the patriots having captured Manila, Spain's ownership of the Archipelago and her sovereignty over it were at an end—obliterated—annihilated—not a rag or shred of either remaining behind. It was then that we conceived the divinely humorous idea of *buying* both of these specters from Spain! [It is quite safe to confess this to the Person Sitting in Darkness, since neither he nor any other sane person will believe it.] In buying those ghosts for twenty millions, we also contracted to take care of the friars and their accumulations. [I think we also agreed to propagate leprosy and smallpox, but as to this there is doubt. But it is not important; persons afflicted with the friars do not mind other diseases.]

"With our Treaty ratified, Manila subdued, and our Ghosts secured, we had no further use for Aguinaldo and the owners of the Archipelago. We forced a war, and we have been hunting America's guest and ally through the woods and swamps ever since."

At this point in the tale, it will be well to boast a little of our war work and our heroisms in the field, so as to make our performance look as fine as England's in South Africa; but I believe it will not be best to emphasize this too much. We must be cautious. Of course, we must read the war telegrams to the Person, in order to keep up our frankness; but we can throw an air of humorousness over them, and that will modify their grim eloquence a little, and their rather indiscreet exhibitions of gory exultation. Before reading to him the following display heads of the dispatches of November 18, 1900, it will be well to practice on them in private first, so as to get the right tang of lightness and gayety into them:

"ADMINISTRATION WEARY OF PROTRACTED HOSTILITIES!"

"REAL WAR AHEAD FOR FILIPINO
REBELS"*
"WILL SHOW NO MERCY!"
"KITCHENER'S PLAN ADOPTED!"

Kitchener knows how to handle disagreeable people who are fighting for their homes and their liberties, and we must let on that we are
merely imitating Kitchener, and have no national interest in the matter, further than to get ourselves admired by the Great Family of
Nations, in which august company our Master of the Game has
bought a place for us in the back row.

Of course, we must not venture to ignore our General MacArthur's
reports—oh, why do they keep on printing those embarrassing things?
—we must drop them trippingly from the tongue and take the
chances:

> During the last ten months our losses have been 268 killed
> and 750 wounded; Filipino loss, *three thousand two hundred
> and twenty-seven killed,* and 694 wounded.

We must stand ready to grab the Person Sitting in Darkness, for he
will swoon away at this confession, saying: "Good God! those 'niggers'
spare their wounded, and the Americans massacre theirs!"

We must bring him to, and coax him and coddle him, and assure
him that the ways of Providence are best, and that it would not become us to find fault with them; and then, to show him that we are
only imitators, not originators, we must read the following passage
from the letter of an American soldier lad in the Philippines to his
mother, published in *Public Opinion,* of Decorah, Iowa, describing the
finish of a victorious battle:

*"We never left one alive. If one was wounded, we would run our
bayonets through him."*

Having now laid all the historical facts before the Person Sitting in
Darkness, we should bring him to again, and explain them to him. We
should say to him:

"They look doubtful, but in reality they are not. There have been
lies; yes, but they were told in a good cause. We have been treacherous;
but that was only in order that real good might come out of apparent

---

* "Rebels!" Mumble that funny word—don't let the Person catch it distinctly.—M.T.

evil. True, we have crushed a deceived and confiding people; we have turned against the weak and the friendless who trusted us; we have stamped out a just and intelligent and well-ordered republic; we have stabbed an ally in the back and slapped the face of a guest; we have bought a Shadow from an enemy that hadn't it to sell; we have robbed a trusting friend of his land and his liberty; we have invited our clean young men to shoulder a discredited musket and do bandits' work under a flag which bandits have been accustomed to fear, not to follow; we have debauched America's honor and blackened her face before the world; but each detail was for the best. We know this. The Head of every State and Sovereignty in Christendom and 90 per cent. of every legislative body in Christendom, including our Congress and our fifty state legislatures, are members not only of the church, but also of the Blessings-of-Civilization Trust. This world-girdling accumulation of trained morals, high principles, and justice cannot do an unright thing, an unfair thing, an ungenerous thing, and unclean thing. It knows what it is about. Give yourself no uneasiness; it is all right."

Now then, that will convince the Person. You will see. It will restore the Business. Also, it will elect the Master of the Game to the vacant place in the Trinity of our national gods; and there on their high thrones the Three will sit, age after age, in the people's sight, each bearing the Emblem of his service: Washington, the Sword of the Liberator; Lincoln, the Slave's Broken Chains; the Master, the Chains Repaired.

It will give the Business a splendid new start. You will see.

Everything is prosperous, now; everything is just as we should wish it. We have got the Archipelago, and we shall never give it up. Also, we have every reason to hope that we shall have an opportunity before very long to slip out of our congressional contract with Cuba and give her something better in the place of it. It is a rich country, and many of us are already beginning to see that the contract was a sentimental mistake. But now—right now—is the best time to do some profitable rehabilitating work—work that will set us up and make us comfortable, and discourage gossip. We cannot conceal from ourselves that, privately, we are a little troubled about our uniform. It is one of our prides; it is acquainted with honor; it is familiar with great deeds and noble; we love it, we revere it; and so this errand it is on makes us uneasy. And our flag—another pride of ours, our chiefest! We have worshipped it so; and when we have seen it in far lands—glimpsing it unexpectedly in that strange sky, waving its welcome and benediction to us—we have caught our breaths, and uncovered our heads, and couldn't speak, for a moment, for the thought of what it was to us and the great ideals it stood for. Indeed, we *must* do something about these things; it is easily managed. We can have a special one—our states do it: we can have just our usual flag, with the white stripes painted black and the stars replaced by the skull and crossbones.

And we do not need that Civil Commission out there. Having no powers, it has to invent them, and that kind of work cannot be effectively done by just anybody; an expert is required. Mr. Croker can be spared. We do not want the United States represented there, but only the Game.

By help of these suggested amendments, Progress and Civilization in that country can have a boom, and it will take in the Persons who are Sitting in Darkness, and we can resume Business at the old stand.

1901

LETTER FROM THE
RECORDING ANGEL

Office of the Recording Angel
Department of Petitions, Jan. 20

Andrew Langdon
Coal Dealer
Buffalo, New York

I have the honor, as per command, to inform you that your recent act of benevolence and self-sacrifice has been recorded upon a page of the Book called *Golden Deeds of Men:* a distinction, I am permitted to remark, which is not merely extraordinary, it is unique.

As regards your prayers, for the week ending the 19th, I have the honor to report as follows:

1. For weather to advance hard coal 15 cents a ton. Granted.

2. For influx of laborers to reduce wages 10 per cent. Granted.

3. For a break in rival soft-coal prices. Granted.

4. For a visitation upon the man, or upon the family of the man, who has set up a competing retail coal-yard in Rochester. Granted, as follows: diphtheria, 2, 1 fatal; scarlet fever, 1, to result in deafness and imbecility. NOTE. This prayer should have been directed against this subordinate's principals, The N. Y. Central R. R. Co.

5. For deportation to Sheol of annoying swarms of persons who apply daily for work, or for favors of one sort or another. Taken under advisement for later decision and compromise, this petition appearing to conflict with another one of the same date, which will be cited further along.

6. For application of some form of violent death to neighbor who threw brick at family cat, whilst the same was serenading. Reserved for consideration and compromise because of conflict with a prayer of even date to be cited further along.

7. To "damn the missionary cause." Reserved also—as above.

8. To increase December profits of $22,230 to $45,000 for January, and perpetuate a proportionate monthly increase thereafter—"which will satisfy you." The prayer granted; the added remark accepted with reservations.

9. For cyclone, to destroy the works and fill up the mine of the North Pennsylvania Co. NOTE: Cyclones are not kept in stock in the winter season. A reliable article of fire-damp can be furnished upon application.

Especial note is made of the above list, they being of particular moment. The 298 remaining supplications classifiable under the head of Special Providences, Schedule A, for the week ending 19th, are granted in a body, except that 3 of the 32 cases requiring immediate death have been modified to incurable disease.

This completes the week's invoice of petitions known to this office under the technical designation of Secret Supplications of the Heart, and which for a reason which may suggest itself, always receive our first and especial attention.

The remainder of the week's invoice falls under the head of what we term Public Prayers, in which classification we place prayers uttered in Prayer Meeting, Sunday School, Class Meeting, Family Worship, etc. These kinds of prayers have value according to classification of Christian uttering them. By rule of this office, Christians are divided into two grand classes, to wit: 1, Professing Christians; 2, Professional Christians. These, in turn, are minutely subdivided and classified by size, species, and family; and finally, standing is determined by carats, the minimum being 1, the maximum 1000.

As per balance-sheet for quarter ending Dec. 31, 1847, you stood classified as follows:

Grand Classification, Professing Christian.

Size, one-fourth of maximum.

Species, Human-Spiritual.

Family, A of the Elect, Division 16.

Standing, 322 carats fine.

As per balance-sheet for quarter just ended—that is to say, forty years later—you stand classified as follows:

Grand Classification, Professional Christian.

Size, six one-hundredths of maximum.

Species, Human-Animal.

Family, W of the Elect, Division 1547.

Standing, 3 carats fine.

I have the honor to call your attention to the fact that you seem to have deteriorated.

To resume report upon your Public Prayers—with the side remark that in order to encourage Christians of your grade and of approximate grades, it is the custom of this office to grant many things to them which would not be granted to Christians of a higher grade—partly because they would not be asked for:

Prayer for weather mercifully tempered to the needs of the poor and the naked. Denied. This was a Prayer-Meeting Prayer. It conflicts with Item 1 of this report, which was a Secret Supplication of the Heart. By a rigid rule of this office, certain sorts of Public Prayers of Professional Christians are forbidden to take precedence of Secret Supplications of the Heart.

Prayer for better times and plentier food "for the hard-handed son of toil whose patient and exhausting labors make comfortable the homes, and pleasant the ways, of the more fortunate, and entitle him to our vigilant and effective protection from the wrongs and injustices which grasping avarice would do him, and to the tenderest offices of our grateful hearts." Prayer-Meeting Prayer. Refused. Conflicts with Secret Supplication of the Heart No. 2.

Prayer "that such as in any way obstruct our preferences may be

generously blessed, both themselves and their families, we here calling
our hearts to witness that in their wordly prosperity we are spiritually
blessed, and our joys made perfect." Prayer-Meeting Prayer. Refused.
Conflicts with Secret Supplications of the Heart Nos. 3 and 4.

"Oh, let none fall heir to the pains of perdition through words or
acts of ours." Family Worship. Received fifteen minutes in advance of
Secret Supplications of the Heart No. 5, with which it distinctly conflicts. It is suggested that one or the other of these prayers be withdrawn, or both of them modified.

"Be mercifully inclined toward all who would do us offense in our
persons or our property." Includes man who threw brick at cat. Family Prayer. Received some minutes in advance of No. 6, Secret Supplications of the Heart. Modification suggested, to reconcile discrepancy.

"Grant that the noble missionary cause, the most precious labor
entrusted to the hands of man, may spread and prosper without let or
limit in all heathen lands that do as yet reproach us with their spiritual
darkness." Uninvited prayer shoved in at meeting of American Board.
Received nearly half a day in advance of No. 7, Secret Supplications of
the Heart. This office takes no stock in missionaries, and is not connected in any way with the American Board. We should like to grant
one of these prayers but cannot grant both. It is suggested that the
American Board one be withdrawn.

This office desires for the twentieth time to call urgent attention to
your remark appended to No. 8. It is a chestnut.

Of the 464 specifications contained in your Public Prayers for the
week, and not previously noted in this report, we grant 2, and deny the
rest. To wit: Granted, (1), "that the clouds may continue to perform
their office; (2), and the sun his." It was the divine purpose anyhow; it
will gratify you to know that you have not disturbed it. Of the 462
details refused, 61 were uttered in Sunday School. In this connection I
must once more remind you that we grant no Sunday School Prayers
of Professional Christians of the classification technically known in
this office as the John Wanamaker grade. We merely enter them as
"words," and they count to his credit according to number uttered
within certain limits of time; 3000 per quarter-minute required, or no
score; 4200 in a possible 5000 is a quite common Sunday School score
among experts, and counts the same as two hymns and a bouquet
furnished by young ladies in the assassin's cell, execution-morning.
Your remaining 401 details count for wind only. We bunch them and

use them for head-winds in retarding the ships of improper people, but it takes so many of them to make an impression that we cannot allow anything for their use.

I desire to add a word of my own to this report. When certain sorts of people do a sizable good deed, we credit them up a thousand-fold more for it than we would in the case of a better man—on account of the strain. You stand far away above your classification-record here, because of certain self-sacrifices of yours which greatly exceed what could have been expected of you. Years ago, when you were worth only $100,000, and sent $2 to your impoverished cousin the widow when she appealed to you for help, there were many in heaven who were not able to believe it, and many more who believed that the money was counterfeit. Your character went up many degrees when it was shown that these suspicions were unfounded. A year or two later, when you sent the poor girl $4 in answer to another appeal, everybody believed it, and you were the talk here for days together. Two years later you sent $6, upon supplication, when the widow's youngest child died, and that act made perfect your good fame. Everybody in heaven said, "Have you heard about Andrew?"—for you are now affectionately called Andrew here. Your increasing donation, every two or three years, has kept your name on all lips, and warm in all hearts. All heaven watches you Sundays, as you drive to church in your handsome carriage; and when your hand retires from the contribution plate, the glad shout is heard even to the ruddy walls of remote Sheol, "Another nickel from Andrew!"

But the climax came a few days ago, when the widow wrote and said she could get a school in a far village to teach if she had $50 to get herself and her two surviving children over the long journey; and you counted up last month's clear profit from your three coal mines—$22,230—and added to it the certain profit for the current month—$45,000 and a possible fifty—and then got down your pen and your check-book and mailed her *fifteen whole dollars!* Ah, Heaven bless and keep you forever and ever, generous heart! There was not a dry eye in the realms of bliss; and amidst the hand-shakings, and embracings, and praisings, the decree was thundered forth from the shining mount, that this deed should out-honor all the historic self-sacrifices of men and angels, and be recorded by itself upon a page of its own, for that the strain of it upon you had been heavier and bitterer than the strain it costs ten thousand martyrs to yield up their lives at the fiery stake;

and all said, "What is the giving up of life, to a noble soul, or to ten thousand noble souls, compared with the giving up of fifteen dollars out of the greedy grip of the meanest white man that ever lived on the face of the earth?"

And it was a true word. And Abraham, weeping, shook out the contents of his bosom and pasted the eloquent label there, "RE-SERVED"; and Peter, weeping, said, "He shall be received with a torchlight procession when he comes"; and then all heaven boomed, and was glad you were going there. And so was hell.

[Signed]

THE RECORDING ANGEL [Seal]

By command.

1946

LETTERS

TO THE CALIFORNIA PIONEERS[*]

Elmira, October 11, 1869

To the California Pioneers:

Gentlemen: Circumstances render it out of my power to take advantage of the invitation extended to me through Mr. Simonton, and be present at your dinner at New York. I regret this very much, for there are several among you whom I would have a right to join hands with on the score of old friendship, and I suppose I would have a sublime general right to shake hands with the rest of you on the score of kinship in California ups and downs in search of fortune.

If I were to tell some of my experience, you would recognize California blood in me; I fancy the old, old story would sound familiar no doubt. I have the usual stock of reminiscences. For instance: I went to Esmeralda early. I purchased largely in the "Wide West," "Winnemucca," and other fine claims, and was very wealthy. I fared sumptuously on bread when flour was $200 a barrel and had beans for dinner every Sunday, when none but bloated aristocrats could afford such grandeur. But I finished by feeding batteries in a quartz mill at $15 a week, and wishing I was a battery myself and had somebody to feed me. My claims in Esmeralda are there yet. I suppose I could be persuaded to sell.

I went to Humboldt District when it was new; I became largely interested in the "Alba Nueva" and other claims with gorgeous names, and was rich again—in prospect. I owned a vast mining property there. I would not have sold out for less than $400,000 at that

* A letter written in reply to an invitation from the New York Society of California Pioneers to attend a banquet to be given to the visiting members of the Society of California Pioneers of the Pacific Coast. The letter was read at the banquet in New York and was published in the Buffalo *Express* on October 19, 1869.

time. But I will now. Finally I walked home—200 miles—partly for exercise, and partly because stage fare was expensive. Next I entered upon an affluent career in Virginia City, and by a judicious investment of labor and the capital of friends, became the owner of about all the worthless wild cat mines there were in that part of the country. Assessments did the business for me there. There were a hundred and seventeen assessments to one dividend, and the proportion of income to outlay was a little against me. My financial barometer went down to 32 Fahrenheit, and the subscriber was frozen out.

I took up extensions on the main lead—extensions that reached to British America in one direction, and to the Isthmus of Panama in the other—and I verily believe I would have been a rich man if I had ever found those infernal extensions. But I didn't. I ran tunnels till I tapped the Arctic Ocean, and I sunk shafts till I broke through the roof of perdition; but those extensions turned up missing every time. I am willing to sell all that property and throw in the improvements.

Perhaps you remember that celebrated "North Ophir?" I bought that mine. It was very rich in pure silver. You could take it out in lumps as large as a filbert. But when it was discovered that those lumps were melted half dollars, and hardly melted at that, a painful case of "salting" was apparent, and the undersigned adjourned to the poorhouse again.

I paid assessments on "Hale and Norcross" until they sold me out, and I had to take in washing for a living—and the next month that infamous stock went up to $7000 a foot.

I own millions and millions of feet of affluent silver leads in Nevada —in fact the entire undercrust of that country nearly, and if Congress would move that State off my property so that I could get at it, I would be wealthy yet. But no, there she squats—and here am I. Failing health persuades me to sell. If you know of any one desiring a permanent investment, I can furnish one that will have the virtue of being eternal.

I have been through the California mill, with all its "dips, spurs and angles, variations and sinuosities." I have worked there at all the different trades and professions known to the catalogues. I have been everything, from a newspaper editor down to a cowcatcher on a locomotive, and I am encouraged to believe that if there had been a few more occupations to experiment on, I might have made a dazzling success at last, and found out what mysterious designs Providence had in creating me.

But you perceive that although I am not a Pioneer, I have had a sufficiently variegated time of it to enable me to talk Pioneer like a native, and feel like a Forty-Niner. Therefore, I cordially welcome you to your old remembered homes and your long deserted firesides, and close this screed with the sincere hope that your visit here will be a happy one, and not embittered by the sorrowful surprises that absence and lapse of years are wont to prepare for wanderers; surprises which come in the form of old friends missed from their places; silence where familiar voices should be; the young grown old; change and decay everywhere; home a delusion and a disappointment; strangers at hearthstone; sorrow where gladness was; tears for laughter; the melancholy pomp of death where the grace of life has been!

With all good wishes for the Returned Prodigals, and regrets that I cannot partake of a small piece of the fatted calf (rare and no gravy,)

I am yours, cordially,

MARK TWAIN

TO MOLLIE CLEMENS*

Memphis, Tenn., *Friday, June 18th, 1858*

Dear Sister Mollie,

Long before this reaches you, my poor Henry, my darling, my pride, my glory, my all, will have finished his blameless career, and the light of my life will have gone out in utter darkness. O, God! this is hard to bear. Hardened, hopeless—aye, lost—lost—lost and ruined sinner as I am—*I*, even *I*, have humbled myself to the ground and prayed as never man prayed before that the great God might let this cup pass from me, that he would strike me to the earth but spare my brother, that he would pour out the fulness of his just wrath upon my wicked head but have mercy, mercy, mercy upon that unoffending boy. The horrors of three days have swept over me. They have blasted

---

* Clemens's sister-in-law, married to his older brother, Orion.

my youth and left me an old man before my time. Mollie, there are gray hairs in my head tonight. For forty-eight hours I labored at the bedside of my poor burned and bruised but uncomplaining brother, and then the star of my hope went out and left me in the gloom of despair. Men take me by the hand and *congratulate* me and call me "lucky" because I was not on the *Pennsylvania* when she blew up! May God forgive them, for they know not what they say.

Mollie, you do not understand why I was not on that boat. I will tell you. I left Saint Louis on her but on the way down, Mr. Brown, the pilot that was killed by the explosion (poor fellow), quarreled with Henry without cause, while I was steering. Henry started out of the pilot house. Brown jumped up and collared him—turned him half away around and *struck him in the face!*—and him nearly six feet high—struck my little brother. I was wild from that moment. I left the boat to steer herself and avenged the insult. And the Captain said I was right, that he would discharge Brown in N. Orleans if he could get another pilot, and would do it in St. Louis, anyhow. Of course both of us could not return to St. Louis on the same boat. No pilot could be found, and the Captain sent me to the *A. T. Lacey* with orders to her Captain to bring me to Saint Louis. Had another pilot been found, poor Brown would have been the "lucky" man.

I was on the *Pennsylvania* five minutes before she left N. Orleans, and I must tell you the truth, Mollie—*three hundred* human beings perished by that fearful disaster. Henry was asleep—was blown up—then fell back on the hot boilers, and I suppose that rubbish fell on him, for he is injured internally. He got into the water and swam to shore, and got into the flatboat with the other survivors.* He had nothing on but his wet shirt and he lay there burning up with a southern sun and freezing in the wind till the *Kate Frisbee* came along. His wounds were not dressed till he got to Memphis 15 hours after the explosion. He was senseless and motionless for 12 hours after that.

But may God bless Memphis, the noblest city on the face of the earth. She has done her duty by these poor afflicted creatures, especially Henry, for he has had five—aye, ten, fifteen, *twenty* times the care and attention that anyone else has had. Dr. Peyton, the best physician in Memphis (he is exactly like the portraits of Webster), sat by him for 36 hours. There are 32 scalded men in that room, and you

---

* Henry had returned once to the *Pennsylvania* to render assistance to the passengers. Later he had somehow made his way to the flatboat.—A.B.P.

would know Dr. Peyton better than I can describe him if you could follow him around and hear each man murmur as he passed, "May the God of Heaven bless you, Doctor!" The ladies have done well too. Our second Mate, a handsome, noble-hearted young fellow, will die. Yesterday a beautiful girl of 15 stooped timidly down by his side and handed him a pretty bouquet. The poor suffering boy's eyes kindled, his lips quivered out a gentle, "God bless you, Miss," and he burst into tears. He made them write her name on a card for him, that he might not forget it.

Pray for me, Mollie, and pray for my poor sinless brother.

Your unfortunate Brother,
Saml. L. Clemens

P. S. I got here two days after Henry.

The *Pennsylvania*'s boilers had exploded early on a mid-June morning while the ship was being loaded with wood some sixty miles below Memphis. Henry was just about a month short of twenty when he was killed. Clemens was in his twenty-third year at the time.—C.N.

TO PAMELA MOFFETT,* ST. LOUIS

Esmeralda, Cal., *Aug. 15, 1862*

My Dear Sister,

I mailed a letter to you and Ma this morning, but since then I have received yours to Orion and me. Therefore I must answer right away, else I may leave town without doing it at all. What in thunder are pilot's wages to me? Which question, I beg humbly to observe, is of a *general* nature and not discharged particularly at you. But it is singular, isn't it, that such a matter should interest Orion when it is of no earthly consequence to me? I never have *once* thought of returning home to go on the river again, and I never expect to do any more piloting at any price. My livelihood must be made in this country, and if I have to wait longer than I expected, let it be so, I have no fear of

* Clemens's sister.

failure. You know I have extravagant hopes, for Orion tells you everything which he ought to keep to himself, but it's his nature to do that sort of thing, and I let him alone. I did think for awhile of going home this fall but when I found that that was and had been the cherished intention and the darling aspiration every year of these old careworn Californians for twelve weary years, I felt a little uncomfortable, but I stole a march on Disappointment and said I would *not* go home this fall. I will spend the winter in San Francisco if possible. Do not tell anyone that I had any idea of piloting again at present, for it is all a mistake. This country suits me and—it *shall* suit me, whether or no. . . .

Dan Twing and I and Dan's dog "cabin" together, and will continue to do so for awhile until I leave for—

The mansion is 10 × 12, with a "domestic" roof. Yesterday it rained, the first shower for five months. "Domestic," it appears to me, is not waterproof. We went outside to keep from getting wet. Dan makes the bed when it is his turn to do it, and when it is my turn I don't, you know. The dog is not a good hunter and he isn't worth shucks to watch but he scratches up the dirt floor of the cabin and catches flies and makes himself generally useful in the way of washing dishes. Dan gets up first in the morning and makes a fire, and I get up last and sit by it while he cooks breakfast. We have a cold lunch at noon and I cook supper—very much against my will. However, one must have *one* good meal a day, and if I were to live on Dan's abominable cookery I should lose my appetite, you know.

Dan attended Dr. Chorpenning's funeral yesterday and he felt as though he ought to wear a white shirt and we had a jolly good time finding such an article. We turned over all our traps and he found one at last but I shall always think it was suffering from yellow fever. He also found an old black coat, greasy and wrinkled to that degree that it appeared to have been quilted at some time or other. In this gorgeous costume he attended the funeral. And when he returned, his own dog drove him away from the cabin, not recognizing him. This is true.

You would not like to live in a country where flour was $40 a barrel? Very well then, I suppose you would not like to live here, where flour was $100 a barrel when I first came here. And shortly afterwards it couldn't be had at any price, and for one month the people lived on barley, beans and beef and nothing beside. Oh no, we didn't luxuriate then! Perhaps not. But we said wise and severe things about the vanity and wickedness of high living. We preached our doctrine and practised it. Which course I respectfully recommend to the clergymen of St. Louis.

Where is Beack Jolly? And Bixby?*

Your Brother
Sam

TO JANE CLEMENS†AND FAMILY, ST. LOUIS

New York, *June 7th, 1867*

Dear Folks,

I suppose we shall be many a league at sea tomorrow night, and goodness knows I shall be unspeakably glad of it.

I haven't got *any*thing to write, else I *would* write it. I have just written myself clear out in letters to the *Alta,* and I think they are the stupidest letters that were ever written from New York. Corresponding has been a perfect drag ever since I got to the states. If it continues abroad I don't know what the *Tribune* and *Alta* folks will think.

I have withdrawn the Sandwich Island book. It would be useless to publish it in these dull publishing times. As for the Frog book, I don't believe that will ever pay anything worth a cent. I published it simply to advertise myself, not with the hope of making anything out of it.

Well, I haven't anything to write except that I am tired of staying in one place, that I am in a fever to get away. Read my *Alta* letters. They contain everything I could possibly write to you. Tell Zeb and John Leavenworth‡ to write me. They can get plenty of gossip from the pilots.

An importing house sent two cases of exquisite champagne aboard the ship for me today—Veuve Clicquot and Lac d'Or. I and my room-

* Beack Jolly was a pilot. Bixby was Horace Bixby.

† Clemens's mother.

‡ Zeb and John Leavenworth were river pilots whom Clemens had known on the Mississippi. Orion had lost his Nevada job and was trying to practice law. Bill Stewart was U.S. Senator Stewart of Nevada.

mate have set apart every Saturday as a solemn fast day, wherein we will entertain no light matters of frivolous conversation but only get drunk. (That is a joke.) His mother and sisters are the best and most homelike people I have found in a brownstone front. There is no style about them except in house and furniture.

I wish Orion were going on this voyage, for I believe he could not help but be cheerful and jolly. I often wonder if his law business is going satisfactorily to him, but knowing that the dull season is setting in now (it looked like it had already set in before) I have felt as if I could almost answer the question myself, which is to say in plain words, I was afraid to ask. I wish I had gone to Washington in the winter instead of going West. I could have gouged an office out of Bill Stewart for him and that would atone for the loss of my home visit. But I am so worthless that it seems to me I never do anything or accomplish anything that lingers in my mind as a pleasant memory. My mind is stored full of unworthy conduct toward Orion and towards you all, and an accusing conscience gives me peace only in excitement and restless moving from place to place. If I could say I had done one thing for any of you that entitled me to your good opinion (I say nothing of your love, for I am sure of *that*, no matter how unworthy of it I may make myself, from Orion down you have always given me that, all the days of my life, when God Almighty knows I seldom deserve it), I believe I could go home and stay there and I *know* I would care little for the world's praise or blame. There is no satisfaction in the world's praise anyhow, and it has no worth to me save in the way of business. I tried to gather up its compliments to send to you but the work was distasteful and I dropped it.

You observe that under a cheerful exterior I have got a spirit that is angry with me and gives me freely its contempt. I can get away from that at sea and be tranquil and satisfied. And so, with my parting love and benediction for Orion and all of you, I say goodbye and God bless you all, and welcome the wind that wafts a weary soul to the sunny lands of the Mediterranean!

Yrs Forever,
Sam

TO JANE CLEMENS AND FAMILY, ST. LOUIS

Lockport, N. Y. *Feb. 27, 1869*

Dear Folks,

I enclose $20 for Ma. I thought I was getting ahead of her little assessments of $35 a month but find I am falling behind with her instead and have let her go without money. Well, I did not mean to do it. But you see when people have been getting ready for months in a quiet way to get married, they are bound to grow stingy and go to saving up money against that awful day when it is sure to be needed.

I am particularly anxious to place myself in a position where I can carry on my married life in good shape on *my own hook*, because I have paddled my own canoe so long that I could not be satisfied now to let anybody help me, and my proposed father-in-law is naturally so liberal that it would be just like him to want to give us a start in life. But I don't want it that way. I can start myself. I don't want any help. I can run this institution without any outside assistance, and I shall have a wife who will stand by me like a soldier through thick and thin and never complain.

She is only a little body but she hasn't her peer in Christendom. I gave her only a plain gold engagement ring, when fashion imperatively demands a two-hundred-dollar diamond one, and told her it was typical of her future lot—namely, that she would have to flourish on substantials rather than luxuries. (But you see I know the girl—she don't care anything about luxuries.) She is a splendid girl. She spends no money but her usual year's allowance, and she spends nearly every cent of that on other people. She will be a good sensible little wife, without any airs about her. I don't make intercession for her beforehand and ask you to love her, for there isn't any use in that, you couldn't help it if you were to try.

I warn you that whoever comes within the fatal influence of her beautiful nature is her willing slave for evermore. I take my affidavit on that statement. Her father and mother and brother embrace and pet her constantly, precisely as if she were a *sweetheart* instead of a blood relation. She has unlimited power over her father and yet she never uses it except to make him help people who stand in need of help. . . .

But if I get fairly started on the subject of my bride I never shall get through, and so I will quit right here. I went to Elmira a little over a week ago and staid four days and then had to go to New York on business.

TO JAMES REDPATH,*BOSTON

Hartford, *Tuesday Aug. 8, 1871*

Dear Red,

I am different from other women. My mind changes oftener. People who have no mind can easily be steadfast and firm, but when a man is loaded down to the guards with it, as I am, every heavy sea of foreboding or inclination, maybe of indolence, shifts the cargo. See? Therefore, if you will notice, one week I am likely to give rigid instructions to confine me to New England. Next week send me to Arizona. The next week withdraw my name. The next week give you full untrammelled swing. And the week following modify it. You must try to keep the run of my mind, Redpath, it is your business, being the agent, and it always was too many for me. It appears to me to be one of the finest pieces of mechanism I have ever met with. Now about the West, this week I am willing that you shall retain all the Western engagements. But what I shall want *next* week is still with God.

Let us not profane the mysteries with soiled hands and prying eyes of sin.

Yours,
Mark

P. S. Shall be here 2 weeks. Will run up there when Nasby comes.

---

* Clemens's lecture agent.

TO WILLIAM DEAN HOWELLS, BOSTON

Hartford, *June 15, 1872*

Friend Howells,

Could you tell me how I could get a copy of your portrait as published in *Hearth and Home?* I hear so much talk about it as being among the finest works of art which have yet appeared in that journal that I feel a strong desire to see it. Is it suitable for framing? I have written the publishers of H & H time and again but they say that the demand for the portrait immediately exhausted the edition and now a copy cannot be had even for the European demand, which has now begun. Bret Harte has been here and says his family would not be without that portrait for any consideration. He says his children get up in the night and yell for it. I would give anything for a copy of that portrait to put up in my parlor. I have Oliver Wendell Holmes's and Bret Harte's as published in *Every Saturday,* and of all the swarms that come every day to gaze upon them none go away that are not softened and humbled and made more resigned to the will of God. If I had yours to put up alongside of them I believe the combination would bring more souls to earnest reflection and ultimate conviction of their lost condition than any other kind of warning would.

Where in the nation can I get that portrait? Here are heaps of people that want it, that *need* it. There is my uncle. *He* wants a copy. He is lying at the point of death. He has *been* lying at the point of death for two years. He wants a copy, and I want him to *have* a copy. And I want you to send a copy to the man that shot my dog. I want to see if he is dead to every human instinct.

Now you send me that portrait. I am sending you mine in this letter, and am glad to do it, for it has been greatly admired. People who are judges of art find in the execution a grandeur which has not been equalled in this country, and an expression which has not been approached in *any.*

Yrs truly,
S. L. Clemens

P. S. 62,000 copies of *Roughing It* sold and delivered in 4 months.

TO JANE CLEMENS AND PAMELA MOFFETT, FREDONIA, N. Y.

Hartford, *Sunday, 1874*

My dear Mother and Sister,

I saw Gov. Jewell today and he said he was still moving in the matter of Sammy's appointment* and would stick to it till he got a result of a positive nature one way or the other, but thus far he did not know whether to expect success or defeat.

Ma, whenever you need money I hope you won't be backward about saying so—you can always have it. We stint ourselves in some ways but we have no desire to stint you. And we don't intend to, either.

I *can't* "encourage" Orion. Nobody can do that conscientiously, for the reason that before one's letter has time to reach him he is off on some new wild-goose chase. Would you encourage in literature a man who the older he grows the worse he writes? Would you encourage Orion in the glaring insanity of studying law? If he were packed and crammed full of law it would be worthless lumber to him, for his is such a capricious and ill-regulated mind that he would apply the principles of the law with no more judgment than a child of ten years. I know what I am saying. I laid one of the plainest and simplest of legal questions before Orion once, and the helpless and hopeless mess he made of it was absolutely astonishing. Nothing aggravates me so much as to have Orion mention law or literature to me.

Well, I cannot encourage him to try the ministry, because he would change his religion so fast that he would have to keep a traveling agent under wages to go ahead of him to engage pulpits and board for him.

I cannot conscientiously encourage him to do *anything* but potter around his little farm and put in his odd hours contriving new and impossible projects at the rate of 365 a year, which is his customary average. He says he did well in Hannibal! Now there is a man who

* As a West Point cadet.

ought to be entirely satisfied with the grandeurs, emoluments and activities of a hen farm.

If you ask me to pity Orion I can do that. I can do it every day and all day long. But one can't "encourage" quicksilver, because the instant you put your finger on it it isn't there. No, I am saying too much —he *does* stick to his literary and legal aspirations, and he naturally *would* select the very two things which he is wholly and preposterously unfitted for. If I ever become able, I mean to put Orion on a regular pension without revealing the fact that it is a pension. That is best for him. Let him consider it a periodical loan and pay interest out of the principal. Within a year's time he would be looking upon himself as a benefactor of mine, in the way of furnishing me a good permanent investment for money, and that would make him happy and satisfied with himself. If he had money he would share with me in a moment, and I have no disposition to be stingy with *him*.

Affly
Sam

Livy sends love.

TO W. D. HOWELLS, BOSTON

Hartford, July 5th, 1875

My dear Howells,

I have finished the story* and didn't take the chap beyond boyhood. I believe it would be fatal to do it in any shape but autobiographically, like Gil Blas. I perhaps made a mistake in not writing it in the first person. If I went on now and took him into manhood he would just lie like all the one-horse men in literature and the reader would conceive a hearty contempt for him. It is *not* a boy's book at all. It will only be read by adults. It is only written for adults.

Moreover the book is plenty long enough as it stands. It is about

* The "story" was *Tom Sawyer*. Osgood was James R. Osgood, the publisher of some of Clemens's works, among them *Life on the Mississippi*.

900 pages of MS, and may be 1000 when I shall have finished "working up" vague places, so it would make from 130 to 150 pages of the *Atlantic,* about what the *Foregone Conclusion* made, isn't it?

I would dearly like to see it in the *Atlantic,* but I doubt if it would pay the publishers to buy the privilege or me to sell it. Bret Harte has sold his novel (same size as mine, I should say) to *Scribner's Monthly* for $6,500 (publication to begin in September, I think) and he gets a royalty of 7½ per cent from Bliss in book form afterwards. He gets a royalty of ten per cent on it in England (issued in serial numbers) and the same royalty on it in book form afterwards, and is to receive an advance payment of five hundred pounds the day the first No. of the serial appears. If I could do as well, here, and there, with mine it might possibly pay me but I seriously doubt it, though it is likely I could do better in England than Bret, who is not widely known there.

You see I take a vile, mercenary view of things, but then my household expenses are something almost ghastly.

By and by I shall take a boy of twelve and run him on through life (in the first person), but not Tom Sawyer, he would not be a good character for it.

I wish you would promise to read the MS of *Tom Sawyer* some time and see if you don't really decide that I am right in closing with him as a boy, and point out the most glaring defects for me. It is a tremendous favor to ask and I expect you to refuse and would be ashamed to expect you to do otherwise. But the thing has been so many months in my mind that it seems a relief to snake it out. I don't know any other person whose judgment I could venture to take fully and entirely. Don't hesitate about saying no, for I know how your time is taxed, and I would have honest need to blush if you said yes.

Osgood and I are "going for" the puppy G——— on infringement of trademark. To win one or two suits of this kind will set literary folks on a firmer bottom. I wish Osgood would sue for stealing Holmes's poem. Wouldn't it be gorgeous to sue R——— for *petty larceny?* I will promise to go into court and swear I think him capable of stealing peanuts from a blind pedlar.

Yrs ever,
Clemens

TO FRANK E. BURROUGH,* ST. LOUIS

Hartford, *Nov. 1 '76*

My dear Burrough,

As you describe me I can picture myself as I was 22 years ago. The portrait is correct. You think I have grown some. Upon my word there was room for it. You have described a callow fool, a self-sufficient ass, a mere human tumble-bug imagining that he is remodeling the world and is entirely capable of doing it right. Ignorance, intolerance, egotism, self-assertion, opaque perception, dense and pitiful chuckleheadedness—and an almost pathetic unconsciousness of it all. That is what I was at 19 and 20 and that is what the average Southerner is at 60 today. Northerners too of a certain grade. It is of children like this that voters are made. And such is the primal source of our government! A man hardly knows whether to swear or cry over it.

I think I comprehend the position there—perfect freedom to vote just as you choose, provided you choose to vote as *other* people think —social ostracism otherwise. The same thing exists here among the Irish. An Irish Republican is a pariah among his people. Yet that race find fault with the same spirit in Know-Nothingism.

Fortunately a good deal of experience of men enabled me to choose my residence wisely. I live in the freest corner of the country. There are no social disabilities between me and my Democratic personal friends. We break the bread and eat the salt of hospitality freely together and never dream of such a thing as offering impertinent interference in each other's political opinions.

Don't you ever come to New York again and not run up here to see me. I suppose we were away for the summer when you were East, but no matter, you could have telegraphed and found out. We were at Elmira, N.Y. and right on your road and could have given you a good time if you had allowed us the chance.

Yes, Will Bowen and I have exchanged letters now and then for several years, but I suspect that I made him mad with my last—

* Burrough was an old friend who had roomed with Clemens when the latter had worked in the composing room of the St. Louis *Evening News.*

shortly after you saw him in St. Louis, I judge. There is one thing which I can't stand and *won't* stand, from many people. That is sham sentimentality, the kind a schoolgirl puts into her graduating composition, the sort that makes up the Original Poetry column of a country newspaper, the rot that deals in the "happy days of yore," the "sweet yet melancholy past," with its "blighted hopes" and its "vanished dreams"—and all that sort of drivel.

Will's were always of this stamp. I stood it for years. When I get a letter like that from a grown man and he a widower with a family, it gives me the stomach ache. And I just told Will Bowen so last summer. I told him to stop being 16 at 40, told him to stop drooling about the sweet yet melancholy past, and take a pill. I said there was but one solitary thing about the past worth remembering, and that was the fact that it *is* the past—can't be restored. Well, I exaggerated some of these truths a little, but only a little, but my idea was to kill his sham sentimentality once and forever and so make a good fellow of him again. I went to the unheard-of trouble of rewriting the letter and saying the same harsh things softly so as to sugarcoat the anguish and make it a little more endurable, and I asked him to write and thank me honestly for doing him the best and kindliest favor that any friend ever *had* done him—but he hasn't done it yet. Maybe he will sometime. I am grateful to God that I got that letter off before he was married (I get that news from you), else he would just have slobbered all over me and drowned me when that event happened.

I enclose a photograph for the young ladies. I will remark that I do not wear sealskin for grandeur but because I found, when I used to lecture in the winter, that nothing else was able to keep a man warm sometimes in these high latitudes. I wish you had sent pictures of yourself and family. I'll trade picture for picture with you straight through if you are commercially inclined.

Your old friend,
Saml L. Clemens

UNDATED: ADDRESSEE UNKNOWN

In order to relieve himself of strong emotions, Clemens sometimes wrote letters which he had no intention of mailing. The following is in his best manner.—C.N.

An enthusiast who had a new system of musical notation wrote to me and suggested that a magazine article from me, contrasting the absurdities of the old system with the simplicities of his new one would be sure to make a "rousing hit." He shouted and shouted over the marvels wrought by his system and quoted the handsome compliments which had been paid it by famous musical people but he forgot to tell me what his notation was like or what its simplicities consisted in. So I could not have written the article if I had wanted to—which I didn't, because I hate strangers with axes to grind. I wrote him a courteous note explaining how busy I was—I always explain how busy I am—and casually dropped this remark:

"I judge the X-X notation to be a rational mode of representing music, in place of the prevailing fashion, which was the invention of an idiot."

Next mail he asked permission to print that meaningless remark. I answered no—courteously but still no, explaining that I could not afford to be placed in the attitude of trying to influence people with a mere worthless *guess.* What a scorcher I got, next mail! Such irony! Such sarcasm, such caustic praise of my superhonorable loyalty to the public! And withal, such compassion for my stupidity, too, in not being able to understand my own language. I cannot remember the words of this letter broadside but there was about a page used up in turning this idea round and round and exposing it in different lights.

UNMAILED ANSWER

Dear Sir,

What is the trouble with you? If it is your viscera, you cannot have them taken out and reorganized a moment too soon. I mean, if they are inside. But if you are composed of them, that is another matter. Is it your brain? But it could not be your brain. Possibly it is your skull: you want to look out for that. Some people, when they get an idea, it pries the structure apart. Your system of notation has got in there and couldn't find room. Without a doubt that is what the trouble is. Your skull was not made to put ideas in, it was made to throw potatoes at.

Yours Truly

MAILED ANSWER

Dear Sir,

Come, come—take a walk. You disturb the children.

Yours Truly

TO ORION, KEOKUK

Hartford, *Jan.* 5, '89

Dear Orion,

At 12:20 this afternoon a line of movable types was spaced and justified by machinery for the first time in the history of the world! And I was there to see. It was done *automatically*—instantly—perfectly. This is indeed the first line of movable types that ever *was* perfectly spaced and perfectly justified on this earth.

This was the last function that remained to be tested, and so by long odds the most amazing and extraordinary invention ever born of the brain of man stands completed and perfect. Livy is downstairs celebrating.

But it's a cunning devil, is that machine, and knows more than any man that ever lived. You shall see. We made the test in this way. We set up a lot of random letters in a stick—three-fourths of a line—then filled out the line with quads representing 14 spaces, each space to be $35/1000$ of an inch thick. Then we threw aside the quads and put the letters into the machine and formed them into 15 two-letter words, leaving the words separated by two-inch vacancies. Then we started up the machine slowly, by hand, and fastened our eyes on the space-selecting pins. The first pin-block projected its third pin as the first word came traveling along the race-way. Second block did the same. But the third block projected its *second* pin!

"Oh, hell! Stop the machine—something wrong—it's going to set a $30/1000$ space!"

General consternation. "A foreign substance has got into the spacing plates." This from the head mathematician.

"Yes, that is the trouble," assented the foreman.

Paige examined. "No—look in, you can see that there's nothing of the kind." Further examination. *"Now* I know what it is—what it *must* be. One of those plates projects and binds. It's too bad—the first test is a failure." A *pause.* "Well, boys, no use to cry. Get to work—take the machine down.—No—Hold on! Don't touch a thing! Go right ahead! We are fools, the machine isn't. The machine knows what it's about. There is a *speck of dirt* on one of those types, and the machine is putting in a thinner space to *allow* for it!"

That was just it. The machine went right ahead, spaced the line, justified it to a hair, and shoved it into the galley complete and perfect! We took it out and examined it with a glass. You could not tell by your eye that the third space was thinner than the others but the glass and the calipers showed the difference. Paige had always said that the machine would measure invisible particles of dirt and allow for them but even he had forgotten that vast fact for the moment.

All the witnesses made written record of the immense historical birth—the first justification of a line of movable type by machinery—

and also set down the hour and the minute. Nobody had drunk anything and yet everybody seemed drunk. Well—dizzy, stupefied, stunned.

All the other wonderful inventions of the human brain sink pretty nearly into commonplace contrasted with this awful mechanical miracle. Telephones, telegraphs, locomotives, cotton gins, sewing machines, Babbage calculators, Jacquard looms, perfecting presses, Arkwright's frames—all mere toys, simplicities! The Paige Compositor marches alone and far in the lead of human inventions.

In two or three weeks we shall work the stiffness out of her joints and have her performing as smoothly and softly as human muscles, and then we shall speak out the big secret and let the world come and gaze.

Return me this letter when you have read it.

Sam

TO LIVY,* PARIS

Sunday, 9:30 a.m.

Livy dear, when we got out to the house last night Mrs. Rogers, who is up and around now, didn't want to go downstairs to dinner but Mr. R persuaded her and we had a very good time indeed. By 8 o'clock we were down again and bought a fifteen-dollar box in the Madison Square Garden (Rogers bought it, not I), then he went and fetched Dr. Rice while I went to the Players and picked up two artists, Reid and Simmons. And thus we filled 5 of the 6 seats.

There was a vast multitude of people in the brilliant place. Stanford White came along presently and invited me to go to the World Champion's dressing room, which I was very glad to do. Corbett has a fine face and is modest and diffident, besides being the most perfectly and beautifully constructed human animal in the world. I said,

* Clemens's wife.

"You have whipped Mitchell and maybe you will whip Jackson in June but you are not done then. You will have to tackle me."

He answered, so gravely that one might easily have thought him in earnest,

"No—I am not going to meet you in the ring. It is not fair or right to require it. You might chance to knock me out by no merit of your own but by a purely accidental blow, and then my reputation would be gone and you would have a double one. You have got fame enough and you ought not to want to take mine away from me."

Corbett was for a long time a clerk in the Nevada Bank in San Francisco.

There were lots of little boxing matches to entertain the crowd. Then at last Corbett appeared in the ring and the 8,000 people present went mad with enthusiasm. My two artists went mad about his form. They said they had never seen anything that came reasonably near equaling its perfection except Greek statues, and *they* didn't surpass it.

Corbett boxed 3 rounds with the middleweight Australian champion—oh, beautiful to see!—then the show was over and we struggled out through a perfect *wash* of humanity. When we reached the street I found I had left my arctics in the box. I had to have them, so Simmons said he would go back and get them, and I didn't dissuade him. I couldn't see how he was going to make his way a single yard into that solid oncoming wave of people, yet he must plow through it full 50 yards. He was back with the shoes in 3 minutes!

How do you reckon he accomplished that miracle? By saying,

"Way, gentlemen, please. Coming to fetch Mr. Corbett's overshoes."

The word flew from mouth to mouth, the Red Sea divided and Simmons walked comfortably through and back, dry shod. Simmons (this was revealed to me under seal of secrecy by Reid) is the hero of "Gwen," and he and Gwen's author were once engaged to marry. This is "fire-escape" Simmons, the inveterate talker, you know: *"Ex—in case of Simmons."*

I had an engagement at a beautiful dwelling close to the P— for ladies 10:30. I was there by 10:45. Thirty cultivated and very much them and gentlemen present, all of them acquaintances and most there personal friends of mine. That wonderful Hungarian Band til mid- (they charge $500 for an evening). Conversation and compactly night. Then a bite of supper. Then the company grouped before me and I told about Dr. B. E. Martin and the etchings, and followed it with the Scotch-Irish Christening. My, but the Martin is a darling story! Next, the head tenor from the Opera sang half a dozen great songs that set the company wild, yes, mad with delight, that nobly handsome young Damrosch accompanying on the piano.

Just a little pause. Then the Band burst out into an explosion of weird and tremendous dance music. A Hungarian celebrity and his wife took the floor. I followed. I couldn't help it. The others drifted in one by one and it was Onteora over again.

By half past 4 I had danced all those people down and yet was not tired, merely breathless. I was in bed at 5 and asleep in ten minutes. Up at 9 and presently at work on this letter to you. I think I wrote until 2 or half past. Then I walked leisurely out to Mr. Rogers's (it is called 3 miles but it is short of it), arriving at 3:30, but he was out, to return at 5:30 (and a person was *in,* whom I don't particularly like), so I didn't stay, but dropped over and chatted with the Howellses until 6.

First Howells and I had a chat together. I asked about Mrs. H. He said she was fine, still steadily improving and nearly back to her old best health. I asked (as if I didn't know):

"What do you attribute this strange miracle to?"

"Mind-cure—simply mind-cure."

"Lord, what a conversion! You were a scoffer three months ago."

"I? I wasn't."

"You were. You made elaborate fun of me in this very room."

"I did *not,* Clemens."

"It's a lie. Howells, you *did.*"

I detailed to him the conversation of that time—with the stately argument furnished by Boyesen in the fact that a patient had actually been killed by a mind-curist, and Howells's own smart remark that when the mind-curist is done with you, you *have* to call in a "regular" last because the former can't procure you a burial permit.

At last he gave in. He said he remembered that talk but had now been a mind-curist so long it was difficult for him to realize that he had ever been anything else.

H came skipping in presently, the very person to a dot that she used to be so many years ago.

N said, "People may *call* it what they like but it is just *hypnotism*—that's *all* it is—hypnotism pure and simple. Mind-cure!—the *idea!* Why, this woman that cured me hasn't got any mind. She's a good creature but she's dull and dumb and illiterate and—"

"Now *Eleanor!*"

"I know what I'm talking about! Don't I go there twice a week? And Mr. Clemens, if you could only *see* her wooden and satisfied face when she snubs me for forgetting myself and showing by a thoughtless remark that to *me* weather is still *weather,* instead of being just an abstraction and a superstition—oh, it's the *funniest* thing you *ever* saw! A-n-d—when she tilts up her nose—well, it's—it's—Well it's that kind of a nose that—"

"Now *Eleanor!*—the woman is not *responsible* for her nose—" and so on and so on. It didn't seem to me that I had any right to be having this feast and you not there.

She convinced *me,* before she got through, that she and William James are right, hypnotism and mind-cure are the same thing, no difference between them. Very well. The very source, the very *center* of hypnotism is *Paris.* Dr. Charcot's pupils and disciples are right there and ready to your hand without fetching poor dear old Susy across the stormy sea. Let Mrs. Mackay (to whom I send my best respects) tell you whom to go to to learn all you need to learn and how to proceed. *Do,* do it, honey. Don't lose a minute.

. . . At 11 o'clock last night Mr. Rogers said:

"*I* am able to feel physical fatigue and I feel it now. You never show any, either in your eyes or your movements. Do you ever feel any?"

I was able to say that I had forgotten what that feeling was like. Don't you remember how almost impossible it was for me to tire myself at the Villa? Well, it is just so in New York. I go to bed unfatigued at 3, I get up fresh and fine six hours later. I believe I have taken only one daylight nap since I have been here.

When the anchor is down then I shall say:

"Farewell—a long farewell—to *business!* I will *never* touch it again!"

I will live in literature, I will wallow in it, revel in it, I will swim in ink! Joan of Arc—but all this is premature. The anchor is not down yet.

Tomorrow (Tuesday) I will add a P. S. if I've any to add. But, whether or no, I must mail this tomorrow, for the mail steamer goes next day.

5:30 p.m. Great Scott, *this* is Tuesday! I must rush this letter into the mail instantly.

Tell that sassy Ben I've got her welcome letter and I'll write her as soon as I get a daylight chance. I've most time at night but I'd druther write daytimes.

Saml

In the foregoing letter, Rice was Clarence C. Rice, who had introduced Rogers to Clemens. The Players was and is a famous New York club. Reid and Simmons were Robert Reid and Edward Simmons, painters. Paine has described Simmons as "a brilliant, fluent and industrious talker. The title, 'Fire-escape Simmons,' . . . originated when Oliver Herford . . . one day pinned up by the back door of the Players the notice: 'Exit in case of Simmons.' "

Stanford White was a famous American architect of the late nineteenth century who designed Madison Square Garden, in the tower of which he built himself an apartment where he threw parties. He also designed the Washington Arch in Washington Square, New York, the New York Herald Building and a number of buildings at the University of Virginia in Charlottesville. He was shot and killed in 1906 by Harry K. Thaw, who has been described as the jealous and wealthy playboy husband of a woman with whom White was involved. A great trial ensued, the conclusion of which was that Thaw was found innocent by reason of insanity.

James J. Corbett became the world's heavyweight boxing champion when he defeated John L. Sullivan in 1892. He lost the title to Bob Fitzsimmons in 1897. He is considered to be one of the first scientific boxers, and the first boxer to win a championship under the Queensberry rules. After retiring from boxing he became an actor. In his day he was often referred to as Gentleman Jim.

Gwen, a popular novel of the time, was written by Blanche Willis Howard. Damrosch was Walter Damrosch, who later became a well-known orchestra conductor.—C.N.

TO TWICHELL,* HARTFORD

London, *Jan. 19,* '97

Dear Joe,

Do I want you to write to me? Indeed I do. I do not want most people to write but I do want you to do it. The others break my heart but you will not. You have a something divine in you that is not in other men. You have the touch that heals, not lacerates. And you know the secret places of our hearts. You know our life—the outside of it—as the others do—and the inside of it—which they do not. You have seen our whole voyage. You have seen us go to sea, a cloud of sail, and the flag at the peak. And you see us now, chartless, adrift— derelicts, battered, water-logged, our sails a ruck of rags, our pride gone. For it is gone. And there is nothing in its place. The vanity of life was all we had, and there is no more vanity left in us. We are even ashamed of that we had, ashamed that we trusted the promises of life and builded high—to come to this!

I did know that Susy was part of us. I did *not* know that she could go away. I did not know that she could go away and take our lives with her, yet leave our dull bodies behind. And I did not know what she was. To me she was but treasure in the bank, the amount known, the need to look at it daily, handle it, weigh it, count it, *realize* it, not necessary. And now that I would do it, it is too late. They tell me it is not there, has vanished away in a night, the bank is broken, my fortune is gone, I am a pauper. How am I to comprehend this? How am I to *have* it? Why am I robbed, and who is benefited?

Ah well, Susy died at *home.* She had that privilege. Her dying eyes rested upon nothing that was strange to them, but only upon things which they had known and loved always and which had made her young years glad. And she had you and Sue and Katy and John and Ellen. This was happy fortune. I am thankful that it was vouchsafed to her. If she had died in another house—well, I think I could not have borne that. To us, our house was not unsentient matter. It had a heart

---

* Clemens's Hartford neighbor, pastor and good friend.

and a soul and eyes to see us with and approvals and solicitudes and deep sympathies. It was of us and we were in its confidence and lived in its grace and in the peace of its benediction. We never came home from an absence that its face did not light up and speak out its eloquent welcome. And we could not enter it unmoved. And could we now, oh now, in spirit we should enter it unshod.

I am trying to add to the "assets" which you estimate so generously. No, I am not. The thought is not in my mind. My purpose is other. I am working but it is for the sake of the work—the "surcease of sorrow" that is found there. I work all the days, and trouble vanishes away when I use that magic. This book will not long stand between it and me now. But that is no matter, I have many unwritten books to fly to for my preservation. The interval between the finishing of this one and the beginning of the next will not be more than an hour, at most. *Continuances,* I mean, for two of them are already well along. In fact have reached exactly the same stage in their journey: 19,000 words each. The present one will contain 180,000 words—130,000 are done. I am well protected.

But Livy! She has nothing in the world to turn to, nothing but housekeeping and doing things for the children and me. She does not see people and cannot. Books have lost their interest for her. She sits solitary, and all the day and all the days wonders how it all happened and why. We others were always busy with our affairs but Susy was her comrade—had to be driven from her loving persecutions—sometimes at 1 in the morning. To Livy the persecutions were welcome. It was heaven to her to be plagued like that. But it is ended now. Livy stands so in need of help, and none among us all could help her like you.

Some day you and I will walk again, Joe, and talk. I hope so. We could have *such* talks! We are all grateful to you and Harmony—*how* grateful it is not given to us to say in words. We pay as we can, in love, and in this coin practicing no economy. Goodbye, dear old Joe!

Mark

TO BRANDER MATTHEWS, NEW YORK

New York City, *May 4, '03*

Dear Brander,

I haven't been out of my bed for four weeks but—well, I have been reading a good deal and it occurs to me to ask you to sit down some time or other when you have 8 or 9 months to spare, and jot me down a certain few literary particulars for my help and elevation. Your time need not be thrown away, for at your further leisure you can make Columbian lectures out of the results and do your students a good turn.

1. Are there in Sir Walter's novels passages done in good English, English which is neither slovenly or involved?

2. Are there passages whose English is not poor and thin and commonplace, but is of a quality above that?

3. Are there passages which burn with real fire—not punk, foxfire, make believe?

4. Has he heroes and heroines who are not cads and cadesses?

5. Has he personages whose acts and talk correspond with their characters as described by him?

6. Has he heroes and heroines whom the reader admires, admires and knows *why?*

7. Has he funny characters that are funny, and humorous passages that are humorous?

8. Does he ever chain the reader's interest and make him reluctant to lay the book down?

9. Are there pages where he ceases from posing, ceases from admiring the placid flood and flow of his own dilutions, ceases from being artificial, and is for a time, long or short, recognizably sincere and in earnest?

10. Did he know how to write English and didn't do it because he didn't want to?

11. Did he use the right word only when he couldn't think of another one, or did he run so much to wrong because he didn't know the right one when he saw it?

12. Can you read him and keep your respect for him? Of course a person could in *his* day—an era of sentimentality and sloppy romantics—but land! can a body do it today?

Brander, I lie here dying, slowly dying, under the blight of Sir Walter. I have read the first volume of *Rob Roy,* and as far as chapter XIX of *Guy Mannering,* and I can no longer hold my head up nor take my nourishment. Lord, it's all so juvenile! So artificial, so shoddy. And such wax figures and skeletons and spectres. Interest? Why, it is impossible to feel an interest in these bloodless shams, these milk-and-water humbugs. And oh, the poverty of the invention! Not poverty in inventing situations, but poverty in furnishing reasons for them. Sir Walter usually gives himself away when he arranges for a situation—elaborates, and elaborates, and elaborates, till if you live to get to it you don't believe in it when it happens.

I can't find the rest of *Rob Roy,* I can't stand any more *Mannering.* I do not know just what to do but I will reflect and not quit this great study rashly. He *was* great in his day and to his proper audience. And so was God in Jewish times, for that matter, but why should either of them rank high now? And *do* they? Honest, now, *do* they? Damned if I believe it.

My, I wish I could see you and Leigh Hunt!

Sincerely Yours
S. L. Clemens

TO ROBERT FULTON, RENO, NEVADA

In the Mountains
May 24, 1905

Dear Mr. Fulton,

I remember as if it were yesterday that when I disembarked from the overland stage in front of the Ormsby in Carson City in August, 1861, I was not expecting to be asked to come again. I was tired, discouraged, white with alkali dust and did not know anybody. And if you had said then, "Cheer up, desolate stranger, don't be downhearted. Pass on, and come again in 1905," you cannot think how grateful I would have been and how gladly I would have closed the contract. Although I was not expecting to be invited, I was watching out for it and was hurt and disappointed when you started to ask me and changed it to, "How soon are you going away?"

But you have made it all right now, the wound is closed. And so I thank you sincerely for the invitation, and with you all Reno, and if I were a few years younger I would accept it, and promptly. I would go. I would let somebody else do the oration but, as for me, I would talk —just talk. I would renew my youth. And talk—and talk—and talk— and have the time of my life! I would march the unforgotten and unforgettable antiques by and name their names and give them reverent Hail-and-farewell as they passed: Goodman, McCarthy, Gillis, Curry, Baldwin, Winters, Howard, Nye, Stewart, Neely Johnson, Hal Clayton, North, Root—and my brother, upon whom be peace! And then the desperadoes, who made life a joy and the "Slaughter-house" a precious possession: Sam Brown, Farmer Pete, Bill Mayfield, Six-fingered Jake, Jack Williams and the rest of the crimson discipleship— and so on and so on. Believe me, I would start a resurrection it would do you more good to look at than the next one will, if you go on the way you are doing now.

Those were the days!—those old ones. They will come no more. Youth will come no more. They were so full to the brim with the wine of life. There have been no others like them. It chokes me up to think of them. Would you like me to come out there and cry? It would not beseem my white head.

Goodbye. I drink to you all. Have a good time—and take an old man's blessing.

                                                              Mark Twain

SPEECHES

NEW ENGLAND WEATHER

In December of 1876 Clemens attended the seventy-first annual dinner of the New England Society of New York. The toast to which Clemens responded was "The oldest inhabitant—the weather of New England. 'Who can lose it and forget it?/Who can have it and regret it?/Be interposer 'twixt us Twain.' " The last sentence is from *The Merchant of Venice*.—C.N.

I reverently believe that the Maker who made us all makes everything in New England but the weather. I don't know who makes that, but I think it must be raw apprentices in the weather clerk's factory who experiment and learn how, in New England, for board and clothes, and then are promoted to make weather for countries that require a good article and will take their custom elsewhere if they don't get it.

There is a sumptuous variety about the New England weather that compels the stranger's admiration—and regret. The weather is always doing something there, always attending strictly to business, always getting up new designs and trying them on the people to see how they will go. But it gets through more business in spring than any other season.

In the spring I have counted one hundred and thirty-six different kinds of weather inside of four-and-twenty hours. It was I that made the fame and fortune of that man that had that marvelous collection of weather on exhibition at the Centennial, that so astounded the foreigners. He was going to travel all over the world and get specimens from all the climes.

I said, "Don't you do it. You come to New England on a favorable spring day."

I told him what we could do in the way of style, variety and quantity.

Well, he came and he made his collection in four days. As to variety, why, he confessed that he got hundreds of kinds of weather that he had never heard of before. And as to quantity—well, after he had picked out and discarded all that was blemished in any way, he not only had weather enough but weather to spare, weather to hire out, weather to sell, to deposit, weather to invest, weather to give to the poor.

The people of New England are by nature patient and forbearing but there are some things which they will not stand. Every year they kill a lot of poets for writing about "Beautiful Spring." These are generally casual visitors who bring their notions of spring from somewhere else and cannot, of course, know how the natives feel about spring. And so the first thing they know the opportunity to inquire how they feel has permanently gone by.

Old Probabilities has a mighty reputation for accurate prophecy and thoroughly well deserves it. You take up the paper and observe how crisply and confidently he checks off what today's weather is going to be on the Pacific, down South, in the Middle States, in the Wisconsin region. See him sail along in the joy and pride of his power till he gets to New England, and then see his tail drop. *He* doesn't know what the weather is going to be in New England. Well, he mulls over it, and by-and-by he gets out something about like this: Probably northeast to southwest winds, varying to the southward and westward and eastward, and points between, high and low barometer swapping around from place to place; probable areas of rain, snow, hail and drought, succeeded or preceded by earthquakes, with thunder and lightning.

Then he jots down his postscript from his wandering mind, to cover accidents.

"But it is possible that the programme may be wholly changed in the mean time."

Yes, one of the brightest gems in the New England weather is the dazzling uncertainty of it. There is only one thing certain about it. You are certain there is going to be plenty of it—a perfect grand review. But you never can tell which end of the procession is going to move first. You fix up for the drought, you leave your umbrella in the house and sally out, and two to one you get drowned. You make up your mind that the earthquake is due, you stand from under and take hold of something to steady yourself, and the first thing you know you get struck by lightning.

These are great disappointments but they can't be helped.

The lightning there is peculiar. It is so convincing that when it strikes a thing it doesn't leave enough of that thing behind for you to tell whether—Well, you'd think it was something valuable, and a Congressman had been there.

And the thunder. When the thunder begins to merely tune up and scrape and saw, and key up the instruments for the performance, strangers say, "Why, what awful thunder you have here!" But when the baton is raised and the real concert begins you'll find that stranger down in the cellar with his head in the ash barrel.

Now as to the *size* of the weather in New England—lengthways, I mean. It is utterly disproportioned to the size of that little country. Half the time, when it is packed as full as it can stick, you will see that New England weather sticking out beyond the edges and projecting around hundreds and hundreds of miles over the neighboring States. She can't hold a tenth part of her weather. You can see cracks all about where she has strained herself trying to do it.

I could speak volumes about the inhuman perversity of the New England weather but I will give but a single specimen. I like to hear rain on a tin roof. So I covered part of my roof with tin, with an eye to that luxury. Well, sir, do you think it ever rains on that tin? No, sir. Skips it every time.

Mind, in this speech I have been trying merely to do honor to the New England weather—no language could do it justice. But after all there is at least one or two things about that weather (or, if you please, effects produced by it) which we residents would not like to part with. If we hadn't our bewitching autumn foliage we should still have to credit the weather with one feature which compensates for all its bullying vagaries—the ice-storm: when a leafless tree is clothed with ice from the bottom to the top. Ice that is as bright and clear as crystal. When every bough and twig is strung with ice beads, frozen dewdrops, and the whole tree sparkles cold and white like the Shah of Persia's diamond plume.

Then the wind waves the branches and the sun comes out and turns all those myriads of beads and drops to prisms that glow and burn and flash with all manner of colored fires, which change and change again with inconceivable rapidity from blue to red, from red to green, and green to gold. The tree becomes a spraying fountain, a very explosion of dazzling jewels, and it stands there the acme, the climax, the supremest possibility in art or nature of bewildering, intoxicating, intolerable magnificence. One cannot make the words too strong.

1876

WHITTIER'S BIRTHDAY

This speech fell dreadfully flat at the time, in Clemens's opinion, and he feared he had badly damaged his reputation in New England's literary circles. The quotations are from the works of Holmes, Emerson and Longfellow. Clemens was kidding when he ascribed "Barbara Frietchie" (by Whittier) to Emerson, "The Bigelow Papers" (by Lowell) to Longfellow and "Thanatopsis" (by Bryant) to Holmes.—C.N.

This is an occasion peculiarly meet for the digging up of pleasant reminiscences concerning literary folk. Therefore I will drop lightly into history myself.

Standing here on the shore of the Atlantic and contemplating certain of its largest literary billows, I am reminded of a thing which happened to me thirteen years ago when I had just succeeded in stirring up a little Nevadian literary puddle myself, whose spume flakes were beginning to blow thinly Californiaward. I started an inspection tramp through the southern mines of California. I was callow and conceited, and I resolved to try the virtue of my *nom de guerre*.

I very soon had an opportunity. I knocked at a miner's lonely log cabin in the foothills of the Sierras just at nightfall. It was snowing at the time. A jaded, melancholy man of fifty, barefooted, opened the door to me. When he heard my *nom de guerre* he looked more dejected than before. He let me in—pretty reluctantly, I thought—and after the customary bacon and beans, black coffee and hot whisky, I took a pipe. This sorrowful man had not said three words up to this time.

Now he spoke up and said in the voice of one who is secretly suffering, "You're the fourth. I'm going to move."

"The fourth what?" said I.

"The fourth literary man that has been here in twenty-four hours. I'm going to move."

"You don't tell me!" said I. "Who were the others?"

"Mr. Longfellow, Mr. Emerson and Mr. Oliver Wendell Holmes. Consound the lot!"

You can easily believe I was interested. I supplicated. Three hot whiskies did the rest. And finally the melancholy miner began. Said he:

"They came here just at dark yesterday evening and I let them in, of course. Said they were going to the Yosemite. They were a rough lot but that's nothing. Everybody looks rough that travels afoot. Mr. Emerson was a seedy little bit of a chap, red-headed. Mr. Holmes was as fat as a balloon. He weighed as much as three hundred and had double chins all the way down to his stomach. Mr. Longfellow was built like a prizefighter. His head was cropped and bristly, like as if he had a wig made of hair brushes. His nose lay straight down his face like a finger with the end joint tilted up. They had been drinking, I could see that. And what queer talk they used! Mr. Holmes inspected this cabin, then he took me by the buttonhole, and says he:

> " 'Through the deep caves of thought
> I hear a voice that sings,
> Build thee more stately mansions,
> O my soul!'

"Says I, 'I can't afford it, Mr. Holmes. And moreover I don't want to.' Blamed if I liked it pretty well, either, coming from a stranger that way. However, I started to get out my bacon and beans, when Mr. Emerson came and looked on awhile. And then *he* takes me aside by the buttonhole and says:

> " 'Gives me agates for my meat;
> Gives me cantharids to eat;
> From air and ocean bring me foods,
> From all zones and altitudes.'

"Says I, 'Mr. Emerson, if you'll excuse me, this ain't no hotel.' You see it sort of riled me. I warn't used to the ways of littery swells. But I went on a-sweating over my work. And next comes Mr. Longfellow and buttonholes me and interrupts me. Says he:

" 'Honor be to Mudjekeewis!
You shall hear how Pau-Puk-Keewis—'

"But I broke in, and says I, 'Beg your pardon, Mr. Longfellow. If
you'll be so kind as to hold your yawp for about five minutes and let
me get this grub ready, you'll do me proud.' Well sir, after they'd filled
up I set out the jug. Mr. Holmes looks at it and then he fires up all of a
sudden and yells:

" 'Flash out a stream of blood-red wine!
For I would drink to other days.'

"By George, I was getting kind of worked up. I don't deny it, I was
getting kind of worked up. I turns to Mr. Holmes, and says I, 'Looky
here, my fat friend, I'm a-running this shanty, and if the court knows
herself, you'll take whisky straight or you'll go dry.' Them's the very
words I said to him.

"Now I don't want to sass such famous littery people. But you see
they kind of forced me. There ain't nothing onreasonable 'bout me. I
don't mind a passel of guests a-treadin' on my tail three or four times.
But when it comes to *standing* on it it's different. 'And if the court
knows herself,' I says, 'you'll take whisky straight or you'll go dry.'

"Well, between drinks they'd swell around the cabin and strike attitudes and spout. And pretty soon they got out a greasy old deck and
went to playing euchre at ten cents a corner—on trust. I began to
notice some pretty suspicious things. Mr. Emerson dealt, looked at his
hand, shook his head, says:

" 'I am the doubter and the doubt—'

and ca'mly bunched the hands and went to shuffling for a new layout.
Says he:

" 'They reckon ill who leave me out;
They know not well the subtle ways I keep
I pass and deal again!'

"Hang'd if he didn't go ahead and do it, too! Oh, he was a cool one!
Well, in about a minute things were running pretty tight. But all of a
sudden I see by Mr. Emerson's eye he judged he had 'em. He had
already corralled two tricks, and each of the others one. So now he
kind of lifts a little in his chair and says:

> *" 'I tire of globes and aces!—*
> *Too long the game is played!'*

and down he fetched a right bower.

"Mr. Longfellow smiles as sweet as pie and says:

> *" 'Thanks thanks to thee, my worthy friend,*
> *For the lesson thou hast taught,'*

and blamed if he didn't down with *another* right bower!

"Emerson claps his hand on his bowie. Longfellow claps his on his revolver. And I went under a bunk. There was going to be trouble. But that monstrous Holmes rose up, wobbling his double chins, and says he, 'Order, gentlemen. The first man that draws, I'll lay down on him and smother him!'

"All quiet on the Potomac, you bet!

"They were pretty how-come-you-so by now. And they begun to blow. Emerson says, 'The nobbiest thing I ever wrote was "Barbara Frietchie." ' Says Longfellow, 'It don't begin with my "Bigelow Papers." ' Says Holmes, 'My "Thanatopsis" lays over 'em both.'

"They mighty near ended in a fight. Then they wished they had some more company. And Mr. Emerson pointed to me and says:

> *" 'Is yonder squalid peasant all*
> *That this proud nursery could breed?'*

"He was a-whetting his bowie on his boot so I let it pass. Well sir, next they took it into their heads that they would like some music. So they made me stand up and sing 'When Johnny Comes Marching Home' till I dropped—at thirteen minutes past four this morning. That's what I've been through, my friend. When I woke at seven they were leaving, thank goodness, and Mr. Longfellow had my only boots on, and his'n under his arm.

"Says I, 'Hold on there, Evangeline, what are you going to do with them?'

"He says, 'Going to make tracks with 'em. Because:

> *" 'Lives of great men all remind us*
> *We can make our lives sublime;*
> *And, departing, leave behind us*
> *Footprints on the sands of time.'*

"As I said, Mr. Twain, you are the fourth in twenty-four hours. And I'm going to move. I ain't suited to a littery atmosphere."

I said to the miner, "Why, my dear sir, *these* were not the gracious singers to whom we and the world pay loving reverence and homage. These were impostors."

The miner investigated me with a calm eye for awhile. Then said he, "Ah! Impostors, were they? Are *you?*"

I did not pursue the subject. And since then I have not traveled on my *nom de guerre* enough to hurt.

Such was the reminiscence I was moved to contribute, Mr. Chairman. In my enthusiasm I may have exaggerated the details a little but you will easily forgive me that fault since I believe it is the first time I have ever deflected from perpendicular fact on an occasion like this.

1877

There is an epilogue to this event which is very interesting. In January 1906 Clemens answered a letter he had received from a correspondent identified as "Mrs. H" by Albert Bigelow Paine.

"I am forever in your debt for reminding me of that curious passage in my life," he wrote, referring to the Whittier birthday speech. "During the first year or two after it happened I could not bear to think of it. My pain and shame were so intense and my sense of having been an imbecile so settled, established and confirmed, that I drove the episode entirely from my mind. And so all these twenty-eight or twenty-nine years I have lived in the conviction that my performance of that time was coarse, vulgar and destitute of humor. But your suggestion that you and your family found humor in it twenty-eight years ago moved me to look into the matter. So I commissioned a Boston typewriter to delve among the Boston papers of that bygone time and send me a copy of it.

"It came this morning, and if there is any vulgarity about it I am not able to discover it. If it isn't innocently and ridiculously funny, I am no judge. I will see to it that you get a copy."

Clemens then proceeded to reminisce in Paine's presence about the speech, producing one of his autobiographical dictations.

"What I have said to Mrs. H is true. I did suffer during a year or two from the deep humiliations of the episode. But at last in 1888 in Venice my wife and I came across Mr. and Mrs. A.P.C. of Concord, Massachusetts, and a friendship began then of the sort which nothing but death terminates. The C's were very bright people and in every way charming and companionable.

"We were together a month or two in Venice and several months in Rome afterward. And one day that lamented break of mine was mentioned. And when I was on the point of lathering those people for bringing it to my mind when I had gotten the memory of it almost squelched, I perceived with joy that the C's were indignant about the way that my performance had been received in Boston. They poured out their opinions most freely and frankly about the frosty attitude of the people who were present at that performance, and about the Boston newspapers for the position they had taken in regard to the matter. That position was that I had been irreverent beyond belief, beyond imagination.

"Very well. I had accepted that as a fact for a year or two and had been thoroughly miserable about it whenever I thought of it, which was not frequently if I could help it. Whenever I thought of it I wondered how I ever could have been inspired to do so unholy a thing. Well, the C's comforted me. But they did not persuade me to continue to think about the unhappy episode. I resisted that. I tried to get it out of my mind and let it die. And I succeeded. Until Mrs. H's letter came it had been a good twenty-five years since I had thought of that matter. And when she said that the thing was funny I wondered if possibly she might be right. At any rate my curiosity was aroused and I wrote to Boston and got the whole thing copied, as above set forth.

"I vaguely remember some of the details of that gathering. Dimly I can see a hundred people—no, perhaps fifty. Shadowy figures sitting at tables, feeding. Ghosts now to me and nameless forevermore. I don't know who they were but I can very distinctly see, seated at the grand table and facing the rest of us, Mr. Emerson supernaturally grave, unsmiling. Mr. Whittier grave, lovely, his beautiful spirit shining out of his face. Mr. Longfellow with his silken white hair and his benignant face. Dr. Oliver Wendell Holmes flashing smiles and affection and all good fellowship everywhere like a rose diamond whose facets are being turned toward the light first one way and then another—a charming man and always fascinating whether he was talking or whether he was sitting still (what *he* would call still but what would be more or less motion to other people). I can see those figures with entire distinctness across this abyss of time.

"One other feature is clear. Willie Winter (for these past thousand years dramatic editor of the *New York Tribune* and still occupying that high post in his old age) was there. He was much younger then than he is now and he showed it. It was always a pleasure to me to see Willie Winter at a banquet. During a matter of twenty years I was seldom at a banquet where Willie Winter was not also present and where he did not read a charming poem written for the occasion. He did it this time and it was up to standard: dainty, happy, choicely phrased, and as good to listen to as music, and sounding exactly as if it was pouring unprepared out of heart and brain.

"Now at that point ends all that was pleasurable about that notable celebration of Mr. Whittier's seventieth birthday. Because *I* got up at that point and followed Winter with what I have no doubt I supposed would be the gem of the evening—the gay oration above quoted from the Boston paper. I had written it all out the day before and had perfectly memorized it, and I stood up there at my genial and happy and self-satisfied ease and began to deliver it. Those majestic guests, that row of venerable and still active volcanoes, listened, as did everybody else in the house, with attentive interest.

"Well, I delivered myself of—we'll say the first two hundred words of my speech. I was expecting no returns from that part of the speech but this was not the case as regarded the rest of it. I arrived now at the dialogue. 'The old miner said, "You are the fourth, I'm going to move." "The fourth what?" said I. He answered, "The fourth littery man that has been here in twenty-four hours. I am going to move." "Why, you don't tell me," said I. "Who were the others?" "Mr. Longfellow, Mr. Emerson, Mr. Oliver Wendell Holmes, consound the lot—" '

"Now then, the house's *attention* continued but the expression of interest in the faces turned to a sort of black frost. I wondered what the trouble was. I didn't know. I went on but with difficulty. I struggled along and entered upon that miner's fearful description of the bogus Emerson, the bogus Holmes, the bogus Longfellow, always hoping, but with a gradually perishing hope, that somebody would laugh or that somebody would at least smile.

"But nobody did.

"I didn't know enough to give it up and sit down. I was too new to public speaking. And so I went on with this awful performance and carried it clear through to the end in front of a body of people who seemed turned to stone with horror. It was the sort of expression their faces would have worn if I had been making these remarks about the Deity and the rest of the Trinity. There is no milder way in which to describe the petrified condition and the ghastly expression of those people.

"When I sat down it was with a heart which had long ceased to beat. I shall never be as dead again as I was then. I shall never be as miserable again as I was then. I speak now as one who doesn't know what the conditions of things may be in the next world. But in this one I shall never be as wretched again as I was then. Howells, who was near me, tried to say a comforting word but couldn't get beyond a gasp. There was no use. He understood the whole size of the disaster. He had good intentions but the words froze before they could get out. It was an atmosphere that would freeze anything. If Benvenuto Cellini's salamander had been in that place he would not have survived to be put into Cellini's autobiography.

"There was a frightful pause. There was an awful silence. A desolating silence.

"Then the next man on the list had to get up. There was no help for it. That was Bishop. Bishop had just burst handsomely upon the world with a most acceptable novel which had appeared in the *Atlantic Monthly,* a place which would make any novel respectable and any author noteworthy. In this case the novel itself was recognized as being, without extraneous help, respectable. Bishop was away up in the public favor and he was an object of high interest, consequently there was a sort of national expectancy in the air. We may say our American millions were standing from Maine to Texas and from Alaska to Florida, holding their breath, their lips parted, their hands ready to applaud, when Bishop should get up on that occasion and for the first time in his life speak in public. It was under these damaging conditions that he got up to 'make good,' as the vulgar say.

"I had spoken several times before and that is the reason why I was able to go on without dying in my tracks as I ought to have done. But Bishop had had no experience. He was up facing those awful deities, facing those other people, those strangers, facing human beings for the first time in his life, with a speech to utter. No doubt it was well packed away in his memory, no doubt it was fresh and usable until I had been heard from. I suppose that after that, and under the smothering pall of that dreary silence, it began to waste away and disappear out of his head like the rags breaking from the edge of a fog. And presently there wasn't any fog left.

"He didn't go on. He didn't last long. It was not many sentences after his first before he began to hesitate and break and lose his grip and totter and wobble. And at last he slumped down in a limp and mushy pile.

"Well, the program for the occasion was probably not more than one-third finished. But it ended there. Nobody rose. The next man hadn't strength enough to get up. And everybody looked so dazed, so stupefied, paralyzed, it was impossible for anybody to do anything. Or even try. Nothing could go on in that strange atmosphere.

"Howells mournfully and without words hitched himself to Bishop and me and supported us out of the room. It was very kind, he was most generous. He towed us tottering away into some room in that building and we sat down there.

"I don't know what my remark was now but I know the nature of it. It was the kind of remark you make when you know that nothing in the world can help your case.

"But Howells was honest. He had to say the heart-breaking things he did say. That there was no help for this calamity, this shipwreck, this cataclysm. That this was the most disastrous thing that had ever happened in anybody's history.

"And then he added, 'That is, for *you.* And consider what you have done for Bishop. It is bad enough in your case, you deserve to suffer. You have committed this crime, and you deserve to have all you are going to get. But here is an innocent man. Bishop had never done you any harm, and see what you have done to him. He can never hold his head up again. The world can never look upon Bishop as being a live person. He is a corpse.'

"That is the history of that episode of twenty-eight years ago, which pretty nearly killed me with shame during that first year or two whenever it forced its way into my mind.

"Now then, I take that speech up and examine it. As I said, it arrived this morning from Boston. I have read it twice, and unless I am an idiot it hasn't a single defect in it from the first word to the last. It is just as good as good can be. It is smart. It is saturated with humor. There isn't a suggestion of coarseness or vulgarity in it anywhere.

"What could have been the matter with that house? It is amazing, it is incredible, that they didn't shout with laughter, and those deities the loudest of them all.

"Could the fault have been with me? Did I lose courage when I saw those great men up there whom I was going to describe in such a strange fashion? If that happened, if I showed doubt, that can account for it, for you can't be successfully funny if you show that you are afraid of it.

"Well, I can't account for it. But if I had those beloved and revered old literary immortals back here now on the platform at Carnegie Hall I would take that same old speech, deliver it word for word and melt them till they'd run all over that stage.

"Oh, the fault must have been with me, it is not in the speech at all."—C.N.

AN AUTHOR'S SOLDIERING

In April of 1887 Clemens attended a reunion banquet of the Union Veterans Association of Maryland, which was given in Baltimore.

You Union veterans of Maryland have prepared your feast and offered to me, a rebel veteran of Missouri, the wound-healing bread and salt of a gracious hospitality. Do you realize all the vast significance of the situation? Do you sense the whole magnitude of this conjunction and perceive with what opulence of blessing for this nation it is freighted?

What is it we are doing? Reflect! Upon this stage tonight we play the closing scene of the mightiest drama of modern times and ring down for good and all the curtain raised at Sumter six-and-twenty years ago. The two grand divisions of the nation, which we name in general terms the North and the South, have shaken hands long ago and given and taken the kiss of peace.

Was anything lacking to make the reconciliation perfect, the fusion of feeling complete? Yes. The great border States attached to those grand divisions, but belonging to neither of them and independent of both, were silent, had made no forgiving sign to each other across the chasm left by the convulsion of war, and the world grieved that this was so. But tonight the Union veteran of Maryland clasps hands with the rebel veteran of Missouri and the gap is closed. In this supreme moment the imperfect welding of the broken Union is perfected at last, and from this hour the seam of the joining shall no more be visible. The long tragedy is ended—ring down the curtain!

When your secretary invited me to this reunion of the Union Veterans of Maryland he requested me to come prepared to clear up a matter which he said had long been a subject of dispute and bad blood in war circles in this country—to wit, the true dimensions of my military service in the Civil War, and the effect which they had upon the general result. I recognize the importance of this thing to history and I have come prepared. Here are the details.

I was in the Civil War two weeks. In that brief time I rose from private to second lieutenant. The monumental feature of my campaign was the one battle which my command fought—it was in the summer of '61. If I do say it, it was the bloodiest battle ever fought in human history. There is nothing approaching it for destruction of human life in the field, if you take in consideration the forces engaged and the proportion of death to survival.

And yet you do not even know the name of that battle. Neither do I. It had a name but I have forgotten it. It is no use to keep private information which you can't show off.

Now look at the way history does. It takes the battle of Boonville, fought near by about the date of our slaughter and shouts its teeth loose over it and yet never even mentions ours, doesn't even call it an "affair," doesn't call it anything at all, never even heard of it. Whereas what are the facts? Why, these.

In the battle of Boonville there were two thousand men engaged on the Union side and about as many on the other—supposed to be. The casualties all told were two men killed, and not all of these were killed outright but only half of them, for the other man died in hospital next day. I know that, because his great-uncle was second cousin to my grandfather, who spoke three languages and was perfectly honorable and upright though he had warts all over him, and used to—but never mind about that, the facts are just as I say and I can prove it. Two men killed in that battle of Boonville, that's the whole result. All the others got away—on both sides.

Now then, in our battle there were just fifteen men engaged on our side—all brigadier generals but me, and I was a second lieutenant. On the other side there was one man. He was a stranger. We killed him. It was night and we thought he was an army of observation. He looked like an army of observation—in fact he looked bigger than an army of observation would in the daytime. And some of us believed he was trying to surround us, and some thought he was going to try to turn our position, and so we shot him. Poor fellow, he probably wasn't an army of observation after all. But that wasn't our fault. As I say, he had all the look of it in that dim light.

It was a sorrowful circumstance, but he took the chances of war and he drew the wrong card. He overestimated his fighting strength and he suffered the likely result. But he fell as the brave should fall—with his face to the foe and feet to the field—so we buried him with the honors of war and took his things.

So began and ended the only battle in the history of the world where the opposing force was *utterly exterminated,* swept from the face of the earth—to the last man. And yet you don't know the name of that battle. You don't even know the name of that man.

Now then for the argument. Suppose I had continued in the war and gone on as I began and exterminated the opposing force every time—every two weeks—where would your war have been? Why, you see yourself the conflict would have been too one-sided. There was but one honorable course for me to pursue and I pursued it. I withdrew to private life and gave the Union cause a chance.

There, now, you have the whole thing in a nutshell. It was not my presence in the Civil War that determined that tremendous contest—it was my retirement from it that brought the crash. It left the Confederate side too weak.

And yet when I stop and think I cannot regret my course. No, when

I look abroad over this happy land, with its wounds healed and its enmities forgotten; this reunited sisterhood of majestic States; this freest of free commonwealths the sun in his course shines upon; this one sole country nameable in history or tradition where a man is a man and manhood the only royalty; this people ruled by the justest and wholesomest laws and government yet devised by the wisdom of men; this mightiest of the civilized empires of the earth in numbers, in prosperity, in progress and in promise; and reflect that there is no North, no South any more, but that as in the old time it is now and will remain forever in the hearts and speech of Americans our land, our country, our giant empire, and the flag floating in its firmament our flag, I would not wish it otherwise.

No, when I look about me and contemplate these sublime results I feel deep down in my heart that I acted for the best when I took my shoulder out from under the Confederacy and let it come down.

1887

A SPEECH FOR ALL OCCASIONS

This talk was given at the Forefathers' Day dinner of the Congregational Club in Boston. The *Boston Daily Globe* of Wednesday, December 21, 1887, ran headlines and a long story about the affair. "Pilgrims./Their Deeds and Tri-als/Again Recalled./Forefathers' Day in the Con-/gregationalist Club./ Speeches, Poems, Music and/a Big Dinner./Governor Ames and Lieutenant/ Governor Bracket Present./Mark Twain Makes a 'Pat-/tent Adjustable Speech.'/Chauncey M. Depew on the/Meaning of Liberty./Collector Salton-stall, Rev. Dr. Gage/and Other Speakers."

"Ye Congregational Clubbe," the article began, "mette as aforetime in ye Musick Halle to think over and with ye savorie helpe of sundrie goodies of songe and soe forthe to talk about Ye Pilgrim Fathers and their getting ashoare at New Plimmoth two hundred sixty and seven years agone.

"Ye Pilgrim forefathers, could they have filed into Music Hall last night, would have found several things strange to them. First of all, they would have seen something less than a quarter of an acre of heavily laden tables, all ready for the feast which followed. Then they would have noted the crowd of something over 1000 guests. This would have excited their curiosity, and in answer to their query some one would have said it was the Congregational Club gathered to celebrate Forefathers' Day, an event among the descendants of the Pilgrims almost as sacredly commemorated as is Christmas itself.

"It was 'two hundred, sixty and seven years agone' yesterday that the Mayflower dropped her old-fashioned anchor off New Plymouth, and a little time thereafter the voyagers got ashore. There were not a great many of them, but there were enough to found this great Commonwealth. In conjunction with the Puritans they founded much of the good order, established many laws now considered as good enough to govern a people greater in numbers and more advanced than they were. More than all, they gave us institutions which have lived through all the years and are yet considered models.

"The hall was filled. There were 18 large tables, more than could be placed upon the main floor and stage, and so some were put into the first gallery. The guests began to assemble at about 5 o'clock, and spent the ensuing half hour in the usual conversation and in hunting for their seats. Descendants of all the Pilgrims, the Congregationalists of course talked more or less about the brave men who had courage enough in their convictions to follow, even blindly, their consciences. The speeches of the evening, too, were loyal and loving tributes to the bravery and devotion of that little band. It was not a new experience for the people gathered together to commemorate the day, for they have done the same thing year after year since the organization of the club. The Pilgrims landed in 1620, the Congregational Club was founded in 1869. Surely the memory of the day has not grown gray nor been forgotten."

The president of the club introduced Clemens. The article reported, "Mr. Clemens was given quite an ovation, and his remarks which followed were so droll in their nature and the manner in which they were delivered that his hearers were kept upon a broad grin from the first to the last. It would be almost impossible to convey upon paper anything that would give more than an indication of their intense humor, which was derived largely from the peculiar gestures, inflections and actions which accompanied them. This was particularly so of his description of his 'patent adjustable speech.' "—C.N.

In treating of this subject of post-prandial oratory, a subject which I have long been familiar with and may be called an expert in observing in others, I wish to say that a public dinner is the most delightful thing in the whole world—to the guest. That is one fact. And here is another. A public dinner is the most unendurable suffering in the whole world—to the guest.

These two facts don't seem to jibe. But I will explain. Now, at a public dinner when a man knows he is going to be called upon to speak and is thoroughly well prepared, got it all by heart and the pauses marked in his head where the applause is going to come in, that man is simply—is simply in heaven. He won't care to be anywhere else than just where he is. But when at a public dinner it is getting way along toward the end of things and a man is sitting over his glass of wine or his glass of milk, according to the kind of banquet it is, and sitting there not meditating the danger of it, with somebody at his ear bothering him to talk, talk, talk about nothing, why—well, that is just as nearly in the other place as he can be—that man is to be pitied. And the very worst of it is, he *is* pitied.

Now, he could stand the pity of ten people or a dozen but there is no misery in this world that is comparable to the mass of solidifying compassion of five hundred. Why, that wide Sahara of sympathizing faces completely takes the tuck out of him. He stands there in his misery and stammers out the usual stuff of not being prepared and not expecting, and all that kind of folly, and he is wandering and stumbling and getting further and further in, and all the time being unhappy, and at last he fetches out a poor, miserable, crippled joke, and in his grief and confusion he laughs at it himself, and the others look sick. And then he slumps into his chair and wishes he was dead. He knows he is a defeated man, and so do the others.

To a humane person that is a heartrending spectacle. It is indeed. That sort of sacrifice ought to be stopped. And there is only one way to accomplish it that I can think of, and that is for a man to go always prepared, always loaded, always ready, whether he is likely to be called on or not. You can't defeat that man, you can't pity him at all.

My scheme is this: that he shall carry in his head a connected and tried and thoroughly and glibly memorized speech that will fit every conceivable occasion in this life, fit it to a dot, and win success and applause every time. I have completed a speech of that kind and I have brought it along to exhibit here as an example.

We suppose that it is a granger gathering, and this man is suddenly called on. He comes up with some lively hesitancies and deferences and repetitions so as to give the idea that the speech is impromptu. Here, of course, after he has got used to delivering it, he can venture outside and make a genuine impromptu remark to start off with. For instance, if a distinguished person is present he can make a complimentary reference to him, say to Mr. Depew. He could speak about his great talent or his clothes. Such a thing gives him a sort of opening. And about the time that audience is getting to pity that man, he opens his throttle valve and goes for those grangers. That person wants to be gorgeously eloquent. You want to fire the farmer's heart and start him from his mansard down to his cellar.

Now this man is called up, and he says, "I'm called up suddenly, sir, and am indeed not, not prepared to—I was not expecting to be called up, sir, but I will, with what effect I may, add my shout to the jubilations of this spirited, stirring occasion. Agriculture, sir, is, after all, the palladium of our economic liberties. By it, approximately speaking, we may be said to live and move and have our being. All that we have been, all that we are, all that we hope to be, was, is and must continue to be profoundly influenced by that sublimest of the mighty interests of man, thrice glorious agriculture. While we have life, while we have soul, and in that soul the sweet and hallowed sentiment of gratitude, let us with generous accord attune our voices to songs of praise, perennial outpourings of thanksgiving, for that most precious boon whereby we physically thrive, and are made rich and strong and grand and inspiring, imbued with the mighty, far-reaching and all-embracing grace and beauty and purity and loveliness. The least of us knows, the least of us feels, the humblest of us will confess that, whereas—but the hour is late and I will not detain you."

Now then, supposing it is not a granger gathering at all but is a wedding breakfast. Now, of course, then that speech has got to be delivered in an airy, light fashion but it must terminate seriously. It is a mistake to make it any other way.

This person is called up by the minister of the feast and he says, "I am called up suddenly, sir, and am indeed not prepared to—I was not expecting to be called up, sir, but I will, with what effect I may, add my shout to the jubilations of this spirited, stirring occasion. Matrimony, sir, is, after all, the palladium of our domestic liberties. By it, approximately speaking, we may be said to live and move and acquire our being. All that we have been, all that we are, all that we hope to be, was, is and must continue to be profoundly influenced by that sublimest of the mighty interests of man, thrice glorious matrimony. While we have life, while we have soul, and in that soul the sweet and hallowed sentiment of gratitude, let us with generous accord attune our voices to songs of praise, perennial outpourings of thanksgiving for that most precious boon whereby our otherwise sterile existence is made rich and strong and grand and inspiring, and is imbued with a mighty, far-reaching grace and beauty and purity and loveliness. The least of us knows, the least of us feels, the humblest among us will confess that, whereas—but the hour is late and I do not wish to detain you."

Now then, supposing a man with his cut-and-dried speech, this patent adjustable speech, as you may call it, finds himself at a granger gathering or a wedding breakfast or a theological disturbance or a political blowout, an inquest, or funeral anywhere in the world you choose to mention, and be suddenly called up. All he has got to do is to change three or four words in that speech and make his delivery anguishing and tearful, or chippy and facetious, or luridly and thunderously eloquent just as the occasion happens to call for, and just turn himself loose, and he is all right.

Now then, supposing that the occasion—I will make one more illustration so that you will always be perfectly safe here or anywhere—supposing that this is an occasion of an inquest. This is a most elastic speech in a matter of that kind. Where there are grades of men you must observe them. At a private funeral of some friend you want to be just as mournful as you can, but in the case where you don't know the person, grade it accordingly. You want simply to be impressive. That is all.

Now take a case halfway between, about No. 4½, somewhere about there—that is, an inquest on a second cousin, a wealthy second cousin. He has remembered you in the will. Of course all these things count. They all raise the grade a little, and—well, perhaps he hasn't remembered you. Perhaps he has left you a horse, an ordinary horse, a good enough horse, one that can go about three minutes, or perhaps a pair of horses. It may have been one pair of horses at hand, not two pair or two pair and a jack. I don't know whether you understand that, but there are people here.

Well now then, this is a second cousin and he knows all the circumstances. We will say that he has lost his life trying to save somebody from drowning. Well, he saved the mind-cure physician from drowning. He tried to save him but he didn't succeed. Of course he wouldn't succeed. Of course you wouldn't want him to succeed in that way and plan. A person must have some experience and aplomb and all that before he can save anybody from drowning of the mind-cure. I am just making these explanations here.

A person can get so glib in a delivery of this speech, why by the time he has delivered it fifteen or twenty times he could go to any intellectual gathering in Boston even and he would draw like a prizefight. Well, at the inquest of a second cousin under these circumstances a man gets up with graded emotion and he says:

"I am called up suddenly, sir, and am, indeed, not prepared. I was not expecting to be called up, sir, but I will, with what effect I may, add my shout—voice to the lamentations of this spirited, crushing grief. Death, death, sir, is, after all, the palladium of our spiritual liberties. By it, approximately speaking, we may be said to live and move and have ending. All that we may be here, all that we are, all that we hope to be, was, is and must continue to be profoundly influenced by that sublimest of the mighty interests of man, thrice-sorrowful desolation. While we have life, while we have soul, and in that soul the sweet and hallowed sentiment of gratitude, let us with generous accord attune our voices to songs of peace, perennial outpourings of thanksgiving for that most potent boon by which we spiritually save, by which our otherwise sterile existence is made rich and strong and is imbued with a mighty, far-reaching and all-embracing grace and beauty and loveliness. The least of us knows, the least of us feels, the humblest among us will confess—but the hour is late and I will not detain you."

1887

HOW TO REACH SEVENTY

At the close of November 1905 Clemens turned seventy. His birthday occasioned a great banquet in Delmonico's famous red room in New York, complete with music provided by a forty-piece orchestra from the Metropolitan Opera House. As a souvenir of the occasion, each guest was presented with a foot-high plaster bust of the author. The menu included Baltimore terrapin, saddle of lamb, fillet of kingfish, quail, redhead duck, champagne, sauterne and brandy. The host was Colonel George Harvey, editor of *Harper's Weekly* and of the *North American Review*.

The joke at the beginning of the speech refers to a twenty-eight-line "sonnet" which William Dean Howells, the evening's toastmaster, read. "I jolly the whole earth,/But most I love to jolly my own kind,/Joke of a people great, gay, bold, and free,/I type their master-mood. Mark Twain made me." Howells concluded with, "Now, ladies and gentlemen and Colonel Harvey, I will try not to be greedy on your behalf in wishing the health of our honored and, in view of his great age, our revered guest. I will not say, 'Oh King, live forever!' but 'Oh King, live as long as you like!'" Rising amid applause and the waving of napkins, the audience drank to Mark Twain.

"An insurance moral" and "associating with insurance presidents" refer to insurance company scandals of the time, resulting from speculative use of insurance company funds. "Leopold, the pirate King of Belgium"—Clemens savaged him in his *King Leopold's Soliloquy* (1905) for his severe exploitation of Congo native labor.—C.N.

Well, if I made that joke it is the best one I ever made. And it is in the prettiest language, too. I never can get quite to that height. But I appreciate that joke and I shall remember it. And I shall use it when occasion requires.

I have had a great many birthdays in my time. I remember the first one very well and I always think of it with indignation. Everything was so crude, unaesthetic, primeval. Nothing like this at all. No proper appreciative preparation made. Nothing really ready. Now, for a person born with high and delicate instincts—nothing ready at all. I hadn't any hair. I hadn't any teeth. I hadn't any clothes. I had to go to my first banquet just like that.

Well, everybody came swarming in. It was the merest little bit of a village. Hardly that. Just a little hamlet in the backwoods of Missouri, where nothing ever happened. And the people were all interested and they all came. They looked me over to see if there was anything fresh in my line.

Why, nothing ever happened in that village. I was the only thing that had really happened there for months and months and months. And although I say it myself that shouldn't, I came the nearest to being a real event that had happened in that village in more than two years.

Well, those people came, they came with that curiosity which is so provincial, with that frankness which also is so provincial, and they examined me all around and gave their opinion. Nobody asked them. And I shouldn't have minded if anybody had paid me a compliment but nobody did. Their opinions were all just green with prejudice. And I feel those opinions to this day. Well, I stood that as long as—well, you know I was born courteous, and I stood it to the limit. I stood it an hour and then the worm turned. I knew very well the strength of my position. I knew that I was the only spotlessly pure and innocent person in that whole town. And I came out and said so. And they could not say a word. It was so true. They blushed. They were embarrassed. Well, that was the first after-dinner speech I ever made. I think it was after dinner.

It's a long stretch between that first birthday speech and this one. That was my cradle song and this is my swan song, I suppose. I am used to swan songs. I have sung them several times. This is my seventieth birthday, and I wonder if you all rise to the size of that proposition, realizing all the significance of that phrase, seventieth birthday.

The seventieth birthday! It is the time of life when you arrive at a new and awful dignity. When you may throw aside the decent reserves which have oppressed you for a generation and stand unafraid and unabashed upon your seven-terraced summit and look down and teach, unrebuked. You can tell the world how you got there. It is what they all do. You shall never get tired of telling by what delicate arts and deep moralities you climbed up to that great place. You will explain the process and dwell on the particulars with senile rapture. I have been anxious to explain my own system this long time. And now at last I have the right.

I have achieved my seventy years in the usual way: by sticking strictly to a scheme of life which would kill anybody else. It sounds like an exaggeration but that is really the common rule for attaining to old age. When we examine the program of any of these garrulous old people we always find that the habits which have preserved them would have decayed us, that the way of life which enabled them to live upon the property of their heirs so long, as Mr. Choate says, would have put us out of commission ahead of time. I will offer here as a sound maxim this: that we can't reach old age by another man's road.

I will now teach, offering my way of life to whomsoever desires to commit suicide by the scheme which has enabled me to beat the doctor and the hangman for seventy years. Some of the details may sound untrue but they are not. I am not here to deceive. I am here to teach.

We have no permanent habits until we are forty. Then they begin to harden. Presently they petrify. Then business begins. Since forty I have been regular about going to bed and getting up. And that is one of the main things. I have made it a rule to go to bed when there wasn't anybody left to sit up with. And I have made it a rule to get up when I had to. This has resulted in an unswerving regularity of irregularity. It has saved me sound. But it would injure another person.

In the matter of diet, which is another main thing, I have been persistently strict in sticking to the things which didn't agree with me until one or the other of us got the best of it. Until lately I got the best of it myself. But last spring I stopped frolicking with mince pie after midnight. Up to then I had always believed it wasn't loaded.

For thirty years I have taken coffee and bread at eight in the morning, and no bite nor sup until seven-thirty in the evening. Eleven hours. That is all right for me, and is wholesome, because I have never had a headache in my life. But headachy people would not reach seventy comfortably by that road and they would be foolish to try it.

And I wish to urge upon you this, which I think is wisdom, that if you find you can't make seventy by any but an uncomfortable road, don't you go. When they take off the Pullman and retire you to the rancid smoker, put on your things, count your checks and get out at the first way station where there's a cemetery.

I have made it a rule never to smoke more than one cigar at a time. I have no other restriction as regards smoking. I do not know just when I began to smoke, I only know that it was in my father's lifetime and that I was discreet. He passed from this life early in 1847 when I was a shade past eleven. Ever since then I have smoked publicly. As an example to others, and not that I care for moderation myself, it has always been my rule never to smoke when asleep and never to refrain when awake. It is a good rule. I mean for me. But some of you know quite well that it wouldn't answer for everybody that's trying to get to be seventy.

I smoke in bed until I have to go to sleep. I wake up in the night, sometimes once, sometimes twice, sometimes three times, and I never waste any of these opportunities to smoke. This habit is so old and dear and precious to me that I would feel as you, sir, would feel if you should lose the only moral you've got—meaning the chairman—if you've got one. I am making no charges. I will grant here that I have stopped smoking now and then for a few months at a time but it was not on principle, it was only to show off. It was to pulverize those critics who said I was a slave to my habits and couldn't break my bonds.

Today it is all of sixty years since I began to smoke the limit. I have never bought cigars with life belts around them. I early found that those were too expensive for me. I have always bought cheap cigars—reasonably cheap, at any rate. Sixty years ago they cost me four dollars a barrel. But my taste has improved latterly and I pay seven now. Six or seven. Seven, I think. Yes, it's seven. But that includes the barrel. I often have smoking parties at my house. But the people that come have always just taken the pledge. I wonder why that is.

As for drinking, I have no rule about that. When the others drink I like to help. Otherwise I remain dry by habit and preference. This dryness does not hurt me but it could easily hurt you. Because you are different. You let it alone.

Since I was seven years old I have seldom taken a dose of medicine and have still seldomer needed one. But up to seven I lived exclusively on allopathic medicines. Not that I needed them, for I don't think I did. It was for economy. My father took a drug store for a debt, and it made cod-liver oil cheaper than the other breakfast foods. We had nine barrels of it and it lasted me seven years. Then I was weaned. The rest of the family had to get along with rhubarb and ipecac and such things. Because I was the pet.

I was the first Standard Oil Trust. I had it all. By the time the drug store was exhausted my health was established, and there has never been much the matter with me since. But you know very well it would be foolish for the average child to start for seventy on that basis. It happened to be just the thing for me but that was merely an accident. It couldn't happen again in a century.

I have never taken any exercise except sleeping and resting, and I never intend to take any. Exercise is loathsome. And it cannot be any benefit when you are tired. And I was always tired. But let another person try my way and see where he will come out.

I desire now to repeat and emphasize that maxim. We can't reach old age by another man's road. My habits protect my life but they would assassinate you.

I have lived a severely moral life. But it would be a mistake for other people to try that or for me to recommend it. Very few would succeed. You have to have a perfectly colossal stock of morals. And you can't get them on a margin. You have to have the whole thing and put them in your box. Morals are an acquirement like music, like a foreign language, like piety, poker, paralysis. No man is born with them. I wasn't myself, I started poor. I hadn't a single moral. There is hardly a man in this house that is poorer than I was then.

Yes, I started like that, the world before me, not a moral in the slot. Not even an insurance moral. I can remember the first one I ever got. I can remember the landscape, the weather, the—I can remember how everything looked. It was an old moral, an old second-hand moral, all out of repair, and didn't fit, anyway. But if you are careful with a thing like that and keep it in a dry place and save it for processions and Chautauquas and World's Fairs and so on, and disinfect it now and then, and give it a fresh coat of whitewash once in a while, you will be surprised to see how well she will last and how long she will keep sweet, or at least inoffensive.

When I got that mouldy old moral she had stopped growing because she hadn't any exercise. But I worked her hard, I worked her Sundays and all. Under this cultivation she waxed in might and stature beyond belief and served me well and was my pride and joy for sixty-three years. Then she got to associating with insurance presidents and lost flesh and character and was a sorrow to look at and no longer competent for business. She was a great loss to me. Yet not all loss. I sold her—ah, pathetic skeleton as she was—I sold her to Leopold, the pirate King of Belgium. He sold her to our Metropolitan Museum, and it was very glad to get her, for without a rag on she stands 57 feet long and 16 feet high and they think she's a brontosaur. Well, she looks it. They believe it will take nineteen geological periods to breed her match.

Morals are of inestimable value, for every man is born crammed with sin microbes, and the only thing that can extirpate these sin microbes is morals. Now you take a sterilized Christian. I mean, you take *the* sterilized Christian, for there's only one. Dear sir, I wish you wouldn't look at me like that.

Threescore years and ten! It is the Scriptural statute of limitations. After that you owe no active duties. For you the strenuous life is over. You are a time-expired man, to use Kipling's military phrase. You have served your term, well or less well, and you are mustered out.

You are become an honorary member of the republic. You are emancipated. Compulsions are not for you, nor any bugle call but "lights out." You pay the time-worn duty bills if you choose, or decline if you prefer, and without prejudice, for they are not legally collectable.

The previous-engagement plea, which in forty years has cost you so many twinges, you can lay aside forever. On this side of the grave you will never need it again. If you shrink at thought of night and winter and the late home-coming from the banquet and the lights and the laughter through the deserted streets—a desolation which would not remind you now, as for a generation it did, that your friends are sleeping and you must creep in a-tiptoe and not disturb them, but would only remind you that you need not tiptoe, you can never disturb them more—if you shrink at thought of these things you need only reply, "Your invitation honors me and pleases me because you still keep me in your remembrance. But I am seventy. Seventy, and would nestle in the chimney-corner and smoke my pipe and read my book and take my rest, wishing you well in all affection, and that when you in your turn shall arrive at pier No. 70 you may step aboard your waiting ship with a reconciled spirit and lay your course toward the sinking sun with a contented heart."

1905

THE *BEGUM OF BENGAL*

Rubert William Boyce was a professor of pathology at the University of Liverpool. The Waterbury was a cheap American watch popular at the time. John Henniker Heaton was a member of Parliament and a leading promotor of penny postage.—C.N.

My Lord Mayor, my Lord Bishop. And gentlemen. I want to thank you, my Lord Mayor, for the welcome which you have given me tonight. And I thank these gentlemen for their hearty response in which they have received the toast. And I will thank—any other name? I only know him by "Tay Pay." I have another name, Langhorne, but it really doesn't belong to me. Then you have a telegram from Professor Boyce, who says he still has a watch. That comes of having a fleeting reputation. I came to this country distinguished for honesty. And then somebody took that Ascot Cup just as I arrived, which has thrown a gloom over my whole stay here and will provide sorrow and lamentations for my friends on the other side. And now I am held responsible for the regalia which has been stolen from Dublin Castle. What will become of my reputation if I do not get out of the country very soon? I do not know. People say it is a curious coincidence that the Ascot Cup and the regalia from Dublin Castle should have been stolen during my stay. And so it is. I was going to Dublin. Fortunately for the rags of my reputation, I could not get there.

And you say, what is this? It is rumor. Nobody comes out and charges me with carrying out that robbery. It is mere human testimony, and it does not amount to testimony, it is merely rumor, circumstantial evidence, mere human speech, assertion, rumor and suspicion. But circumstantial evidence is the best evidence in the world.

Once a month for five hundred years certain officers whose function it is go down the cellars in Dublin Castle and there they find the safe in which the precious jewels are kept, and take them out one by one daily just to see that they are all right, and put them back in the safe. They have been doing this for five hundred years and they have got so used to it that they did not shut up the safe. I should like to know whether that is a good safe and a valuable safe. That is an important feature for me, because with the reputation I have got now, all the circumstantial evidence would point to the fact that if I took anything at all I would not merely have carried off the regalia but the safe along with it.

All this is testimony in my favor, and yet Professor Boyce is afraid to bring along his watch, which is probably only a Waterbury, and an old one at that.

Mr. O'Connor has furnished you information that enabled you to understand that I have been a jack-of-all-trades. That is quite true. He said a word about my father. He was a lawyer, but my father was entitled to more words than that. He was another of my kind. He was not just merely a lawyer, but in that little village on the banks of the Mississippi, when I was a boy, he was mayor of the town, the chief of police, the postmaster, the one policeman, and the sheriff who had to hang all the malefactors. In fact, he was the entire government—concentrated. Now, you can't pass by a man like that with just a word.

Mr. O'Connor spoke of my brother too. Well, my brother and I were twins. He was born ten years before I was, a little discrepancy that never could be accounted for. It was the intention that that brother of mine should be a lazy person. I know that perfectly well. But somehow or other it missed fire and I was born that way instead. I have been lazy ever since and indolent, while that brother, the twin, he was full of energy and the spirit of labor. Whatever he put his hand to he worked at it hard and faithfully, and the result was—the result was he could never make a living anyhow.

I can't help being frivolous tonight, because I have followed out my instructive and natural custom this afternoon by having a sleep and resting myself. Whenever I am rested and feeling good I can't help being frivolous. It is only when I am weary and worn out and discouraged that the time comes for me to take a hold on great national questions and handle them. I wanted to talk real instructive wisdom tonight. But this rest has intervened and put it all out of my mind.

I have been two or three weeks discussing cheap penny international postage with Mr. Henniker Heaton and I have told him all I know about it. And now he knows nothing about it himself. I said I was born lazy, but I was born wise also, and the only time I ever lost a situation, the only time I was ever discharged from a post, was in San Francisco more than forty years ago when I was a reporter on the *Morning Call.* I was discharged just that once in my life, and the only thing they could bring against me was that I was incompetent and incandescent and inharmonious and everything they could think of in three syllables. But mainly I was lazy and inefficient.

That was the only time anybody ever found fault with me for a thing like that. It was occurring all the time. In fact it was monotonous, and it was no use picking out a thing like that.

According to Tay Pay, I have been a little of everything. This time I am an ambassador. I like that position very well. I don't mind it as it has not a salary attached to it, because a salary limits your energy. It does mine always. I would rather be free to do my ambassadorial work after my own fashion, and I intend to keep up this ambassadorial business right along. Whenever I find a chance of encouraging the good feeling between this old mother country and her eldest child over there, I intend to put in my word and keep up the ambassadorial work.

The University of Oxford in making me a doctor has added one more function to my numerous functions. And somebody asked me a rather pointed question. "Was it not rather a delicate thing to make you a Doctor of Literature? Are you competent to doctor literature? Had you not better doctor your own a little?"

That is all wrong. I have been doctoring my own literature. It is only now by the authority of Oxford that I propose to doctor other people's, and I hope you will see results.

Why, I have always had an interest in literature outside my own concern. I have always been ready to give a helping hand to a rising young author. I saved one poet in San Francisco forty years ago and I don't forget it. I did a good turn to that poet. I was ready to doctor him or anybody else. Well, he wasn't much of a poet—a kind of a poet good enough for the early days on the Pacific. He was not prosperous, and he was named Eddystone. We called him Eddystone Lighthouse. That was sarcasm. He was not a lighthouse. He was in trouble and I came to the young man's help. I was a reporter but I was likely to lose the employment at any time, and I knew it would be such a good thing for me if I could do something rather extraordinary to keep ahead of the other papers.

Well, the young poet got discouraged. His poetry began to be a drug. He could not sell it. And by and by when he could not give it away his circumstances were desperate, and he came to me as a friend and wise adviser, and he proposed to commit suicide.

I told him it was a good idea. It was a good idea in various ways. It would relieve him from writing poetry and it would relieve the community from reading it and it would give me a chance with my newspaper, I being the only other person present at the suicide—I would take care of that.

He was a little sorry to see me so enthusiastic. I could not help that. My heart was in it. We discussed methods, and I told him the most picturesque was the revolver to blow his brains out with. He did not like that idea very much but I reconciled him to it.

But we did not have any money to buy a revolver, and we went round to the place with the three balls. There was a revolver there, just the right thing, but we could not borrow that revolver without furnishing some money. I told the gentleman that this was the only chance the young man had. But he was that kind of man that you could not persuade at all—a man who has no human sympathy although it does not cost anything.

Then I suggested drowning to my friend. That would be a neat thing. It could not be as fine for me as the other, but drowning was good enough when you could not get anything better. So we went out to the seashore, and he did not like the looks of the water, and wanted me to try how it would go. But no, I was not in that line at all.

Then a most curious thing—one of the strangest things, a thing you would never imagine at all—happened. From some ship that had foundered perhaps a thousand miles away there came an object of some interest at that moment. There were, in fact, two events gradually coming together. While this young man was brooding and contemplating suicide there was a life preserver floating in from that ship. A life preserver for a man who was about to commit suicide!

It looked ridiculous at first but we took the life preserver to the pawnbroker and traded with him for the revolver. And then we made all the arrangements. But he didn't like to put the firearm to his forehead.

I said, "It will be over in a minute" and this seemed to reassure him, for he bucked up and blew his brains out.

People said it wasn't brains. But it was. There was not much of it. But it was real gray matter, which is supposed to constitute intelligence so far as it can.

Well, that was the making of that boy. Why, when he got well all obstructions were gone! And I have thought many times since that if poets when they get discouraged would blow their brains out they could write very much better when they get well.

I landed in this town of Liverpool thirty years ago, the first time I ever put my foot on English soil, and I had an adventure. As a matter of fact, Liverpool is connected with one or two adventures of a very pleasant sort. I went to the outside edge of the town and I saw the scenery, the blocked-up windows to escape the window tax, and various other exciting things, and finally I took a cab and drove around.

The man was a very good-natured, pleasant, middle-aged Scotchman, and he asked where he should drive me to. I said anywhere, just around for an hour or two hours. He drove me a little way and then stopped and asked me again.

Well, I wanted to think—I was full of some great project. And finally when this had occurred several more times, in desperation I said, "Oh, take me to Balmoral."

I did not say a word, and I did not pay any attention to where he was going. I wanted to think. I did not know where I was. I was away somewhere in the country, and I hailed him and asked him where he was going. And he said, "On the way to Balmoral." So he was.

I got him to turn round and get back to Liverpool if he could, to catch a train for London if possible. When we got back I asked him what I had to pay, and he said—well, it was equivalent to four hundred dollars. I asked him if he was in earnest and he said he was, as outside the city he could charge any reasonable price. He said that Balmoral was four hundred miles away, and it would be four hundred dollars.

It seemed a sorry and embarrassing situation. I proposed to go before the rulers of the city or his Majesty or something of that sort to lay the case and I did. I said he had made a mistake, and the authorities said he had a right to charge anything reasonable. It seemed a large sum he had charged, and they said it was not the cabman's fault —it was four hundred miles to Balmoral and four shillings a mile was not unreasonable, especially as he would have to come back at his own expense.

Well, the man acted very handsomely. He compromised for twelve dollars. Though stupid tradition says that Scotchmen do not possess a sense of humor, I say that that man has a sense of humor.

What was Tay Pay's early statement that requires refutation?

[O'Connor, "I said that you had been a financier."]

I was, but I am not now. I didn't succeed in it. He also mentioned another matter, and he paid me the compliment to mention that at the time when I was bankrupt, heavily in debt, I paid every dollar. This is often mentioned, very pleasing to me to hear, and I feel that I ought to get on my feet and tell you all about it, how my business man, my longheaded commercial friend said, "In this bankruptcy business you pay thirty cents to the dollar and you go free."

Now, a man can easily be persuaded to go outside the strict moral line but it is not so with a woman and a wife.

My wife said, "No, you shall pay a hundred cents to the dollar and I will go with you all the way."

And she kept her word. Let us give credit where credit is due, and it is more due to her than to me.

I don't think I will say anything about the relations of amity existing between our two countries. It is not necessary, it seems to me. The ties between the two nations are so strong that I do not think we need trouble ourselves about them being broken. Anyhow, I am quite sure that in my time and in yours, my Lord Mayor, those ties will hold good, and please God, they always will. English blood is in our veins, we have a common language, a common religion, a common system of morals, and great commercial interest to hold us together.

Home is dear to us all, and now I am departing to my own home beyond the ocean. Oxford has conferred upon me the loftiest honor that has ever fallen to my share of this world's good things. It is the very one I would have chosen as outranking any and all others, the one more precious to me of any and all others within the gift of man or State. During my four weeks' sojourn here I have had another lofty honor, a continuous honor, an honor which has flowed serenely along without obstruction through all these twenty-six days, a most moving and pulse-stirring honor—the heartfelt grip of the hand, and the welcome that does not descend from the pale, gray matter of the brain but rushes up with the red blood of the heart. It makes me proud and it makes me humble too.

Many and many a year ago I read an anecdote in Dana's *Two Years Before the Mast.* It was like this. There was a presumptuous little self-important man in a coasting sloop engaged in the dried apple and kitchen furniture trade, and he was always hailing every ship that came in sight. He did it just to hear himself talk and to air his small grandeur.

One day a majestic Indiaman came plowing by with course on course of canvas towering into the sky, her decks and yards swarming with sailors, bearing a rich freight of precious spices, lading the breezes with gracious and mysterious odors of the Orient. It was a noble spectacle. And of course the little skipper popped into the shroud and squeaked out a hail.

"Ship ahoy! What ship is that? And whence and whither?"

In a deep and thunderous voice the answer came through the speaking trumpet.

"The *Begum of Bengal,* a hundred and twenty-three days out from Canton. What ship is that?"

Well, it just crushed that poor little creature's vanity, and he squeaked back most humbly.

"Only the *Mary Ann,* fourteen days out from Boston, with nothing to speak of."

Oh, what an eloquent word, that "only," to express the depths of his humbleness. That is just my case. Just one hour, perhaps, in the twenty-four—not more—I pause and reflect, and then I am humble. Then I am properly meek, and for a little while I am only the *Mary Ann,* fourteen days out, charged with vegetables and tinware.

But during all the other twenty-three hours my vain self-complacency rides high, and then I am a stately Indiaman, plowing the great seas under a cloud of canvas, and laden with the finest words that have ever been spoken to any wandering alien in this world, and then my twenty-six happy days seem to be multiplied by five, and I am the *Begum of Bengal,* a hundred and twenty-three days out. And homeward bound.

1907

AUTOBIOGRAPHY

A HEAVENLY PLACE

I was born the 30th of November, 1835, in the almost invisible village of Florida, Monroe County, Missouri. My parents removed to Missouri in the early 'thirties; I do not remember just when, for I was not born then and cared nothing for such things. It was a long journey in those days and must have been a rough and tiresome one. The village contained a hundred people and I increased the population by 1 per cent. It is more than many of the best men in history could have done for a town. It may not be modest in me to refer to this but it is true. There is no record of a person doing as much—not even Shakespeare. But I did it for Florida and it shows that I could have done it for any place—even London, I suppose.

Recently some one in Missouri has sent me a picture of the house I was born in. Heretofore I have always stated that it was a palace but I shall be more guarded now.

I used to remember my brother Henry walking into a fire outdoors when he was a week old. It was remarkable in me to remember a thing like that and it was still more remarkable that I should cling to the delusion for thirty years that I *did* remember it—for of course it never happened; he would not have been able to walk at that age. If I had stopped to reflect I should not have burdened my memory with that impossible rubbish so long. It is believed by many people that an impression deposited in a child's memory within the first two years of its life cannot remain there five years but that is an error. The incident of Benvenuto Cellini and the salamander must be accepted as authentic and trustworthy; and then that remarkable and indisputable instance in the experience of Helen Keller. For many years I believed that I remembered helping my grandfather drink his whisky toddy when I was six weeks old but I do not tell about that any more now; I am grown old and my memory is not as active as it used to be. When I was younger I could remember anything, whether it had happened or not; but my faculties are decaying now and soon I shall be so I cannot remember any but the things that never happened. It is sad to go to pieces like this but we all have to do it.

My uncle, John A. Quarles, was also a farmer, and his place was in the country four miles from Florida. He had eight children and fifteen or twenty negroes and was also fortunate in other ways, particularly in his character. I have not come across a better man than he was. I was his guest for two or three months every year, from the fourth year after we removed to Hannibal till I was eleven or twelve years old. I have never consciously used him or his wife in a book but his farm has come very handy to me in literature once or twice. In *Huck Finn* and in *Tom Sawyer, Detective* I moved it down to Arkansas. It was all of six hundred miles but it was no trouble; it was not a very large farm— five hundred acres, perhaps—but I could have done it if it had been twice as large. And as for the morality of it, I cared nothing for that; I would move a state if the exigencies of literature required it.

It was a heavenly place for a boy, that farm of my uncle John's. The house was a double log one, with a spacious floor (roofed in) connecting it with the kitchen. In the summer the table was set in the middle of that shady and breezy floor, and the sumptuous meals—well, it makes me cry to think of them. Fried chicken, roast pig; wild and tame turkeys, ducks and geese; venison just killed; squirrels, rabbits, pheasants, partridges, prairie-chickens; biscuits, hot batter cakes, hot buckwheat cakes, hot "wheat bread," hot rolls, hot corn pone; fresh corn boiled on the ear, succotash, butter-beans, string-beans, tomatoes, peas, Irish potatoes, sweet potatoes; buttermilk, sweet milk, "clabber"; watermelons, muskmelons, cantaloupes—all fresh from the garden; apple pie, peach pie, pumpkin pie, apple dumplings, peach cobbler—I can't remember the rest. The way that the things were cooked was perhaps the main splendor—particularly a certain few of the dishes. For instance, the corn bread, the hot biscuits and wheat bread and the fried chicken. These things have never been properly cooked in the North—in fact, no one there is able to learn the art, so far as my experience goes. The North thinks it knows how to make corn bread but this is gross superstition. Perhaps no bread in the world is quite so good as Southern corn bread and perhaps no bread in the world is quite so bad as the Northern imitation of it. The North seldom tries to fry chicken and this is well; the art cannot be learned north of the line of Mason and Dixon, nor anywhere in Europe. This is not hearsay; it is experience that is speaking. In Europe it is imagined that the custom of serving various kinds of bread blazing hot is "American," but that is too broad a spread; it is custom in the South but is much less than that in the North. In the North and in Europe hot bread is considered unhealthy. This is probably another fussy superstition, like the European superstition that ice-water is unhealthy. Europe does not need ice-water and does not drink it; and yet, notwithstanding this, its word for it is better than ours, because it describes it, whereas ours doesn't. Europe calls it "iced" water. Our word describes water made from melted ice—a drink which has a characterless taste and which we have but little acquaintance with.

It seems a pity that the world should throw away so many good things merely because they are unwholesome. I doubt if God has given us any refreshment which, taken in moderation, is unwholesome, except microbes. Yet there are people who strictly deprive themselves of each and every eatable, drinkable and smokable which has in any way acquired a shady reputation. They pay this price for health. And health is all they get for it. How strange it is! It is like paying out your whole fortune for a cow that has gone dry.

The farmhouse stood in the middle of a very large yard and the yard was fenced on three sides with rails and on the rear side with high palings; against these stood the smoke-house; beyond the palings was the orchard; beyond the orchard were the negro quarters and the tobacco fields. The front yard was entered over a stile made of sawed-off logs of graduated heights; I do not remember any gate. In a corner of the front yard were a dozen lofty hickory trees and a dozen black walnuts, and in the nutting season riches were to be gathered there.

Down a piece, abreast the house, stood a little log cabin against the rail fence; and there the woody hill fell sharply away, past the barns, the corn-crib, the stables and the tobacco-curing house, to a limpid brook which sang along over its gravelly bed and curved and frisked in and out and here and there and yonder in the deep shade of overhanging foliage and vines—a divine place for wading, and it had swimming pools, too, which were forbidden to us and therefore much frequented by us. For we were little Christian children and had early been taught the value of forbidden fruit.

In the little log cabin lived a bedridden white-headed slave woman whom we visited daily and looked upon with awe, for we believed she was upward of a thousand years old and had talked with Moses. The younger negroes credited these statistics and had furnished them to us in good faith. We accommodated all the details which came to us about her; and so we believed that she had lost her health in the long desert trip coming out of Egypt and had never been able to get it back again. She had a round bald place on the crown of her head and we used to creep around and gaze at it in reverent silence and reflect that it was caused by fright through seeing Pharaoh drowned. We called her "Aunt" Hannah, Southern fashion. She was superstitious, like the other negroes; also, like them, she was deeply religious. Like them, she had great faith in prayer and employed it in all ordinary exigencies, but not in cases where a dead certainty of result was urgent. Whenever witches were around she tied up the remnant of her wool in little tufts, with white thread, and this promptly made the witches impotent.

All the negroes were friends of ours, and with those of our own age we were in effect comrades. I say in effect, using the phrase as a modification. We were comrades and yet not comrades; color and condition interposed a subtle line which both parties were conscious of and which rendered complete fusion impossible. We had a faithful and affectionate good friend, ally and adviser in "Uncle Dan'l," a middle-aged slave whose head was the best one in the negro quarter, whose sympathies were wide and warm and whose heart was honest and simple and knew no guile. He has served me well these many, many years. I have not seen him for more than half a century and yet spiritually I have had his welcome company a good part of that time and have staged him in books under his own name and as "Jim," and carted him all around—to Hannibal, down the Mississippi on a raft and even across the Desert of Sahara in a balloon—and he has endured it all with the patience and friendliness and loyalty which were his birthright. It was on the farm that I got my strong liking for his race and my appreciation of certain of its fine qualities. This feeling and this estimate have stood the test of sixty years and more and have suffered no impairment. The black face is as welcome to me now as it was then.

In my schoolboy days I had no aversion to slavery. I was not aware that there was anything wrong about it. No one arraigned it in my hearing; the local papers said nothing against it; the local pulpit taught us that God approved it, that it was a holy thing and that the doubter need only look in the Bible if he wished to settle his mind—and then the texts were read aloud to us to make the matter sure; if the slaves themselves had an aversion to slavery they were wise and said nothing. In Hannibal we seldom saw a slave misused; on the farm never.

There was, however, one small incident of my boyhood days which touched this matter, and it must have meant a good deal to me or it would not have stayed in my memory, clear and sharp, vivid and shadowless, all these slow-drifting years. We had a little slave boy whom we had hired from some one, there in Hannibal. He was from the eastern shore of Maryland and had been brought away from his family and his friends halfway across the American continent and sold. He was a cheery spirit, innocent and gentle, and the noisiest creature that ever was, perhaps. All day long he was singing, whistling, yelling, whooping, laughing—it was maddening, devastating, unendurable. At last, one day, I lost all my temper and went raging to my mother and said Sandy had been singing for an hour without a single break and I couldn't stand it and *wouldn't* she please shut him up. The tears came into her eyes and her lip trembled and she said something like this:

"Poor thing, when he sings it shows that he is not remembering and that comforts me; but when he is still I am afraid he is thinking and I cannot bear it. He will never see his mother again; if he can sing I must not hinder it, but be thankful for it. If you were older you would understand me; then that friendless child's noise would make you glad."

It was a simple speech and made up of small words but it went home, and Sandy's noise was not a trouble to me any more. She never used large words but she had a natural gift for making small ones do effective work. She lived to reach the neighborhood of ninety years and was capable with her tongue to the last—especially when a meanness or an injustice roused her spirit. She has come handy to me several times in my books, where she figures as Tom Sawyer's Aunt Polly. I fitted her out with a dialect and tried to think up other improvements for her but did not find any. I used Sandy once, also; it was in *Tom Sawyer*. I tried to get him to whitewash the fence but it did not work. I do not remember what name I called him by in the book.

I can see the farm yet, with perfect clearness. I can see all its belongings, all its details; the family room of the house, with a "trundle" bed in one corner and a spinning-wheel in another—a wheel whose rising and falling wail, heard from a distance, was the mournfulest of all sounds to me and made me homesick and low spirited and filled my atmosphere with the wandering spirits of the dead; the vast fireplace, piled high on winter nights with flaming hickory logs from whose ends a sugary sap bubbled out but did not go to waste, for we scraped it off and ate it; the lazy cat spread out on the rough hearthstones; the drowsy dogs braced against the jambs and blinking; my aunt in one chimney corner, knitting; my uncle in the other, smoking his corn-cob pipe; the slick and carpetless oak floor faintly mirroring the dancing flame tongues and freckled with black indentations where fire coals had popped out and died a leisurely death; half a dozen children romping in the background twilight; "split"-bottomed chairs here and there, some with rockers; a cradle—out of service but waiting with confidence; in the early cold mornings a snuggle of children in shirts and chemises, occupying the hearthstone and procrastinating—they could not bear to leave that comfortable place and go out on the wind-swept floor space between the house and kitchen where the general tin basin stood, and wash.

Along outside of the front fence ran the country road, dusty in the summertime and a good place for snakes—they liked to lie in it and sun themselves; when they were rattlesnakes or puff adders we killed them; when they were black snakes or racers or belonged to the fabled "hoop" breed we fled without shame; when they were "house snakes" or "garters" we carried them home and put them in Aunt Patsy's work basket for a surprise; for she was prejudiced against snakes, and always when she took the basket in her lap and they began to climb out of it it disordered her mind. She never could seem to get used to them; her opportunities went for nothing. And she was always cold toward bats, too, and could not bear them; and yet I think a bat is as friendly a bird as there is. My mother was Aunt Patsy's sister and had the same wild superstitions. A bat is beautifully soft and silky; I do not know any creature that is pleasanter to the touch or is more grateful for caressings, if offered in the right spirit. I know all about these coleoptera* because our great cave, three miles below Hannibal, was multitudinously stocked with them and often I brought them home to amuse my mother with. It was easy to manage if it was a school day

* Mark Twain meant chiroptera.

because then I had ostensibly been to school and hadn't any bats. She was not a suspicious person but full of trust and confidence; and when I said, "There's something in my coat pocket for you," she would put her hand in. But she always took it out again, herself; I didn't have to tell her. It was remarkable the way she couldn't learn to like private bats. The more experience she had the more she could not change her views.

I think she was never in the cave in her life; but everybody else went there. Many excursion parties came from considerable distances up and down the river to visit the cave. It was miles in extent and was a tangled wilderness of narrow and lofty clefts and passages. It was an easy place to get lost in; anybody could do it—including the bats. I got lost in it myself, along with a lady, and our last candle burned down to almost nothing before we glimpsed the search party's lights winding about in the distance.

"Injun Joe," the half-breed, got lost in there once and would have starved to death if the bats had run short. But there was no chance of that; there were myriads of them. He told me all his story. In the book called *Tom Sawyer* I starved him entirely to death in the cave but that was in the interest of art; it never happened. "General" Gaines, who was our first town drunkard before Jimmy Finn got the place, was lost in there for the space of a week and finally pushed his handkerchief out of a hole in a hilltop near Saverton, several miles down the river from the cave's mouth, and somebody saw it and dug him out. There is nothing the matter with his statistics except the handkerchief. I knew him for years and he hadn't any. But it could have been his nose. That would attract attention.

The cave was an uncanny place, for it contained a corpse—the corpse of a young girl of fourteen. It was in a glass cylinder inclosed in a copper one which was suspended from a rail which bridged a narrow passage. The body was preserved in alcohol and it was said that loafers and rowdies used to drag it up by the hair and look at the dead face. The girl was the daughter of a St. Louis surgeon of extraordinary ability and wide celebrity. He was an eccentric man and did many strange things. He put the poor thing in that forlorn place himself.

Beyond the road where the snakes sunned themselves was a dense young thicket and through it a dim-lighted path led a quarter of a mile; then out of the dimness one emerged abruptly upon a level great prairie which was covered with wild strawberry plants, vividly starred with prairie pinks and walled in on all sides by forests. The strawberries were fragrant and fine, and in the season we were generally there in the crisp freshness of the early morning, while the dew beads still sparkled upon the grass and the woods were ringing with the first songs of the birds.

Down the forest slopes to the left were the swings. They were made of bark stripped from hickory saplings. When they became dry they were dangerous. They usually broke when a child was forty feet in the air and this was why so many bones had to be mended every year. I had no ill luck myself but none of my cousins escaped. There were eight of them and at one time and another they broke fourteen arms among them. But it cost next to nothing, for the doctor worked by the year—twenty-five dollars for the whole family. I remember two of the Florida doctors, Chowning and Meredith. They not only tended an entire family for twenty-five dollars a year but furnished the medicines themselves. Good measure, too. Only the largest persons could hold a whole dose. Castor oil was the principal beverage. The dose was half a dipperful, with half a dipperful of New Orleans molasses added to help it down and make it taste good, which it never did. The next standby was calomel; the next rhubarb; and the next jalap. Then they bled the patient and put mustard plasters on him. It was a dreadful system and yet the death rate was not heavy. The calomel was nearly sure to salivate the patient and cost him some of his teeth. There were no dentists. When teeth became touched with decay or were otherwise ailing, the doctor knew of but one thing to do—he fetched his tongs and dragged them out. If the jaw remained, it was not his fault.

Doctors were not called in cases of ordinary illness; the family grandmother attended to those. Every old woman was a doctor and gathered her own medicines in the woods and knew how to compound doses that would stir the vitals of a cast-iron dog. And then there was the "Indian doctor"; a grave savage, remnant of his tribe, deeply read in the mysteries of nature and the secret properties of herbs; and most backwoodsmen had high faith in his powers and could tell of wonderful cures achieved by him. In Mauritius, away off yonder in the solitudes of the Indian Ocean, there is a person who answers to our Indian doctor of the old times. He is a negro and has had no teaching as a doctor, yet there is one disease which he is master of and can cure and the doctors can't. They send for him when they have a case. It is a child's disease of a strange and deadly sort and the negro cures it with a herb medicine which he makes himself from a prescription which has come down to him from his father and grandfather. He will not let anyone see it. He keeps the secret of its components to himself and it is feared that he will die without divulging it; then there will be consternation in Mauritius. I was told these things by the people there in 1896.

We had the "faith doctor," too, in those early days—a woman. Her specialty was toothache. She was a farmer's old wife and lived five miles from Hannibal. She would lay her hand on the patient's jaw and say, "Believe!" and the cure was prompt. Mrs. Utterback. I remember her very well. Twice I rode out there behind my mother, horseback, and saw the cure performed. My mother was the patient.

Doctor Meredith removed to Hannibal by and by and was our family physician there and saved my life several times. Still, he was a good man and meant well. Let it go.

I was always told that I was a sickly and precarious and tiresome and uncertain child and lived mainly on allopathic medicines during the first seven years of my life. I asked my mother about this, in her old age—she was in her eighty-eighth year—and said:

"I suppose that during all that time you were uneasy about me?"

"Yes, the whole time."

"Afraid I wouldn't live?"

After a reflective pause—ostensibly to think out the facts—"No—afraid you would."

It sounds like plagiarism but it probably wasn't.

The country schoolhouse was three miles from my uncle's farm. It stood in a clearing in the woods and would hold about twenty-five boys and girls. We attended the school with more or less regularity once or twice a week, in summer, walking to it in the cool of the morning by the forest paths and back in the gloaming at the end of the day. All the pupils brought their dinners in baskets—corn dodger, buttermilk and other good things—and sat in the shade of the trees at noon and ate them. It is the part of my education which I look back upon with the most satisfaction. My first visit to the school was when I was seven. A strapping girl of fifteen, in the customary sunbonnet and calico dress, asked me if I "used tobacco"—meaning did I chew it. I said no. It roused her scorn. She reported me to all the crowd and said:

"Here is a boy seven years old who can't chaw tobacco."

By the looks and comments which this produced I realized that I was a degraded object; I was cruelly ashamed of myself. I determined to reform. But I only made myself sick; I was not able to learn to chew tobacco. I learned to smoke fairly well but that did not conciliate anybody and I remained a poor thing and characterless. I longed to be respected but I never was able to rise. Children have but little charity for one another's defects.

As I have said, I spent some part of every year at the farm until I was twelve or thirteen years old. The life which I led there with my cousins was full of charm, and so is the memory of it yet. I can call back the solemn twilight and mystery of the deep woods, the earthy smells, the faint odors of the wild flowers, the sheen of rain-washed foliage, the rattling clatter of drops when the wind shook the trees, the far-off hammering of woodpeckers and the muffled drumming of wood pheasants in the remoteness of the forest, the snapshot glimpses of disturbed wild creatures scurrying through the grass—I can call it all back and make it as real as it ever was, and as blessed. I can call back the prairie, and its loneliness and peace, and a vast hawk hanging motionless in the sky, with his wings spread wide and the blue of the vault showing through the fringe of their end feathers. I can see the woods in their autumn dress, the oaks purple, the hickories washed with gold, the maples and the sumachs luminous with crimson fires, and I can hear the rustle made by the fallen leaves as we plowed through them. I can see the blue clusters of wild grapes hanging among the foliage of the saplings, and I remember the taste of them and the smell. I know how the wild blackberries looked, and how they tasted, and the same with the pawpaws, the hazelnuts, and the persimmons; and I can feel the thumping rain, upon my head, of hickory nuts and walnuts when we were out in the frosty dawn to scramble for them with the pigs, and the gusts of wind loosed them and sent them down. I know the stain of blackberries, and how pretty it is, and I know the stain of walnut hulls, and how little it minds soap and water, also what grudged experience it had of either of them. I know the taste of maple sap, and when to gather it, and how to arrange the troughs and the delivery tubes, and how to boil down the juice, and how to hook the sugar after it is made, also how much better hooked sugar tastes than any that is honestly come by, let bigots say what they will. I know how a prize watermelon looks when it is sunning its fat rotundity among pumpkin vines and "simblins"; I know how to tell when it is ripe without "plugging" it; I know how inviting it looks when it is cooling itself in a tub of water under the bed, waiting; I know how it looks when it lies on the table in the sheltered great floor space between house and kitchen, and the children gathered for the sacrifice and their mouths watering; I know the crackling sound it makes when the carving knife enters its end, and I can see the split fly along in front of the blade as the knife cleaves its way to the other end; I can see its halves fall apart and display the rich red meat and the black seeds, and the heart standing up, a luxury fit for the elect; I know how a boy looks behind a yard-long slice of that melon, and I know how he feels; for I have been there. I know the taste of the watermelon which has been honestly come by, and I know the taste of the watermelon which has been acquired by art. Both taste good, but the experienced know which tastes best. I know the look of green apples and peaches and pears on the trees, and I know how entertaining they are when they are inside of a person. I know how ripe ones look when they are piled in pyramids under the trees, and how pretty they are and how vivid their colors. I know how a frozen apple looks, in a barrel down cellar in the wintertime, and how hard it is to bite, and how the frost makes the teeth ache, and yet how good it is, notwithstanding. I know the disposition of elderly people to select the speckled apples for the children, and I once knew ways to beat the game. I know the look of an apple that is roasting and sizzling on a hearth on a winter's evening, and I know the comfort that comes of eating it hot, along with some sugar and a drench of cream. I know the delicate art and mystery of so cracking hickory nuts and walnuts on a flatiron with a hammer that the kernels will be delivered whole, and I know how the nuts, taken in conjunction with winter apples, cider, and doughnuts, make old people's old tales and old jokes sound fresh and crisp and enchanting, and juggle an evening away before you know what went with the time. I know the look of Uncle Dan'l's kitchen as it was on the privileged nights, when I was a child, and I can see the white and black children grouped on the hearth, with the firelight playing on their faces and the shadows flickering upon the walls, clear back toward the cavernous gloom of the rear, and I can hear Uncle Dan'l telling the immortal tales which Uncle Remus Harris was to gather into his books and charm the world with, by and by; and I can feel again the creepy joy which quivered through me when the time for the ghost story of the "Golden Arm" was reached—and the sense of regret, too, which came over me, for it was always the last story of the evening and there was nothing between it and the unwelcome bed.

I can remember the bare wooden stairway in my uncle's house, and the turn to the left above the landing, and the rafters and the slanting roof over my bed, and the squares of moonlight on the floor, and the white cold world of snow outside, seen through the curtainless window. I can remember the howling of the wind and the quaking of the house on stormy nights, and how snug and cozy one felt, under the blankets, listening; and how the powdery snow used to sift in, around the sashes, and lie in little ridges on the floor and make the place look chilly in the morning and curb the wild desire to get up—in case there was any. I can remember how very dark that room was, in the dark of the moon, and how packed it was with ghostly stillness when one woke up by accident away in the night, and forgotten sins came flocking out of the secret chambers of the memory and wanted a hearing; and how ill chosen the time seemed for this kind of business; and how dismal was the hoo-hooing of the owl and the wailing of the wolf, sent mourning by on the night wind.

I remember the raging of the rain on that roof, summer nights, and how pleasant it was to lie and listen to it, and enjoy the white splendor of the lightning and the majestic booming and crashing of the thunder. It was a very satisfactory room, and there was a lightning rod which was reachable from the window, an adorable and skittish thing to climb up and down, summer nights, when there were duties on hand of a sort to make privacy desirable.

I remember the 'coon and 'possum hunts, nights, with the negroes, and the long marches through the black gloom of the woods, and the excitement which fired everybody when the distant bay of an experienced dog announced that the game was treed; then the wild scramblings and stumblings through briers and bushes and over roots to get to the spot; then the lighting of a fire and the felling of the tree, the joyful frenzy of the dogs and the negroes, and the weird picture it all made in the red glare—I remember it all well, and the delight that everyone got out of it, except the 'coon.

I remember the pigeon seasons, when the birds would come in millions and cover the trees and by their weight break down the branches. They were clubbed to death with sticks; guns were not necessary and were not used. I remember the squirrel hunts, and prairie-chicken hunts, and wild-turkey hunts, and all that; and how we turned out, mornings, while it was still dark, to go on these expeditions, and how chilly and dismal it was, and how often I regretted that I was well enough to go. A toot on a tin horn brought twice as many dogs as were needed, and in their happiness they raced and scampered about, and knocked small people down, and made no end of unnecessary noise. At the word, they vanished away toward the woods, and we drifted silently after them in the melancholy gloom. But presently the gray dawn stole over the world, the birds piped up, then the sun rose and poured light and comfort all around, everything was fresh and dewy and fragrant, and life was a boon again. After three hours of tramping we arrived back wholesomely tired, overladen with game, very hungry and just in time for breakfast.

1907

BECOMING A PILOT

In 1858 I was a steersman on board the swift and popular New Orleans and St. Louis packet, *Pennsylvania*, Captain Kleinfelter. I had been lent to Mr. Brown, one of the pilots of the *Pennsylvania*, by my owner, Mr. Bixby, and I had been steering for Brown about eighteen months, I think. Then in the early days of May, 1858, came a tragic trip—the last trip of that fleet and famous steamboat. I have told all about it in one of my books, called *Life on the Mississippi*. But it is not likely that I told the dream in that book. It is impossible that I can have published it, I think, because I never wanted my mother to know about that dream, and she lived several years after I published that volume.

I had found a place on the *Pennsylvania* for my brother Henry. It was not a place of profit, it was only a place of promise. He was "mud" clerk. Mud clerks received no salary but they were in the line of promotion. They could become, presently, third clerk and second clerk, then chief clerk—that is to say, purser. The dream begins when Henry had been mud clerk about three months. We were lying in port at St. Louis. Pilots and steersmen had nothing to do during the three days that the boat lay in port in St. Louis and New Orleans, but the mud clerk had to begin his labors at dawn and continue them into the night by the light of pine-knot torches. Henry and I, moneyless and unsalaried, had billeted ourselves upon our brother-in-law, Mr. Moffett, as night lodgers while in port. We took our meals on board the boat. No, I mean *I* lodged at the house, not Henry. He spent the *evenings* at the house, from ni..e until eleven, then went to the boat to be ready for his early duties.

On the night of the dream he started away at eleven, shaking hands with the family, and said good-by according to custom. I may mention that handshaking as a good-by was not merely the custom of that family but the custom of the region—the custom of Missouri, I may say. In all my life up to that time I had never seen one member of the Clemens family kiss another one—except once. When my father lay dying in our home in Hannibal he put his arm around my sister's neck and drew her down and kissed her, saying, "Let me die." I remember that, and I remember the death rattle which swiftly followed those words, which were his last. These good-bys were always executed in the family sitting room on the second floor, and Henry went from that room and downstairs without further ceremony. But this time my mother went with him to the head of the stairs and said good-by again. As I remember it, she was moved to this by something in Henry's manner and she remained at the head of the stairs while he descended. When he reached the door he hesitated and climbed the stairs and shook hands good-by again.

In the morning, when I awoke, I had been dreaming, and the dream was so vivid, so like reality, that it deceived me and I thought it *was* real. In the dream I had seen Henry a corpse. He lay in a metallic burial case. He was dressed in a suit of my clothing and on his breast lay a great bouquet of flowers, mainly white roses, with a red rose in the center. The casket stood upon a couple of chairs. I dressed and moved toward that door, thinking I would go in there and look at it, but I changed my mind. I thought I could not yet bear to meet my mother. I thought I would wait awhile and make some preparation for that ordeal. The house was in Locust Street, a little above Thirteenth, and I walked to Fourteenth and to the middle of the block beyond before it suddenly flashed upon me that there was nothing real about this—it was only a dream. I can still feel something of the grateful upheaval of joy of that moment and I can also still feel the remnant of doubt, the suspicion that maybe it was real after all. I returned to the house almost on a run, flew up the stairs two or three steps at a jump and rushed into that sitting room, and was made glad again, for there was no casket there.

We made the usual eventless trip to New Orleans—no, it was not eventless, for it was on the way down that I had the fight with Mr. Brown* which resulted in his requiring that I be left ashore at New Orleans. In New Orleans I always had a job. It was my privilege to watch the freight piles from seven in the evening until seven in the morning, and get three dollars for it. It was a three-night job and occurred every thirty-five days. Henry always joined my watch about nine in the evening, when his own duties were ended, and we often walked my rounds and chatted together until midnight. This time we were to part and so the night before the boat sailed I gave Henry some advice. I said: "In case of disaster to the boat, don't lose your head— leave that unwisdom to the passengers—they are competent—they'll attend to it. But you rush for the hurricane deck, and astern to the solitary lifeboat lashed aft the wheelhouse on the port side, and obey the mate's orders—thus you will be useful. When the boat is launched, give such help as you can in getting the women and children into it, and be sure you don't try to get into it yourself. It is summer weather, the river is only a mile wide as a rule, and you can swim ashore without any trouble." Two or three days afterward the boat's boilers exploded at Ship Island, below Memphis, early one morning—and what happened afterward I have already told in *Life on the Mississippi.* As related there, I followed the *Pennsylvania* about a day later on another boat, and we began to get news of the disaster at every port we touched at, and so by the time we reached Memphis we knew all about it.

I found Henry stretched upon a mattress on the floor of a great building, along with thirty or forty other scalded and wounded persons, and was promptly informed by some indiscreet person that he had inhaled steam, that his body was badly scalded and that he would live but a little while; also, I was told that the physicians and nurses were giving their whole attention to persons who had a chance of being saved. They were short-handed in the matter of physicians and

* See *Life on the Mississippi.*

nurses, and Henry and such others as were considered to be fatally hurt were receiving only such attention as could be spared from time to time from the more urgent cases. But Doctor Peyton, a fine and large-hearted old physician of great reputation in the community, gave me his sympathy and took vigorous hold of the case and in about a week he had brought Henry around. He never committed himself with prognostications which might not materialize, but at eleven o'clock one night he told me that Henry was out of danger and would get well. Then he said, "At midnight these poor fellows lying here and there and all over this place will begin to mourn and mutter and lament and make outcries and if this commotion should disturb Henry it will be bad for him; therefore ask the physicians on watch to give him an eighth of a grain of morphine, but this is not to be done unless Henry shall show signs that he is being disturbed."

Oh, well, never mind the rest of it. The physicians on watch were young fellows hardly out of the medical college and they made a mistake—they had no way of measuring the eighth of a grain of morphine, so they guessed at it and gave him a vast quantity heaped on the end of a knife blade, and the fatal effects were soon apparent. I think he died about dawn, I don't remember as to that. He was carried to the dead-room and I went away for a while to a citizen's house and slept off some of my accumulated fatigue—and meantime something was happening. The coffins provided for the dead were of unpainted white pine, but in this instance some of the ladies of Memphis had made up a fund of sixty dollars and bought a metallic case, and when I came back and entered the dead-room Henry lay in that open case and he was dressed in a suit of my clothing. I recognized instantly that my dream of several weeks before was here exactly reproduced, so far as these details went—and I think I missed one detail, but that one was immediately supplied, for just then an elderly lady entered the place with a large bouquet consisting mainly of white roses, and in the center of it was a red rose and she laid it on his breast.

I don't believe that I ever had any doubts whatever concerning the salient points of the dream, for those points are of such a nature that they are *pictures,* and pictures can be remembered, when they are vivid, much better than one can remember remarks and unconcreted facts. Although it has been so many years since I have told that dream, I can see those pictures now just as clearly defined as if they were before me in this room. I have not told the entire dream. There

was a good deal more of it. I mean I have not told all that happened in
the dream's fulfillment. After the incident in the death-room I may
mention one detail, and that is this. When I arrived in St. Louis with
the casket it was about eight o'clock in the morning, and I ran to my
brother-in-law's place of business, hoping to find him there, but I
missed him, for while I was on the way to his office he was on his way
from the house to the boat. When I got back to the boat the casket was
gone. He had had it conveyed out to his house. I hastened thither and
when I arrived the men were just removing the casket from the vehicle
to carry it upstairs. I stopped that procedure, for I did not want my
mother to see the dead face, because one side of it was drawn and
distorted by the effects of the opium. When I went upstairs there stood
the two chairs which I had seen in my dream and if I had arrived there
two or three minutes later the casket would have been resting upon
those two chairs, just as in my dream of several weeks before.

1907

OLD NEVADA DAYS

In those early days dueling suddenly became a fashion in the new
territory of Nevada and by 1864 everybody was anxious to have a
chance in the new sport, mainly for the reason that he was not able to
thoroughly respect himself so long as he had not killed or crippled
somebody in a duel or been killed or crippled in one himself.

At that time I had been serving as city editor on Mr. Joe Goodman's Virginia City *Enterprise* for a matter of two years. I was twenty-
nine years old. I was ambitious in several ways but I had entirely
escaped the seductions of that particular craze. I had had no desire to
fight a duel. I had no intention of provoking one. I did not feel respectable but I got a certain amount of satisfaction out of feeling safe. I was
ashamed of myself, the rest of the staff were ashamed of me—but I got
along well enough. I had always been accustomed to feeling ashamed
of myself, for one thing or another, so there was no novelty for me in
this situation. I bore it very well.

Plunkett was on the staff. R. M. Daggett was on the staff. These had tried to get into duels but for the present had failed and were waiting. Goodman was the only one of us who had done anything to shed credit upon the paper. The rival paper was the Virginia *Union*. Its editor for a little while was Tom Fitch, called the "silver-tongued orator of Wisconsin"—that was where he came from. He tuned up his oratory in the editorial columns of the *Union* and Mr. Goodman invited him out and modified him with a bullet. I remember the joy of the staff when Goodman's challenge was accepted by Fitch. We ran late that night and made much of Joe Goodman. He was only twenty-four years old; he lacked the wisdom which a person has at twenty-nine and he was as glad of being *it* as I was that I wasn't.

He chose Major Graves for his second (that name is not right but it's close enough, I don't remember the major's name). Graves came over to instruct Joe in the dueling art. He had been a major under Walker, the "gray-eyed man of destiny," and had fought all through that remarkable man's filibustering campaign in Central America. That fact gauges the major. To say that a man was a major under Walker and came out of that struggle ennobled by Walker's praise is to say that the major was not merely a brave man but that he was brave to the very utmost limit of that word. All of Walker's men were like that.

I knew the Gillis family intimately. The father made the campaign under Walker, and with him one son. They were in the memorable Plaza fight and stood it out to the last against overwhelming odds, as did also all of the Walker men. The son was killed at the father's side. The father received a bullet through the eye. The old man—for he was an old man at the time—wore spectacles, and the bullet and one of the glasses went into his skull, and the bullet remained there. There were some other sons—Steve, George and Jim, very young chaps—the merest lads—who wanted to be in the Walker expedition, for they had their father's dauntless spirit. But Walker wouldn't have them; he said it was a serious expedition and no place for children.

The major was a majestic creature, with a most stately and dignified and impressive military bearing, and he was by nature and training courteous, polite, graceful, winning; and he had that quality which I think I have encountered in only one other man—Bob Howland—a mysterious quality which resides in the eye; and when that eye is turned upon an individual or a squad, in warning, that is enough. The man that has that eye doesn't need to go armed; he can move upon an armed desperado and quell him and take him prisoner without saying a single word. I saw Bob Howland do that once—a slender, good-natured, amiable, gentle, kindly little skeleton of a man, with a sweet blue eye that would win your heart when it smiled upon you, or turn cold and freeze it, according to the nature of the occasion.

The major stood Joe up straight; stood Steve Gillis up fifteen paces away; made Joe turn his right side toward Steve, cock his navy six-shooter—that prodigious weapon—and hold it straight down against his leg; told him that *that* was the correct position for the gun—that the position ordinarily in use at Virginia City (that is to say, the gun straight up in the air, then brought slowly down to your man) was all wrong. At the word *"One,"* you must raise the gun slowly and steadily to the place on the other man's body that you desire to convince. Then, after a pause, *"Two, three—fire—Stop!"* At the word "stop," you may fire—but not earlier. You may give yourself as much time as you please *after* that word. Then, when you fire, you may advance and go on firing at your leisure and pleasure, if you can get any pleasure out of it. And, in the meantime, the other man, if he has been properly instructed and is alive to his privileges, is advancing on *you*, and firing —and it is always likely that more or less trouble will result.

Naturally, when Joe's revolver had risen to a level it was pointing at Steve's breast, but the major said: "No, that is not wise. Take all the risks of getting murdered yourself but don't run any risk of murdering the other man. If you survive a duel you want to survive it in such a way that the memory of it will not linger along with you through the rest of your life and interfere with your sleep. Aim at your man's leg; not at the knee, not above the knee, for those are dangerous spots. Aim below the knee; cripple him but leave the rest of him to his mother."

By grace of these truly wise and excellent instructions, Joe tumbled his man down with a bullet through his lower leg, which furnished him a permanent limp. And Joe lost nothing but a lock of hair, which he could spare better then than he could now. For when I saw him here in New York a year ago his crop was gone; he had nothing much left but a fringe, with a dome rising above.

About a year later I got *my* chance. But I was not hunting for it. Goodman went off to San Francisco for a week's holiday and left me to be chief editor. I had supposed that that was an easy berth, there being nothing to do but write one editorial per day; but I was disappointed in that superstition. I couldn't find anything to write an article about, the first day. Then it occurred to me that inasmuch as it was the 22d of April, 1864, the next morning would be the three-hundredth anniversary of Shakespeare's birthday—and what better theme could I want than that? I got the Cyclopaedia and examined it and found out who Shakespeare was and what he had done, and I borrowed all that and laid it before a community that couldn't have been better prepared for instruction about Shakespeare than if they had been prepared by art. There wasn't enough of what Shakespeare had done to make an editorial of the necessary length but I filled it out with what he hadn't done—which in many respects was more important and striking and readable than the handsomest things he had really accomplished.

But next day I was in trouble again. There were no more Shakespeares to work up. There was nothing in past history or in the world's future possibilities to make an editorial out of suitable to that community; so there was but one theme left. That theme was Mr. Laird, proprietor of the Virginia *Union*. *His* editor had gone off to San Francisco too and Laird was trying his hand at editing. I woke up Mr. Laird with some courtesies of the kind that were fashionable among newspaper editors in that region and he came back at me the next day in a most vitriolic way. So we expected a challenge from Mr. Laird, because according to the rules—according to the etiquette of dueling as reconstructed and reorganized and improved by the duelists of that region—whenever you said a thing about another person that he didn't like, it wasn't sufficient for him to talk back in the same offensive spirit; etiquette required him to send a challenge. So we waited for a challenge—waited all day. It didn't come. And as the day wore along, hour after hour, and no challenge came, the boys grew depressed. They lost heart. But I was cheerful; I felt better and better all the time. They couldn't understand it but *I* could understand it. It was my *make* that enabled me to be cheerful when other people were despondent.

So then it became necessary for us to waive etiquette and challenge Mr. Laird. When we reached that decision, they began to cheer up, but I began to lose some of my animation. However, in enterprises of this kind you are in the hands of your friends; there is nothing for you to do but to abide by what they consider to be the best course. Daggett wrote a challenge for me, for Daggett had the language—the right language—the convincing language—and I lacked it. Daggett poured out a stream of unsavory epithets upon Mr. Laird, charged with a vigor and venom of a strength calculated to persuade him; and Steve Gillis, my second, carried the challenge and came back to wait for the return. It didn't come. The boys were exasperated but I kept my temper. Steve carried another challenge, hotter than the other, and we waited again. Nothing came of it. I began to feel quite comfortable. I began to take an interest in the challenges myself. I had not felt any before; but it seemed to me that I was accumulating a great and valuable reputation at no expense and my delight in this grew and grew as challenge after challenge was declined, until by midnight I was beginning to think that there was nothing in the world so much to be desired as a chance to fight a duel. So I hurried Daggett up; made him keep on sending challenge after challenge. Oh, well, I overdid it: Laird accepted. I might have suspected that that would happen—Laird was a man you couldn't depend on.

The boys were jubilant beyond expression. They helped me make my will, which was another discomfort—and I already had enough. Then they took me home. I didn't sleep any—didn't want to sleep. I had plenty of things to think about and less than four hours to do it in —because five o'clock was the hour appointed for the tragedy and I should have to use up one hour—beginning at four—in practicing with the revolver and finding out which end of it to level at the adversary. At four we went down into a little gorge about a mile from town and borrowed a barn door for a mark—borrowed it of a man who was over in California on a visit—and we set the barn door up and stood a fence rail up against the middle of it to represent Mr. Laird. But the rail was no proper representative of him, for he was longer than a rail and thinner. Nothing would ever fetch him but a line shot, and then, as like as not, he would split the bullet—the worst material for dueling purposes that could be imagined. I began on the rail. I couldn't hit the rail; then I tried the barn door; but I couldn't hit the barn door. There was nobody in danger except stragglers around on the flanks of that mark. I was thoroughly discouraged and I didn't cheer up any when we presently heard pistol shots over in the next little ravine. I knew what that was—that was Laird's gang out practicing him. They would hear my shots and of course they could come up over the ridge to see what kind of a record I was making—see what their chances were against me. Well, I hadn't any record; and I knew that if Laird came over that ridge and saw my barn door without a scratch on it, he would be as anxious to fight as I was—or as I had been at midnight, before that disastrous acceptance came.

Now just at this moment a little bird, no bigger than a sparrow, flew along by and lit on a sagebush about thirty yards away. Steve whipped out his revolver and shot its head off. Oh, he was a marksman—much better than I was. We ran down there to pick up the bird and just then, sure enough, Mr. Laird and his people came over the ridge and they joined us. And when Laird's second saw that bird with its head shot off he lost color, he faded, and you could see that he was interested.

He said: "Who did that?"

Before I could answer, Steve spoke up and said quite calmly, and in a matter-of-fact way, "Clemens did it."

The second said, "Why, that is wonderful! How far off was that bird?"

Steve said, "Oh, not far—about thirty yards."

The second said, "Well, that is astonishing shooting. How often can he do that?"

Steve said languidly, "Oh, about four times out of five!"

I knew the little rascal was lying but I didn't say anything. The second said:

"Why, that is *amazing* shooting! Why, I supposed he couldn't hit a church!"

He was supposing very sagaciously but I didn't say anything. Well, they said good morning. The second took Mr. Laird home, a little tottery on his legs, and Laird sent back a note in his own hand declining to fight a duel with me on any terms whatever.

Well, my life was saved—saved by that accident. I don't know what the bird thought about that interposition of Providence but I felt very, very comfortable over it—satisfied and content. Now we found out later that Laird had hit *his* mark four times out of six, right along. If the duel had come off he would have so filled my skin with bullet holes that it wouldn't have held my principles.

By breakfast time the news was all over town that I had sent a challenge and Steve Gillis had carried it. Now that would entitle us to two years apiece in the penitentiary, according to the brand-new law. Governor North sent us no message as coming from himself but a message *came* from a close friend of his. He said it would be a good idea for us to leave the territory by the first stage-coach. This would sail next morning at four o'clock—and in the meantime we would be searched for but not with avidity; and if we were in the territory after that stage-coach left we would be the first victims of the new law. Judge North was anxious to have some victims for that law and he would absolutely keep us in the prison the full two years. He wouldn't pardon us out to please anybody.

Well, it seemed to me that our society was no longer desirable in Nevada; so we stayed in our quarters and observed proper caution all day—except that once Steve went over to the hotel to attend to another customer of mine. That was a Mr. Cutler. You see, Laird was not the only person whom I had tried to reform during my occupancy of the editorial chair. I had looked around and selected several other people and delivered a new zest of life into them through warm criticism and disapproval—so that when I laid down my editorial pen I had four horse-whippings and two duels owing to me. We didn't care for the horse-whippings; there was no glory in them; they were not worth the trouble of collecting. But honor required that some notice should be taken of that other duel. Mr. Cutler had come up from Carson City and had sent a man over with a challenge from the hotel. Steve went over to pacify him. Steve weighed only ninety-five pounds but it was well known throughout the territory that with his fists he could whip anybody that walked on two legs, let his weight and science be what they might. Steve was a Gillis, and when a Gillis confronted a man and had a proposition to make the proposition always contained business. When Cutler found that Steve was my second he cooled down; he became calm and rational and was ready to listen. Steve gave him fifteen minutes to get out of the hotel and half an hour to get out of town or there would be results. So *that* duel went off successfully, because Mr. Cutler immediately left for Carson a convinced and reformed man.

I have never had anything to do with duels since. I thoroughly disapprove of duels. I consider them unwise and I know they are dangerous. Also, sinful. If a man should challenge me now I would go to that man and take him kindly and forgivingly by the hand and lead him to a quiet retired spot and *kill* him. Still, I have always taken a great interest in other people's duels. One always feels an abiding interest in any heroic thing which has entered into his own experience.

1906

BEGINNINGS AS AN AUTHOR

My experiences as an author began early in 1867. I came to New York from San Francisco in the first month of that year and presently Charles H. Webb, whom I had known in San Francisco as a reporter on *The Bulletin* and afterward editor of *The Californian*, suggested that I publish a volume of sketches. I had but a slender reputation to publish it on but I was charmed and excited by the suggestion and quite willing to venture it if some industrious person would save me the trouble of gathering the sketches together. I was loath to do it myself, for from the beginning of my sojourn in this world there was a persistent vacancy in me where the industry ought to be. ("Ought to was" is better, perhaps, though the most of the authorities differ as to this.)

Webb said I had some reputation in the Atlantic states but I knew quite well that it must be of a very attenuated sort. What there was of it rested upon the story of "The Jumping Frog." When Artemus Ward passed through California on a lecturing tour in 1865 or '66, I told him the "Jumping Frog" story in San Francisco and he asked me to write it out and send it to his publisher, Carleton, in New York, to be used in padding out a small book which Artemus had prepared for the press and which needed some more stuffing to make it big enough for the price which was to be charged for it.

It reached Carleton in time but he didn't think much of it and was not willing to go to the typesetting expense of adding it to the book. He did not put it in the wastebasket but made Henry Clapp a present of it and Clapp used it to help out the funeral of his dying literary journal, *The Saturday Press*. "The Jumping Frog" appeared in the last number of that paper, was the most joyous feature of the obsequies, and was at once copied in the newspapers of America and England. It certainly had a wide celebrity and it still had it at the time that I am speaking of—but I was aware that it was only the frog that was celebrated. It wasn't I. I was still an obscurity.

Webb undertook to collate the sketches. He performed this office, then handed the result to me and I went to Carleton's establishment with it. I approached a clerk and he bent eagerly over the counter to inquire into my needs; but when he found that I had come to sell a book and not to buy one, his temperature fell sixty degrees and the old-gold intrenchments in the roof of my mouth contracted three-quarters of an inch and my teeth fell out. I meekly asked the privilege of a word with Mr. Carleton and was coldly informed that he was in his private office. Discouragements and difficulties followed, but after a while I got by the frontier and entered the holy of holies. Ah, now I remember how I managed it! Webb had made an appointment for me with Carleton; otherwise I never should have gotten over that frontier. Carleton rose and said brusquely and aggressively,

"Well, what can I do for you?"

I reminded him that I was there by appointment to offer him my book for publication. He began to swell and went on swelling and swelling and swelling until he had reached the dimensions of a god of about the second or third degree. Then the fountains of his great deep were broken up and for two or three minutes I couldn't see him for the rain. It was words, only words, but they fell so densely that they darkened the atmosphere. Finally he made an imposing sweep with his right hand which comprehended the whole room and said,

"Books—look at those shelves! Every one of them is loaded with books that are waiting for publication. Do I want any more? Excuse me, I don't. Good morning."

Twenty-one years elasped before I saw Carleton again. I was then sojourning with my family at the Schweizerhof, in Lucerne. He called on me, shook hands cordially and said at once without any preliminaries,

"I am substantially an obscure person but I have a couple of such colossal distinctions to my credit that I am entitled to immortality—to wit: I refused a book of yours and for this I stand without competitor as the prize ass of the nineteenth century."

It was a most handsome apology and I told him so and said it was a long delayed revenge but was sweeter to me than any other that could be devised, that during the lapsed twenty-one years I had in fancy taken his life several times every year and always in new and increasingly cruel and inhuman ways, but that now I was pacified, appeased, happy, even jubilant, and that thenceforth I should hold him my true and valued friend and never kill him again.

I reported my adventure to Webb and he bravely said that not all the Carletons in the universe should defeat that book, he would publish it himself on a ten per cent royalty. And so he did. He brought it out in blue and gold and made a very pretty little book of it. I think he named it *The Celebrated Jumping Frog of Calaveras County, and Other Sketches,* price $1.25. He made the plates and printed and bound the book through a job printing house and published it through the American News Company.

In June I sailed in the *Quaker City* Excursion. I returned in November and in Washington found a letter from Elisha Bliss of the American Publishing Company of Hartford, offering me five per cent royalty on a book which should recount the adventures of the Excursion. In lieu of the royalty I was offered the alternative of ten thousand dollars cash upon delivery of the manuscript. I consulted A. D. Richardson and he said, "Take the royalty." I followed his advice and closed with Bliss.

By my contract I was to deliver the manuscript of *The Innocents Abroad* in July of 1868. I wrote the book in San Francisco, as I have said, and delivered the manuscript within contract time. Bliss provided a multitude of illustrations for the book and then stopped work on it. The contract date for the issue went by and there was no explanation of this. Time drifted along and still there was no explanation. I was lecturing all over the country; and about thirty times a day, on an average, I was trying to answer this conundrum: "When is your book coming out?"

I got tired of inventing new answers to that question and by and by I got horribly tired of the question itself. Whoever asked it became my enemy at once and I was usually almost eager to make that appear.

As soon as I was free of the lecture field I hastened to Hartford to make inquiries. Bliss said that the fault was not his; that he wanted to publish the book but the directors of his company were staid old fossils and were afraid of it. They had examined the book and the majority of them were of the opinion that there were places in it of a humorous character. Bliss said the house had never published a book that had a suspicion like that attaching to it and that the directors were afraid that a departure of this kind could seriously injure the house's reputation, that he was tied hand and foot and was not permitted to carry out his contract.

One of the directors, a Mr. Drake—at least he was the remains of what had once been a Mr. Drake—invited me to take a ride with him in his buggy and I went along. He was a pathetic old relic and his ways and his talk were also pathetic. He had a delicate purpose in view and it took him some time to hearten himself sufficiently to carry it out, but at last he accomplished it. He explained the house's difficulty and distress, as Bliss had already explained it. Then he frankly threw himself and the house upon my mercy and begged me to take away *The Innocents Abroad* and release the concern from the contract. I said I wouldn't—and so ended the interview and the buggy excursion.

Then I warned Bliss that he must get to work or I should make trouble. He acted upon the warning and set up the book and I read the proofs. Then there was another long wait and no explanation. At last toward the end of July (1869, I think) I lost patience and telegraphed Bliss that if the book was not on sale in twenty-four hours I should bring suit for damages.

That ended the trouble. Half a dozen copies were bound and placed on sale within the required time. Then the canvassing began and went briskly forward. In nine months the book took the publishing house out of debt, advanced its stock from twenty-five to two hundred and left seventy thousand dollars profit to the good. It was Bliss that told me this—but if it was true it was the first time that he had told the truth in sixty-five years. He was born in 1804.

1906

DUELLING*

In 1878, fourteen years after my unmaterialized duel, Messieurs
Fortu and Gambetta fought a duel which made heroes of both of them
in France, but made them rather ridiculous throughout the rest of the
world. I was living in Munich that fall and winter, and I was so
interested in that funny tragedy that I wrote a long account of it, and
it is in one of my books, somewhere—an account which had some
inaccuracies in it, but as an exhibition of the *spirit* of that duel, I think
it was correct and trustworthy. And when I was living in Vienna,
thirty-four years after my ineffectual duel, my interest in that kind of
incident was still strong; and I find here among my Autobiographical
manuscripts of that day a chapter which I began concerning it, but did
not finish. I wanted to finish it, but held it open in the hope that the
Italian ambassador, M. Nigra, would find time to furnish me the *full*
history of Señor Cavalotti's adventures in that line. But he was a busy
man; there was always an interruption before he could get well
started; so my hope was never fulfilled. The following is the unfinished
chapter:

As concerns duelling. This pastime is as common in Austria to-day
as it is in France. But with this difference, that here in the Austrian
States the duel is dangerous, while in France it is not. Here it is tragedy, in France it is comedy; here it is a solemnity, there it is monkey-
shines; here the duellist risks his life, there he does not even risk his
shirt. Here he fights with pistol or sabre, in France with a hairpin—a
blunt one. Here the desperately wounded man tries to walk to the
hospital; there they paint the scratch so that they can find it again, lay
the sufferer on a stretcher, and conduct him off the field with a band of
music.

At the end of a French duel the pair hug and kiss and cry, and
praise each other's valor; then the surgeons make an examination and
pick out the scratched one, and the other one helps him on to the litter

* Published here in book form for the first time. Source: *North American Review*,
September 1907, pp. 12–17.

and pays his fare; and in return the scratched one treats to champagne and oysters in the evening, and then "the incident is closed," as the French say. It is all polite, and gracious, and pretty, and impressive. At the end of an Austrian duel the antagonist that is alive gravely offers his hand to the other man, utters some phrases of courteous regret, then bids him good-by and goes his way, and that incident also is closed. The French duellist is painstakingly protected from danger, by the rules of the game. His antagonist's weapon cannot reach so far as his body; if he get a scratch it will not be above his elbow. But in Austria the rules of the game do not provide against danger, they carefully provide *for* it, usually. Commonly the combat must be kept up until one of the men is disabled; a non-disabling slash or stab does not retire him.

For a matter of three months I watched the Viennese journals, and whenever a duel was reported in their telegraphic columns I scrapbooked it. By this record I find that duelling in Austria is not confined to journalists and old maids, as in France, but is indulged in by military men, journalists, students, physicians, lawyers, members of the legislature, and even the Cabinet, the Bench and the police. Duelling is forbidden by law; and so it seems odd to see the makers and administrators of the laws dancing on their work in this way. Some months ago Count Bodeni, at that time Chief of the Government, fought a pistol-duel here in the capital city of the Empire with representative Wolf, and both of those distinguished Christians came near getting turned out of the Church—for the Church as well as the State forbids duelling.

In one case, lately, in Hungary, the police interfered and stopped a duel after the first innings. This was a sabre-duel between the chief of police and the city attorney. Unkind things were said about it by the newspapers. They said the police remembered their duty uncommonly well when their own officials were the parties concerned in duels. But I think the underlings showed good bread-and-butter judgment. If their superiors had carved each other well, the public would have asked, Where were the police? and their places would have been endangered; but custom does not require them to be around where mere unofficial citizens are explaining a thing with sabres.

There was another duel—a double duel—going on in the immediate neighborhood at the time, and in this case the police obeyed custom and did not disturb it. Their bread and butter was not at stake there.

In this duel a physician fought a couple of surgeons, and wounded both—one of them lightly, the other seriously. An undertaker wanted to keep people from interfering, but that was quite natural again.

Selecting at random from my record, I next find a duel at Tarnopol between military men. An officer of the Tenth Dragoons charged an officer of the Ninth Dragoons with an offence against the laws of the card-table. There was a defect or a doubt somewhere in the matter, and this had to be examined and passed upon by a Court of Honor. So the case was sent up to Lemberg for this purpose. One would like to know what the defect was, but the newspaper does not say. A man here who has fought many duels and has a graveyard, says that probably the matter in question was as to whether the accusation was true or not; that if the charge was a very grave one—cheating, for instance —proof of its truth would rule the guilty officer out of the field of honor; the Court would not allow a gentleman to fight with such a person. You see what a solemn thing it is; you see how particular they are; any little careless act can lose you your privilege of getting yourself shot, here. The Court seems to have gone into the matter in a searching and careful fashion, for several months elapsed before it reached a decision. It then sanctioned a duel and the accused killed his accuser.

Next I find a duel between a prince and a major; first with pistols— no result satisfactory to either party; then with sabres, and the major badly hurt.

Next, a sabre-duel between journalists—the one a strong man, the other feeble and in poor health. It was brief; the strong one drove his sword through the weak one, and death was immediate.

Next, a duel between a lieutenant and a student of medicine. According to the newspaper report these are the details. The student was in a restaurant one evening; passing along, he halted at a table to speak with some friends; near by sat a dozen military men; the student conceived that one of these was "staring" at him; he asked the officer to step outside and explain. This officer and another one gathered up their caps and sabres and went out with the student. Outside—this is the student's account—the student introduced himself to the offending officer and said, "You seemed to stare at me"; for answer, the officer struck at the student with his fist; the student parried the blow; both officers drew their sabres and attacked the young fellow, and one of them gave him a wound on the left arm; then they withdrew. This was

Saturday night. The duel followed on Monday, in the military riding-school—the customary duelling-ground all over Austria, apparently. The weapons were pistols. The duelling terms were somewhat beyond custom in the matter of severity, if I may gather that from the statement that the combat was fought *"unter sehr schweren Bedingungen"* —to wit, "Distance, 15 steps—with 3 steps advance." There was but one exchange of shots. The student was hit. "He put his hand on his breast, his body began to bend slowly forward, then collapsed in death and sank to the ground."

It is pathetic. There are other duels in my list, but I find in each and all of them one and the same ever-recurring defect—the *principals* are never present, but only their sham representatives. The *real* principals in any duel are not the duellists themselves, but their families. They do the mourning, the suffering, theirs is the loss and theirs the misery. They stake all that, the duellist stakes nothing but his life, and that is a trivial thing compared with what his death must cost those whom he leaves behind him. Challenges should not mention the duellist; he has nothing much at stake, and the real vengeance cannot reach him. The challenge should summon the offender's old gray mother, and his young wife and his little children,—these, or any to whom he is a dear and worshipped possession—and should say, "You have done me no harm, but I am the meek slave of a custom which requires me to crush the happiness out of your hearts and condemn you to years of pain and grief, in order that I may wash clean with your tears a stain which has been put upon me by another person."

The logic of it is admirable: a person has robbed me of a penny; I must beggar ten innocent persons to make good my loss. Surely nobody's "honor" is worth all that.

Since the duellist's family are the real principals in a duel, the State ought to compel them to be present at it. Custom, also, ought to be so amended as to require it; and without it no duel ought to be allowed to go on. If that student's unoffending mother had been present and watching the officer through her tears as he raised his pistol, he—why, he would have fired in the air. We know that. For we know how we are all made. Laws ought to be based upon the ascertained facts of our nature. It would be a simple thing to make a duelling law which would stop duelling.

As things are now, the mother is never invited. She submits to this; and without outward complaint, for she, too, is the vassal of custom, and custom requires her to conceal her pain when she learns the disastrous news that her son must go to the duelling-field, and by the powerful force that is lodged in habit and custom she is enabled to obey this trying requirement—a requirement which exacts a miracle of her, and gets it. Last January a neighbor of ours who has a young son in the army was wakened by this youth at three o'clock one morning, and she sat up in bed and listened to his message:

"I have come to tell you something, mother, which will distress you, but you must be good and brave, and bear it. I have been affronted by a fellow officer, and we fight at three this afternoon. Lie down and sleep, now, and think no more about it."

She kissed him good night and lay down paralyzed with grief and fear, but said nothing. But she did not sleep; she prayed and mourned till the first streak of dawn, then fled to the nearest church and implored the Virgin for help; and from that church she went to another and another and another; church after church, and still church after church, and so spent all the day until three o'clock on her knees in agony and tears; then dragged herself home and sat down comfortless and desolate, to count the minutes, and wait, with an outward show of calm, for what had been ordained for her—happiness, or endless misery. Presently she heard the clank of a sabre—she had not known before what music was in that sound!—and her son put his head in and said:

"X was in the wrong, and he apologized."

So that incident was closed; and for the rest of her life the mother will always find something pleasant about the clank of a sabre, no doubt.

In one of my listed duels—however, let it go, there is nothing particularly striking about it except that the seconds interfered. And prematurely, too, for neither man was dead. This was certainly irregular. Neither of the men liked it. It was a duel with cavalry sabres, between an editor and a lieutenant. The editor walked to the hospital, the lieutenant was carried. In this country an editor who can write well is valuable, but he is not likely to remain so unless he can handle a sabre with charm.

The following very recent telegram shows that also in France duels are humanely stopped as soon as they approach the (French) danger-point:

"*Reuter's Telegram.*—PARIS, *March 5.*—The duel between Colonels

Henry and Picquart took place this morning in the Riding School of the Ecole Militaire, the doors of which were strictly guarded in order to prevent intrusion. The combatants, who fought with swords, were in position at ten o'clock.

"At the first reengagement Lieutenant-Colonel Henry was slightly scratched in the fore arm, and just at the same moment his own blade appeared to touch his adversary's neck. Senator Ranc, who was Colonel Picquart's second, stopped the fight, but as it was found that his principal had not been touched, the combat continued. A very sharp encounter ensued, in which Colonel Henry was wounded in the elbow, and the duel terminated."

After which, the stretcher and the band. In lurid contrast with this delicate flirtation, we have this fatal duel of day before yesterday in Italy, where the earnest Austrian duel is in vogue. I knew Cavalotti slightly, and this gives me a sort of personal interest in his duel. I first saw him in Rome several years ago. He was sitting on a block of stone in the Forum, and was writing something in his note-book—a poem or a challenge, or something like that—and the friend who pointed him out to me said, "That is Cavalotti—he has fought thirty duels; do not disturb him." I did not disturb him.

[May 13, 1907.] It is a long time ago. Cavalotti—poet, orator, satirist, statesman, patriot—was a great man, and his death was deeply lamented by his countrymen: many monuments to his memory testify to this. In his duels he killed several of his antagonists and disabled the rest. By nature he was a little irascible. Once when the officials of the library of Bologna threw out his books the gentle poet went up there and challenged the whole fifteen! His parliamentary duties were exacting, but he proposed to keep coming up and fighting duels between trains until all those officials had been retired from the activities of life. Although he always chose the sword to fight with, he had never had a lesson with that weapon. When game was called he waited for nothing, but always plunged at his opponent and rained such a storm of wild and original thrusts and whacks upon him that the man was dead or crippled before he could bring his science to bear. But his latest antagonist discarded science, and won. He held his sword straight forward like a lance when Cavalotti made his plunge—with the result

that he impaled himself upon it. It entered his mouth and passed out
at the back of his neck. Death was instantaneous.

1907

OF CATS AND BILLIARDS*

From Susy's Biography of Me.
Papa says that if the collera comes here he will take Sour Mash to the mountains. . . . Sour Mash is a constant source of anxiety, care, and pleasure to
papa.

I did, in truth, think a great deal of that old tortoise-shell harlot; but
I haven't a doubt that in order to impress Susy I was pretending
agonies of solicitude which I didn't honestly feel. Sour Mash never
gave me any real anxiety; she was always able to take care of herself,
and she was ostentatiously vain of the fact; vain of it to a degree which
often made me ashamed of her, much as I esteemed her.

Many persons would like to have the society of cats during the
summer vacation in the country, but they deny themselves this pleasure because they think they must either take the cats along when they
return to the city, where they would be a trouble and an encumbrance,
or leave them in the country, houseless and homeless. These people
have no ingenuity, no invention, no wisdom; or it would occur to them
to do as I do: rent cats by the month for the summer and return them
to their good homes at the end of it. Early last May I rented a kitten of
a farmer's wife, by the month; then I got a discount by taking three.
They have been good company for about five months now, and are
still kittens—at least they have not grown much, and to all intents and
purposes are still kittens, and as full of romping energy and enthusiasm as they were in the beginning. This is remarkable. I am an expert
in cats, but I have not seen a kitten keep its kittenhood nearly so long
before.

* Published here in book form for the first time. Source: *North American Review,*
April 5, 1907, pp. 673–682.

These are beautiful creatures—these triplets. Two of them wear the blackest and shiniest and thickest of sealskin vestments all over their bodies except the lower half of their faces and the terminations of their paws. The black masks reach down below the eyes, therefore when the eyes are closed they are not visible; the rest of the face, and the gloves and stockings, are snow white. These markings are just the same on both cats—so exactly the same that when you call one the other is likely to answer, because they cannot tell each other apart. Since the cats are precisely alike, and can't be told apart by any of us, they do not need two names, so they have but one between them. We call both of them Sackcloth, and we call the gray one Ashes. I believe I have never seen such intelligent cats as these before. They are full of the nicest discriminations. When I read German aloud they weep; you can see the tears run down. It shows what pathos there is in the German tongue. I had not noticed before that all German is pathetic, no matter what the subject is nor how it is treated. It was these humble observers that brought the knowledge to me. I have tried all kinds of German on these cats; romance, poetry, philosophy, theology, market reports; and the result has always been the same—the cats sob, and let the tears run down, which shows that all German is pathetic. French is not a familiar tongue to me, and the pronunciation is difficult, and comes out of me encumbered with a Missouri accent; but the cats like it, and when I make impassioned speeches in that language they sit in a row and put up their paws, palm to palm, and frantically give thanks. Hardly any cats are affected by music, but these are; when I sing they go reverently away, showing how deeply they feel it. Sour Mash never cared for these things. She had many noble qualities, but at bottom she was not refined, and cared little or nothing for theology and the arts.

It is a pity to say it, but these cats are not above the grade of human beings, for I know by certain signs that they are not sincere in their exhibitions of emotion, but exhibit them merely to show off and attract attention—conduct which is distinctly human, yet with a difference: they do not know enough to conceal their desire to show off, but the grown human being does. What is ambition? It is only the desire to be conspicuous. The desire for fame is only the desire to be continuously conspicuous and attract attention and be talked about.

These cats are like human beings in another way: when Ashes began to work his fictitious emotions, and show off, the other members of the firm followed suit, in order to be in the fashion. That is the way with human beings; they are afraid to be outside; whatever the fashion happens to be, they conform to it, whether it be a pleasant fashion or the reverse, they lack the courage to ignore it and go their own way. All human beings would like to dress in loose and comfortable and highly colored and showy garments, and they had their desire until a century ago, when a king, or some other influential ass, introduced sombre hues and discomfort and ugly designs into masculine clothing. The meek public surrendered to the outrage, and by consequence we are in that odious captivity to-day, and are likely to remain in it for a long time to come.

Fortunately the women were not included in the disaster, and so their graces and their beauty still have the enhancing help of delicate fabrics and varied and beautiful colors. Their clothing makes a great opera audience an enchanting spectacle, a delight to the eye and the spirit, a Garden of Eden for charm and color. The men, clothed in dismal black, are scattered here and there and everywhere over the Garden, like so many charred stumps, and they damage the effect, but cannot annihilate it.

In summer we poor creatures have a respite, and may clothe ourselves in white garments; loose, soft, and in some degree shapely; but in the winter—the sombre winter, the depressing winter, the cheerless winter, when white clothes and bright colors are especially needed to brighten our spirits and lift them up—we all conform to the prevailing insanity, and go about in dreary black, each man doing it because the others do it, and not because he wants to. They are really no sincerer than Sackcloth and Ashes. At bottom the Sackcloths do not care to exhibit their emotions when I am performing before them, they only do it because Ashes started it.

I would like to dress in a loose and flowing costume made all of silks and velvets, resplendent with all the stunning dyes of the rainbow, and so would every sane man I have ever known; but none of us dares to venture it. There is such a thing as carrying conspicuousness to the point of discomfort; and if I should appear on Fifth Avenue on a Sunday morning, at church-time, clothed as I would like to be clothed, the churches would be vacant, and I should have all the congregations tagging after me, to look, and secretly envy, and publicly scoff. It is the way human beings are made; they are always keeping their real feelings shut up inside, and publicly exploiting their fictitious ones.

Next after fine colors, I like plain white. One of my sorrows, when the summer ends, is that I must put off my cheery and comfortable white clothes and enter for the winter into the depressing captivity of the shapeless and degrading black ones. It is mid-October now, and the weather is growing cold up here in the New Hampshire hills, but it will not succeed in freezing me out of these white garments, for here the neighbors are few, and it is only of crowds that I am afraid. I made a brave experiment, the other night, to see how it would feel to shock a crowd with these unseasonable clothes, and also to see how long it might take the crowd to reconcile itself to them and stop looking astonished and outraged. On a stormy evening I made a talk before a full house, in the village, clothed like a ghost, and looking as conspicuously, all solitary and alone on that platform, as any ghost could have looked; and I found, to my gratification, that it took the house less than ten minutes to forget about the ghost and give its attention to the tidings I had brought.

I am nearly seventy-one, and I recognize that my age has given me a good many privileges; valuable privileges; privileges which are not granted to younger persons. Little by little I hope to get together courage enough to wear white clothes all through the winter, in New York. It will be a great satisfaction to me to show off in this way; and perhaps the largest of all the satisfactions will be the knowledge that every scoffer, of my sex, will secretly envy me and wish he dared to follow my lead.

That mention that I have acquired new and great privileges by grace of my age, is not an uncalculated remark. When I passed the seventieth mile-stone, ten months ago, I instantly realized that I had entered a new country and a new atmosphere. To all the public I was become recognizably old, undeniably old; and from that moment everybody assumed a new attitude toward me—the reverent attitude granted by custom to age—and straightway the stream of generous new privileges began to flow in upon me and refresh my life. Since then, I have lived an ideal existence; and I now believe what Choate said last March, and which at the time I didn't credit: that the best of life begins at seventy; for then your work is done; you know that you have done your best, let the quality of the work be what it may; that you have earned your holiday—a holiday of peace and contentment—and that thenceforth, to the setting of your sun, nothing will break it, nothing interrupt it.

[Dictated January 22, 1907.] Last night, at a dinner-party where I

was present, Mr. Peter Dunne Dooley handed to the host several dollars, in satisfaction of a lost bet. I seemed to see an opportunity to better my condition, and I invited Dooley, apparently disinterestedly, to come to my house Friday and play billiards. He accepted, and I judge that there is going to be a deficit in the Dooley treasury as a result. In great qualities of the heart and brain, Dooley is gifted beyond all propriety. He is brilliant; he is an expert with his pen, and he easily stands at the head of all the satirists of this generation—but he is going to walk in darkness Friday afternoon. It will be a fraternal kindness to teach him that with all his light and culture, he does not know all the valuable things; and it will also be a fraternal kindness to him to complete his education for him—and I shall do this on Friday, and send him home in that perfected condition.

I possess a billiard secret which can be valuable to the Dooley sept, after I shall have conferred it upon Dooley—for a consideration. It is a discovery which I made by accident, thirty-eight years ago, in my father-in-law's house in Elmira. There was a scarred and battered and ancient billiard-table in the garret, and along with it a peck of checked and chipped balls, and a rackful of crooked and headless cues. I played solitaire up there every day with that difficult outfit. The table was not level, but slanted sharply to the southeast; there wasn't a ball that was round, or would complete the journey you started it on, but would always get tired and stop half-way and settle, with a jolty wobble, to a standstill on its chipped side. I tried making counts with four balls, but found it difficult and discouraging, so I added a fifth ball, then a sixth, then a seventh, and kept on adding until at last I had twelve balls on the table and a thirteenth to play with. My game was caroms—caroms solely—caroms plain, or caroms with cushion to help—anything that could furnish a count. In the course of time I found to my astonishment that I was never able to run fifteen, under any circumstances. By huddling the balls advantageously in the beginning, I could now and then coax fourteen out of them, but I couldn't reach fifteen by either luck or skill. Sometimes the balls would get scattered into difficult positions and defeat me in that way; sometimes if I managed to keep them together, I would freeze; and always when I froze, and had to play away from the contact, there was sure to be nothing to play at but a wide and uninhabited vacancy.

One day Mr. Dalton called on my brother-in-law, on a matter of business, and I was asked if I could entertain him awhile, until my brother-in-law should finish an engagement with another gentleman. I said I could, and took him up to the billiard-table. I had played with him many times at the club, and knew that he could play billiards tolerably well—only tolerably well—but not any better than I could. He and I were just a match. He didn't know our table; he didn't know those balls; he didn't know those warped and headless cues; he didn't know the southeastern slant of the table, and how to allow for it. I judged it would be safe and profitable to offer him a bet on my scheme. I emptied the avalanche of thirteen balls on the table and said:

"Take a ball and begin, Mr. Dalton. How many can you run with an outlay like that?"

He said, with the half-affronted air of a mathematician who has been asked how much of the multiplication table he can recite without a break:

"I suppose a million—eight hundred thousand, anyway."

I said "You shall have the privilege of placing the balls to suit yourself, and I want to bet you a dollar that you can't run fifteen."

I will not dwell upon the sequel. At the end of an hour his face was red, and wet with perspiration; his outer garments lay scattered here and there over the place; he was the angriest man in the State, and there wasn't a rag or remnant of an injurious adjective left in him anywhere—and I had all his small change.

When the summer was over, we went home to Hartford, and one day Mr. George Robertson arrived from Boston with two or three hours to spare between then and the return train, and as he was a young gentleman to whom we were in debt for much social pleasure, it was my duty, and a welcome duty, to make his two or three hours interesting for him. So I took him up-stairs and set up my billiard scheme for his comfort. Mine was a good table, in perfect repair; the cues were in perfect condition; the balls were ivory, and flawless—but I knew that Mr. Robertson was my prey, just the same, for by exhaustive tests with this outfit I had found that my limit was thirty-one. I had proved to my satisfaction that whereas I could not fairly expect to get more than six or eight or a dozen caroms out of a run, I could now and then reach twenty and twenty-five, and after a long procession of failures finally achieve a run of thirty-one; but in no case had I ever got beyond thirty-one. Robertson's game, as I knew, was a little better than mine, so I resolved to require him to make thirty-two. I believed it would entertain him. He was one of these brisk and hearty and cheery and self-satisfied young fellows who are brimful of confidence, and who plunge with grateful eagerness into any enterprise that offers a showy test of their abilities. I emptied the balls on the table and said,

"Take a cue and a ball, George, and begin. How many caroms do you think you can make out of that layout?"

He laughed the laugh of the gay and the care-free, as became his youth and inexperience, and said,

"I can punch caroms out of that bunch a week without a break."

I said "Place the balls to suit yourself, and begin."

Confidence is a necessary thing in billiards, but overconfidence is bad. George went at his task with much too much lightsomeness of spirit and disrespect for the situation. On his first shot he scored three caroms; on his second shot he scored four caroms; and on his third shot he missed as simple a carom as could be devised. He was very much astonished, and said he would not have supposed that careful play could be needed with an acre of bunched balls in front of a person.

He began again, and played more carefully, but still with too much lightsomeness; he couldn't seem to learn to take the situation seriously. He made about a dozen caroms and broke down. He was irritated with himself now, and he thought he caught me laughing. He didn't. I do not laugh publicly at my client when this game is going on; I only do it inside—or save it for after the exhibition is over. But he thought he had caught me laughing, and it increased his irritation. Of course I knew he thought I was laughing privately—for I was experienced; they all think that, and it has a good effect; it sharpens their annoyance and debilitates their play.

He made another trial and failed. Once more he was astonished; once more he was humiliated—and as for his anger, it rose to summer-heat. He arranged the balls again, grouping them carefully, and said he would win this time, or die. When a client reaches this condition, it is a good time to damage his nerve further, and this can always be done by saying some little mocking thing or other that has the outside appearance of a friendly remark—so I employed this art. I suggested that a bet might tauten his nerves, and that I would offer one, but that as I did not want it to be an expense to him, but only a help, I would make it small—a cigar, if he were willing—a cigar that he would fail again; not an expensive one, but a cheap native one, of the Crown Jewel breed, such as is manufactured in Hartford for the clergy. It set him afire all over! I could see the blue flame issue from his eyes. He said,

"Make it a hundred!—and no Connecticut cabbage-leaf product, but Havana, $25 the box!"

I took him up, but said I was sorry to see him do this, because it did not seem to me right or fair for me to rob him under our own roof, when he had been so kind to us. He said, with energy and acrimony:

"You take care of your own pocket, if you'll be so good, and leave me to take care of mine."

And he plunged at the congress of balls with a vindictiveness which was infinitely contenting to me. He scored a failure—and began to undress. I knew it would come to that, for he was in the condition now that Mr. Dooley will be in at about that stage of the contest on Friday afternoon. A clothes-rack will be provided for Mr. Dooley to hang his things on as fast as he shall from time to time shed them. George raised his voice four degrees and flung out the challenge—

"Double or quits!"

"Done," I responded, in the gentle and compassionate voice of one who is apparently getting sorrier and sorrier.

There was an hour and a half of straight disaster after that, and if it was a sin to enjoy it, it is no matter—I did enjoy it. It is half a lifetime ago, but I enjoy it yet, every time I think of it. George made failure after failure. His fury increased with each failure as he scored it. With each defeat he flung off one or another rag of his raiment, and every time he started on a fresh inning he made it "double or quits" once more. Twice he reached thirty and broke down; once he reached thirty-one and broke down. These "nears" made him frantic, and I believe I was never so happy in my life, except the time, a few years later, when the Rev. J. H. Twichell and I walked to Boston and he had the celebrated conversation with the hostler at the Inn at Ashford, Connecticut.

At last, when we were notified that Patrick was at the door to drive him to his train, George owed me five thousand cigars at twenty-five cents apiece, and I was so sorry I could have hugged him. But he shouted,

"Give me ten minutes more!" and added stormily, "it's double or quits again, and I'll win out free of debt or owe you ten thousand cigars, and you'll pay the funeral expenses."

He began on his final effort, and I believe that in all my experience among both amateurs and experts, I have never seen a cue so carefully handled in my lifetime as George handled his upon this intensely interesting occasion. He got safely up to twenty-five, and then ceased to breathe. So did I. He labored along, and added a point, another point, still another point, and finally reached thirty-one. He stopped there, and we took a breath. By this time the balls were scattered all down the cushions, about a foot or two apart, and there wasn't a shot in sight anywhere that any man might hope to make. In a burst of anger and confessed defeat, he sent his ball flying around the table at random, and it crotched a ball that was packed against the cushion and sprang across to a ball against the bank on the opposite side, and counted!

His luck had set him free, and he didn't owe me anything. He had used up all his spare time, but we carried his clothes to the carriage, and he dressed on his way to the station, greatly wondered at and admired by the ladies, as he drove along—but he got his train.

I am very fond of Mr. Dooley, and shall await his coming with affectionate and pecuniary interest.

P.S. Saturday. He has been here. Let us not talk about it.

1907

CAPTAIN OSBORN'S ODD ADVENTURE*

[Dictated December 20, 1906.] Six months ago, when I was recalling early days in San Francisco, I broke off at a place where I was about to tell about Captain Osborn's odd adventure at the "What Cheer," or perhaps it was at another cheap feeding-place—the "Miners' Restaurant." It was a place where one could get good food on the cheapest possible terms, and its popularity was great among the multitudes whose purses were light. It was a good place to go to, to observe mixed humanity. Captain Osborn and Bret Harte went there one day and took a meal, and in the course of it Osborn fished up an interesting

* Published here in book form for the first time. Source: *North American Review,* September 1907, pp. 17–21.

reminiscence of a dozen years before and told about it. It was to this effect:

He was a midshipman in the navy when the Californian gold craze burst upon the world and set it wild with excitement. His ship made the long journey around the Horn and was approaching her goal, the Golden Gate, when an accident happened.

"It happened to me," said Osborn. "I fell overboard. There was a heavy sea running, but no one was much alarmed about me, because we had on board a newly patented life-saving device which was believed to be competent to rescue anything that could fall overboard, from a midshipman to an anchor. Ours was the only ship that had this device; we were very proud of it, and had been anxious to give its powers a practical test. This thing was lashed to the garboard-strake of the main-to'gallant mizzen-yard amidships,* and there was nothing to do but cut the lashings and heave it over; it would do the rest. One day the cry of 'Man overboard!' brought all hands on deck. Instantly the lashings were cut and the machine flung joyously over. Damnation, it went to the bottom like an anvil! By the time that the ship was brought to and a boat manned, I was become but a bobbing speck on the waves half a mile astern and losing my strength very fast; but by good luck there was a common seaman on board who had practical ideas in his head and hadn't waited to see what the patent machine was going to do, but had run aft and sprung over after me the moment the alarm was cried through the ship. I had a good deal of a start of him, and the seas made his progress slow and difficult, but he stuck to his work and fought his way to me, and just in the nick of time he put his saving arms about me when I was about to go down. He held me up until the boat reached us and rescued us. By that time I was unconscious, and I was still unconscious when we arrived at the ship. A dangerous fever followed, and I was delirious for three days; then I came to myself and at once inquired for my benefactor, of course. He was gone. We were lying at anchor in the Bay and every man had deserted to the gold-mines except the commissioned officers. I found out nothing about my benefactor but his name—Burton Sanders—a name which I have held in grateful memory ever since. Every time I have been on the Coast, these twelve or thirteen years, I have tried to get track of him, but have never succeeded. I wish I could find him and make him under-

* Can this be correct? I think there must be some mistake—M. T.

stand that his brave act has never been forgotten by me. Harte, I would rather see him and take him by the hand than any other man on the planet."

At this stage or a little later there was an interruption. A waiter near by said to another waiter, pointing,

"Take a look at that tramp that's coming in. Ain't that the one that bilked the house, last week, out of ten cents?"

"I believe it is. Let him alone—don't pay any attention to him; wait till we can get a good look at him."

The tramp approached timidly and hesitatingly, with the air of one unsure and apprehensive. The waiters watched him furtively. When he was passing behind Harte's chair one of them said,

"He's the one!"—and they pounced upon him and proposed to turn him over to the police as a bilk. He begged piteously. He confessed his guilt, but said he had been driven to his crime by necessity—that when he had eaten the plate of beans and slipped out without paying for it, it was because he was starving, and hadn't the ten cents to pay for it with. But the waiters would listen to no explanations, no palliations; he must be placed in custody. He brushed his hand across his eyes and said meekly that he would submit, being friendless. Each waiter took him by an arm and faced him about to conduct him away. Then his melancholy eyes fell upon Captain Osborn, and a light of glad and eager recognition flashed from them. He said,

"Weren't you a midshipman once, sir, in the old 'Lancaster'?"

"Yes," said Osborn. "Why?"

"Didn't you fall overboard?"

"Yes, I did. How do you come to know about it?"

"Wasn't there a new patent machine aboard, and didn't they throw it over to save you?"

"Why, yes," said Osborn, laughing gently, "but it didn't do it."

"No, sir, it was a sailor that done it."

"It certainly was. Look here, my man, you are getting distinctly interesting. Were you of our crew?"

"Yes, sir, I was."

"I reckon you may be right. You do certainly know a good deal about that incident. What is your name?"

"Burton Sanders."

The Captain sprang up, excited, and said,

"Give me your hand! Give me both your hands! I'd rather shake them than inherit a fortune!"—and then he cried to the waiters, "Let him go!—take your hands off! He is my guest, and can have anything and everything this house is able to furnish. I am responsible."

There was a love-feast, then. Captain Osborn ordered it regardless of expense, and he and Harte sat there and listened while the man told stirring adventures of his life and fed himself up to the eyebrows. Then Osborn wanted to be benefactor in his turn, and pay back some of his debt. The man said it could all be paid with ten dollars—that it had been so long since he had owned that amount of money that it would seem a fortune to him, and he should be grateful beyond words if the Captain could spare him that amount. The Captain spared him ten broad twenty-dollar gold pieces, and made him take them in spite of his modest protestations, and gave him his address and said he must never fail to give him notice when he needed grateful service.

Several months later Harte stumbled upon the man in the street. He was most comfortably drunk, and pleasant and chatty. Harte remarked upon the splendidly and movingly dramatic incident of the restaurant, and said,

"How curious and fortunate and happy and interesting it was that you two should come together, after that long separation, and at exactly the right moment to save you from disaster and turn your defeat by the waiters into a victory. A preacher could make a great sermon out of that, for it does look as if the hand of Providence was in it."

The hero's face assumed a sweetly genial expression, and he said,

"Well now, it wasn't Providence this time. I was running the arrangements myself."

"How do you mean?"

"Oh, I hadn't ever seen the gentleman before. I was at the next table, with my back to you the whole time he was telling about it. I saw my chance, and slipped out and fetched the two waiters with me and offered to give them a commission out of what I could get out of the Captain if they would do a quarrel act with me and give me an opening. So, then, after a minute or two I straggled back, and you know the rest of it as well as I do."

1907

OXFORD*

[Dictated July 26, 1907.] In an article entitled "England's Ovation to Mark Twain," Sydney Brooks—but never mind that, now.

I was in Oxford by seven o'clock that evening (June 25, 1907), and trying on the scarlet gown which the tailor had been constructing, and found it right—right and surpassingly becoming. At half past ten the next morning we assembled at All Souls College and marched thence, gowned, mortar-boarded and in double file, down the long street to the Sheldonian Theatre, between solid walls of the populace, very much hurrah'd and limitlessly kodak'd. We made a procession of considerable length and distinction and picturesqueness, with the Chancellor, Lord Curzon, late Viceroy of India, in his rich robe of black and gold, in the lead, followed by a pair of trim little boy train-bearers, and the train-bearers followed by the young Prince Arthur of Connaught, who was to be made a D.C.L. The detachment of D.C.L.'s were followed by the Doctors of Science, and these by the Doctors of Literature, and these in turn by the Doctors of Music. Sidney Colvin marched in front of me; I was coupled with Sidney Lee, and Kipling followed us; General Booth, of the Salvation Army, was in the squadron of D.C.L.'s.

Our journey ended, we were halted in a fine old hall whence we could see, through a corridor of some length, the massed audience in the theatre. Here for a little time we moved about and chatted and made acquaintanceships; then the D.C.L.'s were summoned, and they marched through that corridor and the shouting began in the theatre. It would be some time before the Doctors of Literature and of Science would be called for, because each of those D.C.L.'s had to have a couple of Latin speeches made over him before his promotion would be complete—one by the Regius Professor of Civil Law, the other by the Chancellor. After a while I asked Sir William Ramsay if a person might smoke here and not get shot. He said, "Yes," but that whoever did it and got caught would be fined a guinea, and perhaps hanged later. He said he knew of a place where we could accomplish at least

* Published here in book form for the first time. Source: *North American Review,* October 1907, pp. 169–73.

as much as half of a smoke before any informers would be likely to chance upon us, and he was ready to show the way to any who might be willing to risk the guinea and the hanging. By request he led the way, and Kipling, Sir Norman Lockyer and I followed. We crossed an unpopulated quadrangle and stood under one of its exits—an archway of massive masonry—and there we lit up and began to take comfort. The photographers soon arrived, but they were courteous and friendly and gave us no trouble, and we gave them none. They grouped us in all sorts of ways and photographed us at their diligent leisure, while we smoked and talked. We were there more than an hour; then we returned to headquarters, happy, content, and greatly refreshed. Presently we filed into the theatre, under a very satisfactory hurrah, and waited in a crimson column, dividing the crowded pit through the middle, until each of us in his turn should be called to stand before the Chancellor and hear our merits set forth in sonorous Latin. Meantime, Kipling and I wrote autographs until some good kind soul interfered in our behalf and procured for us a rest.

I will now save what is left of my modesty by quoting a paragraph from Sydney Brooks's "Ovation."

* * *

Let those stars take the place of it for the present. Sydney Brooks has done it well. It makes me proud to read it; as proud as I was in that old day, sixty-two years ago, when I lay dying, the centre of attraction, with one eye piously closed upon the fleeting vanities of this life—an excellent effect—and the other open a crack to observe the tears, the sorrow, the admiration—all for me—all for me!

Ah, that was the proudest moment of my long life—until Oxford!

Most Americans have been to Oxford and will remember what a dream of the Middle Ages it is, with its crooked lanes, its gray and stately piles of ancient architecture and its meditation-breeding air of repose and dignity and unkinship with the noise and fret and hurry and bustle of these modern days. As a dream of the Middle Ages Oxford was not perfect until Pageant day arrived and furnished certain details which had been for generations lacking. These details began to appear at mid-afternoon on the 27th. At that time singles, couples, groups and squadrons of the three thousand five hundred costumed characters who were to take part in the Pageant began to ooze and drip and stream through house doors, all over the old town, and wend toward the meadows outside the walls. Soon the lanes were thronged with costumes which Oxford had from time to time seen and been familiar with in bygone centuries—fashions of dress which marked off centuries as by dates, and mile-stoned them back, and back, and back, until history faded into legend and tradition, when Arthur was a fact and the Round Table a reality. In this rich commingling of quaint and strange and brilliantly colored fashions in dress the dress-changes of Oxford for twelve centuries stood livid and realized to the eye; Oxford as a dream of the Middle Ages was complete now as it had never, in our day, before been complete; at last there was no discord; the mouldering old buildings, and the picturesque throngs drifting past them, were in harmony; soon—astonishingly soon!—the only persons that seemed out of place, and grotesquely and offensively and criminally out of place, were such persons as came intruding along clothed in the ugly and odious fashions of the twentieth century; they were a bitterness to the feelings, an insult to the eye.

The make-ups of illustrious historic personages seemed perfect, both as to portraiture and costume; one had no trouble in recognizing them. Also, I was apparently quite easily recognizable myself. The first corner I turned brought me suddenly face to face with Henry VIII, a person whom I had been implacably disliking for sixty years; but when he put out his hand with royal courtliness and grace and said, "Welcome, well-beloved stranger, to my century and to the hospitalities of my realm," my old prejudices vanished away and I forgave him. I think now that Henry the Eighth has been over-abused, and that most of us, if we had been situated as he was, domestically, would not have been able to get along with as limited a graveyard as he forced himself to put up with. I feel now that he was one of the nicest men in history. Personal contact with a king is more effective in removing baleful prejudices than is any amount of argument drawn from tales and histories. If I had a child I would name it Henry the Eighth, regardless of sex.

Do you remember Charles the First?—and his broad slouch with the plume in it? and his slender, tall figure? and his body clothed in velvet doublet with lace sleeves, and his legs in leather, with long rapier at his side and his spurs on his heels? I encountered him at the next corner, and knew him in a moment—knew him as perfectly and as vividly as I should know the Grand Chain in the Mississippi if I